ÆSTHETIC

ÆSTHETIC

*As science of expression
and general linguistic*

BY BENEDETTO CROCE

translated from the Italian by
DOUGLAS AINSLIE

THE NOONDAY PRESS
New York

THE NOONDAY PRESS
80 EAST 11TH STREET
NEW YORK 3, N.Y.

First edition 1909 (Macmillan & Co.)
Revised edition 1922 (Macmillan & Co.)

2nd impression of revised edition 1953
3rd impression of revised edition 1955
4th impression of revised edition 1956
5th impression of revised edition 1958
6th impression of revised edition 1960
(The Noonday Press)

Printed in the United States of America
by The Murray Printing Company.

THE

ÆSTHETIC

IS DEDICATED BY THE AUTHOR

TO THE MEMORY OF HIS PARENTS

PASQUALE AND LUISA SIPARI

AND OF HIS SISTER

MARIA

CONTENTS

I

THEORY OF ÆSTHETIC

I

INTUITION AND EXPRESSION

II

INTUITION AND ART

III

ART AND PHILOSOPHY

CONTENTS

XI

CRITICISM OF ÆSTHETIC HEDONISM

XII

THE ÆSTHETIC OF THE SYMPATHETIC AND PSEUDO-ÆSTHETIC
CONCEPTS

XIII

THE "PHYSICALLY BEAUTIFUL" IN NATURE
AND IN ART

XIV

ERRORS ARISING FROM THE CONFUSION BETWEEN
PHYSICS AND ÆSTHETIC

CONTENTS

XV

THE ACTIVITY OF EXTERNALIZATION. TECHNIQUE
AND THE THEORY OF THE ARTS

XVI

TASTE AND THE REPRODUCTION OF ART

XVII

THE HISTORY OF LITERATURE AND OF ART

XVIII

CONCLUSION : IDENTITY OF LINGUISTIC AND ÆSTHETIC

II

HISTORY OF ÆSTHETIC

I

ÆSTHETIC IDEAS IN GRÆCO-ROMAN ANTIQUITY

II

ÆSTHETIC IDEAS IN THE MIDDLE AGES AND RENAISSANCE

III

FERMENTS OF THOUGHT IN THE SEVENTEENTH CENTURY

IV

ÆSTHETIC IDEAS OF THE CARTESIAN AND LEIBNITIAN SCHOOLS, AND THE "ÆSTHETIC" OF BAUMGARTEN

V

GIAMBATTISTA VICO

VI

MINOR ÆSTHETIC DOCTRINES OF THE EIGHTEENTH CENTURY

VII

OTHER ÆSTHETIC DOCTRINES OF THE SAME PERIOD

VIII

IMMANUEL KANT

IX

THE ÆSTHETIC OF IDEALISM : SCHILLER, SCHELLING, SOLGER, HEGEL

X

SCHOPENHAUER AND HERBART

CONTENTS

XI

FRIEDRICH SCHLEIERMACHER

XII

THE PHILOSOPHY OF LANGUAGE : HUMBOLDT AND STEINTHAL

XIII

MINOR GERMAN ÆSTHETICIANS

XIV

ÆSTHETIC IN FRANCE, ENGLAND AND ITALY DURING THE FIRST HALF OF THE NINETEENTH CENTURY

XV

FRANCESCO DE SANCTIS

XVI

ÆSTHETIC OF THE EPIGONI

XVII

ÆSTHETIC POSITIVISM AND NATURALISM

XVIII

XIX

EXTRACT FROM INTRODUCTION
TO THE FIRST ENGLISH EDITION, 1909

I CAN lay no claim to having discovered an America, but I do claim to have discovered a Columbus. His name is Benedetto Croce, and he dwells on the shores of the Mediterranean, at Naples, city of the antique Parthenope.

It was at Naples, in the winter of 1907, that I first saw the Philosopher of Æsthetic. Benedetto Croce, although born in the Abruzzi, Province of Aquila (1866), is essentially a Neapolitan, and rarely remains long absent from the city, on the shore of that magical sea where once Ulysses sailed, and where sometimes yet (near Amalfi) we may hear the Syrens sing their song. But more wonderful than the song of any Syren seems to me the Theory of Æsthetic as the Science of Expression, and that is why I have overcome the obstacles that stood between me and the giving of this theory, which in my belief is the truth, to the English-speaking world.

   .   .   .   .   .   .

The solution of the problem of Æsthetic is not in the gift of the Muses.

This Philosophy of the Spirit is symptomatic of the happy reaction of the twentieth century against the crude materialism of the second half of the nineteenth. It is the spirit which gives to the work of art its value, not this or that method of arrangement, this or that tint or cadence, which can always be copied by skilful plagiarists :

not so the *spirit* of the creator.   In England we hear too
much of (natural) science, which has usurped the very
name of Philosophy.   The natural sciences are very well
in their place, but discoveries such as aviation are of
infinitely less importance to the race than the smallest
addition to the philosophy of the spirit.   Empirical
science, with the collusion of positivism, has stolen the
cloak of philosophy and must be made to give it back.

.   .   .   .   .   .

Yet though severe, the editor of *La Critica* is uncom-
promisingly just, and would never allow personal dislike
or jealousy, or any extrinsic consideration, to stand in the
way of fair treatment to the writer concerned.   Many
superficial English critics might benefit considerably by
attention to this quality in one who is in other respects
also so immeasurably their superior.   A good instance of
this impartiality is his critique of Schopenhauer, with
whose system he is in complete disagreement, yet affords
him full credit for what of truth is contained in his
voluminous writings.

.   .   .   .   .   .

This thoroughness it is which gives such importance to
the literary and philosophical criticisms of *La Critica*.
Croce's method is always historical, and his object in
approaching any work of art is to classify the spirit of its
author, as expressed in that work.   There are, he maintains, but two things to be considered in criticizing a book.
These are, *firstly*, what is its *peculiarity*, in what way is it
singular, how is it differentiated from other works ?
Secondly, what is its degree of *purity* ?—That is, to what
extent has its author kept himself free from all considerations alien to the perfection of the work as an expression,
as a lyrical intuition ?   With the answering of these
questions Croce is satisfied.   He does not care to know if
the author keep a motor-car, like Maeterlinck ; or prefer

to walk on Putney Heath, like Swinburne.   This amounts to saying that all works of art must be judged by their own standard.   How far has the author succeeded in doing what he intended ?

As regards Croce's general philosophical position, it is important to understand that he is *not* a Hegelian, in the sense of being a close follower of that philosopher. One of his last works is that in which he deals in a masterly manner with the philosophy of Hegel.   The title may be translated, " What is living and what is dead of the philosophy of Hegel."   Here he explains to us the Hegelian system more clearly than that wondrous edifice was ever before explained, and we realize at the same time that Croce is quite as independent of Hegel as of Kant, of Vico as of Spinoza.   Of course he has made use of the best of Hegel, just as every thinker makes use of his predecessors and is in his turn made use of by those that follow him.   But it is incorrect to accuse of Hegelian-ism the author of an anti-hegelian *Æsthetic*, of a *Logic* where Hegel is only half accepted, and of a *Philosophy of the Practical* which contains hardly a trace of Hegel.   I give an instance.   If the great conquest of Hegel be the dialectic of opposites, his great mistake lies in the con-fusion of opposites with things which are distinct but not opposite.   If, says Croce, we take as an example the application of the Hegelian triad that formulates becoming (affirmation, negation and synthesis), we find it applicable for those opposites which are true and false, good and evil, being and not-being, but *not applicable* to things which are distinct but not opposite, such as art and philosophy, beauty and truth, the useful and the moral.   These confusions led Hegel to talk of the death of art, to con-ceive as possible a Philosophy of History, and to the application of the natural sciences to the absurd task of constructing a Philosophy of Nature. Croce has cleared away these difficulties by showing that if from the meeting of opposites must arise a superior synthesis, such a synthesis cannot arise from things which are distinct *but not opposite*, since the former are connected together as superior and inferior, and the inferior can exist without the superior, but *not vice versa*. Thus we see how philosophy cannot exist without art, while art, occupying the lower place, can and does exist without philosophy. This brief example reveals Croce's independence in dealing with Hegelian problems.

I know of no philosopher more generous than Croce in praise and elucidation of other workers in the same field, past and present. For instance, and apart from Hegel, *Kant* has to thank him for drawing attention to the marvellous excellence of the *Critique of Judgment*, generally neglected in favour of the Critiques of *Pure Reason and of Practical Judgment* ; *Baumgarten* for drawing the attention of the world to his obscure name and for reprinting his Latin thesis in which the word *Æsthetic* occurs for the first time ; and *Schleiermacher* for the tributes paid to his neglected genius in the History of Æsthetic. *La Critica*, too, is full of generous appreciation of contemporaries by Croce and by that profound thinker, Gentile.

There can be no doubt of the great value of Croce's work as an *educative influence*, and if we are to judge of a philosophical system by its action on others, then we must place the *Philosophy of the Spirit* very high. It may be said with perfect truth that since the death of the poet Carducci there has been no influence in Italy to compare with that of Benedetto Croce.

Of the popularity that his system and teaching have

already attained we may judge by the fact that the *Æsthetic*, despite the difficulty of the subject, is already in its third edition in Italy, where, owing to its influence, philosophy sells better than fiction ; while the French and Germans, not to mention the Czechs, have long had translations of the earlier editions. His *Logic* is on the point of appearing in its second edition, and I have no doubt that the *Philosophy of the Practical* will eventually equal these works in popularity. *The importance and value of Italian thought have been too long neglected in Great Britain.* Where, as in Benedetto Croce, we get the clarity of vision of the Latin, joined to the thoroughness and erudition of the best German tradition, we have a combination of rare power and effectiveness, which can by no means be neglected.

The philosopher feels that he has a great mission, which is nothing less than the leading back of thought to belief in the spirit, deserted by so many for crude empiricism and positivism. His view of philosophy is that it sums up all the higher human activities, including religion, and that in proper hands it is able to solve any problem. But there is no finality about problems : the solution of one leads to the posing of another, and so on. Man is the maker of life, and his spirit ever proceeds from a lower to a higher perfection.

I believe that Croce will one day be recognized as one of the very few great teachers of humanity. At present he is not appreciated at nearly his full value. One rises from a study of his philosophy with a sense of having been all the time as it were in personal touch with the truth, which is very far from the case after the perusal of certain other philosophies.

Secure in his strength, Croce will often introduce a joke

or some amusing illustration from contemporary life, in the midst of a most profound and serious argument. This spirit of mirth is a sign of superiority. He who is not sure of himself can spare no energy for the making of mirth. Croce loves to laugh at his enemies and with his friends. So the philosopher of Naples sits by the blue gulf and explains the universe to those who have ears to hear. "One can philosophize anywhere," he says—but he remains significantly at Naples.

Thus I conclude these brief remarks upon the author of the *Æsthetic,* confident that those who give time and attention to its study will be grateful for having placed in their hands this pearl of great price from the diadem of the antique Parthenope.

DOUGLAS AINSLIE.

The Athenæum, Pall Mall,
May 1909.

NOTE BY THE TRANSLATOR
TO THE SECOND ENGLISH EDITION

THIS second edition of the *Æsthetic* will be found to contain the complete translation of the historical portion, which I was obliged to summarize in the first edition. I have made a number of alterations and some additions to the theoretical portion, following closely the fourth (definitive) Italian edition, and in so doing have received much advice and assistance of value from Mrs. Salusbury, to whom I beg to tender my best thanks. I trust that this new edition will enable all those desirous of studying the work to get into direct touch with the thought of the author.

THE ATHENÆUM, PALL MALL, S.W.,
November 1920.

AUTHOR'S PREFACE

THIS volume is composed of a theoretical and of a historical part, which form two independent but complementary books.

The nucleus of the theoretical part is a memoir, bearing the title *Fundamental Theses of an Æsthetic as Science of Expression and General Linguistic*, which was read at the Accademia Pontaniana of Naples during the sessions of February 18 and May 6, 1900, and printed in vol. xxx. of its *Acts*. The author has added few substantial variations, but not a few additions and amplifications in rewriting it, also following a somewhat different sequence with a view to rendering the exposition more plain and easy. The first five chapters only of the historical portion were inserted in the Neapolitan review *Flegrea* (April 1901), under the title *Giambattista Vico, First Discoverer of Æsthetic Science*, and these also reappear amplified and brought into harmony with the rest.

The author has dwelt, especially in the theoretical part, upon general questions which are side-issues in respect to the theme that he has treated. But this will not seem a digression to those who remember that, strictly speaking, there are no particular philosophical sciences, standing by themselves. Philosophy is unity, and when we treat of Æsthetic or of Logic or of Ethics, we treat always of the whole of philosophy, although illustrating for didactic purposes only one side of that inseparable unity. In like manner, owing to this intimate connexion of all the parts of philosophy, the uncertainty and misunderstanding as to the æsthetic activity, the representative and productive imagination, this first-born of the spiritual activities, mainstay of the others, generates everywhere else misunderstandings, uncertainties and errors : in Psychology as in Logic, in History as in the Philosophy of Practice. If language is the first spiritual manifestation, and if the æsthetic form is language itself, taken in all its true scientific extension, it is hopeless to try to understand clearly the later and more complicated phases of the life of the spirit, when their first and simplest moment is ill known, mutilated and disfigured. From the explanation of the æsthetic activity is also to be expected the correction of several concepts and the solution of certain philosophic problems which generally seem to be almost desperate. Such is precisely the spirit animating the present work. And if the present attempt and the historical illustrations which accompany it may be of use in winning friends to these studies, by levelling obstacles and indicating paths to be followed ; if this happen, especially here in Italy, whose æsthetic traditions (as has been demonstrated in its place) are very noble, the author will consider that he has gained his end, and one of his keenest desires will have been satisfied.

NAPLES, *December* 1901.

In addition to a careful literary revision (in which, as well as in the revision of the notes, I have received valuable help from my friend Fausto Nicolini) I have in this third edition made certain alterations of theory, especially in Chapters X. and XI. of Part I., suggested by further reflexion and self-criticism.

But I have refrained from introducing corrections or additions of such a kind as to alter the original plan of the book, which was, or was meant to be, a complete but brief æsthetic theory set in the framework of a general sketch of a Philosophy of the Spirit.

The reader who desires a complete statement of the general or collateral doctrines or a more particular exposition of the other parts of philosophy (*e.g.* the lyrical nature of art) is now referred to the volumes on *Logic* and the *Philosophy of Practice*, which together with the present work compose the *Philosophy of the Spirit* which in the author's opinion exhausts the entire field of Philosophy. The three volumes were not conceived and written simultaneously ; if they had been, some details would have been differently arranged. When I wrote the first I had no idea of giving it, as I have now done, two such companions ; and I therefore designed it to be, as I say, complete in itself. In the second place, the present state of the study of Æsthetic made it desirable to append to the theoretical exposition a somewhat full history of the science, whereas for the other parts of Philosophy I was able to restrict myself to brief historical notes merely designed to show how, from my point of view, such a history would best be composed. Lastly, there are many things which now, after a systematic exposition of the various philosophical sciences, I see in closer connexions and in a clearer, or at least a different, light ; a certain hesitation and even some doctrinal errors visible here and there in the *Æsthetic*, especially where subjects foreign to Æsthetic itself are being treated, would now no longer be justified. For all these reasons the three volumes, in spite of their substantial unity of spirit and of aim, have each its own physiognomy, and show marks of the different periods of life at which they were written, so as to group themselves, and to demand interpretation, as a progressive series according to their dates of publication.

With what may be called the minor problems of Æsthetic, and the objections which have been or might be brought against my theory, I have dealt and am continuing to deal in special essays, of which I shall shortly publish a first collection which will form a kind of explanatory and polemical appendix to the present volume.

November 1907.

In revising this book once more for a fourth edition, I take the opportunity of announcing that the supplementary volume of essays promised above was published in 1910 under the title *Problems of Æsthetic and Contributions to the History of Æsthetic in Italy.*

B. C.

May 1911.

I

THEORY OF ÆSTHETIC

I

INTUITION AND EXPRESSION

KNOWLEDGE has two forms : it is either *intuitive* know- *Intuitive*
ledge or *logical* knowledge ; knowledge obtained through *knowledge.*
the *imagination* or knowledge obtained through the
intellect ; knowledge of the *individual* or knowledge of
the *universal* ; of *individual things* or of the *relations*
between them : it is, in fact, productive either of *images*
or of *concepts*.

In ordinary life, constant appeal is made to intuitive
knowledge. It is said that we cannot give definitions of certain truths ; that they are not demonstrable
by syllogisms ; that they must be learnt intuitively.
The politician finds fault with the abstract reasoner, who
possesses no lively intuition of actual conditions ; the
educational theorist insists upon the necessity of developing the intuitive faculty in the pupil before everything
else ; the critic in judging a work of art makes it a point
of honour to set aside theory and abstractions, and to
judge it by direct intuition ; the practical man professes
to live rather by intuition than by reason.

But this ample acknowledgment granted to intuitive
knowledge in ordinary life, does not correspond to an
equal and adequate acknowledgment in the field of
theory and of philosophy. There exists a very ancient
science of intellectual knowledge, admitted by all without
discussion, namely, Logic ; but a science of intuitive
knowledge is timidly and with difficulty asserted by but
a few. Logical knowledge has appropriated the lion's
share ; and if she does not slay and devour her

companion outright, yet yields to her but grudgingly
the humble place of maid-servant or doorkeeper.—What
can intuitive knowledge be without the light of intellectual knowledge ?   It is a servant without a master ;
and though a master find a servant useful, the master
is a necessity to the servant, since he enables him to
gain his livelihood.   Intuition is blind ; intellect lends
her eyes.

Its independ-
ence with
respect to
intellectual
knowledge.

Now, the first point to be firmly fixed in the mind
is that intuitive knowledge has no need of a master, nor
to lean upon any one ; she does not need to borrow the
eyes of others, for she has excellent eyes of her own.
Doubtless it is possible to find concepts mingled with
intuitions.   But in many other intuitions there is no
trace of such a mixture, which proves that it is not
necessary.   The impression of a moonlight scene by a
painter ; the outline of a country drawn by a carto-
grapher ; a musical motive, tender or energetic ; the
words of a sighing lyric, or those with which we ask,
command and lament in ordinary life, may well all be
intuitive facts without a shadow of intellectual relation.
But, think what one may of these instances, and admitting further the contention that the greater part of
the intuitions of civilized man are impregnated with
concepts, there yet remains to be observed something
more important and more conclusive.   Those concepts
which are found mingled and fused with the intuitions
are no longer concepts, in so far as they are really mingled
and fused, for they have lost all independence and autonomy.   They have been concepts, but have now become
simple elements of intuition.   The philosophical maxims
placed in the mouth of a personage of tragedy or of
comedy, perform there the function, not of concepts, but
of characteristics of such personage ; in the same way
as the red in a painted face does not there represent the
red colour of the physicists, but is a characteristic element
of the portrait.   The whole is that which determines
the quality of the parts.   A work of art may be full of
philosophical concepts ; it may contain them in greater

abundance and they may there be even more profound
than in a philosophical dissertation, which in its turn
may be rich to overflowing with descriptions and intuitions. But notwithstanding all these concepts the
total effect of the work of art is an intuition ; and notwithstanding all those intuitions, the total effect of the
philosophical dissertation is a concept. The *Promessi
Sposi* contains copious ethical observations and distinctions, but does not for that reason lose as a whole its
character of simple story or intuition. In like manner
the anecdotes and satirical effusions to be found in the
works of a philosopher like Schopenhauer do not deprive
those works of their character of intellectual treatises.
The difference between a scientific work and a work of
art, that is, between an intellectual fact and an intuitive
fact, lies in the difference of the total effect aimed at by
their respective authors. This it is that determines and
rules over the several parts of each not these parts
separated and considered abstractly in themselves.

But to admit the independence of intuition as regards *Intuition and*
concept does not suffice to give a true and precise idea *perception.*
of intuition. Another error arises among those who
recognize this, or who at any rate do not explicitly
make intuition dependent upon the intellect, to obscure
and confuse the real nature of intuition. By intuition is
frequently understood *perception*, or the knowledge of
actual reality, the apprehension of something as *real*.

Certainly perception is intuition : the perceptions of
the room in which I am writing, of the ink-bottle and
paper that are before me, of the pen I am using, of the
objects that I touch and make use of as instruments of
my person, which, if it write, therefore exists ;—these
are all intuitions. But the image that is now passing
through my brain of a me writing in another room, in
another town, with different paper, pen and ink, is also
an intuition. This means that the distinction between
reality and non-reality is extraneous, secondary, to the
true nature of intuition. If we imagine a human mind
having intuitions for the first time, it would seem that

it could have intuitions of actual reality only, that is to say, that it could have perceptions of nothing but the real. But since knowledge of reality is based upon the distinction between real images and unreal images, and since this distinction does not at the first moment exist, these intuitions would in truth not be intuitions either of the real or of the unreal, not perceptions, but pure intuitions. Where all is real, nothing is real. The child, with its difficulty of distinguishing true from false, history from fable, which are all one to childhood, can furnish us with a sort of very vague and only remotely approximate idea of this ingenuous state. Intuition is the undifferentiated unity of the perception of the real and of the simple image of the possible. In our intuitions we do not oppose ourselves as empirical beings to external reality, but we simply objectify our impressions, whatever they be.

Intuition and the concepts of space and time. Those, therefore, who look upon intuition as sensation formed and arranged simply according to the categories of space and time, would seem to approximate more nearly to the truth. Space and time (they say) are the forms of intuition ; to have an intuition is to place it in space and in temporal sequence. Intuitive activity would then consist in this double and concurrent function of spatiality and temporality. But for these two categories must be repeated what was said of intellectual distinctions, when found mingled with intuitions. We have intuitions without space and without time : the colour of a sky, the colour of a feeling, a cry of pain and an effort of will, objectified in consciousness : these are intuitions which we possess, and with their making space and time have nothing to do. In some intuitions, spatiality may be found without temporality, in others, *vice versa* ; and even where both are found, they are perceived by later reflexion : they can be fused with the intuition in like manner with all its other elements : that is, they are in it *materialiter* and not *formaliter*, as ingredients and not as arrangement. Who, without an act of reflexion which for a moment breaks in upon his contemplation, can think of space while looking at a drawing or a view? Who is conscious of temporal sequence while listening to a story or a piece of music without breaking into it with a similar act of reflexion? What intuition reveals in a work of art is not space and time, but *character, individual physiognomy*. The view here maintained is confirmed in several quarters of modern philosophy. Space and time, far from being simple and primitive functions, are nowadays conceived as intellectual constructions of great complexity. And further, even in some of those who do not altogether deny to space and time the quality of formative principles, categories and functions, one observes an effort to unite them and to regard them in a different manner from that in which these categories are generally conceived. Some limit intuition to the sole category of spatiality, maintaining that even time can only be intuited in terms of space. Others abandon the three dimensions of space as not philosophically necessary, and conceive the function of spatiality as void of all particular spatial determination. But what could such a spatial function be, a simple arrangement that should arrange even time? It represents, surely, all that criticism and refutation have left standing—the bare demand for the affirmation of some intuitive activity in general. And is not this activity truly determined, when one single function is attributed to it, not spatializing nor temporalizing, but characterizing? Or rather, when it is conceived as itself a category or function which gives us knowledge of things in their concreteness and individuality?

Having thus freed intuitive knowledge from any *Intuition and* suggestion of intellectualism and from every later and *sensation.* external addition, we must now explain it and determine its limits from another side and defend it from a different kind of invasion and confusion. On the hither side of the lower limit is sensation, formless matter, which the spirit can never apprehend in itself as simple matter. This it can only possess with form and in form, but postulates the notion of it as a mere limit. Matter, in its abstraction, is mechanism, passivity ; it is what the spirit of man suffers, but does not produce. Without it no human knowledge or activity is possible ; but mere matter produces animality, whatever is brutal and impulsive in man, not the spiritual dominion, which is humanity. How often we strive to understand clearly what is passing within us ! We do catch a glimpse of something, but this does not appear to the mind as objectified and formed. It is in such moments as these that we best perceive the profound difference between matter and form. These are not two acts of ours, opposed to one another ; but the one is outside us and assaults and sweeps us off our feet, while the other inside us tends to absorb and identify itself with that which is outside. Matter, clothed and conquered by form, produces concrete form. It is the matter, the content, which differentiates one of our intuitions from another : the form is constant : it is spiritual activity, while matter is changeable. Without matter spiritual activity would not forsake its abstractness to become concrete and real activity, this or that spiritual content, this or that definite intuition.

It is a curious fact, characteristic of our times, that this very form, this very activity of the spirit, which is essentially ourselves, is so often ignored or denied. Some confound the spiritual activity of man with the metaphorical and mythological activity of what is called nature, which is mechanism and has no resemblance to human activity, save when we imagine, with Æsop, that " *arbores loquuntur non tantum ferae.*" Some affirm that they have never observed in themselves this " miraculous " activity, as though there were no difference, or only one of quantity, between sweating and thinking, feeling cold and the energy of the will. Others, certainly with greater reason, would unify activity and mechanism in a more general concept, though they are specifically distinct. Let us, however, refrain for the moment from examining if such a final unification be possible, and in what sense, but admitting that the attempt may be made, it is clear that to unify two concepts in a third implies to begin with the admission of a difference between the two first. Here it is this difference that concerns us and we set it in relief.

Intuition has sometimes been confused with simple sensation. But since this confusion ends by being offensive to common sense, it has more frequently been attenuated or concealed with a phraseology apparently designed at once to confuse and to distinguish them. Thus, it has been asserted that intuition is sensation, but not so much simple sensation as *association* of sensations. Here a double meaning is concealed in the word " association." Association is understood, either as memory, mnemonic association, conscious recollection, and in that case the claim to unite in memory elements which are not intuited, distinguished, possessed in some way by the spirit and produced by consciousness, seems inconceivable : or it is understood as association of unconscious elements, in which case we remain in the world of sensation and of nature. But if with certain associationists we speak of an association which is neither memory nor flux of sensations, but a *productive* association (formative, constructive, distinguishing) ; then our contention is admitted and only its name is denied to it. For productive association is no longer association in the sense of the sensationalists, but *synthesis*, that is to say, spiritual activity. Synthesis may be called association ; but with the concept of productivity is already posited the distinction between passivity and activity, between sensation and intuition. *Intuition and association.*

Other psychologists are disposed to distinguish from sensation something which is sensation no longer, but is not yet intellectual concept : the *representation* or *image*. What is the difference between their representation or image and our intuitive knowledge ? Everything and nothing : for "representation" is a very equivocal word. If by representation be understood something cut off and standing out from the psychic basis of the sensations, then representation is intuition. If, on the other *Intuition and representation.*

hand, it be conceived as complex sensation we are back once more in crude sensation, which does not vary in quality according to its richness or poverty, or according to whether the organism in which it appears is rudimentary or highly developed and full of traces of past sensations. Nor is the ambiguity remedied by defining representation as a psychic product of secondary degree in relation to sensation, defined as occupying the first place. What does secondary degree mean here ? Does it mean a qualitative, formal difference ? If so, representation is an elaboration of sensation and therefore intuition. Or does it mean greater complexity and complication, a quantitative, material difference ? In that case intuition is once more confused with simple sensation.

Intuition and expression.

And yet there is a sure method of distinguishing true intuition, true representation, from that which is inferior to it : the spiritual fact from the mechanical, passive, natural fact. Every true intuition or representation is also *expression*. That which does not objectify itself in expression is not intuition or representation, but sensation and mere natural fact. The spirit only intuites in making, forming, expressing. He who separates intuition from expression never succeeds in reuniting them.

Intuitive activity *possesses intuitions to the extent that it expresses them.* Should this proposition sound paradoxical, that is partly because, as a general rule, a too restricted meaning is given to the word " expression." It is generally restricted to what are called verbal expressions alone. But there exist also non-verbal expressions, such as those of line, colour and sound, and to all of these must be extended our affirmation, which embraces therefore every sort of manifestation of the man, as orator, musician, painter, or anything else. But be it pictorial, or verbal, or musical, or in whatever other form it appear, to no intuition can expression in one of its forms be wanting ; it is, in fact, an inseparable part of intuition. How can we really possess an intuition of a geometrical figure, unless we possess so accurate an image of it as to be able to trace it immediately upon paper or on the blackboard ?

How can we really have an intuition of the contour of a region, for example of the island of Sicily, if we are not able to draw it as it is in all its meanderings? Every one can experience the internal illumination which follows upon his success in formulating to himself his impressions and feelings, but only so far as he is able to formulate them. Feelings or impressions, then, pass by means of words from the obscure region of the soul into the clarity of the contemplative spirit. It is impossible to distinguish intuition from expression in this cognitive process. The one appears with the other at the same instant, because they are not two, but one.

The principal reason which makes our view appear *Illusion as* paradoxical as we maintain it, is the illusion or prejudice *to their difference.* that we possess a more complete intuition of reality than we really do. ⌈One often hears people say that they have⌉ many great thoughts in their minds, but that they are not able to express them. But if they really had them, they would have coined them into just so many beautiful, sounding words, and thus have expressed them. If these thoughts seem to vanish or to become few and meagre in the act of expressing them, the reason is that they did not exist or really were few and meagre.⌋ People think that all of us ordinary men imagine and intuite countries, figures and scenes like painters, and bodies like sculptors ; save that painters and sculptors know how to paint and carve such images, while we bear them unexpressed in our souls. They believe that any one could have imagined a Madonna of Raphael; but that Raphael was Raphael owing to his technical ability in putting the Madonna upon canvas. Nothing can be more false than this view. The world which as a rule we intuite is a small thing. It consists of little expressions, which gradually become greater and wider with the increasing spiritual concentration of certain moments. They are the words we say to ourselves, our silent judgments : " Here is a man, here is a horse, this is heavy, this is sharp, this pleases me," etc. It is a medley of light and colour, with no greater pictorial value than would be expressed by a haphazard splash of colours, from among which one could barely make out a few special, distinctive traits. This and nothing else is what we possess in our ordinary life ; this is the basis of our ordinary action. It is the index of a book. The labels tied to things (it has been said) take the place of the things themselves. This index and these labels (themselves expressions) suffice for small needs and small actions. From time to time we pass from the index to the book, from the label to the thing, or from the slight to the greater intuitions, and from these to the greatest and most lofty. This passage is sometimes far from easy. It has been observed by those who have best studied the psychology of artists that when, after having given a rapid glance at any one, they attempt to obtain a real intuition of him, in order, for example, to paint his portrait, then this ordinary vision, that seemed so precise, so lively, reveals itself as little better than nothing. What remains is found to be at the most some superficial trait, which would not even suffice for a caricature. The person to be painted stands before the artist like a world to discover. Michael Angelo said, " One paints, not with the hands, but with the brain." Leonardo shocked the prior of the Convent of the Graces by standing for days together gazing at the " Last Supper," without touching it with the brush. He remarked of this attitude : " The minds of men of lofty genius are most active in invention when they are doing the least external work." The painter is a painter, because he sees what others only feel or catch a glimpse of, but do not see. We think we see a smile, but in reality we have only a vague impression of it, we do not perceive all the characteristic traits of which it is the sum, as the painter discovers them after he has worked upon them and is thus able to fix them on the canvas. We do not intuitively possess more even of our intimate friend, who is with us every day and at all hours, than at most certain traits of physiognomy which enable us to distinguish him from others. The illusion is less easy as regards musical expression ; because it would seem strange to every one to say that the composer had added or attached notes to a motive which was already in the mind of him who is not the composer ; as if Beethoven's Ninth Symphony were not his own intuition and his intuition the Ninth Symphony. Now, just as one who is deluded as to the amount of his material wealth is confuted by arithmetic, which states its exact amount, so he who nourishes delusions as to the wealth of his own thoughts and images is brought back to reality, when he is obliged to cross the *Pons Asinorum* of expression. Let us say to the former, count ; to the latter, speak ; or, here is a pencil, draw, express yourself.

Each of us, as a matter of fact, has in him a little of the poet, of the sculptor, of the musician, of the painter, of the prose writer : but how little, as compared with those who bear those names, just because they possess the most universal dispositions and energies of human nature in so lofty a degree ! How little too does a painter possess of the intuitions of a poet ! And how little does one painter possess those of another painter! Nevertheless, that little is all our actual patrimony of intuitions or representations. Beyond these are only impressions, sensations, feelings, impulses, emotions, or whatever else one may term what still falls short of the spirit and is not assimilated by man ; something postulated for the convenience of exposition, while actually non-existent, since to exist also is a fact of the spirit.

We may thus add this to the various verbal descriptions of intuition, noted at the beginning : intuitive knowledge is expressive knowledge. Independent and autonomous in respect to intellectual function ; indifferent to later empirical discriminations, to reality and to unreality, to formations and apperceptions of space and time, which are also later : intuition or representation is distinguished as *form* from what is felt and suffered, from the flux or wave of sensation, or from psychic matter ; and this form, this taking possession, is expression. To intuite is to express ; and nothing else (nothing more, but nothing less) than *to express*.

Identity of intuition and expression.

II

INTUITION AND ART

Corollaries and explanations. BEFORE proceeding further, it may be well to draw certain consequences from what has been established and to add some explanations.

Identity of art and intuitive knowledge. We have frankly identified intuitive or expressive knowledge with the æsthetic or artistic fact, taking works of art as examples of intuitive knowledge and attributing to them the characteristics of intuition, and *vice versa*. But our identification is combated by a view held even by many philosophers, who consider art to be an intuition of an altogether special sort. " Let us admit " (they say) " that art is intuition ; but intuition is not always art : artistic intuition is a distinct species differing from intuition in general by something *more*."

No specific difference. But no one has ever been able to indicate of what this something more consists. It has sometimes been thought that art is not a simple intuition, but an intuition of an intuition, in the same way as the concept of science has been defined, not as the ordinary concept, but as the concept of a concept. Thus man would attain to art by objectifying, not his sensations, as happens with ordinary intuition, but intuition itself. But this process of raising to a second power does not exist ; and the comparison of it with the ordinary and scientific concept does not prove what is intended, for the good reason that it is not true that the scientific concept is the concept of a concept. If this comparison proves anything, it proves just the opposite. The ordinary concept, if it be really a concept and not a simple representation, is a perfect concept, however poor and limited. Science substitutes concepts for representations ; for those concepts that are poor and limited it substitutes others, larger and more comprehensive ; it is ever discovering new relations. But its method does not differ from that by which is formed the smallest universal in the brain of the humblest of men. What is generally called *par excellence* art, collects intuitions that are wider and more complex than those which we generally experience, but these intuitions are always of sensations and impressions.

Art is expression of impressions, not expression of expression.

For the same reason, it cannot be asserted that the intuition, which is generally called artistic, differs from ordinary intuition as intensive intuition. This would be the case if it were to operate differently on the same matter. But since the artistic function is extended to wider fields, yet does not differ in method from ordinary intuition, the difference between them is not intensive but extensive. The intuition of the simplest popular love-song, which says the same thing, or very nearly, as any declaration of love that issues at every moment from the lips of thousands of ordinary men, may be intensively perfect in its poor simplicity, although it be extensively so much more limited than the complex intuition of a love-song by Leopardi.

No difference of intensity.

The whole difference, then, is quantitative, and as such is indifferent to philosophy, *scientia qualitatum.* Certain men have a greater aptitude, a more frequent inclination fully to express certain complex states of the soul. These men are known in ordinary language as artists. Some very complicated and difficult expressions are not often achieved, and these are called works of art. The limits of the expression-intuitions that are called art, as opposed to those that are vulgarly called non-art, are empirical and impossible to define. If an epigram be art, why not a simple word ? If a story, why not the news-jottings of the journalist ? If a landscape,

The difference is extensive and empirical.

why not a topographical sketch ?   The teacher of philosophy in Molière's comedy was right : " whenever we
speak, we create prose."   But there will always be scholars
like Monsieur Jourdain, astonished at having spoken prose
for forty years without knowing it, who will have difficulty
in persuading themselves that when they call their servant
John to bring their slippers, they have spoken nothing
less than—prose.

We must hold firmly to our identification, because
among the principal reasons which have prevented
Æsthetic, the science of art, from revealing the true
nature of art, its real roots in human nature, has been its
separation from the general spiritual life, the having made
of it a sort of special function or aristocratic club.   No
one is astonished when he learns from physiology that
every cell is an organism and every organism a cell or
synthesis of cells.   No one is astonished at finding in a
lofty mountain the same chemical elements that compose
a small stone fragment.   There is not one physiology of
small animals and one of large animals ; nor is there a
special chemical theory of stones as distinct from moun-
tains.   In the same way, there is not a science of lesser
intuition as distinct from a science of greater intuition,
nor one of ordinary intuition as distinct from artistic
intuition.   There is but one Æsthetic, the science of
intuitive or expressive knowledge, which is the æsthetic
or artistic fact.   And this Æsthetic is the true analogue
of Logic, which includes, as facts of the same nature, the
formation of the smallest and most ordinary concept
and the most complicated scientific and philosophical
system.

Artistic
genius.
Nor can we admit that the word *genius* or artistic
genius, as distinct from the non-genius of the ordinary
man, possesses more than a quantitative signification.
Great artists are said to reveal us to ourselves.   But how
could this be possible, unless there were identity of nature
between their imagination and ours, and unless the
difference were only one of quantity ?   It were better to
change *poeta nascitur* into *homo nascitur poeta* : some men

are born great poets, some small. The cult of the genius
with all its attendant superstitions has arisen from this
quantitative difference having been taken as a difference
of quality. It has been forgotten that genius is not
something that has fallen from heaven, but humanity
itself. The man of genius who poses or is represented as
remote from humanity finds his punishment in becoming
or appearing somewhat ridiculous. Examples of this are
the *genius* of the romantic period and the *superman* of our
time.

But it is well to note here, that those who claim unconsciousness as the chief quality of an artistic genius,
hurl him from an eminence far above humanity to a
position far below it. Intuitive or artistic genius, like
every form of human activity, is always conscious ;
otherwise it would be blind mechanism. The only thing
that can be wanting to artistic genius is the *reflective*
consciousness, the superadded consciousness of the
historian or critic, which is not essential to it.

The relation between matter and form, or between
content and *form*, as is generally said, is one of the most
disputed questions in Æsthetic. Does the æsthetic fact
consist of content alone, or of form alone, or of both
together ? This question has taken on various meanings,
which we shall mention, each in its place. But when
these words are taken as signifying what we have above
defined, and matter is understood as emotionality not
æsthetically elaborated, or impressions, and form as
intellectual activity and expression, then our view cannot
be in doubt. We must, that is to say, reject both the
thesis that makes the æsthetic fact to consist of the
content alone (that is, the simple impressions), and the
thesis which makes it to consist of a junction between
form and content, that is, of impressions plus expressions.
In the æsthetic fact, expressive activity is not added to
the fact of the impressions, but these latter are formed
and elaborated by it. The impressions reappear as it
were in expression, like water put into a filter, which
reappears the same and yet different on the other side.

Content and form in Æsthetic.

The æsthetic fact, therefore, is form, and nothing but form.

From this was inferred not that the content is something superfluous (it is, on the contrary, the necessary point of departure for the expressive fact) ; but that *there is no passage* from the qualities of the content to those of the form. It has sometimes been thought that the content, in order to be æsthetic, that is to say, transformable into form, should possess some determined or determinable qualities. But were that so, then form and content, expression and impression, would be the same thing. It is true that the content is that which is convertible into form, but it has no determinable qualities until this transformation takes place. We know nothing about it. It does not become æsthetic content before, but only after it has been actually transformed. The æsthetic content has also been defined as the *interesting*. That is not an untrue statement ; it is merely void of meaning. Interesting to what ? To the expressive activity ? Certainly the expressive activity would not have raised the content to the dignity of form, had it not been interested in it. Being interested is precisely the raising of the content to the dignity of form. But the word " interesting " has also been employed in another and a illegitimate sense, which we shall explain further on.

Criticism of the imitation of nature and of the artistic illusion. The proposition that art is *imitation of nature* has also several meanings. Sometimes truths have been expressed or at least shadowed forth in these words, sometimes errors have been promulgated. More frequently, no definite thought has been expressed at all. One of the scientifically legitimate meanings occurs when " imitation " is understood as representation or intuition of nature, a form of knowledge. And when the phrase is used with this intention, and in order to emphasize the spiritual character of the process, another proposition becomes legitimate also : namely, that art is the *idealization* or *idealizing* imitation of nature. But if by imitation of nature be understood that art gives mechanical reproductions, more or less perfect duplicates of natural objects, in the presence of which is renewed the same tumult of impressions as that caused by natural objects, then the proposition is evidently false. The coloured waxen effigies that imitate the life, before which we stand astonished in the museums where such things are shown, do not give æsthetic intuitions. Illusion and hallucination have nothing to do with the calm domain of artistic intuition. But on the other hand if an artist paint the interior of a wax-work museum, or if an actor give a burlesque portrait of a man-statue on the stage, we have work of the spirit and artistic intuition. Finally, if photography have in it anything artistic, it will be to the extent that it transmits the intuition of the photographer, his point of view, the pose and grouping which he has striven to attain. And if photography be not quite an art, that is precisely because the element of nature in it remains more or less unconquered and ineradicable. Do we ever, indeed, feel complete satisfaction before even the best of photographs ? Would not an artist vary and touch up much or little, remove or add something to all of them ?

The statements repeated so often, that art is not know- *Criticism of art* ledge, that it does not tell the truth, that it does not *conceived as a fact of feeling,* belong to the world of theory, but to the world of feel- *not a theoretical* ing, and so forth, arise from the failure to realize exactly *fact. Æsthetic appearance,* the theoretic character of simple intuition. This simple *and feeling.* intuition is quite distinct from intellectual knowledge, as it is distinct from perception of the real ; and the statements quoted above arise from the belief that only intellectual cognition is knowledge. We have seen that intuition is knowledge, free from concepts and more simple than the so-called perception of the real. Therefore art is knowledge, form ; it does not belong to the world of feeling or to psychic matter. The reason why so many æstheticians have so often insisted that art is *appearance* (*Schein*), is precisely that they have felt the necessity of distinguishing it from the more complex fact of perception, by maintaining its pure intuitiveness. And if for the same reason it has been claimed that art is *feeling* the reason is the same. For if the concept as content of art, and historical reality as such, be excluded from the sphere of art, there remains no other content than reality apprehended in all its ingenuousness and immediacy in the vital impulse, in its *feeling*, that is to say again, pure intuition.

Criticism of the theory of æsthetic senses. The theory of the *æsthetic senses* has also arisen from the failure to establish, or from having lost to view, the character of expression as distinct from impression, of form as distinct from matter.

This theory can be reduced to the error just indicated of wishing to find a passage from the qualities of the content to those of the form. To ask, in fact, what the æsthetic senses are, implies asking what sensible impressions are able to enter into æsthetic expressions, and which must of necessity do so. To this we must at once reply, that all impressions can enter into æsthetic expressions or formations, but that none are bound to do so of necessity. Dante raised to the dignity of form not only the " sweet colour of the oriental sapphire " (visual impressions), but also tactual or thermic impressions, such as the " dense air " and the " fresh rivulets " which " parch the more " the throat of the thirsty. The belief that a picture yields only visual impressions is a curious illusion. The bloom on a cheek, the warmth of a youthful body, the sweetness and freshness of a fruit, the edge of a sharp knife, are not these, too, impressions obtainable from a picture ? Are they visual ? What would a picture mean to an imaginary man, lacking all or many of his senses, who should in an instant acquire the organ of sight alone ? The picture we are looking at and believe we see only with our eyes would seem to his eyes to be little more than an artist's paint-smeared palette.

Some who hold firmly to the æsthetic character of certain groups of impressions (for example, the visual and auditive), and exclude others, are nevertheless ready to admit that if visual and auditive impressions enter *directly* into the æsthetic fact, those of the other senses also enter into it, but only as *associated*. But this distinction is altogether arbitrary. Æsthetic expression is synthesis, in which it is impossible to distinguish direct and indirect. All impressions are placed by it on a level, in so far as they are æstheticized. A man who absorbs the subject of a picture or poem does not have it before him as a series of impressions, some of which have prerogatives and precedence over the others. He knows nothing as to what has happened prior to having absorbed it, just as, on the other hand, distinctions made after reflexion have nothing whatever to do with art as such.

The theory of the æsthetic senses has also been presented in another way ; as an attempt to establish what physiological organs are necessary for the æsthetic fact. The physiological organ or apparatus is nothing but a group of cells, constituted and disposed in a particular manner ; that is to say, it is a merely physical and natural fact or concept. But expression does not know physiological facts. Expression has its point of departure in the impressions, and the physiological path by which these have found their way to the mind is to it altogether indifferent. One way or another comes to the same thing : it suffices that they should be impressions.

It is true that the want of given organs, that is, of certain groups of cells, prevents the formation of certain impressions (when these are not otherwise obtained through a kind of organic compensation). The man born blind cannot intuite and express light. But the impressions are not conditioned solely by the organ, but also by the stimuli which operate upon the organ. One who has never had the impression of the sea will never be able to express it, in the same way as one who has never had the impression of the life of high society or of the political arena will never express either. This, however, does not prove the dependence of the expressive function on the stimulus or on the organ. It merely repeats what we know already : expression presupposes impression, and particular expressions particular impressions. For the rest, every impression excludes other impressions during the moment in which it dominates; and so does every expression.

Another corollary of the conception of expression as activity is the *indivisibility* of the work of art. Every expression is a single expression. Activity is a fusion of the impressions in an organic whole. A desire to express this has always prompted the affirmation that the work of art should have *unity*, or, what amounts to the same thing, *unity in variety*. Expression is a synthesis of the various, or multiple, in the one.

The fact that we divide a work of art into parts, a poem into scenes, episodes, similes, sentences, or a picture into single figures and objects, background, foreground, etc., may seem opposed to this affirmation. But such division annihilates the work, as dividing the organism into heart, brain, nerves, muscles and so on, turns the living being into a corpse. It is true that there exist organisms in which division gives rise to other living beings, but in such a case we must conclude, maintaining the analogy between the organism and the work of art, that in the latter case too there are numerous germs of life each ready to grow, in a moment, into a single complete expression.

It may be said that expression sometimes arises from other expressions. There are simple and there are *compound* expressions. One must surely admit some difference between the *eureka*, with which Archimedes expressed all his joy at his discovery, and the expressive act (indeed all the five acts) of a regular tragedy.—Not in the least: expression always arises directly from impressions. He who conceives a tragedy puts into a crucible a great quantity, so to say, of impressions: expressions themselves, conceived on other occasions, are fused together with the new in a single mass, in the same way as we can cast into a melting furnace formless pieces of bronze and choicest statuettes. Those choicest statuettes must be melted just like the pieces of bronze, before there can be a new statue. The old expressions must descend again to the level of impressions, in order to be synthesized in a new single expression.

By elaborating his impressions, man *frees* himself from them. By objectifying them, he removes them from him and makes himself their superior. The liberating and purifying function of art is another aspect and another formula of its character as activity. Activity is the deliverer, just because it drives away passivity. *Art as liberator.*

This also explains why it is usual to attribute to artists both the maximum of sensibility or *passion*, and the maximum of insensibility or Olympian *serenity*. The two characters are compatible, for they do not refer to the same object. The sensibility or passion relates to the rich material which the artist absorbs into his psychic organism ; the insensibility or serenity to the form with which he subdues and dominates the tumult of the sensations and passions.

III

ART AND PHILOSOPHY

Inseparability of intellectual from intuitive knowledge.

THE two forms of knowledge, æsthetic and intellectual or conceptual, are indeed different, but this does not altogether amount to separation and disjunction, as of two forces each pulling in its own direction. If we have shown that the æsthetic form is altogether independent of the intellectual and suffices to itself without external support, we have not said that the intellectual can stand without the æsthetic. To describe the independence as *reciprocal* would not be true.

What is knowledge by concepts ? It is knowledge of the relations of things, and things are intuitions. Concepts are not possible without intuitions, just as intuition is itself impossible without the matter of impressions. Intuitions are : this river, this lake, this brook, this rain, this glass of water ; the concept is : water, not this or that appearance and particular example of water, but water in general, in whatever time or place it be realized ; the material of infinite intuitions, but of one single constant concept.

But the concept, the universal, if it be no longer intuition in one respect, is intuition in another respect, and cannot fail of being intuition. The man who thinks has impressions and emotions, in so far as he thinks. His impression and emotion will be not love or hate, not the passion of the man who is not a philosopher, not hate or love for certain objects and individuals, but *the effort of his thought itself*, with the pain and the joy, the love and the hate joined to it. This effort cannot but assume an intuitive form, in becoming objective to the spirit. To speak is not to think logically ; but to *think logically* is also to *speak*.

That thought cannot exist without speech, is a truth *Criticism of* generally admitted. The negations of this thesis are all *the negations of* founded on equivocations and errors. *this thesis.*

The first of the equivocations is that of those who observe that one can likewise think with geometrical figures, algebraical numbers, ideographic signs, without any word, even pronounced silently and almost insensibly within one ; that there are languages in which the word, the phonetic sign, expresses nothing, unless the written sign also be examined, and so on. But when we said "speak," we intended to employ a synecdoche, by which was to be understood " expression " in general, for we have already remarked that expression is not only so-called verbal expression. It may or may not be true that certain concepts may be thought without phonetic manifestations. But the very examples adduced to show this also prove that those concepts never exist without expressions.

Others point out that animals, or certain animals, think and reason without speaking. Now as to how, whether, and what animals think, whether they be rudimentary men, like savages who refuse to be civilized, rather than physiological machines, as the old spiritualists maintained, are questions that do not concern us here. When the philosopher talks of animal, brutal, impulsive, instinctive nature and the like, he does not base himself on such conjectures as to dogs or cats, lions or ants ; but upon observations of what is called animal and brutal in man : of the animal side or basis of what we feel in ourselves. If individual animals, dogs or cats, lions or ants, possess something of the activity of man, so much the better, or so much the worse, for them. This means that in respect to them also we must talk, not of " nature " as a whole, but of its animal basis, as being perhaps larger and stronger in them than the animal basis of man. And if we suppose that animals think and form concepts, what kind of conjecture would justify the assertion that they do so without corresponding expressions ? Analogy with man, knowledge of the spirit, human psychology, the instrument of all our conjectures as to animal psychology, would constrain us on the contrary to suppose that if they think in any way, they also somehow speak.

Another objection is derived from human psychology, and indeed literary psychology, to the effect that the concept can exist without the word, for it is certainly true that we all know books *well thought and ill written* : that is to say, a thought which remains *beyond* the expression, or *notwithstanding* faulty expression. But when we talk of books well thought and ill written, we cannot mean anything but that in such books are parts, pages, periods or propositions well thought and well written, and other parts (perhaps the least important) ill thought and ill written, not really thought and so not really expressed. Where Vico's *Scienza nuova* is really ill written, it is also ill thought. If we pass from the consideration of big books to a short sentence, the error or inaccuracy of such a contention will leap to the eyes. How could a single sentence be clearly thought and confusedly written ?

All that can be admitted is that sometimes we possess thoughts (concepts) in an intuitive form, which is an abbreviated or rather peculiar expression, sufficient for us, but not sufficient to communicate it easily to any other given person or persons. Hence it is incorrect to say that we have the thought without the expression ; whereas we should rather say that we have, indeed, the expression, but in such a form that it is not easy to communicate it to others. This, however, is a very variable, relative fact. There are always those who catch our thought on the wing, prefer it in this abbreviated form, and would be wearied by the greater development of it required by others. In other words, the thought considered abstractly and logically will be the same ; but æsthetically we are dealing with two different intuition-expressions, into which different psychological elements enter. The same argument suffices to destroy, that is,

to interpret correctly, the altogether empirical distinction
between an *internal* and an *external* language.

The most lofty manifestations, the summits of in- *Art and*
tellectual and of intuitive knowledge shining from afar, *science.*
are called, as we know, Art and Science. Art and Science,
then, are different and yet linked together ; they meet
on one side, which is the æsthetic side. Every scientific
work is also a work of art. The æsthetic side may remain
little noticed when our mind is altogether taken up with
the effort to understand the thought of the man of
science and to examine its truth. But it is no longer
unnoticed when we pass from the activity of understanding to that of contemplation and see that thought
either develop itself before us, limpid, exact, well-shaped,
without superfluous or insufficient words, with appropriate
rhythm and intonation ; or confused, broken, embarrassed,
tentative. Great thinkers are sometimes called great
writers, while other equally great thinkers remain more
or less fragmentary writers even if their fragments have
the scientific value of harmonious, coherent, and perfect
works.

We pardon thinkers and men of science their literary
mediocrity. The fragments, the flashes, console us for
the whole, because it is far easier to recover the well-
arranged composition from the fragmentary work of
genius, to liberate the flame latent in the spark, than to
achieve the discovery of genius. But how can we pardon
mediocre expression in pure artists ? " *Mediocribus esse
poetis non di, non homines, non concessere columnae.*"
The poet or painter who lacks form, lacks everything,
because he lacks *himself*. Poetical material permeates
the souls of all : the expression alone, that is to say, the
form, makes the poet. And here appears the truth of *Content and*
the view which denies all content to art, just the in- *form : another*
tellectual concept being understood as content. In this *meaning.*
sense, when we take " content " as equal to " concept " *Prose and*
it is most true, not only that art does not consist of *poetry.*
content, but also that *it has no content*.

The distinction between *poetry and prose* also cannot

be justified, save as that between art and science. It was seen in antiquity that such distinction could not be founded on external elements, such as rhythm and metre, or on rhymed or unrhymed form ; that it was, on the contrary, altogether internal. Poetry is the language of feeling, prose of the intellect ; but since the intellect is also feeling, in its concreteness and reality, all prose has its poetical side.

The relation of first and second degree.

The relation between intuitive knowledge or expression and intellectual knowledge or concept, between art and science, poetry and prose, cannot be otherwise defined than by saying that it is one of *double degree*. The first degree is the expression, the second the concept : the first can stand without the second, but the second cannot stand without the first. There is poetry without prose, but not prose without poetry. Expression, indeed, is the first affirmation of human activity. Poetry is " the mother tongue of the human race " ; the first men " were by nature sublime poets." We assert this in another way, when we observe that the passage from soul to spirit, from animal to human activity, is effected by means of language. And this should be said of intuition or expression in general. But to us it appears somewhat inaccurate to define language or expression as an *intermediate* link between nature and humanity, as though it were a mixture of both. Where humanity appears, the other has already disappeared ; the man who expresses himself, certainly emerges from the state of nature, but he really does emerge : he does not stand half within and half without, as the use of the phrase " intermediate link " would imply.

Non-existence of other forms of knowledge.

The cognitive spirit has no form other than these two. Expression and concept exhaust it completely. The whole speculative life of man is spent in passing from one to the other and back again.

Historicity. Its identity with and difference from art.

Historicity is incorrectly held to be a third theoretical form. Historicity is not form, but content : as form, it is nothing but intuition or æsthetic fact. History does not seek for laws nor form concepts ; it employs neither

induction nor deduction ; it is directed *ad narrandum,
non ad demonstrandum* ; it does not construct universals
and abstractions, but posits intuitions. The this and
here, the *individuum omnimode determinatum,* is its
domain, as it is the domain of art. History, therefore,
is included in the universal concept of art.

As against this doctrine, in view of the impossibility
of conceiving a third mode of knowledge, objections have
been brought forward which would lead to the affiliation
of history to intellectual or scientific knowledge. The
greater portion of these objections is animated by the
prejudice that in refusing to history the character of
conceptual science something of its value and dignity
has been taken from it. This really arises from a false
idea of art, conceived not as an essential theoretic
function, but as an amusement, a superfluity, a frivolity.
Without reopening a long debate, which so far as we
are concerned is finally closed, we will mention here one
sophism which has been and still is widely repeated.
Its purpose is to show the logical and scientific nature
of history. The sophism consists in admitting that historical knowledge has for its object the individual ;
but not the representation, it is added, but rather the
concept of the individual. From this it is argued that
history is also a logical or scientific form of knowledge.
History, in fact, is supposed to work out the concept of
a personage such as Charlemagne or Napoleon ; of an
epoch, like the Renaissance or the Reformation ; of an
event, such as the French Revolution and the Unification
of Italy. This it is held to do in the same way as Geometry works out the concepts of spatial forms, or Æsthetic
that of expression. But all this is untrue. History
cannot do otherwise than *represent* Napoleon and Charlemagne, the Renaissance and the Reformation, the French
Revolution and the Unification of Italy as individual
facts with their individual physiognomy : that is, in the
sense in which logicians use the word " represent " when
they say that one cannot have a concept of the individual,
but only a representation. The so-called concept of the

individual is always a universal or general concept, full
of characteristics, supremely full, if you like, but however full it be, incapable of attaining to that individuality
to which historical knowledge, as æsthetic knowledge,
alone attains.

To show how the content of history comes to be distinguished from that of art in the narrow sense, we must
recall what has already been observed as to the ideal
character of the intuition or first perception, in which
all is real and therefore nothing is real. Only at a later
stage does the spirit form the concepts of external and
internal, of what has happened and what is desired, of
object and subject, and the like : only at this later stage,
that is, does it distinguish historical from non-historical
intuition, the *real* from the *unreal*, real imagination from
pure imagination. Even internal facts, what is desired and
imagined, castles in the air, and countries of Cockaigne,
have their reality, and the soul, too, has its history. His
illusions form part of the biography of every individual
as real facts. But the history of an individual soul is
history, because the distinction between the real and the
unreal is always active in it, even when the illusions
themselves are the real. But these distinctive concepts
do not appear in history like the concepts of science,
but rather like those that we have seen dissolved and
melted in the æsthetic intuitions, although in history
they stand out in a manner altogether special to themselves. History does not construct the concepts of the
real and unreal, but makes use of them. History, in
fact, is not the theory of history. Mere conceptual
analysis is of no use in ascertaining whether an event in
our lives was real or imaginary. We must mentally
reproduce the intuitions in the most complete form, as
they were at the moment of production. Historicity is
distinguished in the concrete from pure imagination as
any one intuition is distinguished from any other : in
memory.

Historical   Where this is not possible, where the delicate and
criticism. fleeting shades between the real and unreal intuitions

are so slight as to mingle the one with the other, we must either renounce for the time being at least the knowledge of what really happened (and this we often do), or we must fall back upon conjecture, verisimilitude, probability. The principle of verisimilitude and of probability in fact dominates all historical criticism. Examination of sources and authorities is devoted to establishing the most credible evidence. And what is the most credible evidence, save that of the best observers, that is, of those who best remember and (be it understood) have not wished to falsify, nor had interest in falsifying the truth of things?

From this it follows that intellectualistic scepticism *Historical* finds it easy to deny the certainty of any history, for the *scepticism.* certainty of history differs from that of science. It is the certainty of memory and of authority, not that of analysis and demonstration. To speak of historical induction or demonstration is to make a metaphorical use of these expressions, which bear a quite different meaning in history to that which they bear in science. The conviction of the historian is the undemonstrable conviction of the juryman, who has heard the witnesses, listened attentively to the case, and prayed Heaven to inspire him. Sometimes, without doubt, he is mistaken, but the mistakes are in a negligible minority compared with the occasions when he grasps the truth. That is why good sense is right against the intellectualists in believing in history, which is not a " fable agreed upon," but what the individual and humanity remember of their past. We strive to enlarge and to render as precise as possible this record, which in some places is dim, in others very clear. We cannot do without it, such as it is, and taken as a whole it is rich in truth. Only in a spirit of paradox can one doubt that there ever was a Greece or a Rome, an Alexander or a Cæsar, a feudal Europe overthrown by a series of revolutions, that on the 1st of November 1517 the theses of Luther were fixed to the door of the church at Wittemberg, or that the Bastile was taken by the people of Paris on the 14th of July 1789.

"What proof hast thou of all this?" asks the sophist, ironically. Humanity replies: "I remember it."

Philosophy as perfect science. The so-called natural sciences, and their limits. The world of what has happened, of the concrete, of historical fact, is the world called real, natural, including in this definition both the reality called physical and that called spiritual and human. All this world is intuition; historical intuition, if it be shown as it realistically is; imaginary or artistic intuition in the narrow sense, if presented in the aspect of the possible, that is to say, of the imaginable.

Science, true science, which is not intuition but concept, not individuality but universality, cannot be anything but science of the spirit, that is, of what reality has of universal: Philosophy. If natural *sciences* be spoken of, apart from philosophy, we must observe that these are not perfect sciences: they are aggregates of cognitions, arbitrarily abstracted and fixed. The so-called natural sciences indeed themselves recognize that they are surrounded by limitations, and these limitations are nothing but historical and intuitive data. They calculate, measure, establish equalities and uniformities, create classes and types, formulate laws, show in their own way how one fact arises out of other facts; but while doing this they are constantly running into facts known intuitively and historically. Even geometry now states that it rests altogether on hypotheses, since three-dimensional or Euclidean space is but one of the possible spaces, selected for purposes of study because more convenient. What is true in the natural sciences is either philosophy or historical fact. What of properly naturalistic they contain, is abstraction and caprice. When the natural sciences wish to become perfect sciences, they must leave their circle and enter philosophy. They do this when they posit concepts which are anything but naturalistic, such as those of the unextended atom, of ether or vibration, of vital force, of non-intuitional space, and the like. These are true and proper attempts at philosophy, when they are not mere words void of meaning. The concepts of natural science are, without doubt, most useful ; but one cannot obtain from them that *system* which belongs only to the spirit.

These historical and intuitive data which cannot be eliminated from the natural sciences furthermore explain not only how, with the advance of knowledge, what was once believed to be true sinks gradually to the level of mythological belief and fantastic illusion, but also how among natural scientists some are to be found who call everything in their sciences upon which reasoning is founded *mythical facts, verbal expedients*, or *conventions*. Natural scientists and mathematicians who approach the study of the energies of the spirit without preparation, are apt to carry thither such mental habits and to speak in philosophy of such and such conventions as " decreed by man." They make conventions of truth and morality, and a supreme convention of the Spirit itself ! But if there are to be conventions, something must exist which is no convention, but is itself the author of conventions. This is the spiritual activity of man. The limitation of the natural sciences postulates the illimitability of philosophy.

These explications have firmly established that the *The phenomenon and the noumenon.* pure or fundamental forms of knowledge are two : the intuition and the concept—Art, and Science or Philosophy. With these are to be included History, which is, as it were, the product of intuition placed in contact with the concept, that is, of art receiving in itself philosophic distinctions, while remaining concrete and individual. All other forms (natural sciences and mathematics) are impure, being mingled with extraneous elements of practical origin. Intuition gives us the world, the phenomenon ; the concept gives us the noumenon, the Spirit.

HISTORICISM AND INTELLECTUALISM IN
ÆSTHETIC

THESE relations between intuitive or æsthetic knowledge
and the other fundamental or derivative forms of knowledge having been definitely established, we are now in
a position to reveal the errors of a series of theories which
have been, or are, presented as theories of Æsthetic.

Criticism of probability and of naturalism. From the confusion between the demands of art in
general and the particular demands of history has resulted
the theory (which has lost ground to-day, but was
once dominant) of the *probable* as the object of art.
As is generally the case with erroneous propositions,
the meaning of those who employed and employ the
concept of probability has no doubt often been much
more reasonable than their definition of the word. By
probability used really to be meant the artistic *coherence*
of the representation, that is to say, its completeness
and effectiveness, its actual presence. If "probable" be
translated "coherent," a very just meaning will often
be found in the discussions, examples, and judgements
of the critics who employ this word. An improbable
personage, an improbable ending to a comedy, are
really badly-drawn personages, badly-arranged endings,
happenings without artistic motive. It has been said
with reason that even fairies and sprites must have
probability, that is to say, be really sprites and fairies,
coherent artistic intuitions. Sometimes the word "possible" has been used instead of "probable." As we
have already remarked in passing, this word possible is

synonymous with the imaginable or intuitible. Everything truly, that is to say coherently, imagined, is possible.
But also, by a good many critics and theorists, the
probable was taken to mean the historically credible, or
that historical truth which is not demonstrable but
conjecturable, not true but probable. This was the
character which these theorists sought to impose upon
art. Who does not remember how great a part was
played in literary history by criticism based on probability, for example, censure of *Jerusalem Delivered*,
based upon the history of the Crusades, or of the Homeric
poems, upon the probable customs of emperors and kings ?
Sometimes too the æsthetic reproduction of historical
reality has been imposed upon art. This is another of
the erroneous forms taken by the theory of the *imitation
of nature*. Verism and naturalism also have afforded the
spectacle of a confusion of the æsthetic fact with the
processes of the natural sciences, by aiming at some sort
of *experimental* drama or romance.

Confusions between the methods of art and those
of the philosophic sciences have been far more frequent.
Thus it has often been held to be the task of art to expound
concepts, to unite an intelligible with a sensible, to represent *ideas* or *universals* ; putting art in the place of science,
that is, confusing the artistic function in general with the
particular case in which it becomes æsthetico-logical.

Criticism of ideas in art, of theses in art and of the typical.

The theory of art as supporting *theses*, of art considered
as an individual representation exemplifying scientific
laws, can be proved false in like manner. The example,
as example, stands for the thing exemplified, and is
thus an exposition of the universal, that is to say, a form
of science, more or less popular or vulgarizing.

The same may be said of the æsthetic theory of the
typical, when by type is understood, as it frequently is,
the abstraction or the concept, and it is affirmed that
art should make the *species* shine in the *individual*. If
individual be here understood by typical, we have here
too a merely verbal variation. To typify would signify,
in this case, to characterize ; that is, to determine and

to represent the individual. Don Quixote is a type ; but
of what is he a type, save of all Don Quixotes ? A type,
so to speak, of himself. Certainly he is not a type of
abstract concepts, such as the loss of the sense of reality,
or of the love of glory. An infinite number of personages
can be thought of under these concepts, who are not Don
Quixotes. In other words, we find our own impressions
fully determined and realized in the expression of a poet
(for example in a poetical personage). We call that
expression typical, which we might call simply æsthetic.
Thus poetical or artistic universals have sometimes been
spoken of, only to show that the artistic product is
altogether spiritual and ideal.

Criticism of the symbol and of the allegory. Continuing to correct these errors, or to clear up misunderstandings, we shall also remark that the *symbol* has
sometimes been given as the essence of art. Now, if the
symbol be conceived as inseparable from the artistic
intuition, it is a synonym for the intuition itself, which
always has an ideal character. There is no double
bottom to art, but one only ; in art all is symbolical,
because all is ideal. But if the symbol be conceived as
separable—if the symbol can be on one side, and on the
other the thing symbolized, we fall back again into the
intellectualist error : the so-called symbol is the exposition of an abstract concept, an *allegory* ; it is science,
or art aping science. But we must also be just toward
the allegorical. Sometimes it is altogether harmless.
Given the *Gerusalemme liberata*, the allegory was imagined
afterwards ; given the *Adone* of Marino, the poet of the
lascivious afterwards insinuated that it was written to
show how " immoderate indulgence ends in pain " ; given
a statue of a beautiful woman, the sculptor can attach a
label to the statue saying that it represents *Clemency* or
Goodness. This allegory that arrives attached to a
finished work *post festum* does not change the work of
art. What then is it ? It is an expression externally
added to another expression. A little page of prose is
added to the *Gerusalemme*, expressing another thought
of the poet ; a verse or a strophe is added to the *Adone*,

expressing what the poet would like to make a part of his public believe ; to the statue nothing but the single word : *Clemency* or *Goodness*.

But the greatest triumph of the intellectualist error lies in the theory of artistic and literary kinds, which still has vogue in literary treatises and disturbs the critics and the historians of art.   Let us observe its genesis.

Criticism of the theory of artistic and literary kinds.

The human mind can pass from the æsthetic to the logical, just because the former is a first step in respect to the latter.   It can destroy expression, that is, the thought of the individual, by thinking of the universal. It can gather up expressive facts into logical relations. We have already shown that this operation becomes in its turn concrete in an expression, but this does not mean that the first expressions have not been destroyed. They have yielded their place to the new æsthetico-logical expressions.   When we are on the second step, we have left the first.

One who enters a picture-gallery, or who reads a series of poems, having looked and read, may go further : he may seek out the nature and the relations of the things there expressed.   Thus those pictures and compositions, each of which is an individual inexpressible in logical terms, are gradually resolved into universals and abstractions, such as *costumes, landscapes, portraits, domestic life, battles, animals, flowers, fruit, seascapes, lakes, deserts; tragic, comic, pathetic, cruel, lyrical, epic, dramatic, chivalrous, idyllic facts,* and the like.   They are often also resolved into merely quantitative categories, such as *miniature, picture, statuette, group, madrigal, ballad, sonnet, sonnet-sequence, poetry, poem, story, romance,* and the like.

When we think the concept *domestic life*, or *chivalry*, or *idyll*, or *cruelty*, or one of the quantitative concepts mentioned above, the individual expressive fact from which we started has been abandoned.   From æsthetes that we were, we have changed into logicians ; from contemplators of expression, into reasoners.   Certainly no objection can be made to such a process.   In what other way could science arise, which, if it have æsthetic expressions presupposed in it, must yet go beyond them in order to fulfil its function ? The logical or scientific form, as such, excludes the æsthetic form. He who begins to think scientifically has already ceased to contemplate æsthetically ; although his thought assumes of necessity in its turn an æsthetic form, as has already been said, and as it would be superfluous to repeat.

Error begins when we try to deduce the expression from the concept, and to find in what takes its place the laws of the thing whose place is taken ; when the difference between the second and the first step has not been observed, and when, in consequence, we declare that we are standing on the first step, when we are really standing on the second. This error is known as the *theory of artistic and literary kinds*.

" What is the *æsthetic* form of domestic life, of chivalry, of the idyll, of cruelty, and so forth ? How should these contents be *represented* ? " Such is the absurd problem implied in the theory of artistic and literary classes, when it has been shorn of excrescences and reduced to a simple formula. It is in this that consists all search after laws or rules of classes. Domestic life, chivalry, idyll, cruelty and the like, are not impressions, but concepts. They are not contents, but logical-æsthetic forms. You cannot express the form, for it is already itself expression. For what are the words cruelty, idyll, chivalry, domestic life, and so on, but the expression of those concepts ?

Even the most refined of such distinctions, which possess the most philosophic appearance, do not resist criticism ; as when works of art are divided into subjective and objective kinds, into lyric and epic, into works of feeling and decorative works. In æsthetic analysis it is impossible to separate subjective from objective, lyric from epic, the image of feeling from that of things.

Errors derived from this theory in judgements on art. From the theory of artistic and literary kinds derive those erroneous modes of judgement and of criticism, thanks to which, instead of asking before a work of art if it be expressive and what it expresses, whether it speak or stammer or is altogether silent, they ask if it obey the *laws* of epic or of tragedy, of historical painting or of landscape. While making a verbal pretence of agreeing, or yielding a feigned obedience, artists have, however, really always disregarded these *laws of the kinds*. Every true work of art has violated some established kind and upset the ideas of the critics, who have thus been obliged to broaden the kinds, until finally even the broadened kind has proved too narrow, owing to the appearance of new works of art, naturally followed by new scandals, new upsettings and—new broadenings.

To the same theory are due the prejudices, owing to which at one time (is it really passed ?) people used to lament that Italy had no tragedy (until one arose who bestowed such a wreath, which alone of adornments was wanting to her glorious locks), nor France the epic poem (until the *Henriade*, which slaked the thirsty throats of the critics). Eulogies accorded to the inventors of new kinds are connected with these prejudices, so much so, that in the seventeenth century the invention of the *mock-heroic* poem seemed an important event, and the honour of it was disputed, as though it were the discovery of America. But the works adorned with this name (the *Secchia rapita* and the *Scherno degli Dei*) were still-born, because their authors (a slight drawback) had nothing new or original to say. Mediocrities racked their brains to invent new kinds artificially. The *piscatorial* eclogue was added to the *pastoral*, and finally the *military* eclogue. The *Aminta* was dipped and became the *Alceo*. Finally, there have been historians of art and literature, so much fascinated with these ideas of kinds, that they claimed to write the history, not of individual and real literary and artistic works, but of those empty phantoms, their kinds. They have claimed to portray, not the evolution of the *artistic spirit*, but the *evolution of kinds*.

The philosophical condemnation of artistic and literary kinds is found in the formulation and demonstration of what artistic activity has always done and good taste always recognized. What are we to do if good taste and

the real fact, when reduced to formulas, sometimes assume
the air of paradoxes ?

*Empirical
sense of the
divisions of
kinds.*

It is not scientifically incorrect to talk of tragedies,
comedies, dramas, romances, pictures of everyday life,
battle - pieces, landscapes, seascapes, poems, versicles,
lyrics, and the like, if it be only with a view to be understood, and to draw attention to certain groups of works,
in general and approximately, to which, for one reason or
another, it is desired to draw attention. To employ
words and *phrases* is not to establish *laws* and *definitions*.
The mistake only arises when the weight of a scientific
definition is given to a word, when we ingenuously let
ourselves be caught in the meshes of that phraseology.
Pray permit me a comparison. The books in a library
must be arranged in one way or another. This used
generally to be done by a rough classification of subjects
(among which the categories of miscellaneous and eccentric
were not wanting) ; they are now generally arranged by
sizes or by publishers. Who can deny the necessity and
the utility of such arrangements ? But what should we
say if some one began seriously to seek out the literary
laws of miscellanies and of eccentricities, of the Aldines or
Bodonis, of shelf A or shelf B, that is to say, of those
altogether arbitrary groupings whose sole object was their
practical utility. Yet should any one attempt such an
undertaking, he would be doing neither more nor less than
those do who seek out the *æsthetic laws* which must in
their belief control literary and artistic kinds.

V

ANALOGOUS ERRORS IN THE THEORY OF HISTORY AND IN LOGIC

THE better to confirm these criticisms, it will be useful to cast a rapid glance over analogous and opposite errors, due to ignorance as to the true nature of art and its relation to history and to science. These errors have injured alike the theory of history and that of science, Historic (or Historiology) and Logic.

Historical intellectualism has opened the way to the many attempts, made especially during the last two centuries and continued to-day, to discover *a philosophy of history*, an *ideal history*, a *sociology*, a *historical psychology*, or whatever else a science may be called, whose object is to extract from history concepts and universal laws. What must these laws, these universals be ? Historical laws and historical concepts ? In that case, an elementary acquaintance with the theory of knowledge suffices to make clear the absurdity of the attempt. When such expressions as a *historical law*, a *historical concept* are not simply metaphors colloquially employed, they are truly contradictory terms : the adjective is as unsuitable to the substantive as in the expressions "qualitative quantity" or "pluralistic monism." History implies concreteness and individuality, law and concept mean abstractness and universality. But if the attempt to extract *historical* laws and concepts from history be abandoned, and it be merely desired to draw from it laws and concepts, the attempt is certainly not frivolous ; but the science thus obtained will be, not a philosophy of

Criticism of the philosophy of history.

39

history, but rather, according to circumstances, either philosophy in its various forms of Ethics, Logic, etc., or empirical science with its infinite divisions and sub-divisions. The search is in fact either for those philo-sophical concepts which, as already remarked, are the basis of every historical construction and differentiate perception from intuition, historical intuition from pure intuition, history from art ; or already formed historical intuitions are collected and arranged in types and classes, which is exactly the method of the natural sciences. Great thinkers have sometimes donned the ill-fitting cloak of the philosophy of history, and notwithstanding the covering, they have attained philosophical truths of the greatest magnitude. The cloak discarded, the truth has remained. Modern sociologists are rather to be blamed, not so much for the illusion in which they are involved when they talk of an impossible science of sociology, as for the infecundity which almost always accompanies their illusion. It matters little that Æsthetic should be called " sociological Æsthetic," or Logic, " sociological Logic." The grave evil is that such Æsthetic is an old-fashioned expression of sensationalism, such Logic verbal and incoherent. The philosophical movement to which we have referred has however borne two good fruits in relation to history. First of all, a keener desire has arisen for a theory of history, that is, a theory of the nature and the limits of history, a theory which, in conformity with the analysis made above, cannot obtain satisfaction save in a general science of intuition, in an Æsthetic, in which the theory of history would form a special chapter, distinguished by the insertion of universal functions. Furthermore, concrete truths relating to historical events have often been expressed beneath the false and presumptuous cloak of a philosophy of history ; rules and warnings have been formulated, empirical no doubt, yet by no means useless to students and critics. It does not seem possible to deny this utility even to the most recent of philosophies of history, known as historical materialism, which has thrown a very vivid light upon many sides of social life formerly neglected or ill understood.

The principle of authority, of the *ipse dixit*, is an intrusion by historicity into the domains of science and philosophy which has dominated the schools and substitutes for introspection and philosophical analysis this or that evidence, document, or authoritative statement, with which history certainly cannot dispense. But Logic, the science of thought and of intellectual knowledge, has suffered the most grave and destructive of all disturbances and errors through an imperfect understanding of the æsthetic fact. How could it be otherwise, if logical activity come after and contain in itself æsthetic activity ? An inexact Æsthetic must of necessity drag after it an inexact Logic. *Æsthetic intrusions into Logic.*

Whoever opens a logical treatise, from the *Organon* of Aristotle to the modern works on the subject, must agree that all contain a haphazard mixture of verbal facts and facts of thought, of grammatical forms and of conceptual forms, of Æsthetic and of Logic. Not that attempts have been wanting to escape from verbal expression and to seize thought in its true nature. Aristotelian logic itself did not become mere syllogistic and verbalism without some hesitation and indecision. The problem proper to logic was often touched upon in their disputes by the nominalists, realists and conceptualists of the Middle Ages. With Galileo and with Bacon, the natural sciences gave an honourable place to induction. Vico combated formalist and mathematical logic in favour of inventive methods. Kant called attention to the *a priori* synthesis. Absolute idealism despised the Aristotelian Logic. The followers of Herbart, though still loyal to Aristotle, emphasized those judgements which they called narrative and which have a character altogether differing from that of other logical judgements. Finally, the linguists insisted upon the irrationality of the word, in relation to the concept. But a conscious, sure and radical movement of reform can find no basis or point of departure, save in the science of Æsthetic.

Logic in its essence.   In a Logic suitably reformed on this basis, this truth must first and foremost be proclaimed, and all its consequences deduced : the logical fact, *the only logical fact*, is *the concept*, the universal, the spirit that forms, and in so far as it forms, the universal. And if by induction be understood, as sometimes it has been, the formation of universals, and by deduction their verbal development, then it is clear that true Logic can be nothing but inductive Logic. But since by the word " deduction " has been more frequently understood the special processes of mathematics, and the word " induction " those of the natural sciences, it will be best to avoid both words and say that true Logic is Logic of the concept. The Logic of the concept, while employing a method which is both induction and deduction, will employ neither exclusively, that is, it will employ the speculative method which is intrinsic to it.

The concept, the universal, considered abstractly in itself, is *inexpressible*. No word is proper to it. So true is this, that the logical concept remains always the same, notwithstanding the variation of verbal forms. In respect to the concept, expression is a simple *sign* or *indication*. There must be an expression, it cannot be absent ; but what it is to be, this or that, is determined by the historical and psychological conditions of the individual who is speaking. The quality of the expression is not deducible from the nature of the concept. There does not exist a true (logical) sense of words. The true sense of words is that which is conferred upon them on each occasion by the person forming a concept.

Distinction between logical and non-logical judgements.   This being so, the only truly logical (that is, æstheticological) propositions, the only rigorously logical judgements, must be those whose proper and sole content is the determination of a concept. These propositions or judgements are *definitions*. Science itself is nothing but a collection of definitions, unified in a supreme definition ; a system of concepts, or highest concept.

It is therefore necessary (at least as a preliminary) to exclude from Logic all those propositions which do not affirm universals. Narrative judgements, not less than those termed non-enunciative by Aristotle, such as the expression of desires, are not properly logical judgements. They are either purely æsthetic propositions or historical propositions. " Peter is passing ; it is raining to-day ; I am sleepy ; I want to read " : these and an infinity of propositions of the same kind are nothing but either a mere enclosing in words the impression of the fact that Peter is passing, of the falling rain, of my organism inclining to sleep, and of my will directed to reading, or an existential affirmation concerning those facts. They are expressions of the real or of the unreal, historical-imaginative or pure-imaginative ; they are certainly not definitions of universals.

This exclusion cannot meet with great difficulties. It *Syllogistic.* is already almost an accomplished fact, and the only thing required is to render it explicit, decisive and coherent. But what is to be done with all that part of human thought called *syllogistic*, consisting of judgements and reasonings based upon concepts ? What is syllogistic ? Is it to be looked down upon with contempt, as something useless, as has so often been done by the humanists in their reaction against scholasticism, by absolute idealism, by the enthusiastic admiration of our times for the methods of observation and experiment of the natural sciences ?— Syllogistic, reasoning *in forma*, is not the discovery of truth ; it is the art of expounding, debating, disputing with oneself and others. Proceeding from concepts already formed, from facts already observed, and appealing to the persist-ence of the true or of thought (such is the meaning of the laws of identity and contradiction), it infers consequences from those data, that is, it re-states what has already been discovered. Therefore, if it be an *idem per idem* from the point of view of invention, it is most efficacious in teaching and in exposition. To reduce affirmations to a syllogistic form is a way of controlling one's own thought and of criticizing the thought of others. It is easy to laugh at syllogizers, but, if syllogistic has been born and persists, it must have good reasons of its own. Satire on it can concern only its abuses, such as the attempt to prove syllogistically questions of fact, observation and intuition, or the neglect of profound meditation and unprejudiced investigation of problems, in favour of syllogistic externality.   And if so-called *mathematical Logic* can sometimes aid us in our attempt to remember with ease, rapidly to control the results of our own thought, let us welcome this form of syllogistic also, anticipated by Leibnitz among others and again attempted by some in our own days.

But precisely because syllogistic is the art of exposition and debate, its theory cannot hold the first place in a philosophical Logic, thus usurping that belonging to the doctrine of the concept, which is the central and dominating doctrine, to which everything logical in syllogistic is reducible, without leaving a residuum (relations of concepts, subordination, co-ordination, identification and so on).   Nor must it ever be forgotten that concept and (logical) judgement and syllogism are not in the same line.   The first alone is the logical fact, the second and third are the forms in which the first manifests itself.   These, in so far as they are forms, can only be examined æsthetically (grammatically), and in so far as they possess logical content, only by ignoring the forms themselves and passing to the doctrine of the concept.

Logical falsehood and æsthetic truth.

This confirms the truth of the ordinary remark to the effect that he who reasons ill, also speaks and writes ill, that exact logical analysis is the basis of good expression.   This truth is a tautology, for to reason well is in fact to express oneself well, because the expression is the intuitive possession of one's own logical thought. The principle of contradiction itself is at bottom nothing but the æsthetic principle of coherence.   It may be maintained that it is possible to write and to speak exceedingly well, as it is also possible to reason well though starting from erroneous concepts ; that some, though lacking the acuteness that makes a great discoverer, are nevertheless exceedingly lucid writers ; because to write well depends upon having a clear intuition of one's own thought, even if it be erroneous ; not of its scientific, but of its æsthetic truth, which indeed is the same thing as writing well. A philosopher like Schopenhauer can imagine that art is a representation of the Platonic ideas. This doctrine is scientifically false, yet he may develop this false knowledge in excellent prose, æsthetically most true. But we have already replied to these objections, when observing that at that precise point where a speaker or a writer enunciates an ill-thought concept, he is at the same time a bad speaker and a bad writer, although he may afterwards recover himself in the many other parts of his thought which contain true propositions not connected with the preceding error, and therefore lucid expressions following upon confused expressions.

All researches as to the forms of judgements and of *Reformed logic.* syllogisms, their conversions and their various relations, which still encumber treatises on Logic, are therefore destined to diminish, to be transformed, to be converted into something else. The doctrine of the concept and of the organism of concepts, of definition, of system, of philosophy and the various sciences, and the like, will occupy the field and alone will constitute true and proper Logic.

Those who first had some suspicion of the intimate connexion between Æsthetic and Logic and conceived Æsthetic as a *Logic of sensible knowledge* were peculiarly addicted to applying logical categories to the new knowledge, talking of *æsthetic concepts, æsthetic judgements, æsthetic syllogisms,* and so on. We who are less superstitious as regards the permanence of the traditional Logic of the schools, and better informed as to the nature of Æsthetic, do not recommend the application of Logic to Æsthetic, but the liberation of Logic from æsthetic forms. These have given rise to non-existent forms or categories of Logic, due to the adoption of altogether arbitrary and ill-considered distinctions.

Logic thus reformed will still be *formal* Logic ; it will study the true form or activity of thought, the concept, excluding individual and particular concepts. The old Logic is ill called formal ; it would be better to call it *verbal* or *formalistic*. Formal Logic will drive out formalistic Logic. To attain this object, it will not be necessary to have recourse, as some have done, to a real or material Logic, which is no longer a science of thought, but thought itself in action ; not only a Logic, but the whole of Philosophy, in which Logic is also included. The science of thought (Logic) is that of the concept, as that of imagination (Æsthetic) is that of expression. The well-being of both sciences lies in exactly carrying out in every particular the distinction between the two domains.

Note to the Fourth Italian Edition.—The observations contained in this chapter on Logic, which are not all of them clear or accurate, should be clarified and corrected by means of the further treatment of the theme in the second volume of the *Philosophy of the Spirit*, dedicated to Logic, where the distinction between logical and historical propositions is again examined and their synthetic unity demonstrated.

THE THEORETIC ACTIVITY AND THE PRACTICAL ACTIVITY

THE intuitive and intellectual forms contain between them, as we have said, the whole theoretic domain of the spirit. But it is not possible to know them thoroughly, nor to criticize another series of erroneous æsthetic theories, without first establishing clearly the relations of the theoretic spirit with the *practical* spirit.

The practical form or activity is the *will*. We do not *The will.* here employ this word in the sense of some philosophical systems, where the will is the foundation of the universe, the ground of things and the true reality. Nor do we employ it in the wide sense of other systems, which understand by will the energy of the spirit, spirit or activity in general, making of every act of the human spirit an act of will. Neither such metaphysical nor such metaphorical meaning is ours. For us, the will is, as generally understood, that activity of the spirit which differs from the merely theoretical contemplation of things, and is productive, not of knowledge, but of actions. Action is really action, in so far as it is voluntary. It is not necessary to remark that in the will to do, we include, in the scientific sense, also what is usually called not-doing: the will to resist, to reject, the will of a Prometheus, which also is action.

Man understands things with the theoretical form, *The will as an* with the practical form he changes them; with the one *ulterior stage* he appropriates the universe, with the other he creates *knowledge.* it. But the first form is the basis of the second; and

47

the relation of *double degree*, which we have already found existing between æsthetic and logical activity, is repeated between these two on a larger scale. A knowing independent of the will is thinkable, at least in a certain sense ; will independent of knowing is unthinkable. Blind will is not will ; true will has eyes.

How can we will, without having before us historical intuitions (perceptions) of objects, and knowledge of (logical) relations, which enlightens us as to the nature of those objects ? How can we really will, if we do not know the world which surrounds us or how to change things by acting upon them ?

Objections and explanations. It has been objected that men of action, practical men *par excellence*, are the least disposed to contemplate and to theorize : their energy is not delayed in contemplation, it rushes at once intó will. And conversely, that contemplative men, philosophers, are often very mediocre in practical matters, weak willed, and therefore neglected and thrust aside in the tumult of life. It is easy to see that these distinctions are merely empirical and quantitative. Certainly, the practical man has no need of a philosophical system in order to act, but in the spheres where he does act, he starts from intuitions and concepts which are perfectly clear to him. Otherwise the most ordinary actions could not be willed. It would not be possible to will to feed oneself, for instance, without knowledge of the food, and of the link of cause and effect between certain movements and certain satisfactions. Rising gradually to the more complex forms of action, for example to the political, how could we will anything politically good or bad without knowing the real conditions of society, and consequently the means and expedients to be adopted ? When the practical man feels himself in the dark about one or more of these points, or when he is seized with doubt, action either does not begin or stops. It is then that the theoretical moment, which in the rapid succession of human actions is hardly noticed and rapidly forgotten, becomes important and occupies consciousness for a longer time. And if this moment be prolonged, then the practical man may become a Hamlet, divided between desire for action and his deficient theoretical clarity as regards the situation and the means to be employed. And if he develop a taste for contemplation and discovery, and leave willing and acting, to a greater or less extent, to others, there is formed in him the calm disposition of the artist, of the man of science, or of the philosopher, who in practice are sometimes incompetent or downright immoral. These observations are all obvious. Their exactitude cannot be denied. Let us, however, repeat that they are founded on quantitative distinctions and do not disprove but confirm the fact that an action, however slight it be, cannot really be an action, that is, an action that is willed, unless it be preceded by the cognitive activity.

Some psychologists, on the other hand, place before practical action an altogether special class of judgements, which they call *practical* judgements or *judgements of value*. They say that in order to resolve on performing an action there must have been a judgement to the effect : " this action is useful, this action is good." And at first sight this seems to have the testimony of consciousness on its side. But closer observation and analysis of greater subtlety reveal that such judgements follow instead of preceding the affirmation of the will, and are nothing but the expression of the volition already exercised. A good or useful action is an action willed. It will always be impossible to distil a single drop of usefulness or goodness from the objective study of things. We do not desire things because we know them to be good or useful ; but we know them to be good and useful, because we desire them. Here too, the rapidity with which the facts of consciousness follow one another has given rise to an illusion. Practical action is preceded by knowledge, but not by practical knowledge, or rather, knowledge of the practical : to obtain this, we must first have practical action. The third moment, therefore, of practical judgements, or judgements of value, is altogether imaginary. It does not come between the two moments or degrees

Criticism of practical judgements or judgements of value.

of theory and practice. For the rest, normative sciences in general, which regulate or command, discover and indicate values to the practical activity, do not exist ; indeed none exist for any sort of activity, since every science presupposes that activity to be already realized and developed, which it afterwards takes as its object.

Exclusion of the practical from the æsthetic.

These distinctions established, we must condemn as erroneous every theory which annexes the æsthetic activity to the practical, or introduces the laws of the second into the first. That science is theory and art practice has been many times affirmed. Those who make this statement, and look upon the æsthetic fact as a practical fact, do not do so capriciously or because they are groping in the void ; but because they have their eye on something which is really practical. But the practical which they aim is not Æsthetic, nor within Æsthetic ; it is *outside and beside it* ; and although often found united, they are not united necessarily or by the bond of identity of nature.

The æsthetic fact is altogether completed in the expressive elaboration of impressions. When we have achieved the word within us, conceived definitely and vividly a figure or a statue, or found a musical motive, expression is born and is complete ; there is no need for anything else. If after this we should open our mouths —*will* to open them to speak, or our throats to sing, that is to say, utter by word of mouth and audible melody what we have completely said or sung to ourselves ; or if we should stretch out—*will* to stretch out our hands to touch the notes of the piano, or to take up the brush and chisel, thus making on a large scale movements which we have already made in little and rapidly, in a material in which we leave more or less durable traces ; this is all an addition, a fact which obeys quite different laws from the former, with which we are not concerned for the moment, although we recognize henceforth that this second movement is a production of things, a *practical* fact, or fact of *will*. It is usual to distinguish the internal from the external work of art : the terminology seems to us infelicitous, for the work of art (the æsthetic work) is always *internal*; and what is called *external* is no longer a work of art. Others distinguish between *æsthetic* fact and *artistic* fact, meaning by the second the external or practical stage, which may follow and generally does follow the first. But in this case, it is simply a question of a linguistic usage, doubtless permissible, though perhaps not advisable.

For the same reasons the search for the *end of art* is ridiculous, when it is understood of art as art. And since to fix an end is to choose, the theory that the content of art must be *selected* is another form of the same error. A selection among impressions and sensations implies that these are already expressions, otherwise how could a selection be made among the continuous and indistinct? To choose is to will: to will this and not to will that: and this and that must be before us, expressed. Practice follows, it does not precede theory; expression is free inspiration. *Criticism of the theory of the end of art and of the choice of content.*

The true artist, in fact, finds himself big with his theme, he knows not how; he feels the moment of birth drawing near, but he cannot will it or not will it. If he were to wish to act in opposition to his inspiration, to make an arbitrary choice, if, born Anacreon, he should wish to sing of Atreus and of Alcides, his lyre would warn him of his mistake, sounding only of Venus and of Love, notwithstanding his efforts to the contrary.

The theme or content cannot, therefore, be practically or morally charged with epithets of praise or blame. When critics of art remark that a theme is *badly selected*, in cases where that observation has a just foundation, it is a question of blaming, not the selection of the theme (which would be absurd), but the manner in which the artist has treated it, the failure of the expression due to the contradictions which it contains. And when the same critics object to the theme or content of works which they proclaim to be artistically perfect as being unworthy of art and blameworthy; if these expressions really are perfect, there is nothing to be done but to *Practical innocence of art.*

advise the critics to leave the artists in peace, for they can only derive inspiration from what has moved their soul. They should rather direct their attention towards effecting changes in surrounding nature and society, that such impressions and states of soul should not recur. If ugliness were to vanish from the world, if universal virtue and felicity were established there, perhaps artists would no longer represent perverse or pessimistic feelings, but calm, innocent and joyous feelings, Arcadians of a real Arcady. But so long as ugliness and turpitude exist in nature and impose themselves upon the artist, to prevent the expression of these things also is impossible ; and when it has arisen, *factum infectum fieri nequit.* We speak thus entirely from the æsthetic point of view, and of pure criticism of art.

We are not concerned to estimate the damage which the criticism of " choice " does to artistic production, with the prejudices which it produces or maintains among the artists themselves, and with the conflict to which it gives rise between artistic impulse and critical demands. It is true that sometimes it seems also to do some good, by aiding artists to discover themselves, that is, their own impressions and their own inspiration, and to acquire consciousness of the task which is, as it were, imposed upon them by the historical moment in which they live, and by their individual temperament. In these cases, criticism of " choice," while believing that it generates, merely recognizes and aids the expressions which are already being formed. It believes itself to be the mother, where, at most, it is only the midwife.

The independ-ence of art. The impossibility of choice of content completes the theorem of the *independence of art*, and is also the only legitimate meaning of the expression : *art for art's sake.* Art is independent both of science and of the useful and the moral. There should be no fear lest frivolous or cold art should thus be justified, since what is truly frivolous or cold is so because it has not been raised to expression ; or in other words, frivolity and frigidity come always from the form of the æsthetic treatment, from failure to grasp a content, not from the material qualities of the content itself.

The saying: *the style is the man*, can also not be completely criticized, save by starting from the distinction between the theoretic and the practical, and from the theoretic character of the æsthetic activity. Man is not simply knowledge and contemplation: he is will, which contains the cognitive moment in itself. Hence the saying is either altogether void, as when it is taken to mean that the style is the man *qua* style—is the man, that is, but only so far as he is expressive activity; or it is erroneous, as when the attempt is made to deduce what a man has done and willed from what he has seen and expressed, thereby asserting that there is a logical connexion between knowing and willing. Many legends in the biographies of artists have sprung from this erroneous identification, since it seemed impossible that a man who gives expression to generous feelings should not be a noble and generous man in practical life; or that the dramatist whose plays are full of stabbing, should not himself have done a little stabbing in real life. Artists protest vainly: "*Lasciva est nobis pagina, vita proba.*" They are merely taxed in addition with lying and hypocrisy. How far more prudent you were, poor women of Verona, when you founded your belief that Dante had really descended to hell upon his blackened countenance! Yours was at any rate a historical conjecture.

Finally, *sincerity* imposed as a duty upon the artist (a law of ethics also said to be a law of æsthetic) rests upon another double meaning. For by sincerity may be meant, in the first place, the moral duty not to deceive one's neighbour; and in that case it is foreign to the artist. For indeed he deceives no one, since he gives form to what is already in his soul. He would only deceive if he were to betray his duty as an artist by failing to execute his task in its essential nature. If lies and deceit are in his soul, then the form which he gives to these things cannot be deceit or lies, precisely because it is æsthetic. If the artist be a charlatan, a

Criticism of the saying: the style is the man.

Criticism of the concept of sincerity in art.

liar, or a miscreant, he purifies his other self by reflecting it in art. If by sincerity be meant, in the second place, fulness and truth of expression, it is clear that this second sense has no relation to the ethical concept. The law, called both ethical and æsthetic, reveals itself here as nothing but a word used both by Ethics and Æsthetic.

VII

ANALOGY BETWEEN THE THEORETIC AND THE PRACTICAL

THE double degree of the theoretical activity, æsthetic *The two forms* and logical, has an important parallel in the practical *of the practical activity.* activity, which has not yet been placed in due relief. The practical activity is also divided into a first and second degree, the second implying the first. The first practical degree is the simply *useful* or *economical* activity ; the second the *moral* activity.

Economy is, as it were, the Æsthetic of practical life ; Morality its Logic.

If this has not been clearly seen by philosophers ; *The economic-* if the correct place in the system of the spirit has not *ally useful.* been given to the economic activity, if it has been left to wander about in the prolegomena to treatises on political economy, often vague and but little developed, this is due, among other reasons, to the fact that the useful or economic has been confused, sometimes with the concept of the *technical*, sometimes with that of the *egoistical.*

Technique is certainly not a special activity of the *Distinction* spirit. Technique is knowledge ; or rather, it is know- *between the useful and the* ledge itself in general which takes this name when it serves *technical.* as basis, as we have seen it does, for practical action. Knowledge which is not followed, or is supposed not to be easily followed by practical action, is called " pure " : the same knowledge, if effectively followed by action, is called " applied " ; if it is supposed that it can be easily followed by a particular action, it is called " applicable "

55

or " technical." This word, then, indicates a *situation* in which knowledge is, or may easily be, not a special form of knowledge. So true is this, that it would be altogether impossible to establish whether a given order of knowledge were, intrinsically, pure or applied. All knowledge, however abstract and philosophical it may be believed to be, may be a guide to practical acts ; a theoretical error in the ultimate principles of morality may be reflected and always in some way is reflected in practical life. One can only speak roughly and unscientifically of certain truths as pure and of others as applied.

The same knowledge that is called technical may also be called *useful*. But the word " *useful*," in conformity with the criticism of judgements of value made above, is to be understood as used here in a verbal or metaphorical sense. When we say that water is useful for putting out fire, the word " useful " is used in a non-scientific sense. Water thrown on the fire is the cause of its going out : this is the knowledge that serves for basis to the action, let us say, of firemen. There is a link, not of nature, but of simple succession, between the useful action of the person who extinguishes the conflagration and that knowledge. The technique of the effects of the water is the theoretical activity which precedes ; the only useful thing is the *action* of the man who extinguishes the fire.

Distinction of the useful from the egoistic. Some economists identify utility, that is to say, merely economic action or will, with the *egoistic*, that is to say, with what is profitable to the individual, in so far as individual, without regard to and indeed in complete opposition to the moral law. The egoistic is the immoral. In this case Economics would be a very strange science, standing not beside but opposite Ethics, like the devil facing God, or at least like the *advocatus diaboli* in the processes of canonization. Such a conception is altogether inadmissible : the science of immorality is implied in that of morality, as the science of the false is implied in Logic, science of the true, and a science of unsuccessful expression in Æsthetic, science of successful expression. If, then, Economics were the scientific treatment of egoism, it would be a chapter of Ethics, or Ethics itself ; because every moral determination implies, at the same time, a negation of its contrary.

Further, conscience tells us that to conduct oneself economically is not to conduct oneself egoistically ; that even the most morally scrupulous man must conduct himself usefully (economically), if he does not wish to act at hazard and consequently in a manner quite the reverse of moral. If utility were egoism, how could it be the duty of the altruist to behave like an egoist ?

If we are not mistaken, the difficulty is solved in a manner perfectly analogous to that in which is solved the problem of the relations between expression and concept, Æsthetic and Logic. *Economic will and moral will.*

To will economically is to *will an end* ; to will morally is to *will the rational end*. But whoever wills and acts morally, cannot but will and act usefully (economically). How could he will the *rational* end, unless he also willed it *as his particular end* ?

The converse is not true ; as it is not true in æsthetic science that the expressive fact must of necessity be linked with the logical fact. It is possible to will economically without willing morally ; and it is possible to conduct oneself with perfect economic coherence, while pursuing an end which is objectively irrational (immoral), or, rather, an end which would be held to be so at a higher grade of consciousness. *Pure economicity.*

Examples of the economic, without the moral character, are Machiavelli's hero Cæsar Borgia, or the Iago of Shakespeare. Who can help admiring their strength of will, although their activity is only economic, and is developed in opposition to what we hold moral ? Who can help admiring the Ser Ciappelletto of Boccaccio, who pursues and realizes his ideal of the perfect rascal even on his death-bed, making the petty and timid little thieves who are present at his burlesque confession exclaim : " What manner of man is this, whose perversity neither age, nor infirmity, nor the fear of death which he sees at hand, nor the fear of God before whose judgement-seat he must stand in a little while, have been able to remove, nor to make him wish to die otherwise than as he has lived ? "

The economic side of morality.

The moral man unites with the pertinacity and fearlessness of a Cæsar Borgia, of an Iago, or of a Ser Ciappelletto, the good will of the saint or of the hero. Or, rather, good will would not be will, and consequently not good, if it did not possess, in addition to the side which makes it *good*, also that which makes it *will*. So a logical thought which does not succeed in expressing itself is not thought, but at the most a confused presentiment of a thought beyond yet to come.

It is not correct, then, to conceive of the amoral man as also anti-economical, or to make of morality an element of coherence in the acts of life, and therefore of economicity. Nothing prevents us from conceiving (an hypothesis which is verified at least during certain periods and moments, if not during whole lifetimes) a man altogether without moral conscience. In a man thus organized, what for us is immorality is not so for him, because it is not felt as such. The consciousness of the contradiction between what is desired as a rational end and what is pursued egoistically cannot arise in him. This contradiction is anti-economicity. Immoral conduct becomes also anti - economical only in the man who possesses moral conscience. The moral remorse which is the indication of this, is also economical remorse ; that is to say, sorrow at not having known how to will completely and to attain that moral ideal which was willed at first, instead of allowing himself to be led astray by the passions. *Video meliora proboque, deteriora sequor*. The *video* and the *probo* are here an initial *volo* immediately contradicted and overthrown. In the man without moral sense, we must admit a remorse that is *merely economic* ; like that of a thief or of an assassin who, when on the point of robbing or of assassinating should abstain from doing so, not owing to a conversion of his being, but to nervousness and bewilderment, or even to a momentary awakening of moral consciousness. When he has come back to himself, such a thief or assassin will regret and be ashamed of his incoherence ; his remorse will not be due to having done wrong, but to *not* having done wrong ; it is therefore economic, not moral, since the latter is excluded by hypothesis. But since a lively moral consciousness is generally found among the majority of men and its total absence is a rare and perhaps non-existent monstrosity, it may be admitted that morality, in general, coincides with economicity in the conduct of life.

There need be no fear lest the parallelism that we support should introduce afresh into science the category of the *morally indifferent*, of that which is in truth action and volition, but is neither moral nor immoral ; the category in short of the *licit* and of the *permissible*, which has always been the cause or reflexion of ethical corruption, as was the case with Jesuitical morality, which it dominated. It remains quite certain that indifferent moral actions do not exist, because moral activity pervades and must pervade every least volitional movement of man. But far from upsetting the established parallelism, this confirms it. Are there by any chance intuitions which science and the intellect do not pervade and analyse, resolving them into universal concepts, or changing them into historical affirmations ? We have already seen that true science, philosophy, knows no external limits which bar its way, as happens with the so-called natural sciences. Science and morality entirely dominate, the one the æsthetic intuitions, the other the economic volitions of man, although neither of them can appear in the concrete, save the one in the intuitive, the other in the economic form. *The merely economic and the error of the morally indifferent.*

This combined identity and difference of the useful and the moral, of the economic and the ethical, explains the success at the present time and formerly of the utilitarian theory of Ethics. Indeed it is easy to discover and to illustrate a utilitarian side in every moral action ; as it is easy to reveal the æsthetic side in every logical proposition. The criticism of ethical utilitarianism cannot begin by denying this truth and seeking out absurd and *Criticism of utilitarianism and the reform of Ethics and of Economics.*

non-existent examples of *useless* moral actions. It must admit the utilitarian side and explain it as the concrete form of morality, which consists in this, that it is *inside* this form. Utilitarians do not see this inside. This is not the place for the fuller development that such ideas deserve. Ethics and Economics cannot however fail to be gainers (as we have said of Logic and Æsthetic) by a more exact determination of the relations that exist between them. Economic science is now rising to the activistical concept of the useful, as it attempts to surpass the mathematical phase in which it is still entangled ; a phase which was in its turn a progress when it super-seded historicism, or the confusion of the theoretical with the historical, and destroyed a number of capricious distinctions and false economic theories. With this con-ception, it will be easy on the one hand to absorb and to verify the semi-philosophical theories of so-called pure economics, and on the other, by the introduction of successive complications and additions, to effect a transi-tion from the philosophical to the empirical or naturalistic method and thus to embrace the particular theories ex-pounded in the so-called political or national economy of the schools.

Phenomenon and noumenon in practical activity.   As æsthetic intuition knows the phenomenon or nature, and the philosophic concept the noumenon or spirit ; so the economic activity wills the phenomenon or nature, and the moral activity the noumenon or spirit. *The spirit which wills itself,* its true self, the universal which is in the empirical and finite spirit : that is the formula which perhaps defines the essence of morality with the least impropriety. This will for the true self is *absolute freedom.*

VIII

EXCLUSION OF OTHER SPIRITUAL FORMS

IN this summary sketch that we have given of the entire *The system of* philosophy of the spirit in its fundamental moments, the *the spirit.* spirit is thus conceived as consisting of four moments or degrees, disposed in such a way that the theoretical activity is to the practical as the first theoretical degree is to the second theoretical, and the first practical degree to the second practical. The four moments imply one another regressively by their concreteness. The concept cannot exist without expression, the useful without both and morality without the three preceding degrees. If the æsthetic fact is in a certain sense alone independent while the others are more or less dependent, then the logical is the least dependent and the moral will the most. Moral intention acts on given theoretic bases, with which it cannot dispense, unless we are willing to accept that absurd procedure known to the Jesuits as *direction of intention,* in which people pretend to themselves not to know what they know only too well.

If the forms of human activity are four, four also *The forms of* are the forms of *genius.* Men endowed with genius in *genius.* art, in science, and in moral will or heroes, have always been recognized. But the genius of pure econo- micity has met with repugnance. It is not altogether without reason that a category of bad geniuses or of *geniuses of evil* has been created. The practical, merely economic genius, which is not directed to a rational end, cannot but excite an admiration mingled with alarm. To dispute as to whether the word " genius " should be applied only to creators of æsthetic expression or also to men of scientific research and of action would be a mere question of words. To observe, on the other hand, that " genius," of whatever kind it be, is always a quantitative conception and an empirical distinction, would be to repeat what has already been explained as regards artistic genius.

Non-existence of a fifth form of activity. Law ; sociability.

A fifth form of spiritual activity does not exist. It would be easy to show how all the other forms either do not possess the character of activity, or are verbal variants of the activities already examined, or are complex and derivative facts, in which the various activities are mingled, and are filled with particular and contingent contents.

The *juridical* fact, for example, considered as what is called objective law, is derived both from the economic and from the logical activities. Law is a rule, a formula (whether oral or written matters little here) in which is fixed an economic relation willed by an individual or by a community, and this economic side at once unites it with and distinguishes it from moral activity. Take another example. Sociology (among the many meanings the word bears in our times) is sometimes conceived as the study of an original element, which is called *sociability*. Now what is it that distinguishes sociability, or the relations which are developed in a meeting of men, and not in a meeting of sub-human beings, if it be not just the various spiritual activities which exist among the former and which are supposed not to exist, or to exist only in a rudimentary degree, among the latter ? Sociability, then, far from being an original, simple, irre-ducible conception, is very complex and complicated. A proof of this would be the impossibility, generally recognized, of enunciating a single law which could be described as purely sociological. Those that are im-properly so called are shown to be either empirical historical observations, or spiritual laws, that is to say judgements into which the conceptions of the spiritual activities are translated, when they are not simply empty and indeterminate generalities, like the so-called law of evolution. Sometimes, too, nothing more is understood by " sociability " than " social rule," and so law ; thus confounding sociology with the science or theory of law itself. Law, sociability, and similar concepts, are to be dealt with in a mode analogous to that employed by us in the consideration and analysis of historicity and technique.

It may seem that *religious* activity should be judged *Religion.* otherwise. But religion is nothing but knowledge, and does not differ from its other forms and sub-forms. For it is in turn either the expression of practical aspirations and ideals (religious ideals), or historical narrative (legend), or conceptual science (dogma).

It can therefore be maintained with equal truth either that religion is destroyed by the progress of human knowledge, or that it is always present there. Their religion was the whole intellectual patrimony of primitive peoples : our intellectual patrimony is our religion. The content has been changed, bettered, refined, and it will change and become better and more refined in the future also ; but its form is always the same. We do not know what use could be made of religion by those who wish to preserve it side by side with the theoretic activity of man, with his art, with his criticism and with his philosophy. It is impossible to preserve an imperfect and inferior kind of knowledge, such as religion, side by side with what has surpassed and disproved it. Catholicism, which is always consistent, will not tolerate a Science, a History, an Ethics, in contradiction to its views and doctrines. The rationalists are less coherent : they are disposed to allow a little space in their souls for a religion in contradiction with their whole theoretic world.

The religious affectations and weaknesses prevalent among the rationalists of our time have their origin in the superstitious worship so recklessly lavished upon the natural sciences. We know ourselves and their chief representatives admit that these sciences are all surrounded by *limits*. Science having been wrongly identified with the so-called natural sciences, it could be foreseen that the remainder would be sought in religion ; that remainder with which the human spirit cannot dispense. We are therefore indebted to materialism, to positivism, to naturalism for this unhealthy and often disingenuous recrudescence of religious exaltation, which belongs to the hospital, when it does not belong to the politician.

Metaphysic. Philosophy removes from religion all reason for existing, because it substitutes itself for religion. As the science of the spirit, it looks upon religion as a phenomenon, a transitory historical fact, a psychic condition that can be surpassed. Philosophy shares the domain of knowledge with the natural sciences, with history and with art. To the first it leaves enumeration, measurement and classification ; to the second, the chronicling of what has individually happened ; to the third, the individually possible. There is nothing left to allot to religion. For the same reason, philosophy, as the science of the spirit, cannot be philosophy of the intuitive datum ; nor, as has been seen, *philosophy of history*, nor *philosophy of nature* ; and therefore there cannot be a philosophical science of what is not form and universal, but material and particular. This amounts to affirming the impossibility of *Metaphysic*.

The methodology or logic of history has supplanted the philosophy of history ; an epistemology of the concepts employed in the natural sciences succeeded the Philosophy of Nature. What philosophy can study of history is its mode of construction (intuition, perception, document, probability, etc.) ; of the natural sciences the forms of the concepts which constitute them (space, time, motion, number, types, classes, etc.). Philosophy as metaphysic in the sense above described would, on the other hand, claim to compete with history and with the natural sciences, which alone are legitimate and effective in their field. Such a challenge could do nothing but reveal the incompetence of those who made it. In this sense we are *antimetaphysicans*, while declaring ourselves to be *ultra-*

metaphysicians, when the word is used to claim and to affirm the office of philosophy as self-consciousness of the spirit, distinguished from the merely empirical and classificatory office of the natural sciences.

Metaphysic has been obliged to assert the existence of a specific spiritual activity producing it, in order to maintain itself side by side with the sciences of the spirit. This activity, called in antiquity *mental or superior imagination*, and more often in modern times *intuitive intellect or intellectual intuition*, was held to unite the characters of imagination and intellect in an altogether special form. It was supposed to provide the means of passing by deduction or dialectic from the infinite to the finite, from form to matter, from the concept to the intuition, from science to history, acting by a method which was held to penetrate both the universal and the particular, the abstract and the concrete, intuition and intellect. A faculty marvellous indeed and most valuable to possess ; but we, who do not possess it, have no means of establishing its existence.

Mental imagination and the intuitive intellect.

Intellectual intuition has sometimes been considered to be the true æsthetic activity. At others a no less marvellous æsthetic activity has been placed beside, below, or above it, a faculty altogether different from simple intuition. The glories of this faculty have been celebrated, and the production of art attributed to it, or at least of certain groups of artistic production, arbitrarily chosen. Art, religion and philosophy have seemed in turn to be one only, or three distinct faculties of the spirit, sometimes one, sometimes another of them being supreme in the dignity shared by all.

Mystical Æsthetic.

It is impossible to enumerate all the various attitudes assumed or capable of being assumed by this conception of Æsthetic, which we will call *mystical*. We are here in the kingdom, not of the science of imagination, but of imagination itself, which creates its world out of varying elements drawn from impressions and feelings. Suffice it to mention that this mysterious faculty has been conceived, sometimes as practical, sometimes as a mean between the theoretic and the practical, at others again as a theoretic form side by side with philosophy and religion.

Mortality and immortality of art.

The immortality of art has sometimes been deduced from this last conception, as belonging with its sisters to the sphere of absolute spirit. At other times, on the other hand, when religion has been looked upon as mortal and as dissolved in philosophy, then has been proclaimed the mortality, even the death, actual or at least imminent, of art. This question has no meaning for us, because, seeing that the function of art is a necessary degree of the spirit, to ask if art can be eliminated is the same as to ask if sensation or intelligence can be eliminated. But Metaphysic, in the above sense, transplanting itself into an arbitrary world, is not to be criticized in its particulars, any more than we can criticize the botany of the garden of Alcina or the navigation of the voyage of Astolfo. Criticism can only exist when we refuse to join in the game ; that is to say, when we reject the very possibility of Metaphysic, always in the sense above indicated.

There is therefore no intellectual intuition in philosophy, as there is no surrogate or equivalent of it in art, or any other mode by which this imaginary function may be called and represented. There does not exist (if we may repeat ourselves) a fifth degree, a fifth or supreme faculty, theoretic or practical-theoretic, imaginative-intellectual, or intellectual-imaginative, or however otherwise it may be attempted to conceive such a faculty.

IX

INDIVISIBILITY OF EXPRESSION INTO MODES OR DEGREES AND CRITICISM OF RHETORIC

IT is customary to give long catalogues of the *characters* of art. Having reached this point of the treatise, after having studied art as spiritual activity, as theoretic activity, and as special theoretic activity (intuitive), we are able to discover that those varied and numerous determinations of characters, where they refer to anything real, do nothing but represent what we have already met with as genera, species and individuality of the æsthetic form. To the generic are reducible, as we have already observed, the characters, or rather, the verbal variants of *unity*, and of *unity* in *variety*, of *simplicity*, or *originality*, and so on ; to the specific, the characters of *truth*, of *sincerity*, and the like ; to the individual, the characters of *life*, of *vivacity*, of *animation*, of *concreteness*, of *individuality*, of *characteristicality*. The words may change again, but they will not contribute anything scientifically new. The analysis of expression as such is completely effected in the results expounded above.

It might, on the other hand, be asked at this point if there be *modes* or *degrees* of expression ; if, having distinguished two degrees of activity of the spirit, each of which is subdivided into two other degrees, one of these, the intuitive-expressive, is not in its turn subdivided into two or more intuitive modes, into a first, second or third degree of expression. But this further division is impossible ; a classification of intuition-expressions is certainly permissible, but is not philosophical : individual

The characters of art.

Non-existence of modes of expression.

67

expressive facts are so many individuals, not one of which is interchangeable with another, save in its common quality of expression. To employ the language of the schools : expression is a species which cannot function in its turn as a genus. Impressions or contents vary ; every content differs from every other content, because nothing repeats itself in life ; and the irreducible variety of the forms of expression corresponds to the continual variation of the contents, the æsthetic synthesis of impressions.

Impossibility of translations.

A corollary of this is the impossibility of *translations*, in so far as they pretend to effect the re-moulding of one expression into another, like a liquid poured from a vase of a certain shape into a vase of another shape. We can elaborate logically what we have already elaborated in æsthetic form only ; but we cannot reduce what has already possessed its æsthetic form to another form also æsthetic. Indeed, every translation either diminishes and spoils, or it creates a new expression, by putting the former back into the crucible and mingling it with the personal impressions of the so-called translator. In the former case, the expression always remains one, that of the original, the translation being more or less deficient, that is to say, not properly expression : in the other case, there would certainly be two expressions, but with two different contents. " Faithful ugliness or faithless beauty " is a proverb that well expresses the dilemma with which every translator is faced. Un-æsthetic translations, such as those that are word for word, or paraphrastic, are to be looked upon as simple commentaries upon the original.

Criticism of the rhetorical categories.

The illegitimate division of expressions into various grades is known in literature by the name of doctrine of *ornament* or of *rhetorical categories*. But similar attempts at distinctions in other artistic groups are not wanting : suffice it to recall the *realistic* and *symbolic* forms, so often mentioned in relation to painting and sculpture.

Realistic and *symbolic*, *objective* and *subjective*, *classical*

and *romantic, simple* and *ornate, proper* and *metaphorical,*
the fourteen forms of metaphor, the figures of *word* and
sentence, pleonasm, eilipse, inversion, repetition, synonyms
and *homonyms,* these and all other determinations of
modes or degrees of expression reveal their philosophical
nullity when the attempt is made to develop them in
precise definitions, because they either grasp the void
or fall into the absurd. A typical example of this is
the very common definition of metaphor as of *another
word used in place of the proper word.* Now why give
oneself this trouble ? Why substitute the improper for
the proper word ? Why take the worse and longer road
when you know the shorter and better road ? Perhaps,
as is commonly said, because the proper word is in certain
cases not so *expressive* as the so-called improper word or
metaphor ? But if this be so the metaphor is exactly
the proper word in that case, and the so-called " proper "
word, if it were used, would be *inexpressive* and therefore
most improper. Similar observations of elementary good
sense can be made regarding the other categories, as, for
example, the general one of the *ornate.* Here for instance
it may be asked how an ornament can be joined to expression. Externally ? In that case it is always separated
from the expression. Internally ? In that case, either
it does not assist the expression and mars it ; or it does
form part of it and is not an ornament, but a constituent
element of the expression, indivisible and indistinguishable
in its unity.

It is needless to say how much harm has been done
by rhetorical distinctions. Rhetoric has often been de-
claimed against, but although there has been rebellion
against its consequences, its principles have, at the same
time, been carefully preserved (perhaps in order to show
proof of philosophic consistency). In literature the
rhetorical categories have contributed, if not to make
dominant, at least to justify theoretically, that particular
kind of *bad writing* which is called *fine writing* or writing
according to rhetoric.

The terms above mentioned would never have gone

Empirical sense of the rhetorical categories.

beyond the schools, where we all of us learned them (only we never found an opportunity of using them in strictly æsthetic discussions, or at most of doing so jocosely and with a comic intention), were it not that they can sometimes be employed in one of the following significations : as *verbal variants* of the æsthetic concept ; as indications of the *anti-æsthetic*, or, finally (and this is their most important use), no longer in the service of art and æsthetic, but of *science* and *logic*.

Use of these categories as synonyms of the æsthetic fact.

First. Expressions considered directly or positively are not divisible into classes, but some are successful, others half-successful, others failures. There are perfect and imperfect, successful and unsuccessful expressions. The words recorded, and others of the same sort, may therefore sometimes indicate the successful expression, and the various forms of the failures. But they do this in the most inconstant and capricious manner, so much so that the same word serves sometimes to proclaim the perfect, sometimes to condemn the imperfect.

For example, some will say of two pictures—one without inspiration, in which the author has copied natural objects without intelligence ; the other inspired, but without close relation to existing objects—that the first is *realistic*, the second *symbolic*. Others, on the contrary, utter the word *realistic* before a picture strongly felt representing a scene of ordinary life, while they apply that of *symbolic* to another picture that is but a cold allegory. It is evident that in the first case symbolic means artistic and realistic inartistic, while in the second, realistic is synonymous with artistic and symbolic with inartistic. What wonder, then, that some hotly maintain the true art form is the symbolic, and that the realistic is inartistic ; others, that the realistic is artistic and the symbolic inartistic ? We cannot but grant that both are right, since each uses the same words in such a different sense.

The great disputes about *classicism* and *romanticism* were frequently based upon such equivocations. Sometimes the former was understood as the artistically perfect, and the second as lacking balance and imperfect ; at others " classic " meant cold and artificial, " romantic " pure, warm, powerful, truly expressive. Thus it was always possible reasonably to take the side of the classic against the romantic, or of the romantic against the classic.

The same thing happens as regards the word *style*. Sometimes it is said that every writer must have style. Here style is synonymous with form of expression. At others the form of a code of laws or of a mathematical work is said to be without style. Here the error is again committed of admitting diverse modes of expression, an ornate and a naked form, because, if style is form, the code and the mathematical treatise must also be asserted, strictly speaking, to have each its style. At other times, one hears the critics blaming some one for " having too much style " or for " writing a style." Here it is clear that style signifies, not the form, nor a mode of it, but improper and pretentious expression, a form of the inartistic.

Second. The second not altogether meaningless use of these words and distinctions is to be found when we hear in the examination of a literary composition such remarks as these : here is a pleonasm, here an ellipse, there a metaphor, here again a synonym or an ambiguity. The meaning is : Here is an error consisting of using a larger number of words than necessary (pleonasm) ; here, on the other hand, the error arises from too few having been used (ellipse), here from the use of an unsuitable word (metaphor), here of two words which seem to say two different things, but really say the same thing (synonym) ; here, on the contrary, of one word which seems to express the same thing, whereas it says two different things (ambiguity). This depreciatory and pathological use of the terms is, however, less common than the preceding.

Thirdly and finally, when rhetorical terminology possesses no æsthetic signification similar or analogous to those passed in review, and yet one feels that it is not void of meaning and designates something that

Their use to indicate various æsthetic imperfections.

Their use transcending æsthetic, in the service of science.

deserves to be noted, this means that it is used in the service of logic and of science. Granted that a concept used by a writer in a scientific sense is designated by a definite term, it is natural that other terms found in use by that writer on which he incidentally employs himself to signify the same thought, become *in respect to* the vocabulary fixed upon by him as true, metaphors, synecdoches, synonyms, elliptical forms and the like. We ourselves in the course of this treatise have several times made use of, and intend again to make use of such language, in order to make clear the sense of the words we employ, or may find employed. But this proceeding, which is of value in discussions pertaining to the criticism of science and philosophy, has none whatever in literary and artistic criticism. There are words and metaphors proper to science : the same concept may be psychologically formed in various circumstances and therefore differ in its intuitional expression. When the scientific terminology of a given writer has been established and one of these modes fixed as correct, then all other uses of it become improper or tropical. But in the æsthetic fact there are none but proper words : the same intuition can be expressed in one way only, precisely because it is intuition and not concept.

Rhetoric in the schools. Some, while admitting the æsthetic non-existence of the rhetorical categories, yet make a reservation as to their utility and the service they are supposed to render, especially in schools of literature. We confess that we fail to understand how error and confusion can educate the mind to logical distinction, or aid the teaching of a science which they disturb and obscure. Perhaps what is meant is that such distinctions, as empirical classes, can aid memory and learning, as was admitted above for literary and artistic kinds. To this there is no objection. There is certainly another purpose for which the rhetorical categories should continue to appear in schools : to be criticized there. The errors of the past must not be forgotten and no more said, and truths cannot be kept alive save by making them combat errors. Unless an account of the rhetorical categories be given, accompanied by a criticism of them, there is a risk of their springing up again, and it may be said that they are already springing up among certain philologists as the latest *psychological* discoveries.

It might seem that we thus wished to deny all bond of resemblance between different expressions and works of art. Resemblances exist, and by means of them, works of art can be arranged in this or that group. But they are likenesses such as are observed among individuals, and can never be rendered with abstract determinations. That is to say, it would be incorrect to apply identification, subordination, co-ordination and the other relations of concepts to these resemblances, which consist wholly of what is called a *family likeness*, derived from the historical conditions in which the various works have appeared and from relationship of soul among the artists. *The resemblances of expressions.*

It is in these resemblances that lies the *relative* possibility of translations ; not as reproductions of the same original expressions (which it would be vain to attempt), but as productions of *similar* expressions more or less nearly resembling the originals. The translation called good is an approximation which has original value as a work of art and can stand by itself. *The relative possibility of translations.*

X

ÆSTHETIC FEELINGS AND THE DISTINCTION BETWEEN THE BEAUTIFUL AND THE UGLY

Various signi-fications of the word feeling. PASSING to the study of more complex concepts, where the æsthetic activity is to be considered in conjunction with other orders of facts, and showing the mode of their union or complication, we find ourselves first face to face with the concept of *feeling* and with those feelings that are called *æsthetic*.

The word " feeling " is one of the richest in meanings in philosophic terminology. We have already had occasion to meet with it once, among those used to designate the spirit in its passivity, the matter or content of art, and so as synonym of *impressions*. Once again (and then the meaning was altogether different), we have met with it as designating the *non-logical* and *non-historical* character of the æsthetic fact, that is to say, pure intuition, a form of truth which defines no concept and affirms no fact.

Feeling as activity. But here it is not regarded in either of these two meanings, nor in the others which have also been con-ferred upon it to designate other *cognitive* forms of the spirit, but only in that where feeling is understood as a special activity, of non-cognitive nature, having its two poles, positive and negative, in *pleasure* and *pain*.

This activity has always greatly embarrassed philo-sophers, who have therefore attempted either to deny it as activity, or to attribute it to *nature*, excluding it from the spirit. But both these solutions bristle with diffi-culties of such a kind as to prove them finally unaccept-able to any one who examines them with care. For what could a non-spiritual activity ever be, an *activity of nature*, when we have no other knowledge of activity save as spirituality, nor of spirituality save as activity? Nature is in this case, by definition, the merely passive, inert, mechanical, material. On the other hand, the negation of the character of activity to feeling is energetically disproved by those very poles of pleasure and of pain which appear in it and manifest activity in its concreteness, or, so to say, quivering.

This critical conclusion should place us especially in the greatest embarrassment, for in the sketch of the system of the spirit given above we have left no room for the new activity of which we are now obliged to recognize the existence. But the activity of feeling, if it is activity, is not new. It has already had its place assigned to it in the system that we have sketched, where, however, it has been given another name, *economic* activity. What is called the activity of feeling is nothing but that more elementary and fundamental practical activity which we have distinguished from the ethical activity and made to consist of the appetition and volition for some individual end, apart from any moral determination. *[Identification of feeling with economic activity.]*

If feeling has been sometimes considered to be an organic or natural activity, this has happened just because it does not coincide either with logical, æsthetic or ethical activity. Looked at from the standpoint of those three (which were the only ones admitted), it has seemed to lie *outside* the true and real spirit, spirit in its aristocracy, and to be almost a determination of nature, or of the soul in so far as it is nature. From this too results the truth of another thesis, often maintained, that the æsthetic activity, like the ethical and intellectual activities, is not feeling. This thesis is inexpugnable, when feeling has already been understood implicitly and unconsciously as economic volition. The view refuted in this thesis is known as *hedonism*. This consists in reducing all the various forms of the spirit to one, which thus also loses its own distinctive character and *[Criticism of hedonism.]*

becomes something obscure and mysterious, like "the night in which all cows are black." Having brought about this reduction and mutilation, the hedonists naturally do not succeed in seeing anything else in any activity but pleasure and pain. They find no substantial difference between the pleasure of art and that of easy digestion, between the pleasure of a good action and that of breathing the fresh air with wide-expanded lungs.

Feeling as a concomitant of every form of activity.   But if the activity of feeling in the sense here defined must not be substituted for all the other forms of spiritual activity, we have not said that it cannot *accompany* them. Indeed it accompanies them of necessity, because they are all in close relation both with one another and with the elementary volitional form. Therefore each of them has for concomitants individual volitions and volitional pleasures and pains, known as feeling. But we must not confound a concomitant with the principal fact, and substitute the one for the other. The discovery of a truth, or the fulfilment of a moral duty, produces in us a joy which makes vibrate our whole being, which, by attaining the aim of those forms of spiritual activity, attains at the same time that to which it was *practically* tending, as its end. Nevertheless, *economic* or *hedonistic* satisfaction, *ethical* satisfaction, *æsthetic* satisfaction, *intellectual* satisfaction, though thus united, remain always distinct.

A question often asked is thus answered at the same time, one which has correctly seemed to be a matter of life or death for æsthetic science, namely, whether feeling and pleasure precede or follow, are cause or effect of the æsthetic fact. We must widen this question to include the relation between the various spiritual forms, and answer it by maintaining that one cannot talk of cause and effect and of a chronological before and after in the unity of the spirit.

And once the relation above expounded is established, all necessity for inquiry as to the nature of æsthetic, moral, intellectual and even what was sometimes called economic feelings, must disappear. In this last case, it is clear that it is a question, not of two terms, but of one, and inquiry as to economic feeling must be the same as that relating to economic activity. But in the other cases also, we must attend, not to the substantive, but to the adjective : the æsthetic, moral and logical character will explain the colouring of the feelings as æsthetic, moral and intellectual, whereas feeling, studied alone, will never explain those refractions and colorations.

A further consequence is, that we no longer need retain the well-known distinctions between values or feelings *of value*, and feelings that are merely hedonistic and *without value* ; *disinterested* and *interested* feelings, *objective* feelings and feelings not *objective* but simply *subjective* feelings of *approbation* and of *mere pleasure* (cf. the distinction of *Gefallen* and *Vergnügen* in German). Those distinctions were used to save the three spiritual forms, which were recognized as the triad of the *True*, the *Good* and the *Beautiful*, from confusion with the fourth form, still unknown, and therefore insidious in its indeterminateness and mother of scandals. For us this triad has completed its task, because we are capable of reaching the distinction far more directly, by receiving also the selfish, subjective, merely pleasurable feelings among the respectable forms of the spirit ; and where formerly antitheses were conceived (by ourselves and others), between value and feelings, as between spirituality and naturality, henceforth we see nothing but differences between value and value. *Meaning of certain ordinary distinctions of feelings.*

As has already been said, feeling or the economic activity presents itself as divided into two poles, positive and negative, pleasure and pain, which we can now translate into useful and disuseful (or hurtful). This bipartition has already been noted above, as a mark of the activistic character of feeling, and one which is to be found in all forms of activity. If each of these is *value*, each has opposed to it *antivalue* or *disvalue*. Absence of value is not sufficient to cause disvalue, but activity and passivity must be struggling between themselves, with- *Value and disvalue : the contraries and their union.*

out the one getting the better of the other ; hence the contradiction and disvalue of the activity that is embarrassed, impeded, or interrupted. Value is activity that unfolds itself freely : disvalue is its contrary.

We will content ourselves with this definition of the two terms, without entering into the problem of the relation between value and disvalue, that is, the problem of contraries (that is to say, whether they are to be thought of dualistically, as two beings or two orders of beings, like Ormuzd and Ahriman, angels and devils, enemies to one another ; or as a unity, which is also contrariety). This definition of the two terms will be sufficient for our purpose, which is to make clear the nature of æsthetic activity, and at this particular point one of the most obscure and disputed concepts of Æsthetic : the concept of the *Beautiful*.

The Beautiful as the value of expression, or expression without qualification. Æsthetic, intellectual, economic and ethical values and disvalues are variously denominated in current speech : *beautiful, true, good, useful, expedient, just, right* and so on—thus designating the free development of spiritual activity, action, scientific research, artistic production, when they are successful ; *ugly, false, bad, useless, inexpedient, unjust, wrong* designating embarrassed activity, the product that is a failure. In linguistic usage, these denominations are being continually shifted from one order of facts to another. *Beautiful*, for instance, is said not only of a successful expression, but also of a scientific truth, of an action successfully achieved, and of a moral action : thus we talk of an *intellectual beauty*, of a *beautiful action*, of a *moral beauty*. The attempt to keep up with these infinitely varying usages leads into a trackless labyrinth of verbalism in which many philosophers and students of art have lost their way. For this reason we have thought it best studiously to avoid the use of the word " beautiful " to indicate successful expression in its positive value. But after all the explanations that we have given, all danger of misunderstanding being now dissipated, and since on the other hand we cannot fail to recognize that the prevailing

tendency, both in current speech and in philosophy, is
to limit the meaning of the word " beautiful " precisely
to the æsthetic value, it seems now both permissible and
advisable to define beauty as *successful expression*, or
rather, as *expression* and nothing more, because expression
when it is not successful is not expression.

Consequently, the ugly is unsuccessful expression. *The ugly, and*
The paradox is true, for works of art that are failures, *the elements of*
that the beautiful presents itself as *unity*, the ugly as *compose it.*
multiplicity. Hence we hear of *merits* in relation to
works of art that are more or less failures, that is to say,
of *those parts of them that are beautiful*, which is not the
case with perfect works. It is in fact impossible to
enumerate the merits or to point out what parts of the
latter are beautiful, because being a complete fusion they
have but one value. Life circulates in the whole organism : it is not withdrawn into the several parts.

Unsuccessful works may have merit in various degrees,
even the greatest. The beautiful does not possess
degrees, for there is no conceiving a more beautiful,
that is, an expressive that is more expressive, an adequate
that is more than adequate. Ugliness, on the other
hand, does possess degrees, from the rather ugly (or
almost beautiful) to the extremely ugly. But if the ugly
were *complete*, that is to say, without any element of
beauty, it would for that very reason cease to be ugly,
because it would be without the contradiction in which
is the reason of its existence. The disvalue would become non-value ; activity would give place to passivity,
with which it is not at war, save when activity is really
present to oppose it.

And because the distinctive consciousness of the *Illusion that*
beautiful and of the ugly is based on the conflicts and *there exist*
contradictions in which æsthetic activity is developed, it *expressions*
is evident that this consciousness becomes attenuated to *neither beauti-*
the point of disappearing altogether, as we descend from *ful nor ugly.*
the more complicated to the more simple and to the
simplest instances of expression. Hence the illusion that
there are expressions neither beautiful nor ugly, those

which are obtained without sensible effort and appear easy and natural being considered such.

The whole mystery of the *beautiful* and the *ugly* is reduced to these henceforth most easy definitions. Should any one object that there exist perfect æsthetic expressions before which no pleasure is felt, and others, perhaps even failures, which give him the greatest pleasure, we must recommend him to concentrate his attention in the æsthetic fact, upon that which is truly æsthetic pleasure. Æsthetic pleasure is sometimes reinforced or rather complicated by pleasures arising from extraneous facts, which are only accidentally found united with it. The poet or any other artist affords an instance of purely æsthetic pleasure at the moment when he sees (or intuites) his work for the first time ; that is to say, when his impressions take form and his countenance is irradiated with the divine joy of the creator. On the other hand, a mixed pleasure is experienced by one who goes to the theatre, after a day's work, to witness a comedy : when the pleasure of rest and amusement, or that of laughingly snatching a nail from his coffin, accompanies the moment of true æsthetic pleasure in the art of the dramatist and actors. The same may be said of the artist who looks upon his labour with pleasure when it is finished, experiencing, in addition to the æsthetic pleasure, that very different one which arises from the thought of self-complacency satisfied, or even of the economic gain which will come to him from his work. Instances could be multiplied.

A category of *apparent* æsthetic feelings has been formed in modern Æsthetic, not arising from the form, that is to say, from the works of art as such, but from their content. It has been remarked that artistic representations arouse pleasure and pain in their infinite shades of variety. We tremble with anxiety, we rejoice, we fear, we laugh, we weep, we desire, with the personages of a drama or of a romance, with the figures in a picture and with the melody of music. But these feelings are not such as would be aroused by the real fact outside art ; or rather, they are the same in quality, but are quantitatively an attenuation of real things. Æsthetic and *apparent* pleasure and pain show themselves to be light, shallow, mobile. We have no need to treat here of these *apparent feelings*, for the good reason that we have already amply discussed them ; indeed, we have hitherto treated of nothing but them. What are these apparent or manifested feelings, but feelings objectified, intuited, expressed ? And it is natural that they do not trouble and afflict us as passionately as those of real life, because those were matter, these are form and activity ; those true and proper feelings, these intuitions and expressions. The formula of *apparent feelings* is therefore for us nothing but a tautology, through which we can run the pen without scruple.

XI

CRITICISM OF ÆSTHETIC HEDONISM

As we are opposed to hedonism in general, that is to say, to the theory based upon the pleasure and pain intrinsic to the economic activity and accompanying every other form of activity, which, confounding container and content, fails to recognize any process but the hedonistic; so we are opposed to æsthetic hedonism in particular, which looks at any rate upon the æsthetic, if not also upon all other activities, as a simple fact of feeling, and confounds the pleasurable expression, which is the beautiful, with the simply pleasurable and all its other species.

Criticism of the beautiful as that which pleases the higher senses. The æsthetic-hedonistic point of view has been presented in several forms. One of the most ancient conceives the beautiful as that which pleases sight and hearing, that is to say, the so-called *higher senses.* When analysis of æsthetic facts first began, it was, indeed, difficult to avoid the false belief that a picture and a piece of music are impressions of sight or hearing and correctly to interpret the obvious remark that the blind man does not enjoy the picture, nor the deaf man the music. To show, as we have shown, that the æsthetic fact does not depend upon the nature of the impressions, but that all sensible impressions can be raised to æsthetic expression and that none need of necessity be so raised, is an idea which presents itself only when all other doctrinal constructions of this problem have been tried. Any one who holds that the æsthetic fact is something pleasing to the eyes or to the hearing, has no line of defence against

him who consistently proceeds to identify the beautiful
with the pleasurable in general, and includes in Æsthetic
cooking, or (as some positivists have called it) the
viscerally beautiful.

The theory of *play* is another form of æsthetic hedonism.
The concept of play has sometimes helped towards the
realization of the activistic character of the expressive
fact : man (it has been said) is not really man, save when
he begins to play (that is to say, when he frees himself
from natural and mechanical causality and works spiritually) ; and his first game is art. But since the word
" play " also means that pleasure which arises from the
expenditure of the exuberant energy of the organism
(which is a practical fact), the consequence of this theory
has been that every game has been called an æsthetic
fact, or that the æsthetic function has been called a
game, because like science and everything else, it may
form part of a game. Morality alone cannot ever be
caused by the will to play (for it will never consent
to such an origin), but on the contrary itself dominates
and regulates the act itself of playing.

Criticism of the theory of play.

Finally, some have tried to deduce the pleasure of
art from the echo of that of the sexual organs. And
some of the most recent æstheticians confidently find
the genesis of the æsthetic fact in the pleasure of *conquering* and in that of *triumphing*, or, as others add, in the
wish of the male to conquer the female. This theory is
seasoned with much anecdotal erudition, heaven knows
of what degree of credibility, as to the customs of savage
peoples. But there was really no need for such assistance,
since in ordinary life one often meets poets who adorn
themselves with their poetry, like cocks raising their
crests, or turkeys spreading out their tails. But any one
who does this, in so far as he does it, is not a poet but a
poor fool, in fact, a poor fool of a cock or turkey, and the
desire for the victorious conquest of women has nothing
to do with the fact of art. It would be just as correct to
look upon poetry as *economic*, because there once were
court poets and salaried poets, and there are poets now

Criticism of the theories of sexuality and of triumph.

who find in the sale of their verses an aid to life if not a complete living.   This deduction and definition has not failed to attract some zealous neophytes in historical materialism.

Criticism of the Æsthetic of the sympathetic. Meaning in it of content and form.

Another less vulgar current of thought considers Æsthetic as the science of the *sympathetic*, as that with which we sympathize, which attracts, rejoices, arouses pleasure and admiration.   But the sympathetic is nothing but the image or representation of what pleases.   And as such it is a complex fact, resulting from a constant element, the æsthetic element of representation, and a variable element, the pleasing in its infinite forms, arising from all the various classes of values.

In ordinary language, there is sometimes a feeling of repugnance at calling an expression " beautiful," unless it is an expression of the sympathetic.   Hence the continual conflicts between the point of view of the æsthetician or art critic and that of the ordinary person, who cannot succeed in persuading himself that the image of pain and baseness can be beautiful or at least that it has as much right to be beautiful as the pleasing and the good.

The conflict could be put an end to by distinguishing two different sciences, one of expression and the other of the sympathetic, if the latter could be the object of a special science ; that is to say, if it were not, as has been shown, a complex and equivocal concept.   If predominance be given to the expressive fact, it enters Æsthetic as science of expression ; if to the pleasurable content, we fall back to the study of facts essentially hedonistic (utilitarian), however complicated they may appear.   The particular origin of the doctrine which conceives the relation between form and content as the sum of two values is also to be sought in the doctrine of the sympathetic.

Æsthetic hedonism and moralism.

In all the doctrines just now discussed, art is considered as a merely hedonistic thing.   But æsthetic hedonism cannot be maintained, save by uniting it with a general philosophical hedonism, which does not admit any other form of value.   Hardly has this hedonistic conception of art been received by philosophers who admit one or more spiritual values, truth or morality, when the following question must necessarily be asked : What must be done with art ? To what use should it be put ? Should a free course be allowed to the pleasures it procures ? And if so, to what extent ? The question of the *end of art*, which in the Æsthetic of expression is inconceivable, has a clear significance in the Æsthetic of the Sympathetic and demands a solution.

Now it is evident that such solution can have but two forms, one altogether negative, the other of a restrictive nature. The first, which we shall call *rigoristic* or *ascetic*, appears several times, although not frequently, in the history of ideas. It looks upon art as an inebriation of the senses and therefore as not only useless but harmful. According to this theory, then, we must exert all our strength to liberate the human soul from its disturbing influence. The other solution, which we shall call *pedagogic* or *moralistic-utilitarian*, admits art, but only in so far as it co-operates with the end of morality ; in so far as it assists with innocent pleasure the work of him who points the way to the true and the good ; in so far as it anoints the edge of the cup of wisdom and morality with sweet honey.

The rigoristic negation, and the pedagogic justification of art.

It is well to observe that it would be an error to divide this second view into intellectualistic and moralistic-utilitarian, according as to whether be assigned to art the end of leading to the true or to what is practically good. The educational task which is imposed upon it, precisely because it is an end which is sought after and advised, is no longer merely a theoretical fact, but a theoretical fact already become the ground for practical action ; it is not, therefore, intellectualism, but pedagogism and practicism. Nor would it be more exact to subdivide the pedagogic view into pure utilitarian and moralistic-utilitarian ; because those who admit only the satisfaction of the individual (the desire of the individual), precisely because they are absolute hedonists, have no motive for seeking an ulterior justification for art.

But to enunciate these theories at the point to which we have attained is to confute them. We prefer to restrict ourselves to observing that in the pedagogic theory of art is to be found another of the reasons why the claim has erroneously been made that the content of art should be *chosen* with a view to certain practical effects.

Criticism of pure beauty. The thesis that art consists of *pure beauty* has often been brought forward against hedonistic and pedagogic Æsthetic, and eagerly taken up by artists : " Heaven places all our joy in *pure beauty*, and the Verse is everything." If by this be understood that art is not to be confounded with sensual pleasure (utilitarian practicism), nor with the exercise of morality, then our Æsthetic also must be permitted to adorn itself with the title of *Æsthetic of pure beauty.* But if (as is often the case) something mystical and transcendent be meant by this, something unknown to our poor human world, or something spiritual and beatific, but not expressive, we must reply that while applauding the conception of a beauty *free from all that is not the spiritual form of expression*, we are unable to conceive a beauty superior to this and still less that it should be *purified of expression*, or severed from itself.

XII

THE ÆSTHETIC OF THE SYMPATHETIC AND PSEUDO-ÆSTHETIC CONCEPTS

THE doctrine of the sympathetic (very often animated and seconded in this by the capricious metaphysical and mystical Æsthetic, and by that blind traditionalism which assumes an intimate connection between things fortuitously treated together by the same authors in the same books), has introduced and rendered familiar in systems of Æsthetic a series of concepts a rapid mention of which suffices to justify our resolute expulsion of them from our own treatise.

Pseudo-æsthetic concepts, and the æsthetic of the sympathetic.

Their catalogue is long, not to say interminable : *tragic, comic, sublime, pathetic, moving, sad, ridiculous, melancholy, tragi-comic, humorous, majestic, dignified, serious, grave, imposing, noble, decorous, graceful, attractive, piquant, coquettish, idyllic, elegiac, cheerful, violent, ingenuous, cruel, base, horrible, disgusting, dreadful, nauseating ;* the list can be increased at will.

Since that doctrine took the sympathetic as its special object, it was naturally unable to neglect any of the varieties of the sympathetic, any of the mixtures or gradations by means of which, starting from the sympathetic in its loftiest and most intense manifestation, its contrary, the antipathetic and repugnant, is finally reached. And since the sympathetic content was held to be the *beautiful* and the antipathetic the *ugly*, the varieties (tragic, comic, sublime, pathetic, etc.) constituted for that conception of Æsthetic the shades and gradations intervening between the beautiful and the ugly.

*Criticism
of the theory
of the ugly in
art and of the
overcoming
of it.*

Having enumerated and defined as well as it could, the chief of these varieties, the Æsthetic of the sympathetic set itself the problem of the place to be assigned to the *ugly in art*. This problem is without meaning for us, who do not recognize any ugliness save the anti-æsthetic or inexpressive, which can never form *part* of the æsthetic fact, being, on the contrary, its *antithesis*. But in the doctrine which we are here criticizing the positing and discussion of that problem meant neither more nor less than the necessity of reconciling in some way the false and defective idea of art from which it started—art reduced to the representation of the pleasurable—with real art, which occupies a far wider field. Hence the artificial attempt to settle what examples of the *ugly* (antipathetic) could be admitted in artistic representation, and for what reasons, and in what ways.

The answer was : that the ugly is admissible, only when it can be *overcome* ; an unconquerable ugliness, such as the *disgusting* or the *nauseating*, being altogether excluded. Further, that the duty of the ugly, when admitted in art, is to contribute towards heightening the effect of the beautiful (sympathetic), by producing a series of contrasts, from which the pleasurable may issue more efficacious and joy-giving. It is, indeed, a common observation that pleasure is more vividly felt when preceded by abstinence and suffering. Thus the ugly in art was looked upon as adapted for the service of the beautiful, a stimulant and condiment of æsthetic pleasure.

That special refinement of hedonistic theory which used to be pompously called the doctrine of the *overcoming of the ugly* falls with the Æsthetic of the sympathetic, and with it the enumeration and definition of the concepts mentioned above, which show themselves to be completely foreign to Æsthetic. For Æsthetic does not recognize the sympathetic or the antipathetic or their varieties, but only the spiritual activity of representation.

*Pseudo-
æsthetic
concepts belong
to Psychology.*

Nevertheless, the important place which, as we have said, those concepts have hitherto occupied in æsthetic treatises makes it advisable to supply a rather more

XII PSEUDO-ÆSTHETIC CONCEPTS 89

complete explanation as to their nature. What shall be
their lot ? Excluded from Æsthetic, in what other part
of Philosophy will they be received ?

In truth, nowhere ; for all those concepts are without
philosophical value. They are nothing but a series of
classes, which can be fashioned in the most various ways
and multiplied at pleasure, to which it is sought to
reduce the infinite complications and shadings of the
values and disvalues of life. Of these classes, some have
an especially positive significance, like the beautiful, the
sublime, the majestic, the solemn, the serious, the weighty,
the noble, the elevated ; others a significance chiefly
negative, like the ugly, the painful, the horrible, the
dreadful, the tremendous, the monstrous, the insipid,
the extravagant ; finally in others a mixed significance
prevails, such as the comic, the tender, the melancholy,
the humorous, the tragi-comic. The complications are
infinite, because the individuations are infinite ; hence
it is not possible to construct the concepts, save in the
arbitrary and approximate manner proper to the natural
sciences, satisfied with making the best classification they
can of that reality which they can neither exhaust by
enumeration, nor understand and conquer speculatively.
And since *Psychology* is the naturalistic science which
undertakes to construct types and schemes of the spiritual
life of man (a science whose merely empirical and descriptive character becomes more evident day by day), these
concepts do not belong to Æsthetic, nor to Philosophy
in general, but must simply be handed over to Psychology.

The case of those concepts is that of all other psycho- *Impossibility*
logical constructions : no rigorous definitions of them *of rigorous*
are possible ; and consequently they cannot be deduced *definitions*
from one another nor be connected in a system, though *of them.*
this has often been attempted, with great waste of time
and without obtaining thereby any useful results. Nor
can it be claimed as possible to obtain empirical definitions, universally acceptable as precise and true in the
place of those philosophical definitions recognized as
impossible. For no single definition of a single fact

can be given, but there are innumerable definitions of it, according to the cases and the purposes for which they are made ; and it is clear that if there were only one which had the value of truth it would no longer be an empirical, but a rigorous and philosophical definition. And as a matter of fact whenever one of the terms to which we have referred has been employed (or indeed any other belonging to the same class), a new definition of it has been given at the same time, expressed or understood. Each one of those definitions differed somehow from the others, in some particular, however minute, and in its implied reference to some individual fact or other, which thus became a special object of attention and was raised to the position of a general type. Thus it is that not one of such definitions satisfies either the hearer or the constructor of it. For a moment later he finds himself before a new instance to which he recognizes that his definition is more or less insufficient, ill-adapted, and in need of retouching. So we must leave writers and speakers free to define the sublime or the comic, the tragic or the humorous, on every occasion as they please and as may suit the end they have in view. And if an empirical definition of universal validity be demanded, we can but submit this one :—The sublime (or comic, tragic, humorous, etc.) is *everything* that is or shall be so *called* by those who have employed or shall employ these *words*.

*Examples :
definitions of
the sublime,
the comic,
the humorous.*
　　What is the sublime ? The unexpected affirmation of an overwhelming moral force : that is one definition. But the other definition is equally good, which recognizes the sublime also where the force which affirms itself is certainly overwhelming, but immoral and destructive. Both remain vague and lack precision, until applied to a concrete case, to an example which makes clear what is meant by " overwhelming," and what by unexpected. They are quantitative concepts, but falsely quantitative, since there is no way of measuring them ; they are at bottom metaphors, emphatic phrases, or logical tautologies. The humorous will be laughter amid tears, bitter laughter, the sudden spring from the comic to the tragic

and from the tragic to the comic, the romantic comic, the opposite of the sublime, war declared against every attempt at insincerity, compassion ashamed to weep, a laugh, not at the fact, but at the ideal itself ; and what you will beside, according as it is wished to get a view of the physiognomy of this or that poet, of this or that poem, which, in its uniqueness, is its own definition, and though momentary and circumscribed, is alone adequate. The comic has been defined as the displeasure arising from the perception of a deformity immediately followed by a greater pleasure arising from the relaxation of our psychical forces, strained in expectation of a perception looked upon as important.   While listening to a narrative, which might, for example, be a description of the magnificently heroic purpose of some individual, we anticipate in imagination the occurrence of a magnificent and heroic action, and we prepare for its reception by concentrating our psychic forces.   All of a sudden, however, instead of the magnificent and heroic action, which the preliminaries and the tone of the narrative had led us to expect, there is an unexpected change to a small, mean, foolish action, which does not satisfy to our expectation. We have been deceived, and the recognition of the deceit brings with it an instant of displeasure.   But this instant is as it were conquered by that which immediately follows : we are able to relax our strained attention, to free ourselves from the provision of accumulated psychic energy henceforth superfluous, to feel ourselves light and well.   This is the pleasure of the comic, with its physiological equivalent of laughter.   If the unpleasant fact that has appeared should painfully affect our interests, there would not be pleasure, laughter would be at once suffocated, the psychic energy would be strained and overstrained by other more weighty perceptions.   If on the other hand such more weighty perceptions do not appear, if the whole loss be limited to a slight deception of our foresight, then the feeling of our psychic wealth that ensues affords ample compensation for this very slight disappointment.   Such, expressed in a few words, is one of the most accurate modern definitions of the comic. It boasts of containing in itself, justified or corrected and verified, the manifold attempts to define the comic, from Hellenic antiquity to our own day, from Plato's definition in the *Philebus*, and from Aristotle's, which is more explicit, and looks upon the comic as an *ugliness without pain*, to that of Hobbes, who replaced it in the feeling of *individual superiority* ; of Kant, who saw in it the *relaxation of a tension* ; or from the other proposals of those for whom it was *the conflict between great and small, between the finite and the infinite* and so on. But on close observation, the analysis and definition above given, although in appearance most elaborate and precise, yet enunciates characteristics which are applicable, not only to the comic, but to every spiritual process ; such as the succession of painful and pleasing moments and the satisfaction arising from the consciousness of strength and of its free expansion. The differentiation is here given by quantitative determinations whose limits cannot be laid down. They therefore remain vague words, possessing some degree of meaning from their reference to this or that particular comic fact, and from the psychic disposition of qualities of the speaker. If such definitions be taken too seriously, there happens to them what Jean Paul Richter said of all the definitions of the comic : namely, that their sole merit is *to be themselves comic* and to produce in reality the fact which they vainly try to fix logically. And who will ever logically determine the dividing line between the comic and the non-comic, between laughter and smiles, between smiling and gravity, or cut the ever varying continuum into which life melts into clearly divided parts ?

Relation between these concepts and æsthetic concepts.

The facts, classified as far as possible in these psychological concepts, bear no relation to the artistic fact, beyond the general one, that all of them, in so far as they constitute the material of life, can become the object of artistic representation ; and the other, an accidental relation, that æsthetic facts also may sometimes enter the processes described, such as the impression of the sublime aroused

by the work of a Titanic artist, such as Dante or Shakespeare, and of the comic produced by the attempts of a
dauber or scribbler.

But here too the process is external to the æsthetic
fact, to which is linked only the feeling of æsthetic
value and disvalue, of the beautiful and of the ugly.
Dante's Farinata is æsthetically beautiful and nothing
but beautiful : if the force of will of that personage
seem also sublime, or the expression that Dante gives
him seem, by reason of his great genius, sublime in comparison with that of a less energetic poet, these are things
altogether outside æsthetic consideration. We repeat
again that this last pays attention always and only to
the adequateness of the expression, that is to say, to
beauty.

THE " PHYSICALLY BEAUTIFUL " IN NATURE
AND IN ART

Æsthetic activity and physical concepts.

ÆSTHETIC activity, distinct from the practical activity, is always accompanied by it in its manifestations. Hence its utilitarian or hedonistic side, and the pleasure and pain which are, as it were, the practical echo of æsthetic value and disvalue, of the beautiful and of the ugly. But this practical side of the æsthetic activity has in its turn a *physical* or *psychophysical* accompaniment, which consists of sounds, tones, movements, combinations of lines and colours, and so on.

Does it *really* possess this side, or does it only seem to possess it, through the construction which we put on it in physical science, and the useful and arbitrary methods which we have already several times set in relief as proper to the empirical and abstract sciences ? Our reply cannot be doubtful, that is, it must affirm to the second of the two hypotheses.

However, it will be better to leave this point in suspense, since it is not at present necessary to press this line of inquiry further. The mere mention suffices to secure our speaking (for reasons of simplicity and adhesion to ordinary language) of the physical element as something objective and existing, against leading to hasty conclusions as to the concepts of spirit and nature and their relation.

Expression in the æsthetic sense, and expression in the naturalistic sense.

It is important, on the other hand, to make clear that as the existence of the hedonistic side in every spiritual activity has given rise to the confusion between the

XIII PHYSICAL BEAUTY

æsthetic activity and the useful or pleasurable, so the existence of, or rather the possibility of constructing, this physical side, has caused the confusion between *æsthetic* expression and expression *in a naturalistic sense* ; that is to say, between a spiritual fact and a mechanical and passive fact (not to say, between a concrete reality and an abstraction or fiction). In common speech, sometimes it is the words of the poet that are called *expressions*, the notes of the musician, or the figures of the painter ; sometimes the blush which generally accompanies the feeling of shame, the pallor often due to fear, the grinding of the teeth proper to violent anger, the shining of the eyes and certain movements of the muscles of the mouth, which manifest cheerfulness. We also say that a certain degree of heat is the *expression* of fever, that the falling of the barometer is the *expression* of rain, and even that the height of the exchange *expresses* the depreciation of the paper currency of a State, or social discontent the approach of a revolution. One can well imagine what sort of scientific results would be attained by allowing oneself to be governed by verbal usage and classing together facts so widely different. But there is, in fact, an abyss between a man who is the prey of anger with all its natural manifestations and another man who expresses it æsthetically ; between the appearance, the cries and contortions of some one grieving at the loss of a dear one and the words or song with which the same individual portrays his suffering at another time ; between the grimace of emotion and the gesture of the actor. Darwin's book on the expression of the emotions in man and animals does not belong to Æsthetic ; because there is nothing in common between the science of spiritual expression and a *Semiotic*, whether it be medical, meteorological, political, physiognomic, or chiromantic.

Expression in the naturalistic sense simply lacks *expression in the spiritual sense*, that is to say, the very character of activity and of spirituality, and therefore the bipartition into the poles of beauty and of ugliness.

It is nothing but a relation between cause and effect, fixed by the abstract intellect. The complete process of æsthetic production can be symbolized in four stages, which are : *a*, impressions ; *b*, expression or spiritual æsthetic synthesis ; *c*, hedonistic accompaniment, or pleasure of the beautiful (æsthetic pleasure) ; *d*, translation of the æsthetic fact into physical phenomena (sounds, tones, movements, combinations of lines and colours, etc.). Any one can see that the capital point, the only one that is properly speaking æsthetic and truly real, is in *b*, which is lacking to the merely naturalistic manifestation or construction also metaphorically called expression.

The expressive process is exhausted when these four stages have been passed through. It begins again with new impressions, a new æsthetic synthesis, and the accompaniments that belong to it.

Representations and memory. Expressions or representations follow one another, the one drives out the other. Certainly, this passing away, this being driven out, is not a perishing, it is not total elimination : nothing that is born dies with that complete death which would be identical with never having been born. If all things pass away, nothing can die. Even the representations that we have forgotten persist somehow in our spirit, for without this we could not explain acquired habits and capacities. Indeed the strength of life lies in this apparent forgetting : one forgets what has been absorbed and what life has superseded.

But other representations are also powerful elements in the present processes of our spirit ; and it is incumbent upon us not to forget them, or to be capable of recalling them when they are wanted. The will is always vigilant in this work of preservation, which aims at preserving (we may say) the greater, the more fundamental part of all our riches. But its vigilance does not always suffice. Memory, as we say, abandons or betrays us in different ways. For this very reason, the human spirit devises expedients which succour the weakness of memory and are its *aids*.

How these aids are possible we have been informed *The production* from what has been said. Expressions or representations *of aids to* are *also* practical facts, which are also called physical *memory.* in so far as physics classifies and reduces them to types. Now it is clear that if we can succeed in making those practical or physical facts somehow permanent, it will always be possible (all other conditions remaining equal) on perceiving them to reproduce in ourselves the already produced expression or intuition.

If that be called the object or physical stimulus in which the practical concomitant acts, or (to use physical terms) in which the movements have been isolated and made in some sort permanent, and if that object or stimulus be designated by the letter e ; the process of reproduction will take place in the following order : e, the physical stimulus ; d-b, perception of physical facts (sounds, tones, mimetic, combinations of lines and colours, etc.), which is together the æsthetic synthesis, already produced ; c, the hedonistic accompaniment, which is also reproduced.

And what else are those combinations of words called poetry, prose, poems, novels, romances, tragedies or comedies, but *physical stimulants of reproduction* (the stage e) ; what else are those combinations of sound called operas, symphonies, sonatas ; or those combinations of lines and colours called pictures, statues, architecture ? The spiritual energy of memory, with the assistance of the physical facts above mentioned, makes possible the preservation and the reproduction of the intuitions produced by man. The physiological organism and with it the memory become weakened ; the monuments of art are destroyed, and lo, all that æsthetic wealth, the fruit of the labours of many generations, diminishes and rapidly disappears.

Monuments of art, the stimulants of æsthetic reproduc- *Physical* tion, are called *beautiful things* or *physical beauty*. This *beauty.* combination of words constitutes a verbal paradox, for the beautiful is not a physical fact ; it does not belong to things, but to the activity of man, to spiritual energy.

But it is now clear through what transferences and associations, physical things and facts which are simply aids to the reproduction of the beautiful are finally called elliptically beautiful things and physical beauty. And now that we have explained this elliptical usage, we shall ourselves employ it without hesitation.

Content and form : another meaning.   The intervention of " physical beauty " serves to explain another meaning of the words " *content* " and " *form*," as used by æstheticians. Some call " content " the internal fact or expression (for us, on the other hand, form), and " form " the marble, the colours, the rhythm, the sounds (for us the antithesis of form) ; thus looking upon the physical fact as the form, which may or may not be joined to the content. It also serves to explain another aspect of what is called æsthetic " ugliness." Somebody who has nothing definite to express may try to conceal his internal emptiness in a flood of words, in sounding verse, in deafening polyphony, in painting that dazzles the eye, or by heaping together great architectural masses which arrest and astonish us without conveying anything whatever. Ugliness, then, is the capricious, the charlatanesque ; and, in reality, if practical caprice did not intervene in the theoretic function, there might be absence of beauty, but never the real presence of something deserving the adjective " ugly."

Natural and artificial beauty.   Physical beauty is usually divided into *natural* and *artificial* beauty. Thus we reach one of the facts which have given the greatest trouble to thinkers : *natural beauty*. These words often designate facts of merely practical pleasure. Any one who calls a landscape beautiful where the eye rests upon verdure, where the body moves briskly and the warm sun envelops and caresses the limbs, does not speak of anything æsthetic. But it is nevertheless indubitable that on other occasions the adjective " beautiful," applied to objects and scenes existing in nature, has a completely æsthetic signification.

It has been observed that in order to enjoy natural objects æsthetically, we must abstract from their external and historical reality, and separate their simple semblance or appearance from existence ; that if we contemplate a landscape with our head between our legs, so as to cancel our wonted relations with it, the landscape appears to us to be an ideal spectacle ; that nature is beautiful only for him who contemplates her *with the eye of the artist* ; that zoologists and botanists do not recognize *beautiful* animals and flowers ; that natural beauty is *discovered* (and examples of discovery are the points of view, pointed out by men of taste and imagination, to which more or less æsthetic travellers and excursionists afterwards have recourse in pilgrimage, whence a kind of collective *suggestion*) ; that, without the *aid of the imagination*, no part of nature is beautiful, and that with such aid the same natural object or fact is, according to the disposition of the soul, now expressive, now insignificant, now expressive of one definite thing, now of another, sad or glad, sublime or ridiculous, sweet or laughable ; finally, that a *natural beauty* which an artist would not *to some extent correct, does not exist.*

All these observations are just, and fully confirm the fact that natural beauty is simply a *stimulus* to æsthetic reproduction, which presupposes previous production. Without the previous æsthetic intuitions of the imagination, nature cannot awaken any at all. As regards natural beauty, man is like the mythical Narcissus at the fountain. Leopardi said that natural beauty is " rare, scattered, and fugitive " : it is imperfect, equivocal, variable. Each refers the natural fact to the expression in his mind. One artist is thrown into transports by a smiling landscape, another by a rag-shop, another by the pretty face of a young girl, another by the squalid countenance of an old rascal. Perhaps the first will say that the rag-shop and the ugly face of the old rascal are *repulsive* ; the second, that the smiling landscape and the face of the young girl are *insipid*. They may dispute for ever ; but they will never agree, save when they are supplied with a sufficient dose of æsthetic knowledge to enable them to recognize that both are right. *Artificial* beauty, created by man, supplies an aid that is far more ductile and efficacious.

Mixed beauty.   In addition to these two classes, æstheticians also sometimes talk in their treatises of a *mixed* beauty. A mixture of what ? Precisely of natural and artificial. Whoever fixes and externalizes, operates with natural data which he does not create but combines and transforms. In this sense, every artificial product is a mixture of nature and artifice ; and there would be no occasion to speak of a mixed beauty, as of a special category. But it sometimes happens that combinations already given in nature can be used a great deal more than in others ; as, for instance, when we design a beautiful garden and include in our design groups of trees or ponds already in place. On other occasions externalization is limited by the impossibility of producing certain effects artificially. Thus we can mix colouring matters, but we cannot create a powerful voice or a face and figure appropriate to this or that character in a play. We must therefore seek them among already existing things, and make use of them when found. When, therefore, we employ a great number of combinations already existing in nature, such as we should not be able to produce artificially if they did not exist, the resulting fact is called *mixed* beauty.

Writings.   We must distinguish from artificial beauty those instruments of reproduction called *writings*, such as alphabets, musical notes, hieroglyphics, and all pseudo-languages, from the language of flowers and flags to the language of patches (so much in vogue in the society of the eighteenth century). Writings are not physical facts which arouse directly impressions answering to æsthetic expressions ; they are simple *indications* of what must be done in order to produce such physical facts. A series of graphic signs serves to remind us of the movements which we must execute with our vocal apparatus in order to emit certain definite sounds. If, through practice, we become able to hear the words without opening our mouths and (what is much more difficult) to hear the sounds by running the eye along the stave, all this does not alter in any way the nature of the writings, which are altogether different from direct physical beauty. No one calls the book which contains the *Divine Comedy*, or the score which contains *Don Giovanni*, beautiful in the same sense in which the block of marble which contains Michael Angelo's *Moses*, or the piece of coloured wood which contains the *Transfiguration*, is metaphorically called beautiful. Both serve the reproduction of the beautiful, but the former by a far longer and more indirect route than the latter.

Another division of the beautiful, still found in treatises, is that into *free and not free*. By not-free *Free and non-free beauty.* beauties have been understood those objects which have to serve a double purpose, extra-æsthetic and æsthetic (stimulants of intuitions) ; and since it seems that the first purpose sets limits and barriers in the way of the second, the resulting beautiful object has been considered as not-free beauty.

Architectural works are especially cited ; and just for this reason, architecture has often been excluded from the number of what are called the fine arts. A temple must above all things be for the use of a cult ; a house must contain all the rooms needed for the convenience of life, and they must be arranged with a view to this convenience; a fortress must be a construction capable of resisting the attacks of given armies and the blows of given instruments of war. It is therefore concluded that the architect's field is restricted : he may *embellish* to some extent the temple, the house, the fortress ; but he is bound by the *object* of those edifices, and he can only manifest that part of his vision of beauty which does not impair their extra-æsthetic but fundamental objects.

Other examples are taken from what is called art applied to industry. Plates, glasses, knives, guns and combs can be made beautiful ; but it is held that their beauty must not be pushed so far as to prevent our eating from the plate, drinking from the glass, cutting with the knife, firing off the gun, or combing one's hair with the comb. The same is said of the art of typography : a book should be beautiful, but not to the extent of being difficult or impossible to read.

Criticism of non-free beauty. In respect of all this we must observe in the first place that the extrinsic purpose is not necessarily, precisely because it is such, a limit or impediment to the other purpose of being a stimulus to æsthetic reproduction. It is therefore quite false to maintain that architecture, for example, is by its nature imperfect and not free, since it must also obey other practical purposes ; in fact, the mere presence of fine works of architecture is enough to dispel any such illusion.

In the second place, not only are the two purposes not necessarily contradictory, but we must add that the artist always has the means of preventing this contradiction from arising. How ? by simply making the *destination* of the object which serves a practical end enter as material into his æsthetic intuition and externalization. He will not need to add anything to the object, in order to make it the instrument of æsthetic intuitions : it will be so, if perfectly adapted to its practical purpose. Rustic dwellings and palaces, churches and barracks, swords and ploughs, are beautiful, not in so far as they are embellished and adorned, but in so far as they express their end. A garment is only beautiful because it is exactly suitable to a given person in given conditions. The sword bound to the side of the warrior Rinaldo by the amorous Armida was not beautiful : " so adorned that it may seem a useless ornament, not the free instrument of war," or it was beautiful, if you will, but to the eyes and imagination of the sorceress, who liked to see her lover equipped in that effeminate way. The æsthetic activity can always agree with the practical, because expression is truth.

It cannot however be denied that æsthetic contemplation sometimes hinders practical usage. For instance, it is a quite common experience to find certain new objects seem so well adapted to their purpose, and therefore so beautiful, that people occasionally feel scruples in maltreating them by passing from their contemplation to their use. It was for this reason that King Frederick

William of Prussia showed such repugnance to sending his magnificent grenadiers, so well adapted to war, into the mud and fire of battle, while his less æsthetic son, Frederick the Great, obtained from them excellent service.

It might be objected to the explanation of the physically beautiful as a simple aid to the reproduction of the internally beautiful, or expressions, that the artist creates his expressions by painting or by sculpturing, by writing or by composing, and that therefore the physically beautiful, instead of following, sometimes precedes the æsthetically beautiful. This would be a somewhat superficial mode of understanding the procedure of the artist, who never in reality makes a stroke with his brush without having previously seen it with his imagination ; and if he has not yet seen it, he will make the stroke, not in order to externalize his expression (which does not yet exist), but as a kind of experiment and in order to have a point of departure for further meditation and internal concentration. The physical point of departure is not the physically beautiful instrument of reproduction, but a means that may be called *pedagogic*, like retiring into solitude, or the many other expedients frequently very strange, adopted by artists and scientists, who vary in these according to their various idiosyncrasies. The old æsthetician Baumgarten advised poets seeking inspiration to ride on horseback, to drink wine in moderation, and (provided they were chaste) to look at beautiful women.

Stimulants of production.

XIV

ERRORS ARISING FROM THE CONFUSION BETWEEN PHYSICS AND ÆSTHETIC

WE must mention a series of fallacious scientific doctrines which have arisen from the failure to understand the purely external relation between the æsthetic fact or artistic vision and the physical fact or instrument which aids in its reproduction, together with brief criticisms of them deduced from what has already been said.

Criticism of æsthetic associationism. That form of associationism which identifies the æsthetic fact with the *association* of two images finds support in such lack of apprehension. By what path has it been possible to arrive at such an error, so repugnant to our æsthetic consciousness, which is a consciousness of perfect unity, never of duality ? Precisely because the physical and æsthetic facts have been considered separately, as two distinct images, which enter the·spirit, the one drawn in by the other, first one and then the other. A picture has been divided into the image of the *picture* and the image of the *meaning* of the picture ; a poem, into the image of the *words* and the image of the *meaning* of the words. But this dualism of images is non-existent : the physical fact does not enter the spirit as an image, but causes the reproduction of the image (the only image, which is the æsthetic fact), in so far as it blindly stimulates the psychic organism and produces the impression which answers to the æsthetic expression already produced.

The efforts of the associationists (the usurpers of to-day in the field of Æsthetic) to emerge from the difficulty, and to reaffirm in some way the unity which has been destroyed by their principle of association, are highly instructive. Some maintain that the image recalled is unconscious ; others, leaving unconsciousness alone, hold that, on the contrary, it is vague, vaporous, confused, thus reducing the *force* of the æsthetic fact to the *weakness* of bad memory. But the dilemma is inexorable : either keep association and give up unity, or keep unity and give up association. No third way out of the difficulty exists.

From the failure to analyse so-called natural beauty thoroughly and to recognize that it is simply an incident of æsthetic reproduction, and from having looked upon it, on the contrary, as given in nature, is derived all that portion of treatises upon Æsthetic entitled *Beauty of Nature* or *Æsthetic Physics* ; sometimes even subdivided, save the mark, into æsthetic Mineralogy, Botany and Zoology. We do not wish to deny that such treatises contain many just observations, and are sometimes themselves works of art, in so far as they represent beautifully the imaginings and fancies or impressions of their authors. But we must affirm it to be scientifically false to ask oneself if the dog be beautiful and the ornithorhynchus ugly, the lily beautiful and the artichoke ugly. Indeed, the error is here double. On the one hand, æsthetic Physics falls back into the equivocation of the theory of artistic and literary kinds, of attempting to attach æsthetic determinations to the abstractions of our intellect ; on the other, it fails to recognize, as we said, the true formation of so-called natural beauty, a formation which excludes even the possibility of the question as to whether some given individual animal, flower or man be beautiful or ugly. What is not produced by the æsthetic spirit, or cannot be referred to it, is neither beautiful nor ugly. The æsthetic process arises from the ideal connexions in which natural objects are placed. *Criticism of æsthetic physics.*

The double error can be exemplified by the question as to the *Beauty of the human body*, upon which whole volumes have been written. Here we must before everything turn those who discuss this subject from the abstract toward the concrete, by asking : " What do you mean by *Criticism of the theory of the beauty of the human body.*

the human body, that of the male, the female, or the hermaphrodite?" Let us assume that they reply by dividing the inquiry into two distinct inquiries, as to male and female beauty (there really are writers who seriously discuss whether man or woman is the more beautiful); and let us continue: "Masculine or feminine beauty; but of what race of men—the white, the yellow or the black, or any others that may exist, according to the division you prefer?" Let us assume that they limit themselves to the white race, and drive home the argument: "To what sub-species of the white race?" And when we have restricted them gradually to one corner of the white world, going, let us say, from the Italian to the Tuscan, the Siennese, the Porta Camollía quarter, we will proceed: "Very good; but at what age of the human body, and in what condition and stage—that of the new-born babe, of the child, of the boy, of the adolescent, of the man of middle age, and so on? and of him who is at rest or of him who is at work, or of him who is occupied like Paul Potter's bull, or the Ganymede of Rembrandt?"

Having thus arrived, by successive reductions, at the individual *omnimode determinatum*, or rather at "this man here," pointed out with the finger, it will be easy to expose the other error, by recalling what we have said about the natural fact, which is now beautiful, now ugly, according to the point of view and to what is passing in the soul of the artist. If even the Gulf of Naples have its detractors, and if there be artists who declare it inexpressive, preferring the "gloomy firs," the "clouds and perpetual north winds," of northern seas; is it really possible that such relativity does not exist for the human body, source of the most varied suggestions?

Criticism of the beauty of geometrical figures.

The question of the *beauty of geometrical figures* is connected with æsthetic Physics. But if by geometrical figures be understood the concepts of geometry (the concepts of the triangle, the square, the cone), these are neither beautiful nor ugly, just because they are concepts. If, on the other hand, by such figures be understood bodies which possess definite geometrical forms, they will be beautiful or ugly, like every natural fact, according to the ideal connexions in which they are placed. Some hold that those geometrical figures are beautiful which point upwards, since they give the suggestion of firmness and of power. We do not deny that this may be so. But it must not be denied on the other hand that those also may possess beauty which give the impression of instability and weakness, where they represent just the insecure and the feeble ; and that in these last cases the firmness of the straight line and the lightness of the cone or of the equilateral triangle would seem to be on the contrary elements of ugliness.

Certainly, such questions as to the beauty of nature and the beauty of geometry, like others analogous as to the historically beautiful and human beauty, seem less absurd in the Æsthetic of the sympathetic, which really means by the words " æsthetic beauty " the representation of the pleasing. But the claim to determine scientifically what are sympathetic contents and what are irremediably antipathetic is none the less erroneous, even in the sphere of that doctrine and after laying down those premises. One can only answer such questions by repeating with an infinitely long postscript the *Sunt quos* of the first ode of the first book of Horace, and the *Havvi chi* of Leopardi's letter to Carlo Pepoli. To each man his beautiful (=sympathetic), as to each man his fair one. Philography is not science.

The artist sometimes has naturally existing facts before him, in producing the artificial instrument, or physically beautiful. These are called his *models* : bodies, stuffs, flowers and so on. Let us run over the sketches, studies and notes of artists : Leonardo noted down in his pocket-book, when he was working on the Last Supper : " Giovannina, weird face, is at St. Catherine's, at the Hospital ; Cristofano di Castiglione is at the Pietà, he has a fine head ; Christ, Giovan Conte, of Cardinal Mortaro's suite." And so on. From this comes the illusion that the artist *imitates nature*, when it would perhaps be more exact to say that nature imitates the artist, and

Criticism of another aspect of the imitation of nature.

obeys him. The illusion that *art imitates nature* has sometimes found ground and support in this illusion, as also in
its variant, more easily maintained, which makes of art
the *idealizer of nature*. This last theory presents the
process out of its true order, which indeed is not merely
upset but actually inverted ; for the artist does not
proceed from external reality, in order to modify it by
approximating it to the ideal ; he goes from the impression
of external nature to expression, that is to say, his ideal,
and from this passes to the natural fact, which he employs
as instrument of reproduction of the ideal fact.

Criticism of the theory of the elementary forms of the beautiful.

Another consequence of the confusion between the
æsthetic fact and the physical fact is the theory of the
elementary forms of the beautiful. If expression, if the
beautiful, be indivisible, the physical fact on the contrary,
in which it externalizes itself, can easily be divided and
subdivided : for example, a painted surface, into lines and
colours, groups and curves of lines, kinds of colours, and
so on ; a poem, into strophes, verses, feet, syllables ; a
piece of prose, into chapters, paragraphs, headings,
periods, phrases, words and so on. The parts thus
obtained are not æsthetic facts, but smaller physical facts,
arbitrarily divided. If this path were followed and
the confusion persisted in, we should end by concluding
that the true elementary forms of the beautiful are *atoms*.

The æsthetic law, several times promulgated, that
beauty must have *bulk*, could be invoked against the
atoms. It cannot be the imperceptibility of the too small,
or the inapprehensibility of the too large. But a greatness determined by perceptibility, not by measurement,
implies a concept widely different from the mathematical.
Indeed, what is called imperceptible and inapprehensible
does not produce an impression, because it is not a real
fact, but a concept : the demand for bulk in the beautiful
is thus reduced to the actual presence of the physical fact,
which serves for the reproduction of the beautiful.

Criticism of the search for the objective conditions of the beautiful.

Continuing the search for the *physical laws* or for the
objective conditions of the beautiful, it has been asked : To
what physical facts does the beautiful correspond ? To

what the ugly ?   To what unions of tones, colours, sizes,
mathematically determinable ?   Such inquiries are as if
in Political Economy one were to seek for the laws of
exchange in the physical nature of the objects exchanged.
The persistent fruitlessness of the attempt should have
given rise before long to some suspicion of its vanity.   In
our times, especially, necessity for an *inductive* Æsthetic
has been often proclaimed, of an Æsthetic starting *from
below*, proceeding like natural science and not jumping to
its conclusions.   Inductive ?   But Æsthetic has always
been both inductive and deductive, like every philosophical
science ; induction and deduction cannot be separated, nor
can they separately avail to characterize a true science.
But the word " induction " was not pronounced here by
chance.   The intention was to imply that the æsthetic
fact is really nothing but a physical fact, to be studied by
the methods proper to the physical and natural sciences.

With such a presupposition and in such a faith did
inductive Æsthetic or Æsthetic *from below* (what pride in
this modesty !) begin its labours.   It conscientiously
began by making a collection of *beautiful things*, for
example, a great number of envelopes of various shapes
and sizes, and asked which of these give the impression of
beauty and which of ugliness.   As was to be expected, the
inductive æstheticians speedily found themselves in a
difficulty, for the same objects that appeared ugly in one
aspect appeared beautiful in another.   A coarse yellow
envelope, which would be extremely ugly for the purpose
of enclosing a love-letter, is just what is wanted for a writ
served by process on stamped paper, which in its turn
would look very bad, or seem at any rate an irony,
enclosed in a square envelope of English paper.   Such
considerations of simple common sense should have
sufficed to convince inductive æstheticians that the
beautiful has no physical existence, and cause them to
desist from their vain and ridiculous quest.   But no :
they had recourse to an expedient, as to which we should
hardly like to say how far it belongs to the strict method
of natural science.   They sent their envelopes round

and opened a *referendum*, trying to settle in what beauty
or ugliness consists by the votes of the majority.

We will not waste time over this subject, lest we
should seem to be turning ourselves into tellers of comic
tales rather than expositors of æsthetic science and of its
problems. It is a matter of fact that the inductive
æstheticians have not yet discovered *one single law*.

The Astrology of Æsthetic.

He who despairs of doctors is apt to abandon himself
to charlatans. This has befallen those who have believed
in the naturalistic laws of the beautiful. Artists sometimes adopt empirical canons, such as that of the proportions of the human body, or of the golden section, that
is to say, of a line divided into two parts in such a manner
that the less is to the greater as is the greater to the whole
line ($bc : ac = ac : ab$). Such canons easily become their
superstitions, and they attribute to them the success of
their works. Thus Michael Angelo left as a precept to
his disciple Marco del Pino da Siena that " he should
always make a pyramidal serpentine figure multiplied by
one two and three," a precept which did not enable Marco
da Siena to emerge from that mediocrity which we can yet
observe in many of his paintings that exist here in Naples.
Others took Michael Angelo's words as authority for the
precept that serpentine undulating lines were the true
lines of beauty. Whole volumes have been composed on
these laws of beauty, on the golden section and on the
undulating and serpentine lines. These should in our
opinion be looked upon as the *astrology of Æsthetic*.

XV

THE ACTIVITY OF EXTERNALIZATION.
TECHNIQUE AND THE THEORY OF THE ARTS

THE fact of the production of physical beauty implies, as *The practical* *activity of ex-* *ternalization.* has already been remarked, a vigilant will, which persists in not allowing certain visions, intuitions or representations to be lost. Such a will must be able to act with the utmost rapidity and as it were instinctively, and may also need long and laborious deliberations. In any case, thus and thus only does the practical activity enter into relations with the æsthetic, that is to say, no longer as its simple accompaniment, but as a really distinct moment of it. We cannot will or not will our æsthetic vision : we can however will or not will to externalize it, or rather, to preserve and communicate to others, or not, the externalization produced.

This volitional fact of externalization is preceded by a *The technique* *of externaliza-* *tion.* complex of various kinds of knowledge. These are known as *technique*, like all knowledge which precedes a practical activity. Thus we talk of an *artistic technique* in the same metaphorical and elliptic manner that we talk of the physically beautiful, that is to say (in more precise language), *knowledge at the service of the practical activity directed to producing stimuli to aesthetic reproduction.* In place of employing so lengthy a phrase, we shall here avail ourselves of ordinary terminology, whose meaning we now understand.

The possibility of this technical knowledge, at the service of artistic reproduction, is what has led minds astray to imagine the existence of an æsthetic technique of internal expression, which is tantamount to saying, a doctrine of the *means of internal expression*, a thing that is altogether inconceivable. And we know well the reason of its inconceivability ; expression, considered in itself, is a primary theoretic activity, and as such precedes practice and intellectual knowledge which illumines practice and is independent alike of both. It aids for its part to illumine practice, but is not illuminated by it. Expression does not possess *means*, because it has not an *end* ; it has intuitions of things, but it does not will and is therefore unanalysable into the abstract components of volition, means and end. Sometimes a certain writer is said to have invented a new technique of fiction or of drama, or a painter is said to have discovered a new technique of distributing light. The word is used here at hazard ; because the so-called *new technique* is really *that romance itself, or that new picture* itself and nothing else. The distribution of light belongs to the vision of the picture itself ; as the technique of a dramatist is his dramatic conception itself. On other occasions, the word " technique " is used to designate certain merits or defects in a work that is a failure ; and it is euphemistically said that the conception is bad but the technique good, or that the conception is good but the technique bad.

On the other hand, when we talk of the different ways of painting in oils, or of etching, or of sculpturing in alabaster, then the word " technique " is in its place ; but in such a case the adjective " artistic " is used metaphorically. And if a dramatic technique in the æsthetic sense be impossible, a theatrical technique of processes of externalization of certain particular æsthetic works is not impossible. When, for instance, women were introduced on the stage in Italy in the second half of the sixteenth century, in place of men dressed as women, this was a true and real discovery in theatrical technique ; such too was the perfecting in the following century of machines for the rapid changing of scenery by the impresarios of Venice.

The collection of technical knowledge at the service of artists desirous of externalizing their expressions, can

be divided into groups, which may be entitled *theories* Technical
of the arts. Thus arises a theory of Architecture, com- theories of the
prising mechanical laws, information relating to the different arts.
weight or resistance of the materials of construction or
of fortification, manuals relating to the method of mixing
lime or stucco ; a theory of Sculpture, containing advice
as to the instruments to be used for sculpturing the various
sorts of stone, for obtaining a successful mixture of
bronze, for working with the chisel, for the accurate casting
of the clay or plaster model, for keeping clay damp ; a
theory of Painting, on the various techniques of tempera,
of oil-painting, of water-colour, of pastel, on the proportions of the human body, on the laws of perspective ;
a theory of Oratory, with precepts as to the method of
producing, of exercising and of strengthening the voice,
of attitude in impersonation and gesture ; a theory of
Music, on the combinations and fusions of tones and
sounds ; and so on. Such collections of precepts abound
in all literatures. And since it is impossible to say what
is useful and what useless to know, books of this sort
become very often a sort of encyclopædias or *catalogues of
desiderata*. Vitruvius, in his treatise on Architecture,
claims for the architect a knowledge of letters, of drawing,
of geometry, of arithmetic, of optic, of history, of natural
and moral philosophy, of jurisprudence, of medicine,
of astrology, of music, and so on. Everything is worth
knowing : learn the art and have done with it.

It should be evident that such empirical collections
are not reducible to science. They are composed of
notions, taken from various sciences and disciplines, and
their philosophical and scientific principles are to be
found in the latter. To propose to construct a scientific
theory of the different arts would be to wish to reduce
to the single and homogeneous what is by nature multiple
and heterogeneous ; to wish to destroy the existence as
a collection of what was put together precisely to form
a collection. Were we to try to give scientific form to
the manuals of the architect, the painter, or the musician,
it is clear that nothing would remain in our hands but

the general principles of Mechanics, Optics, or Acoustics. And if we were to extract and isolate what may be scattered among them of properly artistic observations, to make of them a scientific system, then the sphere of the individual art would be abandoned and that of Æsthetic entered, for Æsthetic is always general Æsthetic, or rather it cannot be divided into general and special. This last case (that is, the attempt to furnish a technique which ends in composing an Æsthetic) arises when men possessing strong scientific instincts and a natural tendency to philosophy set themselves to work to produce such theories and technical manuals.

Criticism of æsthetic theories of particular arts. But the confusion between Physics and Æsthetic has attained to its highest degree, when æsthetic theories of particular arts are imagined, to answer such questions as : What are the *limits* of each art ? What can be represented with colours, and what with sounds ? What with simple monochromatic lines and what with touches of various colours ? What with tones, and what with metres and rhythms ? What are the limits between the figurative and the auditive arts, between painting and sculpture, poetry and music ?

This, translated into scientific language, is tantamount to asking : What is the connexion between Acoustics and æsthetic expression ? What between the latter and Optics ?—and the like. Now, if *there is no passage* from the physical fact to the æsthetic, how could there be from the æsthetic to particular groups of physical facts, such as the phenomena of Optics or of Acoustics ?

Criticism of the classification of the arts. The so-called *arts* have no æsthetic limits, because, in order to have them, they would need to have also æsthetic existence in their particularity ; and we have demonstrated the altogether empirical genesis of those partitions. Consequently, any attempt at an æsthetic classification of the arts is absurd. If they be without limits, they are not exactly determinable, and consequently cannot be philosophically classified. All the books dealing with classifications and systems of the arts could be burned without any loss whatever. (We say this with the utmost respect to the writers who have expended their labours upon them.)

The impossibility of such systematizations finds something like a proof in the strange attempts made to carry it out. The first and most common partition is that into arts of *hearing, sight,* and *imagination* ; as if eyes, ears, and imagination were on the same level and could be deduced from the same logical variable as *fundamentum divisionis.* Others have proposed the division into arts of *space* and arts of *time,* arts of *rest* and *movement* ; as if the concepts of space, time, rest and motion could determine special æsthetic forms and possess anything in common with art as such. Finally, others have amused themselves by dividing them into *classic* and *romantic,* or into *oriental, classic,* and *romantic,* thereby conferring the value of scientific concepts upon simple historical denominations, or falling into those rhetorical partitions of expressive forms, already criticized above ; or into arts *that can only be seen from one side,* like painting, and arts *that can be seen from all sides,* like sculpture —and similar extravagances, which hold good neither in heaven nor on earth.

The theory of the limits of the arts was perhaps at the time when it was put forward a beneficial critical reaction against those who believed in the possibility of remodelling one expression into another, as the *Iliad* or *Paradise Lost* into a series of paintings, and indeed held a poem to be of greater or lesser value according as it could or could not be translated into pictures by a painter. But if the rebellion were reasonable and resulted in victory, this does not mean that the arguments employed and the systems constructed for the purpose were sound.

Another theory which is a corollary to that of the arts and their limits, falls with them ; that of the *union of the arts.* Given particular arts, distinct and limited, it was asked : Which is the most *powerful* ? Do we not obtain *more powerful* effects by *uniting* several ? We know nothing of this : we know only that in each particular case certain given artistic intuitions have need of

Criticism of the theory of the union of the arts.

definite physical means for their reproduction and other artistic intuitions of other means. We can obtain the effect of certain plays by simply reading them ; others need declamation and scenic display : there are some artistic intuitions which need for their full externalization words, song, musical instruments, colours, statuary, architecture, actors ; while others are quite complete in a slight outline made with the pen, or a few strokes of the pencil. But it is false to suppose that declamation and scenic effects and all the other things together that we have mentioned are *more powerful* than a simple reading or a simple outline of pen or pencil ; because each of those facts or groups of facts has, so to say, a different purpose, and the power of the means cannot be compared when the purposes are different.

Relation of the activity of externalization to utility and morality.

Finally, it is only from the point of view of a clear and rigorous distinction between the true and proper æsthetic activity and the practical activity of externalization that we can solve the complicated and confused questions as to the relations between *art and utility* and *art and morality*.

We have demonstrated above that art as art is independent both of utility and of morality, as also of all practical value. Without this independence, it would not be possible to speak of an intrinsic value of art, nor indeed to conceive an æsthetic science, which demands the autonomy of the æsthetic fact as its necessary condition.

But it would be erroneous to maintain that this independence of the vision or intuition or *internal expression* of the artist should be simply extended to the practical activity of externalization and communication which may or may not follow the æsthetic fact. If by art be understood the externalization of art, then utility and morality have a perfect right to enter into it ; that is to say, the right to be master in one's own house.

Indeed we do not externalize and fix all the many expressions and intuitions which we form in our spirit ; we do not declare our every thought in a loud voice, or write it down, or print, or draw, or paint, or expose it to the public. We *select* from the crowd of intuitions which are formed or at least sketched within us ; and the selection is ruled by the criteria of the economic disposition of life and of its moral direction. Therefore, when we have fixed an intuition, we have still to decide whether or no we should communicate it to others, and to whom, and when, and how ; all which deliberations come equally under the utilitarian and ethical criterion.

Thus we find the concepts of *selection*, of the *interesting*, of *morality*, of an *educational end*, of *popularity*, etc., to some extent justified, although these can in no way be justified when imposed upon art as art, and we have ourselves rejected them in pure Æsthetic. Error always contains an element of truth. He who formulated those erroneous æsthetic propositions in reality had his eye on practical facts, which attach themselves externally to the æsthetic fact and belong to economic and moral life.

It is well to advocate yet greater freedom in making known the means of æsthetic reproduction ; we are of the same opinion, and leave projects for legislation and for legal action against immoral art, to hypocrites, to the ingenuous and to wasters of time. But the proclamation of this freedom, and the fixing of its limits, how wide soever they be, is always the task of morality. And it would in any case be out of place to invoke that highest principle, that *fundamentum aesthetices*, which is the independence of art, to deduce from it the guiltlessness of the artist who calculates like an immoral speculator upon the unhealthy tastes of his readers in the externalization of his imaginings, or the freedom of hawkers to sell obscene statuettes in the public squares. This last case is the affair of the police, as the first must be brought before the tribunal of the moral consciousness. The æsthetic judgement on the work of art has nothing to do with the morality of the artist as a practical man, or with the provisions to be taken that the things of art may not be diverted to evil ends alien to her nature, which is pure theoretic contemplation.

TASTE AND THE REPRODUCTION OF ART

WHEN the entire æsthetic and externalizing process has
been completed, when a beautiful expression has been
produced and it has been fixed in a definite physical
material, what is meant by *judging it* ? *To reproduce
it in oneself,* answer the critics of art, almost with one
voice. Very good. Let us try thoroughly to understand
this fact, and with that object in view, let us represent
it schematically.

The individual A is seeking the expression of an impression which he feels or anticipates, but has not yet
expressed. See him trying various words and phrases
which may give the sought-for expression, that expression
which must exist, but which he does not possess. He tries
the combination *m,* but rejects it as unsuitable, inexpressive, incomplete, ugly : he tries the combination
n, with a like result. *He does not see at all, or does not
see clearly.* The expression still eludes him. After other
vain attempts, during which he sometimes approaches,
sometimes retreats from the mark at which he aims, all
of a sudden (almost as though formed spontaneously of
itself) he forms the sought-for expression, and *lux facta
est.* · He enjoys for an instant æsthetic pleasure or the
pleasure of the beautiful. The ugly, with its correlative
displeasure, was the æsthetic activity which had not
succeeded in conquering the obstacle ; the beautiful is
the expressive activity which now displays itself
triumphant.

We have taken this example from the domain of

speech, as being nearer and more accessible, and because we all talk, though we do not all draw or paint. Now if another individual, whom we shall call B, is to judge that expression and decide whether it be beautiful or ugly, he *must of necessity place himself at A's point of view*, and go through the whole process again, with the help of the physical sign supplied to him by A. If A has seen clearly, then B (who has placed himself at A's point of view) will also see clearly and will see this expression as beautiful. If A has not seen clearly, then B also will not see clearly, and will find the expression more or less ugly, *just as A did*.

It may be observed that we have not taken into consideration two other cases : that of A having a clear and B an obscure vision ; and that of A having an obscure and B a clear vision. Strictly speaking, these two cases are *impossible*. *Impossibility of divergences.*

Expressive activity, just because it is activity, is not caprice, but spiritual necessity ; it cannot solve a definite æsthetic problem save in one way, which is the right way. It will be objected to this plain statement that works which seem beautiful to the artists are afterwards found to be ugly by the critics ; while other works with which the artists were discontented and held to be imperfect or failures are, on the contrary, held to be beautiful and perfect by the critics. But in this case, one of the two is wrong : either the critics or the artists, sometimes the artists, at other times the critics. Indeed, the producer of an expression does not always fully realize what is happening in his soul. Haste, vanity, want of reflexion, theoretic prejudices, make people say, and others sometimes almost believe, that works of ours are beautiful, which, if we really looked into ourselves, we should see to be ugly, as they are in reality. Thus poor Don Quixote, when he had reattached to his helmet as well as he could the vizor of cardboard—the vizor that had showed itself to possess but the feeblest force of resistance at the first encounter,—took good care not to test it again with a well-delivered sword-thrust, but simply declared and maintained it to be (says the author) *por celada finisima de encaxe.* And in other cases, the same reasons, or opposite but analogous ones, trouble the consciousness of the artist, and cause him to value badly what he has successfully produced, or to strive to undo and do again for the worse what he has done well in artistic spontaneity. An instance of this is Tasso and his passage from the *Gerusalemme liberata* to the *Gerusalemme conquistata.* In the same way, haste, laziness, want of reflexion, theoretic prejudices, personal sympathies or animosities, and other motives of a similar sort, sometimes cause the critics to proclaim ugly what is beautiful, and beautiful what is ugly. Were they to eliminate such disturbing elements, they would feel the work of art as it really is, and would not leave it to posterity, that more diligent and more dispassionate judge, to award the palm, or to do that justice which they have refused.

Identity of taste and genius. It is clear from the preceding theorem that the activity of judgement which criticizes and recognizes the beautiful is identical with what produces it. The only difference lies in the diversity of circumstances, since in the one case it is a question of æsthetic production, in the other of reproduction. The activity which judges is called *taste* ; the productive activity is called *genius* : genius and taste are therefore substantially *identical.*

The common remark that the critic should possess something of the genius of the artist and that the artist should possess taste, gives a glimpse of this identity ; or the remark that there exists an active (productive) and a passive (reproductive) taste. But it is also negated in other equally common remarks, as when people speak of taste without genius, or of genius without taste. These last observations are meaningless, unless they allude to quantitative or psychological differences, those being called geniuses without taste who produce works of art, inspired in their chief parts and neglected or defective in their secondary parts, and men of taste without genius, those who, while they succeed in obtaining certain isolated or secondary merits, do not possess sufficient power for a great artistic synthesis. Analogous explanations can easily be given of other similar expressions. But to posit a substantial difference between genius and taste, between artistic production and reproduction, would render both communication and judgement alike inconceivable. How could we judge what remained external to us? How could that which is produced by a given activity be judged by a *different* activity? The critic may be a small genius, the artist a great one; the former may have the strength of ten, the latter of a hundred; the former, in order to reach a certain height, will have need of the assistance of the other; but the nature of both must remain the same. To judge Dante, we must raise ourselves to his level: let it be well understood that empirically we are not Dante, nor Dante we; but in that moment of contemplation and judgement, our spirit is one with that of the poet, and in that moment we and he are one thing. In this identity alone resides the possibility that our little souls can echo great souls, and grow great with them in the universality of the spirit.

Let us remark in passing that what has been said of the æsthetic judgement holds good equally for every other activity and for every other judgement; and that scientific, economic, and ethical criticism is effected in a like manner. To limit ourselves to this last, only if we place ourselves ideally in the same conditions in which he found himself who took a given resolution, can we form a judgement as to whether his decision were moral or immoral. An action would otherwise remain incomprehensible and therefore impossible to judge. A homicide may be a rascal or a hero: if this be, within limits, indifferent as regards the defence of society, which condemns both to the same punishment, it is not indifferent to one who wishes to distinguish and judge from the moral point of view, and we therefore cannot dispense with reconstructing the individual psychology of the homicide, in order to determine the true nature of his deed, not merely in its legal, but also in its moral aspect. In Ethics, a moral taste or tact is sometimes mentioned, answering to what is

Analogy with other activities.

generally called the moral consciousness, that is to say, to the activity of the good will itself.

Criticism of æsthetic absolutism (intellectualism) and relativism. The explanation above given of æsthetic judgement or reproduction both agrees with and condemns the absolutists and relativists, those who affirm and those who deny the absoluteness of taste.

In affirming that the beautiful can be judged, the absolutists are right; but the theory on which they found their affirmation is not tenable, because they conceive of the beautiful, that is, æsthetic value, as something placed outside the æsthetic activity, as a concept or a model which an artist realizes in his work, and of which the critic avails himself afterwards in judging the work itself. These concepts and models have no existence in art, for when proclaiming that every art can be judged only in itself and that it has its model in itself, they implicitly denied the existence of objective models of beauty, whether these are intellectual concepts, or ideas suspended in a metaphysical heaven.

In proclaiming this, their adversaries, the relativists, are perfectly right, and effect an advance upon them. However, the initial rationality of their thesis in its turn becomes converted into a false theory. Repeating the ancient adage that there is no accounting for tastes, they believe that æsthetic expression is of the same nature as the pleasant and the unpleasant, which every one feels in his own way, and about which there is no dispute. But we know that the pleasant and the unpleasant are utilitarian, practical facts. Thus the relativists deny the specific character of the æsthetic fact, and again confound expression with impression, the theoretic with the practical.

The true solution lies in rejecting alike relativism or psychologism and false absolutism ; and in recognizing that the criterion of taste is absolute, but absolute in a different way from that of the intellect, which expresses itself in ratiocination. The criterion of taste is absolute, with the intuitive absoluteness of the imagination. Thus any act of expressive activity, which is so really, is to be recognized as beautiful, and any fact as ugly in which expressive activity and passivity are found engaged with one another in an unfinished struggle.

Between absolutists and relativists is a third class, which may be called that of the relative relativists. These affirm the existence of absolute values in other fields, such as Logic and Ethic, but deny it in the field of Æsthetic. To dispute about science or morals seems to them to be rational and justifiable, because science depends upon the universal, common to all men, and morality upon duty, which is also a law of human nature ; but how dispute about art, which depends upon imagination ? Not only, however, is the imaginative activity universal and no less inherent in human nature than the logical concept and practical duty ; but there is a preliminary objection to the thesis in question. If the absoluteness of the imagination be denied, we must also deny intellectual or conceptual truth and implicitly morality. Does not morality presuppose logical distinctions ? How could these be known, otherwise than in expressions and words, that is to say, in imaginative form ? If the absoluteness of the imagination were removed, the life of the spirit would tremble to its foundations. One individual would no longer understand another, nor indeed his own self of a moment before, which is already another individual considered a moment after. *Criticism of relative relativism.*

Nevertheless, variety of judgements is an indubitable fact. Men disagree as to logical, ethical, and economical valuations ; and they disagree equally or even more as to the æsthetic. If certain reasons recorded by us above, such as haste, prejudices, passions, etc., may lessen the importance of this disagreement, they do not on that account annul it. When speaking of the stimuli of reproduction we have added a caution, for we said that reproduction takes place, *if all the other conditions remain equal.* Do they remain equal ? Does the hypothesis correspond to reality ? *Objection founded on the variation of the stimulus and of psychic disposition.*

It would appear not. In order to reproduce an impression several times by means of a suitable physical stimulus it is necessary that this stimulus be not changed, and that the organism remain in the same psychical conditions as those in which was experienced the impression that it is desired to reproduce. Now it is a fact that the physical stimulus is continually changing, and in like manner the psychological conditions.

Oil-paintings grow dark, frescoes fade, statues lose noses, hands and legs, architecture becomes totally or partially a ruin, the tradition of the execution of a piece of music is lost, the text of a poem is corrupted by bad copyists or bad printing. These are obvious instances of the changes which daily occur in objects or physical stimuli. · As regards psychological conditions, we will not dwell upon the cases of deafness or blindness, that is to say, upon the loss of entire orders of psychical impressions ; these cases are secondary and of less importance compared with the fundamental, daily, inevitable and perpetual changes of the society around us and of the internal conditions of our individual life. The phonetic manifestations or words and verses of Dante's *Commedia* must produce a very different impression on an Italian citizen engaged in the politics of the third Rome, from that experienced by a well-informed and intimate contemporary of the poet. The Madonna of Cimabue is still in the Church of Santa Maria Novella ; but does she speak to the visitor of to-day as to the Florentines of the thirteenth century ? Even though she were not also darkened by time, must we not suppose that the impression which she now produces is altogether different from that of former times ? And even in the case of the same individual poet, will a poem composed by him in youth make the same impression upon him when he re-reads it in his old age, with psychic conditions altogether changed ?

Criticism of the distinction of signs into natural and conventional. It is true that certain æstheticians have attempted a distinction between stimuli and stimuli, between *natural* and *conventional* signs. The former are held to have a constant effect upon all ; the latter only upon a limited circle. In their belief, signs employed in painting are natural, those used in poetry conventional. But the difference between them is at the most only one of degree.

It has often been said that painting is a language under-stood by all, while with poetry it is otherwise. Here, for example, Leonardo found one of the prerogatives of his art, "which hath not need of interpreters of different tongues as have letters," and it pleases man and beast. He relates the anecdote of that portrait of the father of a family "which the little grandchildren were wont to caress while they were still in swaddling-clothes, and the dogs and cats of the house in like manner." But other anecdotes, such as those of the savages who took the portrait of a soldier for a boat, or considered the portrait of a man on horseback to be furnished with only one leg, are apt to shake one's faith in the understanding of paint-ing by sucklings, dogs and cats. Fortunately, no arduous researches are necessary to convince oneself that pictures, poetry and all works of art only produce effects upon souls prepared to receive them. Natural signs do not exist ; because all are equally conventional, or, to speak with greater exactness, *historically conditioned*.

Granting this, how are we to succeed in causing the *The surmount-ing of variety.* expression to be reproduced by means of the physical object ? How obtain the same effect, when the conditions are no longer the same ? Would it not, rather, seem necessary to conclude that expressions cannot be repro-duced, despite the physical instruments made for the purpose, and that what is called reproduction consists in ever new expressions ? Such would indeed be the con-clusion if the varieties of physical and psychical condi-tions were intrinsically insurmountable. But since the insuperability has none of the characteristics of necessity we must on the contrary conclude that reproduction always occurs when we can replace ourselves in the conditions in which the stimulus (physical beauty) was produced.

Not only can we replace ourselves in these conditions as an abstract possibility, but as a matter of fact we do so continually. Individual life, which is communion with ourselves (with our past), and social life, which is communion with our like, would not otherwise be possible.

Restorations and historical interpretation.

As regards the physical object, palæographers and philologists, who *restore* to texts their original physiognomy, *restorers* of pictures and of statues and other industrious toilers strive precisely to preserve or to restore to the physical object all its primitive energy. These efforts are certainly not always successful, or are not completely successful, for it is never or hardly ever possible to obtain a restoration complete in its smallest details. But the insurmountable is here only present accidentally and must not lead us to overlook the successes which actually are achieved.

Historical interpretation labours for its part to re-integrate in us the psychological conditions which have changed in the course of history. It revives the dead, completes the fragmentary, and enables us to see a work of art (a physical object) as its author saw it in the moment of production.

A condition of this historical labour is tradition, with the help of which it is possible to collect the scattered rays and concentrate them in one focus. With the help of memory we surround the physical stimulus with all the facts among which it arose ; and thus we enable it to act upon us as it acted upon him who produced it.

Where the tradition is broken, interpretation is arrested ; in this case, the products of the past remain silent for us. Thus the expressions contained in the Etruscan or Mexican inscriptions are unattainable ; thus we still hear discussions among ethnographers as to whether certain products of the art of savages are pictures or writings ; thus archæologists and prehistorians are not always able to establish with certainty whether the figures found on the pottery of a certain region, and on other instruments employed, are of a religious or profane nature. But the arrest of interpretation, as that of restoration, is never a definitely insurmountable barrier ; and the daily discoveries of new historical sources and of new methods of better exploiting the old, which we may hope to see ever improving, link up again broken traditions.

We do not wish to deny that erroneous historical interpretation sometimes produces what may be called *palimpsests*, new expressions imposed upon the ancient, artistic fancies instead of historical reproductions. The so-called " fascination of the past " depends in part upon these expressions of ours, which we weave upon the historical. Thus has been discovered in Greek plastic art the calm and serene intuition of life of those peoples, who nevertheless felt the universal sorrow so poignantly ; thus " the terror of the year 1000 " has recently been discerned on the faces of the Byzantine saints, a terror which is a misunderstanding, or an artificial legend invented later by men of learning. But *historical criticism* tends precisely to circumscribe fancies and to establish exactly the point of view from which we must look.

By means of the above process we live in communication with other men of the present and of the past ; and we must not conclude because we sometimes, and indeed often, meet with an unknown or an ill-known, that therefore, when we believe we are engaged in a dialogue, we are always speaking a monologue ; or that we are unable even to repeat the monologue which we formerly held with ourselves.

XVII

THE HISTORY OF LITERATURE AND ART

Historical criticism in literature and art. Its importance.

THIS brief exposition of the method by which is obtained the reintegration of the original conditions in which the work of art was produced, and consequently reproduction and judgement are made possible, shows how important is the function fulfilled by historical research in relation to artistic and literary works which is what is usually called *historical criticism* or method in literature and art.

Without tradition and historical criticism the enjoyment of all or nearly all the works of art produced by humanity would be irrevocably lost : we should be little more than animals, immersed in the present alone, or in the most recent past. It is fatuous to despise and laugh at one who reconstitutes an authentic text, explains the sense of forgotten words and customs, investigates the conditions in which an artist lived, and accomplishes all those labours which revive the qualities and the original colouring of works of art.

Sometimes a depreciatory or negative judgement is passed upon historical research because of the presumed or proved inability of such researches, in many cases, to give us a true understanding of works of art. But it must be observed, in the first place, that historical research does not only fulfil the task of helping to reproduce and judge artistic works : the biography of a writer or of an artist, for example, and the study of the customs of a period, have an interest of their own, that is to say, extraneous to the history of art, but not to other forms of historiography. If allusion be made to

128

those researches which do not appear to have interest of any kind, nor to fulfil any purpose, it must be replied that the historical student must often reconcile himself to the useful but inglorious function of a collector of facts. These facts remain for the time being formless, incoherent and meaningless, but they are preserves or mines for the historian of the future and for whosoever may afterwards want them for any purpose. In the same way in a library, books which nobody asks for are placed on the shelves and catalogued, because they may be asked for at some time or other. Certainly, just as an intelligent librarian gives the preference to the acquisition and cataloguing of those books which he foresees may be of more or better service, so intelligent students possess an instinct as to what is or may more probably be of use among the material of facts which they are examining; while others less well endowed, less intelligent or more hasty in producing, accumulate useless rubbish, refuse and sweepings, and lose themselves in details and petty discussions. But this appertains to the economy of research, and does not concern us. It concerns at most the master who selects the subjects, the publisher who pays for the printing, and the critic who is called upon to praise or to blame the research workers.

On the other hand, it is clear that historical research directed to illuminate a work of art does not alone suffice to bring it to birth in our spirit and place us in a position to judge it, but presupposes taste, that is to say, an alert and cultivated imagination. The greatest historical erudition may accompany a gross or otherwise defective taste, a slow imagination, or, as they say, a cold hard heart closed to art. Which is the lesser evil, great erudition with defective taste, or natural taste and much ignorance? The question has often been asked, and perhaps it will be best to deny that it has any meaning, because one cannot tell which of two evils is the less, or what exactly that means. The merely learned man never succeeds in entering into direct communion with great spirits; he keeps wandering for ever about the outer courts, the staircases and antechambers of their palaces; but the gifted ignoramus either passes by masterpieces to him inaccessible, or instead of understanding works of art as they really are, invents others with his fancy. Now, the labour of the former may at least serve to enlighten others; but the genius of the latter remains altogether sterile in relation to knowledge. How then can we in a certain respect fail to prefer the conscientious learned man to the inconclusive though gifted man, who is not really gifted, if he resign himself and in so far as he resigns himself, to his inconclusiveness?

Literary and artistic history. Its distinction from historical criticism and from the æsthetic judgement.

We must accurately distinguish *the history of art and literature* from those historical labours where works of art are used, but for extraneous purposes (such as biography, civil, religious and political history, etc.), and also from historical erudition directed to the preparation of the æsthetic synthesis of reproduction.

The difference of the first two is obvious. The history of art and literature has the works of art themselves as its principal subject; those other labours invoke and interrogate works of art, but only as witnesses from whom to discover the truth of facts which are not æsthetic. The second difference to which we have referred may seem less profound. It is, however, very great. Erudition directed to illuminate the understanding of works of art aims simply at calling into existence a certain internal fact, an æsthetic reproduction. Artistic and literary history, on the other hand, does not appear until after such reproduction has been obtained. It implies, therefore, a further stage of labour.

Like all other history, its object is to record precisely such facts as have really taken place, in this case artistic and literary facts. A man who, after having acquired the requisite historical erudition, reproduces in himself and tastes a work of art, may remain simply a man of taste, or at the most express his own feeling with an exclamation of praise or condemnation. This does not

suffice for the making of a historian of literature and
art.   Something else is needed, namely, that a new mental
operation succeed in him the simple reproduction.   This
new operation is in its turn an expression : the expression
of the reproduction ; the historical description, exposition or representation.   There is this difference, then,
between the man of taste and the historian : the first
merely reproduces in his spirit the work of art ; the
second, after having reproduced it, represents it historically, or applies those categories by which, as we know,
history is differentiated from pure art.   Artistic and
literary history is therefore *a historical work of art founded
upon one or more works of art.*

The name " artistic " or " literary " critic is used in
various senses : sometimes it is applied to the scholar who
devotes his services to literature ; sometimes to the historian who reveals the works of art of the past in their
reality ; more often to both.   By critic is sometimes
understood in a more restricted sense he who judges and
describes contemporary literary works, and by historian,
he who treats of those less recent.   These are linguistic
uses and empirical distinctions, which may be neglected ;
because the true difference lies between *the scholar, the man
of taste* and *the historian of art.*   These words designate
three successive stages of work, each one independent
relatively to the one that follows, but not to that which
precedes.   As we have seen, a man may be a mere
scholar, and possess little capacity for understanding
works of art ; he may even both be learned and possess
taste, yet be unable to portray them by writing a page
of artistic and literary history.   But the true and complete
historian, while containing in himself both the scholar
and the man of taste as necessary pre-requisites, must
add to their qualities the gift of historical comprehension
and representation.

The theory of artistic and literary historical method *The method
of artistic
and literary
history.*
presents problems and difficulties, some common to the
theory of historical method in general, others peculiar to
it, because derived from the concept of art itself.

Criticism of the problem of the origin of art.

History is commonly divided into human history, natural history, and the mixture of both. Without examining here the question of the solidity of this distinction, it is clear that artistic and literary history belongs in any case to the first, since it concerns a spiritual activity, that is to say, an activity proper to man. And since this activity is its subject, the absurdity of propounding the historical problem of the *origin* of *art* becomes at once evident. We should note that by this formula many different things have in turn been included on many different occasions. *Origin* has often meant *nature* or *character* of the artistic fact, in which case an attempt was made to deal with a real scientific or philosophic problem, the very problem in fact which our treatise has attempted to solve. At other times, by origin has been understood the *ideal genesis*, the search for the reason of art, the deduction of the artistic fact from a first principle containing in itself both spirit and nature. This is also a philosophical problem, complementary to the preceding, coinciding indeed with it, although it has sometimes been strangely interpreted and solved by means of an arbitrary and semi-imaginary metaphysic. But when the object was to discover further exactly in what way the artistic function was *historically formed*, the result has been the absurdity which we have mentioned. If expression be the first form of consciousness, how can we look for the historical origin of what is not a product of nature and is presupposed by human history? How can we assign a historical genesis to a thing which is a category by means of which all historical processes and facts are understood? The absurdity has arisen from the comparison with human institutions, which have been formed in the course of history, and have disappeared or may disappear in its course. Between the æsthetic fact and a human institution (such as monogamic marriage or the fief) there exists a difference comparable with that between simple and compound bodies in chemistry. It is impossible to indicate the formation of the former, otherwise they would not be simple, and if this be discovered, they cease to be simple and become compound.

The problem of the origin of art, historically understood, is only justified when it is proposed to investigate, not the formation of the artistic category, but where and when art has appeared for the first time (appeared, that is to say, in a striking manner), at what point or in what region of the globe and at what point or epoch of its history ; when, that is to say, not the origin of art, but its earliest or primitive history is the object of research. This problem forms one with that of the appearance of human civilization on the earth. Data for its solution are certainly wanting, but there yet remains the abstract possibility of a solution, and certainly tentative and hypothetical solutions abound.

Every representation of human history has the concept of *progress* as foundation. But by progress must not be understood the imaginary *law of progress* which is supposed to lead the generations of man with irresistible force to some unknown destiny, according to a providential plan which we can divine and then understand logically. A supposed law of this sort is the negation of history itself, of that accidentality, that empiricity, that contingency, which distinguish concrete fact from abstraction. And for the same reason, progress has nothing to do with the so-called law of *evolution*, which, if it mean that reality evolves (and it is only reality in so far as it evolves or becomes), cannot be called a law, and if it be given as a law, becomes identical with the law of progress in the sense just described. The progress of which we speak here is nothing but *the very concept of human activity*, which, working upon the material supplied to it by nature, conquers its obstacles and bends it to its own ends. *The criterion of progress and history.*

Such conception of progress, that is to say, of human activity applied to a given material, is the *point of view* of the historian of humanity. No one but a mere collector of unrelated facts, a mere antiquary or inconsequent annalist, can put together the smallest narrative of human doings unless he have a determined point of view, that is to say, a personal conviction of his own regarding the facts whose history he has undertaken to relate. No one can start from the confused and discordant mass of crude facts and arrive at the historical work of art save by means of this apperception, which makes it possible to carve a definite representation in that rough and formless mass. The historian of a practical action should know what is economy and what is morality ; the historian of mathematics, what is mathematics ; the historian of botany, what is botany ; the historian of philosophy, what is philosophy. If he does not really know these things, he must at least have the illusion of knowing them ; otherwise he will not even be able to delude himself into believing that he is writing history.

We cannot here expand the demonstration of the necessity and inevitability of this subjective criterion in every narrative of human affairs (which is compatible with the utmost objectivity, impartiality and scrupulousness in dealing with data of fact and indeed forms a constitutive element in these virtues), in every narrative of human doings and happenings. It suffices to read any book of history to discover at once the point of view of the author, if he be a historian worthy of the name and know his own business. There are liberal and reactionary, rationalist and catholic historians, who deal with political or social history ; for the history of philosophy there are metaphysical, empirical, sceptical, idealist and spiritualist historians. Purely historical historians do not and cannot exist. Were Thucydides and Polybius, Livy and Tacitus, Machiavelli and Guicciardini, Giannone and Voltaire, wholly without moral and political views ; and, in our time, was Guizot or Thiers, Macaulay or Balbo, Ranke or Mommsen ? And in the history of philosophy, from Hegel, who was the first to raise it to a great height, to Ritter, Zeller, Cousin, Lewes and our Spaventa, was there one who did not possess his conception of progress and his criterion of judgement ? Is there one single work of any value on the history of

Æsthetic which has not been written from this or that point of view, with this or that bias (Hegelian or Herbartian), from a sensationalist or from an eclectic or some other point of view ? If the historian is to escape from the inevitable necessity of taking a side, he must become a political or scientific eunuch ; and history is not an occupation for eunuchs. Such would at most be of use in compiling those great tomes of not useless erudition, *elumbis atque fracta,* which are called, not without reason, monkish.

If, then, a concept of progress, a point of view, a criterion, be inevitable, the best to be done is not to try and escape from it, but to obtain the best possible. Every one tends to this end when he forms his own convictions, seriously and laboriously. Historians who profess to wish to interrogate the facts without adding anything of their own to them are not to be trusted. This is at best the result of ingenuousness and illusion on their part : they will always add something of their own, if they be truly historians, even without knowing it, or they will only believe that they have avoided doing so because they have conveyed it only by hints, which is the most insinuating, penetrative and effective of methods.

Artistic and literary history cannot dispense with the criterion of progress any more easily than other history. We cannot show what a given work of art is, save by proceeding from a conception of art, in order to fix the artistic problem which the author of such work of art had to solve, and by determining whether or no he has solved it, or by how much and in what way he has failed to do so. But it is important to note that the criterion of progress assumes a different form in artistic and literary history to that which it assumes (or is believed to assume) in the history of science. *Non-existence of a single line of progress in artistic and literary history.*

It is customary to represent the whole history of knowledge by one single line of progress and regress. Science is the universal, and its problems are arranged in one single vast system or comprehensive problem.

All thinkers labour upon the same problem as to the nature of reality and of knowledge : contemplative Indians and Greek philosophers, Christians and Mohammedans, bare heads and turbaned heads, wigged heads and college-capped heads (as Heine said) ; and future generations will weary themselves with it, as ours has done. It would take too long to inquire here if this be true or not of science. But it is certainly not true of art ; art is intuition, and intuition is individuality, and individuality does not repeat itself. To conceive of the history of the artistic production of the human race as developed along a single line of progress and regress would therefore be altogether erroneous.

At the most, and working to some extent with generalizations and abstractions, it may be asserted that the history of æsthetic productions shows progressive cycles, but each cycle with its own problem and each progressive only in respect to that problem. When many are at work in a general way upon the same subject, without succeeding in giving to it the suitable form, yet drawing always more near to it, there is said to be progress, and when appears the man who gives it definite form, the cycle is said to be complete, and progress is ended. A typical example of this would here be the progress in the elaboration of the mode of using the subject-matter of chivalry, during the Italian Renaissance, from Pulci to Ariosto (using this as an example and excusing excessive simplification). Nothing but repetition and imitation, diminution or exaggeration, a spoiling of what had already been done, in short decadence could be the result of employing that same material after Ariosto. The epigoni of Ariosto prove this. Progress begins with the beginning of a new cycle. Cervantes, with his more open and conscious irony, is an instance of this. In what did the general decadence of Italian literature at the end of the sixteenth century consist ? Simply in having nothing more to say and in repeating and exaggerating motives already discovered. If the Italians of this period had even been able to express their own decadence, they would not have been altogether failures, but would have anticipated the literary movement of the Risorgimento. Where the matter is not the same, a progressive cycle does not exist. Shakespeare does not represent an advance on Dante, nor Goethe upon Shakespeare. Dante, however, represents an advance on the visionaries of the Middle Ages, Shakespeare on the Elizabethan dramatists, Goethe, with *Werther* and the first part of *Faust*, on the writers of the *Sturm und Drang* period. This mode of presenting the history of poetry and art contains, however, as we have remarked, something of the abstract, of the merely practical, and is without strict philosophical value. Not only is the art of savages not inferior, as art, to that of civilized peoples, if it be correlative to the impressions of the savage ; but every individual, indeed every moment of the spiritual life of an individual, has its artistic world ; none of these worlds can be compared with any other in respect of artistic value.

Many have sinned and continue to sin against this special form of the criterion of progress in artistic and literary history. Some, for instance, talk of the infancy of Italian art in Giotto, and of its maturity in Raphael or in Titian ; as though Giotto were not complete and absolutely perfect, granted the material of feeling with which his mind was furnished. He was certainly incapable of drawing a figure like Raphael, or of colouring it like Titian ; but was Raphael or Titian capable of creating the *Marriage of Saint Francis with Poverty* or the *Death of Saint Francis* ? The spirit of Giotto had not felt the attraction of the body beautiful, which the Renaissance studied and raised to a place of honour ; the spirits of Raphael and of Titian were no longer interested in certain movements of ardour and of tenderness with which the man of the fourteenth century was in love. How, then, can a comparison be made, where there is no comparative term ?

Errors committed against this law.

The celebrated divisions of the history of art into an oriental period, representing a lack of equilibrium between idea and form, the latter dominating, a classical

representing an equilibrium between idea and form, a
romantic representing a new lack of equilibrium between
idea and form, the former dominating, suffer from the
same defect.   The same is true of the division into
oriental art, representing imperfection of form ; classical,
perfection of form ; romantic or modern, perfection of
content and of form.   Thus classic and romantic have
also received, among their many other meanings, that
of progressive or regressive periods, in respect to the
realization of some alleged artistic ideal of all humanity.

*Other meanings
of the word
" progress "
in respect to
Æsthetic.*

There is no such thing, then, as an *æsthetic* progress of
humanity.   However, by æsthetic progress is sometimes
meant, not what the two words coupled together really
signify, but the ever-increasing accumulation of our
historical knowledge, which makes us able to sympathize
with all the artistic products of all peoples and of all
times, or, as they say, makes our taste more catholic.
The difference appears very great if the eighteenth
century, so incapable of escaping from itself, be compared
with our own time, which enjoys alike Greek and Roman
art, now better understood, Byzantine, mediæval, Arabic
and Renaissance art, the art of the Cinquecento, baroque
art, and the art of the eighteenth century.   Egyptian,
Babylonian, Etruscan, and even prehistoric art are more
profoundly studied every day.   Certainly, the difference
between the savage and civilized man does not lie in
the human faculties.   The savage has speech, intellect,
religion and morality in common with civilized man,
and is a complete man.   The only difference lies in this,
that civilized man penetrates and dominates a larger
portion of the universe with his theoretic and practical
activity.   We cannot claim to be more spiritually alert
than, for example, the contemporaries of Pericles ; but
no one can deny that we are richer than they—rich with
their riches and with those of how many other peoples
and generations besides our own ?

By æsthetic progress is also meant, in another sense,
which is also improper, the greater abundance of artistic
intuitions and the smaller number of imperfect or inferior

works which one epoch produces in respect to another. Thus it may be said that there was æsthetic progress, an artistic awakening in Italy, at the end of the thirteenth or of the fifteenth century.

Finally, æsthetic progress is talked of in a third sense, with an eye to the refinement and complications of soul-states exhibited in the works of art of the most civilized peoples, as compared with those of less civilized peoples, barbarians and savages. But in this case the progress is of the comprehensive psycho-social conditions, not of the artistic activity, to which the material is indifferent.

These are the most important points to note concerning the method of artistic and literary history.

XVIII

CONCLUSION :
IDENTITY OF LINGUISTIC AND ÆSTHETIC

Summary of the study. A GLANCE over the path traversed will show that we have completed the entire programme of our treatise. We have studied the nature of intuitive or expressive knowledge, which is the æsthetic or artistic fact (I. and II.), and described the other form of knowledge, the intellectual, and the successive complications of these forms (III.) ; it thus became possible for us to criticize all erroneous æsthetic theories arising from the confusion between the various forms and from the illicit transference of the characteristics of one form to another (IV.), noting at the same time the opposite errors to be found in the theory of intellectual knowledge and of historiography (V.). Passing on to examine the relations between the æsthetic activity and the other activities of the spirit, no longer theoretic but practical, we indicated the true character of the practical activity and the place which it occupies in respect to the theoretic activity : hence the criticism of the intrusion into æsthetic theory of practical concepts (VI.) ; we have distinguished the two forms of the practical activity, as economic and ethical (VII.), reaching the conclusion that there are no other forms of the spirit beyond the four which we have analyzed ; hence (VIII.) the criticism of every mystical or imaginative Æsthetic. And since there are no other spiritual forms co-ordinate with these, so there are no original subdivisions of the four established, and in particular of Æsthetic. From this arises the impossibility of classes of expressions and the criticism of Rhetoric, that is, of ornate expression distinct from simple expression, and of other similar distinctions and sub-distinctions (IX.). But by the law of the unity of the spirit, the æsthetic fact is also a practical fact, and as such, occasions pleasure and pain. This led us to study the feelings of value in general, and those of æsthetic value or of the beautiful in particular (X.), to criticize æsthetic hedonism in all its various manifestations and complications (XI.), and to expel from the system of Æsthetic the long series of psychological concepts which had been introduced into it (XII.). Proceeding from æsthetic production to the facts of reproduction, we began by investigating the external fixing of the æsthetic expression, for the purpose of reproduction. This is called the physically beautiful, whether natural or artificial (XIII.). We derived from this distinction the criticism of the errors which arise from confounding the physical with the æsthetic side of facts (XIV.). We determined the meaning of artistic technique, or that technique which is at the service of reproduction, thus criticizing the divisions, limits and classifications of the individual arts, and establishing the relations of art, economy and morality (XV.). Since the existence of physical objects does not suffice to stimulate æsthetic reproduction to the full, and since, in order to obtain it, we must recall the conditions in which the stimulus first operated, we have also studied the function of historical erudition, directed toward re-establishing the communication between the imagination and the works of the past, and to serve as the basis of the æsthetic judgement (XVI.). We have concluded our treatise by showing how the reproduction thus obtained is afterwards elaborated by the categories of thought, that is to say, by an examination of the method of literary and artistic history (XVII.).

The æsthetic fact has in short been considered both in itself and in its relations with the other spiritual activities, with the feelings of pleasure and pain, with what are called physical facts, with memory and with historical treatment. It has passed before us as *subject* until it became *object*, that is to say, from the moment of *its birth* until it becomes gradually changed for the spirit into *subject-matter of history*.

Our treatise may appear to be somewhat meagre when externally compared with the great volumes usually dedicated to Æsthetic. But it will not seem so when we perceive that those volumes are nine-tenths full of matter that is not pertinent, such as definitions, psychological or metaphysical, of pseudo-æsthetic concepts (the sublime, the comic, the tragic, the humorous, etc.), or of the exposition of the supposed Zoology, Botany and Mineralogy of Æsthetic, and of universal history æsthetically judged ; that the whole history of concrete art and literature has also been dragged into those Æsthetics and generally mangled, and that they contain judgements upon Homer and Dante, Ariosto and Shakespeare, Beethoven and Rossini, Michael Angelo and Raphael. When all this has been deducted from them, we flatter ourselves that our treatise will no longer be held to be too meagre, but, on the contrary, far richer than ordinary treatises, which either omit altogether, or hardly touch at all, the greater part of the difficult problems proper to Æsthetic which we have felt it to be our duty to study.

Identity of Linguistic and Æsthetic. But although Æsthetic as science of expression has been studied by us in its every aspect, it remains to justify the sub-title which we have added to the title of our book, *General Linguistic*, to state and make clear the thesis that the science of art and that of language, Æsthetic and Linguistic, conceived as true sciences, are not two distinct things, but one thing only. Not that there is a special Linguistic ; but the much-sought-for science of language, general Linguistic, *in so far as what it contains is reducible to philosophy*, is nothing but Æsthetic. Whoever studies general Linguistic, that is to say, philosophical Linguistic, studies æsthetic problems, and *vice versa*. *Philosophy of language and philosophy of art are the same thing.*

Were Linguistic really a *different* science from Æsthetic it would not have for its object expression, which is the essentially æsthetic fact ; that is to say, we must deny that language is expression. But an emission of sounds which expresses nothing is not language. Language is sound articulated, circumscribed and organized for the purposes of expression. If, on the other hand, linguistic were a *special* science in respect to Æsthetic, it would necessarily have for its object a *special class* of expressions. But the non-existence of classes of expression is a point which we have already demonstrated.

The problems which Linguistic tries to solve, and the errors in which Linguistic has been and is involved, are the same that respectively occupy and complicate Æsthetic. If it be not always easy, it is on the other hand always possible to reduce the philosophic questions of Linguistic to their æsthetic formula. *Æsthetic formulation of linguistic problems. Nature of language.*

The disputes themselves as to the nature of the one find their parallel in those as to the nature of the other. Thus it has been disputed whether Linguistic be a historical or a scientific discipline, and, the scientific having been distinguished from the historical, it has been asked whether it belong to the order of the natural or of the psychological sciences, understanding by these latter empirical Psychology as well as the Sciences of the spirit. The same has happened with Æsthetic, which some have looked upon as a natural science (confusing the æsthetic and the physical sense of the word expression). Others have looked upon it as a psychological science (confusing expression in its universality with the empirical classification of expressions). Others again, denying the very possibility of a science of such a subject, change it into a simple collection of historical facts ; not one of these attaining to the consciousness of Æsthetic as a science of activity or of value, a science of the spirit.

Linguistic expression, or speech, has often seemed to be a fact of *interjection*, which belongs to the so-called physical expressions of the feelings, common alike to men and animals. But it was soon perceived that an abyss yawns between the " Ah ! " which is a physical reflex of pain and a word ; as also between that " Ah ! " of pain and the " Ah ! " employed as a word. The theory of the interjection being abandoned (jocosely termed the " Ah ! Ah ! " theory by German linguists), the theory of *association* or *convention* appeared. This is liable to the same objection which destroyed æsthetic associationism in general : speech is unity, not multiplicity of images, and multiplicity does not explain, but indeed presupposes the expression to be explained. A variant of linguistic associationism is the imitative, that is to say, the theory of *onomatopœia*, which the same philologists deride under the name of the " bow-wow " theory, from the imitation of the dog's bark, which, according to the onomatopœists, must have given its name to the dog.

The most usual theory of our times as regards language (apart from mere crass naturalism) consists of a sort of eclecticism or mixture of the various theories to which we have referred. It is assumed that language is in part the product of interjections and in part of onomatopœia and convention. This doctrine is altogether worthy of the philosophical decadence of the second half of the nineteenth century.

Origin of language and its development.
We must here note an error into which have fallen those very philologists who have best discerned the activistic nature of language, when they maintain that although language was *originally a spiritual creation*, yet that it afterwards increased by *association*. But the distinction does not hold, for origin in this case cannot mean anything but nature or character ; and if language be spiritual creation, it must always be creation ; if it be association, it must have been so from the beginning. The error has arisen from having failed to grasp the general principle of Æsthetic, known to us : that expressions already produced must descend to the rank of impressions before they can give rise to new impressions. When we utter new words we generally transform the old ones, varying or enlarging their meaning ; but this process is not associative, it is *creative*, although the

creation has for material the impressions, not of the hypothetical primitive man, but of man who has lived long ages in society, and who has, so to say, stored so many things in his psychic organism, and among them so much language.

The question of the distinction between the æsthetic and the intellectual fact appears in Linguistic as that of the relations between Grammar and Logic. This problem has been solved in two partially true ways : the *inseparability* and the *separability* of Logic and Grammar. But the complete solution is this : if the logical form be inseparable from the grammatical (æsthetic), the grammatical is separable from the logical.

Relation between Grammar and Logic.

If we look at a picture which for instance portrays a man walking on a country road we may say : " This picture represents a fact of *movement*, which, if conceived as voluntary, is called *action* ; and since every movement implies a *material object*, and every action a *being* that acts, this picture also represents a *material object* or *being*. But this movement takes place in a definite place, which is a piece of a definite heavenly body (the Earth), and precisely of a piece of it which is called *terra-firma*, and more precisely of a part of it that is wooded and covered with grass, which is called *country*, cut naturally or artificially into a form called *road*. Now, there is only one example of that star, which is called Earth : the earth is an *individual*. But *terra-firma, country, road* are genera or *universals*, because there are other terra-firmas, other countries, other roads." And it would be possible to continue for a while with similar considerations. By substituting a phrase for the picture that we have imagined, for example one to this effect : " Peter is walking on a country road," and by making the same remarks, we obtain the concepts of *verb* (motion or action), of *noun* (material object or agent), of *proper noun*, of *common noun* ; and so on.

Grammatical kinds or parts of speech.

What have we done in both cases ? Neither more nor less than submit to logical elaboration what first presented itself only æsthetically ; that is to say, we have destroyed the æsthetic for the logical. But since in general Æsthetic error begins when we wish to return from the logical to the æsthetic and ask what is the *expression* of motion, action, matter, being, of the general, of the individual, etc. ; so in the case of language, error begins when motion or action are called *verb*, being or matter, *noun* or *substantive*, and when linguistic categories, or *parts of speech*, are made of all these, noun and verb and so on. The theory of the parts of speech is really identical with that of artistic and literary kinds, already criticized in our Æsthetic.

It is false to say that the verb or noun is expressed in definite words, truly distinguishable from others. Expression is an indivisible whole. Noun and verb do not exist in it, but are abstractions made by us, destroying the sole linguistic reality, which is the *sentence*. This last is to be understood, not in the way common to grammars, but as an organism expressive of a complete meaning, which includes alike the simplest exclamation and a great poem. This sounds paradoxical, but is nevertheless the simplest truth.

And since in Æsthetic the artistic productions of certain peoples have been looked upon as imperfect, owing to the error above mentioned, because the supposed kinds have seemed not yet to have been discriminated, or to be in part wanting ; so in Linguistic, the theory of the parts of speech has caused the analogous error of judging languages as *formed* and *unformed*, according to whether there appear in them or no some of those supposed parts of speech ; for example, the verb.

The individuality of speech and the classification of languages.

Linguistic also discovered the irreducible individuality of the æsthetic fact, when it affirmed that the word is what is really spoken, and that two truly identical words do not exist. Thus were synonyms and homonyms destroyed, and thus was shown the impossibility of really translating one word into another, from so-called dialect into so-called language, or from the so-called mother-tongue into the so-called foreign tongue.

But the attempt to classify languages ill agrees with

this just view. Languages have no reality beyond the propositions and complexes of propositions really written and pronounced by given peoples at definite periods ; that is to say, they have no existence outside the works of art (whether little or great, oral or written, soon forgotten or long remembered, does not matter) in which they exist concretely. And what is the art of a given people but the whole of its artistic products ? What is the character of an art (for example of Greek art or Provençal literature) but the whole physiognomy of those products ? And how can such a question be answered, save by narrating in its particulars the history of the literature, that is to say, of the language in its actuality ?

It may be thought that this argument, although possessing validity as against many of the usual classifications of languages, yet is without any as regards that queen of classifications, the historico-genealogical, that glory of comparative philology. And this it certainly is ; but why ? Precisely because that historico-genealogical method is not a mere classification. He who writes history does not classify, and the philologists themselves have hastened to say that languages which can be arranged in historical series (those whose series have hitherto been traced) are not distinct and separate species but a single whole of facts in the various phases of its development.

Language has sometimes been regarded as a voluntary *Impossibility* or arbitrary act. But at others the impossibility of *of a normative* creating language artificially, by an act of will, has been *grammar.* clearly seen. " *Tu, Caesar, civitatem dare potes homini, verbo non potes* " was once said to a Roman Emperor. And the æsthetic (and therefore theoretic as opposed to practical) nature of expression supplies the method of discovering the scientific error which lies in the conception of a (normative) *Grammar*, establishing the rules of correct speech. Good sense has always rebelled against this error. An example of such rebellion is the " So much the worse for grammar " attributed to Monsieur de Voltaire. But the impossibility of a normative grammar is also recog-

nized by those who teach it, when they confess that to
write well cannot be learned by rules, that there are no
rules without exceptions, and that the study of Grammar
should be conducted practically, by reading and examples,
which should form the literary taste. The scientific
reason of this impossibility lies in the principle that
we have demonstrated : that a technique of the theoretical amounts to a contradiction in terms. And what
could a (normative) grammar be, but precisely a technique of linguistic expression, that is to say of a theoretic
fact ?

Didactic organisms.   The case in which Grammar is understood merely as
an empirical discipline, that is to say, as a collection
of schemes useful for learning languages, without any
claim whatever to philosophic truth, is quite different.
Even the abstractions of the parts of speech are
in this case both admissible and useful. And we
must tolerate as merely didascalic many books entitled
" Treatises of Linguistic," where we generally find a
little of everything, from the description of the vocal
apparatus and of the artificial machines (phonographs)
which can imitate it, to summaries of the most important
results obtained by Indo-European, Semitic, Coptic,
Chinese, or other philologies ; from philosophical generalizations as to the origin or nature of language, to advice
on format, calligraphy and the arrangement of notes
relating to philological work. But this mass of notions,
here administered in a fragmentary and incomplete
manner about language in its essence, about language
as expression, resolves itself into notions of Æsthetic.
Nothing exists outside *Æsthetic*, which gives knowledge of
the nature of language, and *empirical Grammar*, which is
a pedagogic expedient, save the *History of languages* in
their living reality, that is to say, the history of concrete
literary productions, which is substantially identical with
the *History of literature*.

Elementary linguistic facts, or roots.   The same error of taking the physical for the æsthetic,
from which the search for the *elementary forms* of the
beautiful originates, is made by those who go in search

of *elementary linguistic facts*, decorating with that name the divisions of the longer series of physical sounds into shorter series. Syllables, vowels and consonants, and the series of syllables called words, all these elements of speech, which give no definite sense when taken alone, must be called not *facts of language*, but mere sounds, or rather sounds abstracted and classified physically.

Another error of the same sort is that of *roots*, to which the most distinguished philologists now accord but small value. Having confused physical with linguistic or expressive facts, and considering that the simple precedes the complex in the order of ideas, they necessarily ended by thinking that the smallest physical facts indicated the simplest linguistic facts. Hence the imaginary necessity that the most ancient primitive languages had a monosyllabic character, and that historical research must always lead to the discovery of monosyllabic roots. But (to follow up the imaginary hypothesis) the first expression that the first man conceived may have had not a phonetic but a mimetic physical reflex ; may have been externalized not in a sound but in a gesture. And assuming that it was externalized in a sound, there is no reason to suppose that sound to have been monosyllabic rather than polysyllabic. Philologists readily blame their own ignorance and impotence, when they do not always succeed in reducing polysyllabism to monosyllabism, and rely upon the future to accomplish the reduction. But their faith is without foundation, and their blame of themselves is an act of humility arising from an erroneous presumption.

For the rest, the limits of syllables, as those of words, are altogether arbitrary, and distinguished somehow or other by empirical use. Primitive speech, or the speech of uneducated man, is a *continuum*, unaccompanied by any consciousness of divisions of the discourse into words or syllables, imaginary beings created by schools. No true law of Linguistic can be founded on such divisions. Proof of this is to be found in the confession of linguists, that there are no truly phonetic laws of the hiatus, of cacophony, of diæresis or synæresis, but merely laws of taste and convenience ; that is to say, *æsthetic* laws. And what are laws of *words* which are not at the same time laws of *style* ?

Æsthetic judgement and the model language.

Finally, the search for a *model language*, or for a method of reducing linguistic usage to *unity*, arises from the superstition of a rationalistic measure of the beautiful, from that concept which we have called false æsthetic absoluteness. In Italy we call this the question of the *unity of the language*.

Language is perpetual creation. What has been linguistically expressed is not repeated, save by reproduction of what has already been produced. The ever-new impressions give rise to continuous changes of sound and meaning, that is, to ever-new expressions. To seek the model language, then, is to seek the immobility of motion. Everyone speaks and should speak according to the echoes which things arouse in his soul, that is, according to his impressions. It is not without reason that the most convinced supporter of any one of the solutions of the problem of the unity of language (whether by adopting a standard Italian approximating to Latin, or to fourteenth-century usage, or to the Florentine dialect) feels repugnance in applying his theory, when he is speaking to communicate his thoughts and to make himself understood. The reason is that he feels that in substituting the Latin, fourteenth-century Italian, or Florentine word for that of different origin, but which answers to his natural impressions, he would be falsifying the genuine form of truth. He would become a vain listener to himself instead of a speaker, a pedant in place of a serious man, an actor instead of a sincere person. To write according to a theory is not really to write : at the most, it is making *literature*.

The question of the unity of language is always re-appearing, because, stated as it is, it is insoluble, being based upon a false conception of what language is. Language is not an arsenal of arms already made, and it is not a *vocabulary*, a collection of abstractions, or a cemetery of corpses more or less well embalmed.

Our dismissal of the question of the model language, or of the unity of the language, may seem somewhat abrupt, and yet we would not wish to appear otherwise than respectful towards the long line of literary men who have debated this question in Italy for centuries. But those ardent debates were fundamentally concerned with debates of æstheticity, not of æsthetic science, of literature rather than of literary theory, of effective speaking and writing, not of linguistic science. Their error consisted in transforming the manifestation of a need into a scientific thesis, the desirability, for example, of easier mutual understanding among a people divided by dialects into the philosophic demand for a single, ideal language. Such a search was as absurd as that other search for a *universal language*, a language possessing the immobility of the concept and of abstraction. The social need for a better understanding of one another cannot be satisfied save by the spread of education becoming general, by the increase of communications, and by the interchange of thought among men.

These scattered observations must suffice to show that *Conclusion.* all the scientific problems of Linguistic are the same as those of Æsthetic, and that the truths and errors of the one are the truths and errors of the other. If Linguistic and Æsthetic appear to be two different sciences, this arises from the fact that people think of the former as grammar, or as a mixture between philosophy and grammar, that is, an arbitrary mnemonic schematism or a pedagogic medley, and not of a rational science and a pure philosophy of speaking. Grammar, or something not unconnected with grammar, also introduces into the mind the prejudice that the reality of language lies in isolated and combinable words, not in living discourse, in the expressive organisms, rationally indivisible.

Those linguists or philologists, philosophically endowed, who have penetrated deepest into the problems of language, find themselves (to employ a trite but effective simile) like workmen piercing a tunnel : at a certain point they must hear the voices of their companions, the philosophers of Æsthetic, who have been at work on the other side.   At a certain stage of scientific elaboration, Linguistic, in so far as it is philosophy, must merge itself in Æsthetic : and this indeed it does without leaving a residue.

II

HISTORY OF ÆSTHETIC

I

ÆSTHETIC IDEAS IN GRÆCO-ROMAN ANTIQUITY

THE question whether Æsthetic is to be considered as an *Point of view of this history of Æsthetic.* ancient or a modern science has on several occasions been a matter of controversy ; whether, that is to say, it arose for the first time in the eighteenth century, or had previously arisen in the Græco-Roman world. This is a question, not only of facts, but of criteria, as is easily to be understood : whether one answers it in this way or that depends upon one's idea of that science, an idea afterwards adopted as a standard or criterion.[1]

Our view is that Æsthetic is the *science of the expressive* (representative or imaginative) *activity.* In our opinion, therefore, it does not appear until a precise concept is formulated of imagination, representation or expression, or in whatever other manner we prefer to name that attitude of the spirit, which is theoretical but not intellectual, a producer of knowledge, but of the individual, not of the universal. Outside this point of view, we for our part are not able to discover anything but deviations and errors.

These deviations can lead in various directions. Following the distinctions and terminology of an eminent Italian philosopher [2] in an analogous case, we shall be

[1] See above, pp. 128-131. Quotations which give only the name of the author, or are otherwise abbreviated, refer to historical or critical works of which the complete title is given in the Bibliographical Appendix.

[2] Rosmini, *Nuovo saggio sull' origine delle idee*, sections iii. and iv., where theories of knowledge are classified.

inclined to say that they arise either from *excess* or from
defect. The deviation from defect would be that which
denies the existence of a special æsthetic and imaginative
activity, or, which amounts to the same thing, denies its
autonomy, and thus mutilates the reality of the spirit.
Deviation by excess is that which substitutes for it or
imposes upon it another activity, altogether undiscover-
able in the experience of the interior life, a mysterious
activity which does not really exist. Both these deviations, as can be deduced from the theoretical part of this
work, take various forms. The first, that due to defect,
may be : (*a*) *purely hedonistic*, in so far as it considers and
accepts art as a simple fact of sensuous pleasure ; (*b*)
rigoristic-hedonistic, in so far as, looking upon it in the
same way, it declares it to be irreconcilable with the
highest life of man ; (*c*) *hedonistic-moralistic* or *pedagogic*,
in so far as it consents to a compromise, and while still
considering art to be a fact of sense, declares that it
need not be harmful, indeed that it may render some
service to morality, provided always that it is submissive
and obedient.[1] The forms of the second deviation (which
we shall call " mystical ") are not determinable *a priori*,
for they belong to feeling and imagination in their infinite
variety and shades of meaning.[2]

Mistaken tendencies, and attempts towards an Æsthetic, in Græco-Roman antiquity. The Græco-Roman world presents all these fundamental forms of deviation : pure hedonism, moralism or
pedagogism, mysticism, and together with them the
most solemn and celebrated rigoristic negation of art
which has ever been made. It also exhibits attempts
at the theory of expression or pure imagination ; but
nothing more than approaches and attempts. Hence,
since we must now take sides in the controversy as to
whether Æsthetic is an ancient or modern science, we
cannot but place ourselves upon the side of those who
affirm its modernity.

A rapid glance at the theories of antiquity will suffice
to justify what we have said. We say rapid, because to
enter into minute particulars, collecting all the scattered

---

[1] See above, pp. 83-84.   [2] See above, p. 65.

observations of ancient writers upon art, would be to do
again what has been done many times and sometimes
very well.   Further, those ideas, propositions and theories
have passed into the common patrimony of knowledge,
together with what else remains of the classical world.
It is therefore more advisable here than in any other
part of this history merely to indicate the general lines
of development.

Art, the artistic faculty, only became a philosophical *Origin of*
problem in Greece after the sophistical movement and *the æsthetic*
problem in
as a consequence of the Socratic dialectic.   The historians *Greece.*
of literature generally point to the origins of Greek
Æsthetic in the first appearance of criticism and reflection
upon poetical works, painting and sculpture ;   in the
judgements pronounced on the occasion of poetical com-
petitions, in the observations that were made as to the
methods of the different artists, in the analogies between
painting and poetry as expressed in the sayings attributed to Simonides and Sophocles ;   or, finally, in the
appearance of that word which served to group together
the various arts and to indicate in a certain way their
relationship—the word mimesis or mimetic (μίμησις)—
which oscillates between the meaning of " imitation "
and that of " representation."   Others make the origin
of Æsthetic go back to the polemics which were conducted
by the first naturalistic and moralistic philosophers
against the tales, fantasies and morals of poets, and to
the interpretations of the hidden meaning (ὑπόνοια), or,
as the moderns call it, allegory, employed to defend the
good name of Homer and of the other poets ;   finally,
to the *ancient quarrel* between philosophy and poetry, as
Plato was afterwards to call it.[1]   But, to tell the truth,
none of these reflections, observations and arguments
implied a true and proper philosophical discussion of the
nature of art.   Nor was the sophistical movement favourable to its appearance.   For although attention was at
that time certainly given to internal psychical facts, yet
these were conceived as mere phenomena of opinion

[1] *Republic*, x. 607.

and feeling, of pleasure and pain, of illusion, whim or
caprice. And where there is no true and no false, no
good and no evil, there can be no question of beautiful
and ugly, nor of a difference between the true and the
beautiful or between the beautiful and the good. The
most one has in that case is the general problem of the
irrational and the rational, but not that of the nature
of art, which assumes the difference between rational
and irrational, material and spiritual, mere fact and
value, to have been already stated and grasped. If, then,
the sophistical period was the necessary antecedent to
the discoveries of Socrates, the æsthetic problem could
only arise after Socrates. And it did indeed arise
with Plato, author of the first, or indeed of the only
really great negation of art of which there remains docu-
mentary proof in the history of ideas.

Plato's rigoristic negation. Is art, mimesis, a rational or an irrational fact?
Does it belong to the noble region of the soul, where
philosophy and virtue are found, or does it dwell in that
base lower sphere, with sensuality and crude passionality? This is the question asked by Plato,[1] who thus
states the problem of Æsthetic for the first time. The
sophist Gorgias was able to note, with his sceptical acuteness, that tragic representation is a deception, which
(strangely enough) turns out to the honour both of him
who deceives and of him who is deceived, in which it is
shameful not to know how to deceive oneself and not to
let oneself be deceived.[2] With that remark he could rest
content. That was for him a fact like another. But
Plato, the philosopher, was bound to solve the problem:
if it were a deception, then down with tragedy and the
rest of mimetic productions: down with them among
the other things to be despised, among the animal
qualities of man. But if it were not deception, what
was it? What place did art occupy among the lofty
activities of philosophy and of good action?

The answer that he gave is well known. Mimetic does
not realize the ideas, that is to say the truth of things,

[1] *Republic*, x. 607.　　[2] Plutarch, *De audiendis poetis*, ch. i.

but reproduces natural or artificial things, which are pale shadows of them ; it is a diminution of a diminution, a third-hand work. Art, then, does not belong to the lofty and rational region of the soul (τοῦ λογιστικοῦ ἐν ψυχῇ) but to the sensual ; it is not a strengthening but a corruption of the mind (λώβη τῆς διανοίας) ; it can serve only sensual pleasure, which troubles and obscures. For this reason, mimetic, poetry and poets, must be excluded from the perfect Republic.

Plato is the most consistent example of those who do not succeed in discovering any other form of knowledge but the intellectual. It was correctly observed by him that imitation stops at natural things, at the image (τὸ φάντασμα), and does not reach the concept, logical truth (ἀλήθεια), of which poets and painters are altogether ignorant. But his error consisted in believing that there is no other form of truth below the intellectual ; that there is nothing but sensuality and passionality outside or prior to the intellect, that which discovers the ideas. Certainly, the fine æsthetic sense of Plato did not echo that depreciatory judgement of art ; he himself declared that he would have been very glad to have been shown how to justify art and to place it among the forms of the spirit. But since none was able to give him this assistance, and since art with its *appearance* that yet lacks *reality* was repugnant to his ethical consciousness, and reason compelled him (ὁ λόγος ᾕρει) to banish it and place it with its peers, he resolutely obeyed his conscience and his reason.[1]

Others were not troubled with these scruples, and although art was always looked upon as a mere thing of pleasure among the later hedonistic schools of various sorts, among rhetoricians and worldly people the duty of combating or of abolishing it was not felt. Nevertheless, this opposite extreme was also not calculated to meet with the endorsement of public opinion, for the latter, if tender towards art, is no less tender towards rationality and morality. For this reason both rationalists and moralists, compelled to recognize the force of

Æsthetic hedonism and moralism.

[1] *Republic*, x.

such a condemnation as Plato's, sought for a compromise, a half measure. Away with the sensual and with art : certainly. But can we expel the sensual and the pleasurable without more ado ? Can fragile human nature nourish itself exclusively with the strong food of philosophy and morality ? Can we obtain observance of the true and of the good from the young and from the people, without allowing them at the same time some amusement ? And has not man himself always something of the child, has he not always something of the people in him, is he not to be treated with the same precautions ? Is there not a risk that the over-bent bow will break ?— These considerations prepared the way for the justification of art, for they showed that if it were not rational in itself, it could on the other hand serve a rational end. Hence the search for the *external end* of art, which takes the place of the search for the essence or *internal end*. When art had been lowered to the level of a simple pleasurable illusion, an inebriation of the senses, it was necessary to subordinate the practical action of producing such an illusion and inebriation, like any other action, to the moral end. Art, being deprived of any dignity of its own, was obliged to assume a reflected or second-hand dignity. Thus the moralistic and pedagogic theory was constructed upon a hedonistic basis. The artist, who, for the pure hedonist, was comparable to a *hetaira*, became for the moralist a *pedagogue*. Hetaira and pedagogue, these are the symbols of the two conceptions of art that were disseminated in antiquity, and the second was grafted upon the first.

Even before Plato's peremptory negation had directed thought to this way of issue, the literary criticism of Aristophanes was already full of the pedagogic idea : " What schoolmasters are to children, poets are to young men " (τοῖς ἡβῶσιν δὲ ποιηταί), he says in a celebrated verse.[1] But we can find traces of it in Plato himself (in the dialogues in which he seems to withdraw from the too rigid conclusions of the *Republic*) and in

[1] *Frogs*, l. 1055.

Aristotle, both in the *Politics*, where he determines the
use of music in education, and perhaps in the *Poetics*,
where he speaks obscurely of a tragical *catharsis* ; although
as regards this latter, it is not to be altogether denied
that he may have had a sort of glimpse of the modern
idea of the liberating power of art.[1]   Later on, the pedagogic theory takes a form that was much affected by
the Stoics.   Strabo develops and defends this at great
length, in the introduction to his geographical work,
where he combats Eratosthenes, who has made poetry
consist in mere pleasure without any notion of teaching.
Strabo, on the contrary, maintained the opinion of the
ancients, that it was " a first philosophy (φιλοσοφίαν
τινὰ πρώτην), which educated young men for life, and
created customs, affections and actions, by means of
pleasure."   Therefore, he said, poetry has always been
a part of education ; one cannot be a good poet unless
one is a good man (ἄνδρα ἀγαθόν).   Legislators and
founders of cities were the first to employ fables to
admonish and to terrify :   then this duty, which must be
performed for women and children and even for adults,
passed to the poets.   We caress and dominate the
multitude with fiction and with falsehood.[2]   " The poets
tell many lies " (πολλὰ ψεύδονται ἀοιδοί) is a hemistich
recorded by Plutarch, who describes minutely in one of
his lesser works how the poets should be read to youths.[3]
For him too poetry is a preparation for philosophy ; it
is a disguised philosophy, and therefore delights us in
the same way as do fish and meat at feasts, so prepared
as not to seem to be fish and meat ; it is philosophy
softened with fables, like the vine that grows close to
the mandragora, and produces a wine that is the giver
of sweet slumbers.   It is not possible to pass from dense
darkness to sunlight ; one should first accustom the eyes
to moderate light.   Philosophers, in order to exhort and
instruct, take their examples from true things ; poets

---

[1] Plato, *Laws*, bk. ii. ; Aristotle, *Poet.* ch. 14 ; *Polit.* bk. viii.
[2] Strabo, *Geographica*, i. ch. 2, §§ 3-9.
[3] Texts collected in E. Müller, *Gesch. d. Th. d. K.* i. pp. 57-85.

aim at a like result, when they create fictions and fables.[1]
Lucretius, in Roman literature, gives us the well-known
comparison of the boys for whom the doctors " *prius oras
pocula circum Contingunt mellis dulci flavoque liquore,*"
in order to administer the bitter wormwood.[2]   Horace,
in certain verses of the Epistle to the Pisones which
have become proverbial (perhaps his source for them was
the Greek of Neoptolemus of Paros ?), offers both views
(that of art as courtesan and of art as pedagogue) in his
" *Aut prodesse volunt aut delectare poetae . . . omne tulit
punctum qui miscuit utile dulci.*" [3]

Thus looked at, the office of the poet was confounded
with that of the orator, for he too was a practical man
aiming at practical effects ; hence there arose discussions
as to whether Virgil was to be considered as a poet or
as an orator (" *Virgilius poeta an orator ?* ").   To both
was assigned the triple end of *delectare, movere, docere* ;
in any case this tripartition was very empirical, for we
clearly perceive that the *delectare* is here a means and
the *docere* a simple part of the *movere* : to move in the
direction of the good, and therefore, among other goods,
towards that of instruction.   In like manner, it was said
of the orator and poet (recording the meretricious basis
of their task, and with a metaphor significant in its
naïveté) that they were bound to avail themselves of
the *allurements* (*lenocinium*) of form.

*Mystical
æsthetic
in antiquity.*   The mystical view, which considers art as a special
mode of self-beatification, of entering into relation with
the Absolute, with the Summum Bonum, with the ultimate
root of things, appeared only in late antiquity, almost
at the entrance to the Middle Ages.   Its representative
is the founder of the neo-Platonic school, Plotinus.

It is strange that Plato should be usually selected as
the founder and head of this æsthetic tendency, and that
for this very reason to him should be attributed the
honour of being the father of Æsthetic.   But how could
he, who had expounded with such great limpidity and

---

[1] Plutarch, *De aud. poetis*, chs. 1-4, 14.
[2] *De rerum natura*, i. 935-947.   [3] *Ad Pisones*, 333-334.

clearness the reasons for which he was not able to accord
to art a high place among the activities of the spirit, be
credited with having accorded to it one of the highest
places, equal, if not superior, to philosophy itself ? This
misunderstanding has evidently arisen out of the enthusiastic effusions about the Beautiful that we read in the
Gorgias, the *Philebus*, the *Phaedrus*, the *Symposium*, and
other Platonic dialogues. It is well to dissipate it by
declaring that the *Beauty* of which Plato discourses has
nothing to do with art or with *artistic beauty*.

The search for the meaning and scientific content of
the word " beautiful " could not but early attract
the attention of the subtle and elegant Greek dialec-
ticians. Indeed, we find Socrates engaged in discussing
this question in one of the discourses that have been
preserved for us by Xenophon ; and we find him disposed
to stop for the moment at the conclusion that the beautiful is *that which is convenient and which answers to the
end desired*, or at the other conclusion that it is *that which
one loves*.[1] Plato too examines this sort of problem and
proposes various sorts of solutions or attempts at solutions of it. He sometimes speaks of a beauty that
dwells not only in bodies, but also in laws, in actions, in
the sciences ; sometimes he seems to conjoin and almost
to identify it with the true, the good and the divine ;
now he returns to the view of Socrates and confuses it
with the useful ; now he distinguishes between a beautiful
in itself (καλὰ καθ' αὐτά) and a relatively beautiful (πρός
τι καλά) ; or he makes true beauty consist in pure
pleasure (ἡδονὴ καθαρά), free from all shadow of pain ;
or he places it in measure and proportion (μετριότης καὶ
ξυμμετρία) ; or talks of colours and sounds as possessing
a beauty in themselves.[2] It was impossible to find an
independent dominion for the beautiful, if the artistic
or mimetic activity were deserted. This explains his
wandering among so many different conceptions, among
which it is just possible to say that the identification of

Investigations as to the Beautiful.

---

[1] *Memorab.* iii. ch. 8 ; iv. ch. 6.
[2] Texts collected in Müller, *op. cit.* ii. pp. 84-107.

the Beautiful with the Good prevails. Nothing better describes this uncertainty than the dialogue of the *Hippias maior* (which, if it be not Plato's, is Platonic). He here wishes to find out not what things are beautiful things, but what the beautiful is; that is to say, what it is that makes beautiful, not only a beautiful virgin, but also a beautiful mare, a beautiful lyre, a beautiful pot with two graceful ears of clay. Hippias and Socrates himself propose in turn the most various solutions; but the latter ends by confuting them all. "That which makes things beautiful is the gold that is added to them by way of ornament." No: gold only embellishes where it is *fitting* (πρέπων): for instance, a pot should have a wooden rather than a golden handle. "That is beautiful which cannot seem ugly to any one." But it is not a question of *seeming*: the question is to define what the beautiful is, whether it seems so or not. It is the *fitting* which makes things seem to be beautiful. But in that case, the fitting (which makes them *appear*, not *be*) is one thing, and the beautiful another. "The beautiful is what leads to the end, that is to say, the *useful* (χρήσιμον)." But if that were so, then evil would also be beautiful, because the useful leads also to the evil. "The beautiful is the *helpful*, that which leads to the good (ὠφέλιμον)." But in this case, the good would not be beautiful nor the beautiful good; for the cause is not the effect, and the effect is not the cause. "The beautiful is that which delights the sight and hearing." But this fails to persuade for three reasons: firstly, because beautiful studies and laws are beautiful, which have nothing to do with the eye or with the ear; secondly, because we cannot discover a reason for limiting the beautiful to those senses, while excluding the pleasure of eating and smelling, and the extremely vivid pleasures of sex; thirdly, because, if the foundation of the beautiful were *visibility*, it would not be *audibility*, and if it were audibility it would not be visibility; hence that which constitutes the beautiful cannot dwell in either of the two qualities. And the question which has been repeated so insistently in the course of the dialogue : *what is the beautiful?* (τί ἐστι τὸ καλόν;) remains unanswered.[1]

Later writers also conducted inquiries into the beautiful, and we possess the titles of several treatises upon the theme, which have been lost. Aristotle shows himself changeable and uncertain upon the point. In the scanty references which he makes to it, he at one time confounds the beautiful with the good, defining it as that which is both good and pleasing ;[2] at another he notes that the good consists of action (ἐν πράξει) and the beautiful also in things that are immoveable (ἐν τοῖς ἀκινήτοις), drawing from this the argument that mathematics should be studied in order to determine its characters, order, symmetry and limit ;[3] sometimes he places it in bigness and in order (ἐν μεγέθει καὶ τάξει) ;[4] at others he was led to look upon it as something apparently indefinable.[5] Antiquity also established canons of beautiful things, such as that attributed to Polycletus on the proportions of the human body. And Cicero said of the beauty of bodies that they were " *quaedam apta figura membrorum cum coloris quadam suavitate.*"[6] All these affirmations, even when they are not mere empirical observations, oι verbal glosses and substitutions, meet with unsurmountable obstacles.

In any case, not only is the conception of the beautiful, taken as a whole, identified with art in none of them ; but sometimes art and beauty, mimesis and pleasing or displeasing material of mimesis, are clearly distinguished. *Distinction between the theory of Art and the theory of the Beautiful.* Aristotle notes in his *Poetics* that it pleases us to see the most faithful images of things that are repugnant to us in reality, such, for instance, as the most contemptible forms of animals, or corpses (τὰς εἰκόνας τὰς μάλιστα ἠκριβωμένας χαίρομεν θεωροῦντες).[7] Plutarch demonstrates at length that works of art please us not as beautiful but as *resembling* (οὐχ ὡς καλόν, ἀλλ᾽ ὡς ὅμοιον) ; he affirms that

[1] *Hippias maior, passim.*   [2] *Rhet.* i. ch. 9.
[3] *Metaphys.* xii. ch. 3.   [4] *Poet.* ch. 7.
[5] Diog. Laert. v. ch. 1, § 20.   [6] *Tuscul. quaest.* bk. iv. § 13.
[7] *Poet.* ch. iv. 3.

if the artist beautified things that are ugly in nature he would be offending against fitness and resemblance (τὸ πρέπον καὶ τὸ εἰκός) ; and he proclaims the principle that *the beautiful is one thing and beautiful imitation another* (οὐ γάρ ἐστι ταὐτό, τὸ καλὸν καὶ καλῶς τι μιμεῖσθαι). Paintings of horrible events are pleasing, such as *Medea slaying her sons* by Timomachus, *Orestes the matricide* by Theon, and the *Pretended madness of Ulysses* by Parrhasius; and if the grunting of a pig, the grating of a machine, the noise of the winds and the tumult of the sea are unpleasing, they pleased on the contrary in the case of Parmenon, who imitated the pig perfectly, and in Theodorus, who was not less expert in rendering the grating of machines.[1]　If the ancients had really wanted to place the beautiful and art in relation, a secondary and partial connexion of the two conceptions was to hand in the shape of the category of the *relatively* as distinguished from the *absolutely* beautiful.　But where the word καλόν or *pulchrum* is applied to artistic productions in the writings of literary critics, it does not seem to be more than a linguistic usage, as we find, for instance, in the case of Plutarch's *beautiful* imitation, or also in the terminology of the rhetoricians, who sometimes called elegance and adornment of discourse *beauty* of elocution (τὸ τῆς φράσεως κάλλος).

Fusion of the two by Plotinus.　　It is only with Plotinus that the two divided territories are united and *the beautiful and art are fused into a single concept,* not by means of a beneficial absorption of the *equivocal* Platonic conception of beauty into the *unequivocal* conception of art, but by absorption of the clear into the confused, of *imitative art* in the so-called *beautiful.*　And thus we reach an altogether new view : the beautiful and art are now both alike melted into a mystical passion and elevation of the spirit.

Beauty, observes Plotinus, resides chiefly in things visible ; but it is also to be found in things audible, such as verbal and musical compositions, and it is not lacking in things supersensible, such as works, offices, actions,

---

[1] *De aud. poetis*, ch. 3.

habits, sciences and virtues. What is it that makes beautiful sensible and supersensible things alike ? Not, he answers, the symmetry of their parts among themselves, and with the whole (συμμετρία τῶν μερῶν πρὸς ἄλληλα καὶ πρὸς τὸ ὅλον) and their colour (εὔχροια), according to one of the definitions most in vogue, which we have quoted above in the words of Cicero ; because there are proportions in things ugly, and there are things that are simply beautiful without any relation of proportion : beauty, then, is one thing and symmetry another.[1] The beautiful is what we welcome as akin to our own nature ; the ugly is what repels us as our opposite, and the affinity of beautiful things with our souls that perceive them has its origin in the Idea, which produces both. That is beautiful which is *formed* ; the ugly is what is *unformed*, that is to say, something which is capable of receiving form, but does not receive it or is not entirely dominated by it. A beautiful body is such, because of its communion (κοινωνία) with the Divine ; beauty is the Divine, the Idea, shining through ; and matter is beautiful, not in itself, but only when it is illuminated by the Idea. Light and fire, which are nearest to this state, shed beauty upon visible things, as the most spiritual among bodies. But the soul must purify itself, in order to perceive the beautiful, and make the power of the Idea that lies in it efficacious. Moderation, strength, prudence, and every other virtue, what else are they, according to the oracle, but *purification* ? Thus there opens another eye in the soul, beside that of sensible beauty, which permits it to contemplate divine Beauty coincident with the Good, which is the supreme condition of beatitude.[2] Art enters into such contemplation, because beauty, in things made by man, comes from the mind. Compare two blocks of stone, the one placed beside the other : one rough and crude, the other reduced to the statue of a god or of a man, for example of a Grace or of a Muse, or of a human being of such a shape. as art has collected from many particular beauties. The beauty of a block of this shape

---

[1] *Enneads*, I. bk. vi. ch. 1.   [2] *Enneads, loc. cit.* chs. 2-9.

does not consist in its being of stone, but in the form
that art has been able to give to it (παρὰ τοῦ εἴδους
ὃ ἐνῆκεν ἡ τέχνη) ; and when the form is fully impressed
upon it, the thing of art is more beautiful than any other
natural thing. Hence he who despised the arts (Plato),
because they imitated nature, was wrong ; whereas the
truth is, in the first place, that nature itself imitates the
idea, and then that the arts do not simply limit themselves
to imitating what the eyes see, but go back to those
reasons or ideas from which nature itself is derived
(ὡς οὐχ ἁπλῶς τὸ ὁρώμενον μιμοῦνται, ἀλλ᾽ ἀνατρέχουσιν
ἐπὶ τοὺς λόγους ἐξ ὧν ἡ φύσις). Art therefore does not
belong to nature, but adds beauty where it is wanting
in nature : Phidias did not represent Jove because he
had seen him, but such as he would appear if he wished
to reveal himself to mortal eyes.[1] The beauty of natural
things is the archetype existing in the soul, the sole
source of natural beauty.[2]

*The scientific
tendency.
Aristotle.*

This affirmation of Plotinus and of neo-Platonism is
the first true and proper affirmation of mystical Æsthetic,
destined to such high fortunes in modern times, especially
in the first half of the nineteenth century. But the
attempts at a true Æsthetic, excluding certain luminous
but incidental observations to be found even in Plato :
for instance, that the poet should weave fables, not
arguments (μύθους ἀλλ᾽ οὐ λόγους),[3] go back to Aristotle
and are altogether independent of his few and feeble
speculations as to the beautiful. Aristotle by no means
agreed with the Platonic condemnation ; he felt (as
indeed Plato himself had suspected) that such a result
could not be altogether true, and that some aspect of
the problem must have been neglected. When in his
turn he attempted to find a solution, he found himself
in more advantageous conditions than his great predecessor, since he had already overcome the obstacle
that arose from the Platonic doctrine of ideas, a hypostasis
of concepts and abstractions. The ideas were for him

[1] *Enneads*, V. bk. viii. ch. 1.   [2] *Enneads, loc. cit.* chs. 2-3.
[3] *Phaedrus*, ch. 4.

simply concepts, and reality presented itself in a far more
lively manner, not as a diminution of ideas, but as a
synthesis of matter and form. It was thus much more
easy for him to recognize the rationality of mimesis in
his general philosophical doctrine and to assign to it
its right place; and indeed it seems generally clear to
Aristotle that mimesis, being proper to man by nature,
is contemplation or theoretic activity; although he
sometimes seems to forget this (as when he confuses
imitation with the case of boys, who acquire their first
knowledge by following an example [1]), and although
his system, which admits practical sciences and poietic
activities (distinguished from the practical as leaving a
material object behind them), disturbed the firm and
constant consideration of artistic mimesis and poetry as
a theoretical activity. But if it is a theoretical activity,
by what characteristic is poetry distinguished both from
scientific knowledge and from *historical* knowledge ? This
is the way Aristotle states the problem concerning the
nature of art, and this is the true and only way of stating
it. Even we moderns ask ourselves in what way art is
distinguished from history and from science, and what
this artistic form can be, which has the ideality of science
and the concreteness and individuality of history. Poetry,
answers Aristotle, differs from history, because, while
the latter draws things that have happened (τὰ γενόμενα),
poetry draws things that may possibly happen (οἷα ἂν
γένοιτο), and differs from science, because, although it
regards the universal and not the particular (τὰ καθ᾽
ἕκαστον) like history, it does not regard it in the same way
as science, but in a certain measure, which the philosopher
indicates by the word *rather* (μᾶλλον τὰ καθόλου). The
point then is to establish the precise meaning of the
possible, the *rather* and the *historical particular*. But no
sooner does Aristotle attempt to determine the meaning of
these words, than he falls into contradictions and fallacies.
That *universal* of poetry, which is the *possible*, seems to
identify itself for him with the probable or the necessary (τὰ

[1] *Poet.* ch. 4, § 2.

κατὰ τὸ εἰκὸς ἢ τὸ ἀναγκαῖον), and the particular of history
is not explained at all, except by giving instances : " that
which Alcibiades did and what happened to him." [1]
Aristotle, in fact, after having made so good a beginning
in the discovery of the purely imaginative, proper to
poetry, remains half-way, perplexed and uncertain. Thus
he sometimes makes the truth of imitation consist in a
certain learning and syllogizing that takes place when we
look at imitations, by which we recognize that " this is
that," that a copy answers to the original ; [2] or, worse,
he loses the grains of truth that he has found and forgets
that poetry has for its content the possible, admitting, not
only that it may also depict the *impossible* (τὸ ἀδύνατον),
and even the *absurd* (τὸ ἄτοπον), seeing that both are
credible and that they do not injure the end of art, but
even that we must prefer impossible probabilities to
incredible possibilities.[3] Art, since it has to do even
with the impossible and absurd, will not therefore have
in it anything of the rational, but in accordance with the
Platonic theory it will be an imitation of the appearance
in which empty sense indulges itself ; that is to say, a
thing of pleasure. Aristotle does not attain to this result,
because he does not attain to any clear and precise result
in this part of the subject, but it is one of the results
that can be deduced from what he has said, or that at
any rate he is not able to exclude. This means that he
did not fulfil his tacitly assumed task, and that although
he re-examined the problem with marvellous acuteness
after Plato, he failed truly to rid himself of the Platonic
definition, by substituting a firmly-established one of
his own.

The concepts of imitation and of imagination after Aristotle. Philostratus. But the field of investigation toward which Aristotle
had turned was generally neglected in antiquity : the
very *Poetics* of Aristotle does not seem to have been
widely known or influential. Ancient psychology knew
fancy or imagination as a faculty midway between sense
and intellect, but always as conservative and reproductive
of sensuous impressions or conveying conceptions to the

[1] *Poet.* ch. 9, §§ 1-4.   [2] *Poet.* ch. 4, §§ 4-5.   [3] *Poet.* chs. 24-25.

senses, never properly as a productive autonomous
activity. That faculty was rarely and with little result
placed in relation with the problem of art. Several
historians of Æsthetic attach singular importance to
certain passages in the *Life of Apollonius of Tyana* by
the elder Philostratus, in which they believe that they
discover a correction of the theory of *mimesis* and the
first affirmation in history of the conception of *imaginative creation*. Phidias and Praxiteles (says the extract
in question) did not need to go to heaven to see the gods,
in order to be able to depict them in their works, as
would have been necessary according to the theory of
imitation. Imagination, without any need of models,
made them able to do what they did : imagination, which
is a wiser agent than simple imitation (φαντασία . . .
σοφωτέρα μιμήσεως δημιουργός), and gives form, like the
other, not only to what has been seen, but also to what
has never been seen, imagining it on the basis of existing
things and in that way creating Jupiters and Minervas.[1]
However, the imagination of which Philostratus speaks
here is not something different from the Aristotelian
mimesis, which, as has been noted, was concerned not
only with real things but also and chiefly with possible
things. And had not Socrates observed (in the dialogue
with the painter Parrhasius, preserved for us by Xenophon)
that painters work by collecting what they need to form
their figures from several bodies (ἐκ πολλῶν συνάγοντες
τὰ ἐξ ἑκάστου κάλλιστα) ?[2]   And was not the anecdote of
Zeuxis, who was supposed to have taken the best of five
Crotonian maidens in order to paint his Helen, and other
anecdotes of a like sort, sufficiently widespread in antiquity ?
And had not Cicero eloquently explained, some years
before Philostratus, how Phidias, when he was carving
Jupiter, did not copy anything real, but kept his looks
fixed upon " *species pulcritudinis eximia quaedam*,"
which he had in his soul and which directed his art and
his hand ?[3]   Nor can it be said that Philostratus opened

---

[1] *Apoll. vita*, vi. ch. 10.   [2] *Memorab*. iii. ch. 10.
[3] *Orator ad Brutum*, ch. 2.

the way to Plotinus, for whom the superior or intellectual imagination (νοητή), or eye of supersensible beauty, when it is not a new designation for beautiful imitation, is mystical intuition.

The vagueness of the concept of mimesis reached its apex in those writers who gave it as a general title to any sort of work that had nature for its object, employing the Aristotelian phrase to affirm that " *omnis ars naturae imitatio est*," [1] or saying, like the painter Eupompus when he blamed his servile imitators, that " *natura est imitanda, non artifex.*" [2] And those who wished to escape this vagueness did not know how to do so, save by conceiving the activity of imitation as the practical producer of duplicates of natural objects, a prejudice born in the bosom of the pictorial and plastic arts, against which Philostratus perhaps intended to argue, in common with the other advocates of imagination.

Speculations on language. The speculations upon language had a close connexion with those upon the nature of art begun by the sophists, for whom it became a matter for wonder that sounds could signify colours or things inaudible ; that is to say, *speech* presented itself as a *problem*.[3] It was then discussed whether language was by nature (φύσει) or by convention (νόμῳ). By nature was sometimes understood mental necessity, and by convention what we should call a merely natural fact, psychological mechanism or sensationalism. In that sense of the terms, language would have been better called φύσει than νόμῳ. But at other times the distinction led to the question whether language answers to objective or logical truth and to the real relations between things (ὀρθότης τῶν ὀνομάτων) ; and in this case, those would seem to be nearer the truth who proclaimed it to be conventional or arbitrary in respect to logical truth : νόμῳ or θέσει, and not φύσει. Two different questions were consequently being treated

---

[1] For example, Seneca, *Epist.* 65.
[2] Pliny, *Nat. Hist.* xxxiv. ch. 19.
[3] Gorgias in *De Xenoph., Zen. et Gorg.* (in Aristot., ed. Didot), chs. 5-6.

together, and both were confusedly and equivocally
discussed. They find their monument in the obscure
Cratylus of Plato, which seems to fluctuate between
different solutions. Nor did the later affirmation that
the word is a sign (σημεῖον) of the thought solve anything,
for it still remained to be shown in what way the sign
was to be understood, whether φύσει or νόμῳ. Aristotle,
who looked upon words as imitations (μιμήματα), in the
same way as poetry,[1] made an observation of first-rate
importance : in addition to the *enunciative* propositions,
which express the (logically) true or false, there are others
which do not express either the (logically) true or false,
as for example the expressions of aspirations and of
desires (εὐχή), which therefore belong, not to logical
exposition, but to poetical and rhetorical exposition.[2]
And in another place we find him affirming in opposition
to Bryson (who had said that a base thing remained such
with whatever word it were designated) that base things
can be expressed both with words that place them beneath the eye in all their crudity, and with other words
which surround them with a veil.[3] All this might have led
to the separation of the linguistic faculty from the properly
logical, and to its consideration in union with the poetical
and artistic faculty ; but here too the attempt stopped
half-way. The Aristotelian logic assumed a verbal and
formalistic character, which became more and more
accentuated as time went on and formed an obstacle to
the distinction between the two theoretical forms. Nevertheless, Epicurus asserted that the diversity of names
designating the same thing with various peoples was
due, not to convention and caprice, but to the fact that
the impressions produced by things were different in
each one of them.[4] And the Stoics, although they connected language with thought (διάνοια) and not with
imagination, seem to have had a suspicion of the non-
logical nature of language, for they interposed between
thought and sound a *certain something* which was indicated

[1] *Rhet.* bk. iii. ch. 1.   [2] *De interp.* ch. 4.
[3] *Rhet.* bk. iii. ch. 2.   [4] Diog. Laert. bk. x. § 75.

in Greek by the word λεκτόν, and by the words *effatum* or *dicibile* in Latin. But we are not sure what they really meant, and whether that vague concept were intended by them to distinguish the linguistic representation from the abstract concept (which would bring them into touch with the modern view), or the meaning of sound in general.[1]

We cannot collect any other germ of truth from the ancient writers. A philosophical Grammar, like a philosophical Poetics, remained unattainable in antiquity.

[1] Steinthal, *Gesch. d. Sprachw.*, 2nd ed., i. pp. 288, 293, 296-297.

ÆSTHETIC IDEAS IN THE MIDDLE AGES
AND RENAISSANCE

ALMOST all the developments of ancient Æsthetic were *Middle Ages.* continued by tradition or reappeared by spontaneous *Mysticism.* *Ideas on the* generation in the course of the Middle Ages. Neo- *beautiful.* Platonic mysticism continued, entrusted to the care of the pseudo-Dionysius the Areopagite (*De coelesti hierarchia, De ecclesiastica hierarchia, De divinis nominibus*, etc.), to the translations of these works made by John Scotus Eriugena, and to the divulgations of the Spanish Jews (Avicebron). The Christian God took the place of the Summum Bonum or Idea : God, wisdom, goodness, supreme beauty, source of beautiful things in nature, which are a ladder to the contemplation of the Creator. But these speculations continued to recede further and further from the consideration of art, with which Plotinus had connected them ; and the empty definitions of the beautiful by Cicero and other ancient writers were often repeated. Saint Augustine defined beauty in general as unity (*omnis pulchritudinis forma unitas est*), and that of the body as *congruentia partium cum quadam coloris suavitate*, and the old distinction between something that is beautiful in itself and relative beauty reappeared in a book of his, which has been lost, entitled *De pulchro et apto* ; the very name shows that he reasserted the old distinction between the beautiful in itself and the relatively beautiful, *quoniam apte accommodaretur alicui.* Elsewhere he notes that an image is called beautiful *si perfecte implet illud cujus imago est, et coaequatur ei.*[1]

[1] *Confess.* IV. X. ch. 13 ; *De Trinitate,* vi. ch. 10 ; *Epist.* 3, 18 ; *De*

Thomas Aquinas varied but little from him in positing three requisites for beauty : integrity or perfection, due proportion, and clearness ; following Aristotle, he distinguished the beautiful from the good, defining the first as that which pleases in the mere contemplation of it (*pulcrum . . . id cujus ipsa apprehensio placet*) ; he referred to the beauty that even base things possess if well imitated, and applied the doctrine of imitation to the beauty of the Second Person of the Trinity (*in quantum est imago expressa Patris*).[1] If it were wished to discover references to the hedonistic conception of art, it would be possible to do this, with a little goodwill, in some of the sayings of jongleurs and troubadours. Æsthetic rigorism, the total negation of art for religion or for divine and human science, shows itself in Tertullian and among certain Fathers of the Church, at the entrance to the Middle Ages ; at their conclusion, in a certain crude scholastic spirit, for example in Cecco d' Ascoli, who proclaimed against Dante : " I leave trifles behind me and return to the *true* ; fables are always unpleasing to me," and later, in the reactionary Savonarola. But the narcotic theory of pedagogic or moralistic art prevailed over every other. It had contributed to send to sleep the æsthetic doubts and inquiries of the ancients, and was well suited to a period of relative decadence of culture. This was all the more the case, seeing that it accorded well with the moral and religious ideas of the Middle Ages, and afforded a justification not only for the new art of Christian inspiration, but also for the surviving works of classical and pagan art.

The pedagogic theory of art in the Middle Ages. The allegorical interpretation was again a means of salvation for these last. The *De continentia Virgiliana* of Fulgentius (sixth century) is a curious monument to this fact. This work made Virgil compatible with the Middle Ages and opened his way to that great reputation

---

civitate Dei, xxii. ch. 19 (in *Opera*, ed. dei Maurini, Paris, 1679–1690, vols. i. ii. vii. viii.).

[1] *Summa theol.* I. 1. xxxix. 8 ; I. 11. xxvii. 1 (ed. Migne, i. cols. 794-795 ; ii. col. 219).

which he was destined to attain, as the " gentle sage who knew all things." Even John of Salisbury says of the Roman poet, that " *sub imagine fabularum totius philosophiae exprimit veritatem.*" [1] The process of interpretation became fixed in the doctrine of the *four meanings*, literal, allegorical, moral and anagogic, which Dante afterwards transferred to vernacular poetry. It would be easy to accumulate quotations from mediæval writers, repeating in all keys the theory that art inculcates the truths of morality and of faith and constrains hearts to Christian piety, beginning with those well-known verses of Theodulf : " *In quorum dictis* (that is to say, in the utterances of the poets) *quamquam sint frivola multa, Plurima sub falso tegmine vera latent,*" and so on, until we reach the doctrines and opinions of our own great men, Dante and Boccaccio. For Dante, poetry " *nihil aliud est quam fictio rhethorica in musicaque posita.*" [2] The poet should have a " reasoning " in his verses " under a cloak of figure or of rhetorical colour " ; and it would be a shameful thing for him, if, " when asked, he were not able to divest his words of such a garment, in such a way as to show that they possessed a true meaning." [3] Readers sometimes stop at the external vesture alone, and this indeed suffices for those who, like the vulgar, do not succeed in penetrating the hidden meaning. Poetry will say to the vulgar, which does not understand " its argument," what a song of Dante's says at its conclusion, " At least behold how *beautiful* I am " : if you are not able to obtain instruction from me, at least enjoy me as a pleasing thing. Many, indeed, " their beauty more than their goodness will delight," in poems, unless they are assisted by commentaries in the nature of the *Convivio*, " a light which will allow every shade of meaning to reach them." [4] Poetry was the " gay science," " *un fingimiento* " (as the Spanish poet the Marquis of Santillana wrote) " *de cosas útiles, cubiertas ó veladas con*

---

[1] Comparetti, *Virg. nel medio evo*, vol. i. *passim.*
[2] *De vulg. eloq.* (ed. Rajna), bk. ii. ch. 4.
[3] *Vita nuova*, ch. 25.   [4] *Convivio*, i. 1.

*muy fermosa cobertura, compuestas, distinguidas é scan-
didas, por cierto cuento, pesso é medida."* [1]

It would not then be correct to say that the Middle
Ages simply identified art with theology and with philosophy. Indeed it sharply distinguished the one from
the other, defining art and poetry, like Dante, with the
words *fictio rhethorica*, " figure " and " rhetorical colour,"
" cloak," " beauty," or like Santillana with those of
fingimiento or *fermosa cobertura*. This pleasing falsity
was justified from the practical point of view, very much
in the same way as sexual union and love were justified
and sanctified in matrimony. This did not exclude, indeed
it implied, that the perfect state was certainly celibacy—
that is to say, pure science, free from admixture of art.

Hints of an Æsthetic in scholastic philosophy.   The only tendency that had no true and proper representatives was the sound scientific tendency. The
Poetics of Aristotle itself was hardly known or rather it
was ill-known, from the Latin translation that a German
of the name of Hermann made, not earlier than 1256,
of the paraphrase or commentary of Averroes. Perhaps
the best of the mediæval investigations into language is
that supplied by Dante's *De vulgari eloquentia*, where the
word is, however, still looked upon as a sign ("*rationale
signum et sensuale . . . natura sensuale quidem, in quantum sonus est, rationale vero in quantum aliquid significare
videtur ad placitum* ").[2] The study of the expressive,
æsthetic, linguistic faculty would, however, have found
an appropriate occasion and a point of departure in the
secular debate between nominalism and realism, which
could not avoid touching to some extent the relations
between the word and the flesh, thought and language.
Duns Scotus wrote a treatise *De modis significandi seu*
(the addition is due perhaps to the editors) *grammatica
speculativa*.[3] Abelard had defined sensation as *confusa
conceptio*, and *imaginatio* as a faculty that preserved

---

[1] *Prohemio al Condestable de Portugal*, 1445–1449 (in *Obras*, ed.
Amador de los Rios, 1852), § 3.

[2] *De vulg. eloq.* bk. i. ch. 3.

[3] Lately reprinted under the editorship of padre M. Fernandez
Garcia, Ad claras Aquas (Quarracchi), 1902.

sensations ; the intellect renders discursive what is intuitive in the preceding stage, and we have finally the perfection of knowledge in the intuitive knowledge of the discursive. We find the same importance attached to intuitive knowledge, perception, of the individual or *species specialissima*, in Duns Scotus, together with the progressive denominations of the different sorts of knowledge as *confusae*, *indistinctae* and *distinctae*. We shall see this terminology reappear, big with consequences, at the very commencement of modern Æsthetic.[1]

It may be said that the literary and artistic doctrines and opinions of the Middle Ages have, with few exceptions, a value rather for the history of culture than for the general history of science. The like observation holds good of the Renaissance, for here, too, the circle of the ideas of antiquity was not overstepped. Culture increases ; original sources are studied ; the ancient writers are translated and commented upon ; many treatises are written and henceforth printed upon poetry and the arts, grammars, rhetorics, dialogues, and dissertations upon the beautiful : the proportions have increased, the world has become bigger ; but truly original ideas do not yet show themselves in the domain of æsthetic science. The mystical tradition is refreshed and strengthened by the renewed cult of Plato : Marsilio Ficino, Pico della Mirandola, Cattani, Leon Battista Alberti, in the fifteenth century, and Pietro Bembo, Mario Equicola, Castiglione, Nobili, Betussi, and very many others in the following century, wrote upon the Beautiful and upon Love. Among the most noteworthy productions of the sort, a crossing of the mediæval and classical currents, is the book of the *Dialogues of Love* (1535), composed in Italian by the Spanish Jew Leo, and translated into all the cultured languages of the time.[2] The three parts into which it is divided treat of the nature and essence, of the universality, and of the origin of love ; and it is demonstrated that

Renaissance. Philography and philosophical and empirical inquiries concerning the beautiful.

---

[1] Windelband, *Gesch. d. Phil.* ii. pp. 251-270 ; De Wulf, *Philos. médiév.*, Louvain, 1900, pp. 317-320.

[2] *Dialogi di amore, composti per Leone, medico* . . ., Rome, 1535.

every beautiful thing is good, but not every good thing
is beautiful ; that beauty is a grace which dilates the
soul and moves it to love, and that knowledge of lesser
beauties leads to that of higher spiritual beauties. The
author gave the name of " Philography " to these and
similar affirmations and effusions of which the book is
composed. Equicola's [1] work is also interesting, because
it contains historical accounts of those who wrote upon
the subject before he did so himself. The same intuition
was versified and sighed forth by the Petrarchists in
their sonnets and ballads, while others, rebellious and
mocking, derided it in comedies, verses in *terza rima* and
parodies of all sorts. Some mathematicians, reincarna-
tions of Pythagoras, set to work to determine beauty by
exact relations : for instance Leonardo's friend, Luca
Paciolo, in the *De divina proportione* (1509), in which he
laid down the pretended æsthetic law of the golden
section.[2] And side by side with these new Pythagoreans
were those who revived the canon of Polycletus as to
the beauty of the human body, especially of the female
body, such as Firenzuola, Franco, Luigini, and Dolce.
Michael Angelo fixed an empirical canon for painting in
general, when he stated that the means of giving movement and grace to figures [3] consisted in the observance
of a certain arithmetical relation. Others, such as Fulvio
Pellegrino Morato, investigated the symbolism or meaning of colours. The Platonists generally placed beauty
in the soul, the Aristotelians rather in the physical
qualities. The Averroist, Agostino Nifo, amid much
chatter and many inconclusive remarks, demonstrated
the existence of the beautiful in nature by describing
the supremely beautiful body of Joan of Aragon, Princess
of Tagliacozzo, to whom the book is dedicated.[4] Torquato
Tasso, in the " Minturno," [5] imitated the uncertainties of

[1] *Libro di natura e d' amore*, Venice, 1525 (Ven. 1563).
[2] *De divina proportione*, Venice, 1509.
[3] G. P. Lomazzo, *Trattato dell' arte della pittura, scultura ed archi-
tettura*, Milan, 1585, i. 1, pp. 22-23.
[4] Aug. Niphi, *De pulcro et amore*, Rome, 1529.
[5] *Il Minturno o vero de la belleza* (in *Dialoghi*, ed. Guasti, vol. iii.).

the *Hippias* of Plato, not without making a free use of
the speculations of Plotinus. A chapter of the *Poetica*
of Campanella possesses greater importance, where he
describes the good as *signum boni* and the ugly as *signum
mali*, understanding by good the three prime forces of
Power, Wisdom and Love. Although Campanella was
still tied to the Platonic idea of the beautiful, the conception of a sign or symbol, here introduced by him,
represents progress. By this means he succeeded in
perceiving that material things or external facts are
neither beautiful nor ugly in themselves. " Mandricard
called the wounds in the bodies of his friends the Moors
beautiful, for they were large and gave evidence of the
great strength of Roland who dealt them ; Saint
Augustine called the gashes and the dislocations in the
body of Saint Vincent beautiful, because they were
evidence of his endurance, but they were on the other
hand ugly in so far as they were signs of the cruelty of
the tyrant Dacianus and of his executioners. It is
beautiful to die fighting, said Virgil, for it is the sign of
a strong soul. The pet dog of his mistress will seem
beautiful to the lover, and doctors call even urine and
fæces beautiful, when they indicate health. Everything
is both beautiful and ugly " (*quapropter nihil est quod
non sit pulcrum simul et turpe*).[1] In such observations
as these we have not a mere state of mystical exaltation,
but to some extent a movement in the direction of
analysis.

Nothing better serves to demonstrate that the Re- *The pedagogic theory of art and the Poetics of Aristotle.*
naissance did not pass beyond the confines of ancient
æsthetic thought than the fact that notwithstanding the
renewed acquaintance with the thought of Aristotle, the
pedagogic theory of art not only persisted and triumphed,
but was transplanted bodily into the text of Aristotle,
where its interpreters read it with a certainty that we
have to make efforts to achieve. Certainly, a Robortelli
(1548) or a Castelvetro (1570) stopped short at the simple,
purely hedonistic solution, giving simple pleasure as the

[1] *Ration. philos.* part iv.; *Poeticor.* (Paris, 1638), art. vii.

end of art : poetry, says Castelvetro, " was discovered
solely for the purpose of delighting and of recreating
. . . the souls of the rude multitude and of the common
people." [1]   And here and there some were able to free
themselves from both the pleasure theory and that of
the didactic end ; but the majority, such as Segni, Maggi,
Vettori,[2] were for the *docere delectando*.   Scaliger (1561)
declared .that mimesis or imitation was "*finis medius
ad illum ultimum qui est docendi cum delectatione*," and
believing himself to be altogether in agreement with
Aristotle as to this, he continued, "*docet affectus poeta per
actiones, ut bonos amplectamur atque imitemur ad agendum,
malos aspernemur ad abstinendum*." [3]   Piccolomini (1575)
observed that " It must not be thought that so many
excellent poets and artists, ancient and modern, would
have devoted such care and diligence to this most noble
study, had they not known and believed that in so doing
they were aiding human life," and if " they had not
thought that we were to be instructed, directed, and
well established by it." [4]   The " truth preserved in soft
verses, which attracts and persuades the most reluctant "
(Tasso),[5] with the comparison from Lucretius attached,
is the conception that even Campanella repeats.   Poetry
is for him " *Rhetorica quaedam figurata, quasi magica,
quae exempla ministrat ad suadendum bonum et dissua-
dendum malum delectabiliter iis qui simplici verum et bonum
audire nolunt, aut non possunt aut nesciunt*." [6]   Thus returned the comparison of poetry with oratory ; according
to Segni they only differ because the first occupies a
more lofty situation : " for since imitation representing
itself in act by means of poetry, in mighty, chosen words,

---

[1] Fr. Robortelli, *In librum Aris. de arte poet. explicationes*, Florence,
1548 ; Lud. Castelvetro, *Poetica d' Aristotele vulgarizzata ed esposta*,
1570 (Basle, 1576), part i. particella iv. pp. 29-30.

[2] Bern. Segni, *Rettor. e poet. trad.* Florence, 1549 ; Vinc. Madii,
In Arist. . . . explanationes, 1550 ; Petri Victorii, *Commentarii*, etc.,
Florence, 1560.

[3] *Poetica*, 1561 (ed. 3, 1586), i. 1 ; vii. 3.

[4] *Annotationi nel libro della Poetica*, Venice, 1575, preface.

[5] *Gerus. lib.* i. 3.   [6] *Poetic.* ch. 1, art. 1.

in metaphors, images, and indeed the whole of figured
speech, which is to be found more in poetry than in the
art of oratory, the metrical qualities that are also required
in verse, the subjects of which it treats, which have
something of the great and delightful, make it appear
most beautiful and worthy of being held all the greater
marvel."[1] "Three most noble arts" (wrote Tassoni in
1620, and he repeated common opinion), "History,
Poetics, and Oratory, come under the heading of Politics
and depend upon it ; the first of these has reference to
the instruction of princes and gentlemen, the second
of the people, the third of those who give counsel in
public trials or defend private ones that come up for
judgment."[2]

According to these views, the tragical catharsis was
regarded as designed in general to demonstrate the instability of fortune, or to terrify by example, or to proclaim the triumph of justice, or to render the spectators
insensible to the strokes of fortune, owing to their
familiarity with suffering. The pedagogic theory, thus
renewed and sustained by the authority of the ancients,
was popularized in France, Spain, England and Germany,
together with all the Italian poetic doctrines of the
Renaissance. The French writers of the period of Louis
XIV. are altogether penetrated with it. "*Cette science
agréable qui mêle la gravité des préceptes avec la douceur
du langage*," is what La Ménardière calls poetry (1640),
in the same way as Le Bossu (1675), for whom "*le
premier but du poète est d'instruire*,"[3] as Homer taught,
when he wrote two interesting didactic manuals relating
to military and political events : the *Iliad* and the
Odyssey.

This pedagogic theory has therefore been reasonably   *The "Poetics
described by all the modern critics in concert, as if by   of the Renais-
antonomasia, as the *Poetics of the Renaissance*. It must,   sance."*
however, always be understood that it did not appear

---

[1] *Poetica trad*. preface.   [2] *Pensieri diversi*, bk. x. ch. 18.
[3] La Ménardière, *Poétique*, Paris, 1640 ; Le Bossu, *Traité du poème
épique*, Paris, 1675.

for the first time in the fifteenth or sixteenth century, but that it was prevalent and generally accepted at that time. It may even be remarked, as has already been acutely done,[1] that the Renaissance naturally did not distinguish the didactic kind of poetry from the other kinds, since for it every kind of poetry was didactic. But the Renaissance was not a real Renaissance, save when and where it continued the interrupted spiritual work of antiquity, and in this sense it would perhaps be more just to describe as its Poetics, or rather, as the important element in its Poetics, not the repetition of the pedagogic theory of antiquity and of the Middle Ages, but the resumption, which also took place, of the discussions upon the possible, the probable (*verisimile*, εἰκός) of Aristotle, on the reasons of Plato's condemnation and on the procedure of the artist who creates by imagining.

Dispute concerning the universal and the probable in art.

It is in such discussions that is to be found the true contribution of that epoch, not to learning, but to the formation of the science of Æsthetic. The ground was prepared and enriched through the work of the interpreters and commentators of Aristotle and of the new writers on Poetics, especially the Italians, and it was also enriched with some seed that was destined to sprout and to become a vigorous plant in the future. The study of Plato also contributed not a little to call attention to the function of the idea, or of the universal, in poetry. What meaning was to be attached to the statement that poetry should aim at the universal and history at the particular? What was the meaning of the proposition that poetry should proceed according to *probability*? What could that *certain idea* consist of, which Raphael said that he followed in his painting?

G. Fracastoro.

Girolamo Fracastoro was among the first to ask himself this question seriously, in the dialogue *Naugerius, sive De poetica* (1555). He disdainfully rejected the thesis that the end of poetry is pleasure : far be from us,

[1] Borinski, *Poet. d. Renaiss.* p. 26.

he exclaimed, so bad an opinion of the poets, who the
ancients said were the inventors of all the good arts.
Nor did the end of instruction seem to him to be acceptable, which is the task, not of poetry, but of other
faculties, such as geography, history, agronomy, philosophy. The poet's task is to represent or to imitate,
and he differs from the historian, not in the matter, but
in the manner of representation. The others imitate the
particular, the poet the universal : the others are like
the painters of portraits, the poet produces things as he
contemplates the universal and most beautiful idea of
them : the others say only what they need to say for
their purposes, the poet that he may say everything
beautifully and fully.

But the beauty of a poem must always be understood
as relative to the class of subject of which it treats ; it
is the most beautiful in this class, not the supremely
beautiful : one must be careful to guard against the
equivocal or double meaning of this word " beauty "
(aequivocatio illius verbi). A poet never utters what is
false or expresses what does not exist, for his words inevitably harmonize in appearance or signification either
with the opinions of men or with the universal. Nor
can we accept the Platonic axiom that the poet has no
knowledge of the things of which he treats ; he does know
them, but in his own poet's manner.[1]

While Fracastoro strives to elaborate the important
passage in Aristotle touching the universal of poetry,
and though somewhat vague in his treatment, keeps
fairly close to the mark ; Castelvetro, on the contrary, *L. Castelvetro.*
judges the Aristotelian fragment with the freedom and
superior knowledge of the true critic. He recognizes that
the *Poetics* is merely a notebook recording certain principles and methods of compiling the art, not the art fully
compiled. He remarks, moreover, not without logical
acumen, that Aristotle having adopted the criterion of
probability or of that " which presents an appearance of

[1] Hyeron. Frascatorii *Opera*, Venetian edition, Giunti, 1574, pp.
112-120.

historic truth," should have applied his theory in the
first case to history, not to poetry ; for history being a
" narrative according to truth of memorable human
actions," and poetry a narrative according to probability
of events which might possibly occur, the second cannot
receive " all its radiance " from the first. Nor does it
escape him that Aristotle describes two different things
by the one word " imitation " : (a) " following the example of another," which is " acting in exactly the same
way as another without knowing the reason of such
action " : and (b) the imitation " demanded by poetry,"
which " does things in a manner totally different from
that in which they have been done hitherto and proposes
a new example for imitation." Nevertheless Castelvetro
cannot extricate himself from the confusion between the
imaginary and the historical ; for he himself says " the
realm of the former is generally that of certainty," but
" the field of certainty is often crossed with bars of uncertainty just as the field of uncertainty is often crossed
with bars of certainty." Also what can be said of this
curious interpretation of the Aristotelian theory of
pleasure experienced in the imitation of ugly models,
that such pleasure is based on the fact that since an
imitation is always imperfect, it is incapable of exciting
the disgust and fear which would arise from the contemplation of real ugliness ? And what of his remark
that the characteristics of painting and poetry are so
diverse as to be in opposition one to the other ; imitation
of objects giving rise to great pleasure in the former
art and as great displeasure in the latter ? And so on in
numberless cases of bold but scarcely felicitous subtleties.[1]

*Piccolomini
and Pinciano.*   In opposition to Robortelli, who asserted the identity
of the probable and the false, Piccolomini held that the
probable (*verisimile*) is inherently neither false nor true,
only by accident becoming one or other.[2] Of the same
mind is the Spaniard Alfonso Lopez Pinciano (1596), who
says the scope of poetry " *no es la mentira, que seria*

[1] *Poet., ed. cit.* i. 1 ; ii. 1 ; iii. 7 ; v. 1 (pp. 64, 66, 71-72, 208, 580).
[2] *Annotationi*, preface.

*coincider con la sophística, ni la historia que seria tomar
la materia al histórico ; y no siendo historia porque toca
fabúlas ni mentira porque toca historia, tiene por objeto el
verisimil, que todo lo abraza. De aqui resulta que es un
arte superior á la metaphysica, porqué comprende mucho
mas, y se extiende a lo que es y á lo que no es."* [1] What may
lie behind this notion of probability is still indefinite and
impenetrable.

Moved by a wish to place poetry on a foundation other   *Fr. Patrizzi*
than the probable, Francesco Patrizzi, the anti-Aristo-   *(Patricius).*
telian, composed his *Poetica* between 1555 and 1586 in
refutation of all Aristotle's main doctrines. Patrizzi notes
that the word " imitation " is given many meanings by
the Greek philosopher, who uses it now to denote a
single word, now to describe a tragedy ; at times it stands
for a figure of speech, at others for a fiction : whence he
draws the logical conclusion (from which, however, he
shrinks alarmed) " that all philosophic and other kinds
of writing and speaking are poetry, since they are made
of words which themselves are imitations." He observes
further that, according to Aristotle, it is impossible to
distinguish between poetry and history (since both are
imitations), or to prove that verse is not essential to
poetry, or that history, science and art are unsuitable
material for it ; since Aristotle in several passages says
that poetry may comprise " fable, actual occurrences,
belief of others, duty, the best, necessity, the possible,
the probable, the credible, the incredible, the suitable "
as well as " all things worldly." After these objections,
some sound, others sophistical, Patrizzi comes to the
conclusion that " there is no truth in the dogma that
poetry is wholly imitation ; and even if it be imitation
at all, it belongs not to poets alone, nor is it mere imitation of any kind, but something else not mentioned by
Aristotle nor pointed out by any one else, nor yet borne
into the mind of man. The discovery may possibly be
made in course of time, or some one may hit upon the

[1] *Philosophia antiqua poetica*, Madrid, 1596 (reprinted Valladolid,
1894).

truth and bring it to light " ; but up to the present " such
discovery has not been made." [1]

Yet these confessions of ignorance, these endeavours,
though vain, to escape from the Aristotelian circle of
ideas, and the great literary controversies of the sixteenth
century concerning the concept of poetic truth and the
probable had their use in that they stimulated interest
by directing attention to a mystery still unsolved.
Thought had once more begun to move upon the æsthetic
problem, and this time it was not destined to be broken
off or to lose itself.

[1] Francesco Patrici, *Della poetica, la Deca disputata*, " in which by
history, by reason, by authority of the greatest worthies of antiquity,
is shown the falsity of the most received opinions concerning Poetry
down to our own day." Ferrara, 1586.

III

FERMENTS OF THOUGHT
IN THE SEVENTEENTH CENTURY

INTEREST in æsthetic investigation increased rapidly in *New words and new observations in the seventeenth century* the early years of the following century, owing either to the popularity acquired by certain new words or to the novel meanings given to words already familiar, which emphasized new aspects of artistic production and criticism, complicating the problem and rendering it thereby more puzzling and attractive. For example : wit, taste, imagination or fancy, feeling, and several others, which must be examined rather closely.

Wit (*ingegno*) differed somewhat from intellect. Free use of the word arose, if we mistake not, from its convenience in Rhetoric as conceived by antiquity ; that is to say, a suave and facile mode of knowledge, as opposed to the severity of Dialectic ; an " Antistrophe to Dialectic," which substituted for reasons of actual fact those of probability or fancy ; enthymemes for syllogisms, examples for inductions ; so much so that Zeno the Stoic figured Dialectic with her fist clenched and Rhetoric with her hand open. The empty style of the decadent Italian authors in the seventeenth century found its complete justification in this theory of rhetoric ; their prose and verse, Marinesque and Achillinesque, professed to exhibit not the true but the striking, subtly conceited, curious or nice. The word wit, *ingegno*, was now repeated much more frequently than in the preceding century ; wit was hailed as presiding genius of Rhetoric ; its " vivacities " were lauded to the skies ; " *belli ingegni* "

was a phrase seized upon by the French, who rendered it
as " *esprit* " or " *beaux esprits.*" [1] One of the most noteworthy commentators on these matters (although opposed
to the literary excesses of the times), Matteo Pellegrini
of Bologna (1650), defines wit as " that part of the soul
which in a certain way practises, aims, and seeks to find
and create the beautiful and the efficacious " ; [2] he
considers the work of " wit " to be the " conceits " and
" subtleties " noted by him in a previous pamphlet
(1639).[3] Emmanuele Tesauro also descants at considerable length in his *Cannochiale Aristotelico* (1654) upon
wit and subtleties, not alone " verbal " and " lapidary "
conceits, but also " symbolic " and " figurative " (statues,
stories, devices, satires, hieroglyphs, mosaics, emblems,
insignia, sceptres), and even " animated agents " (panto-
mimes, play-scenes, masques and dances) : all things
which may be grouped under " polite quibbling " or
rhetoric as distinct from " dialectic."

Amongst such treatises, product of their age, one
written by the Spaniard Baltasar Gracian (1642) became
celebrated throughout Europe.[4] Wit became in his hands
the strictly inventive or artistic faculty, " genius " ;
génie, " genius " were now used as synonyms of wit,
ingegno and *esprit*. In the following century Mario
Pagano [5] wrote : " Wit may be taken as equivalent to the
génie of the French, a word now commonly used in
Italy." To return to the seventeenth century, Bouhours,
a Jesuit writer of dialogues on the *Manière de bien penser
dans les ouvrages d'esprit* (1687), says that " ' heart ' and
' wit ' are greatly in fashion just now, nothing else is
spoken of in polite conversation, and all discourse is at
last brought round to *l'esprit et le cœur.*" [6]

[1] *E.g.* Molière, *Préc. ridic.* sc. 1, 10.

[2] *I fonti dell' ingegno ridotti ad arte*, Bologna, 1650.

[3] *Delle acutezze che altrimenti spiriti, vivezze e concetti volgarmenti si
appellano*, Genova-Bologna, 1639.

[4] *Agudeza y arte de ingenio*, Madrid, 1642 ; enlarged, Huesca, 1649.

[5] *Saggio del gusto e delle belle arti*, 1783, ch. 1, *note.*

[6] Ital. trans. in Orsi, *Considerazioni*, etc. (Modena, 1735), vol. i.
dial. 1.

The word *taste* or *good taste* was equally widespread Taste.
and fashionable, signifying the faculty of judgement
brought to bear on the beautiful, distinct to some extent
from intellectual power, and sometimes divided into
active and passive, so that it was usual to speak of one
kind of taste as " productive " or " fertile " (thus coinciding with " wit "), and of another as " sterile."

From the rough notes which we possess as to the *Various*
history of the concept of taste, several meanings of the *meanings of*
word, not all of equal importance as indications of the *the word taste.*
development of ideas, detach themselves in a somewhat
confused manner. " Taste," meaning " pleasure " or
" delight," was an old-established word in Italy and
Spain, as is shown in such phrases as " to have a taste
for, to be to one's taste " ; when Lope di Vega and other
Spaniards speak continually of the drama of their country
as seeking to please the popular taste (" *deleita el gusto* " ;
" *para darle gusto* ") they mean only the " pleasure " of
the populace. In Italy there was a very ancient use
of the word in the metaphorical sense of " judgement,"
either literary, scientific, or artistic ; numberless examples of this use occur in writers of the sixteenth century
(Ariosto, Varchi, Michael Angelo, Tasso). To take but one
of these : the lines in *Orlando Furioso* where it is said
of the Emperor Augustus, " *L' aver avuto in poesia buon
gusto La proscrizione iniqua gli perdona,*" "For having
had good taste in poetry he shall be forgiven his iniquitous
proscriptions " ; or the remark of Ludovico Dolce that
some person " had such exquisite taste, he sang no verses
save those of Catullus and Calvus." [1] The word " taste,"
in the sense of a special faculty or attitude of mind,
appears to have been used for the first time in Spain in
the middle of the seventeenth century by Gracian,[2] the
moralist and political writer already quoted. It is
evidently to him that the Italian author Trevisano
alludes in a preface to a book by Muratori (1708) when

---

[1] *Orl. Furioso*, xxxv. 26 ; L. Dolce, *Dial. del pittura* (Venice, 1557) ;
ad init.

[2] Borinski, *Poet. d. Renaiss.* p. 308 *seqq.* ; *B. Gracian*, pp. 39-54.

he speaks of " Spaniards, above all others cunning in metaphor," who express themselves in " that eloquent and laconic phrase, good taste " ; touching further on taste and genius he quotes, " that ingenious Spaniard," Gracian,[1] who gave the word the sense of " practical wit," enabling one to perceive the " true signification " of things ; his " man of good taste " becomes in our language " a man of tact " in the affairs of life.[2]

The transference of the word to the domain of æsthetic seems to have taken place in France during the last quarter of the century. " *Il y a dans l'art un point de perfection, comme de bonté ou de maturité dans la nature : celui qui le sent et qui l'aime a le goût parfait ; celui qui ne le sent pas, et qui aime au deçà ou au delà, a le goût défectueux. Il y a donc un bon et un mauvais goût, et l'on dispute des goûts avec fondement,*" writes La Bruyère[3] (1688). As attributes or variants of taste it was usual to mention *delicacy* and *variety* or *variability*. Bearing its fresh critical-literary content, but not freed from the encumbrance of its earlier practical and moral significance, the word spread from France into other European countries. Thomasius introduced it into Germany in 1687 ;[4] and in England it becomes " good taste." In Italy it appears as early as 1696 as title of a large book written by Camillo Ettori, the Jesuit, *Il buon gusto ne' componimenti rettorici.*[5] The preface notes : " The expression ' good taste,' proper to those who rightly distinguish good from bad flavour in foods, is now in general use and claimed by every one as a title in connexion with literature and the humanities " ; it reappears in 1708 at

[1] *Riflessioni sopra il buon gusto* (Venice, 1766), introd. pp. 72-84.

[2] Gracian, *Obras* (Antwerp, 1669) ; *El héroe, El discreto,* with introd. by A. Farinelli, Madrid, 1900. Cf. Borinski, *Poet. d. Renais. l.c.*

[3] *Les Caractères, ou les mœurs du siècle,* ch. 1 ; *Des ouvrages de l'esprit.*

[4] In the programme : *Von der Nachahmung der Franzosen,* Leipzig, 1687.

[5] *Opera . . . nella quale con alcune certe considerazioni si mostra in che consista il vero buon gusto ne' suddetti componimenti,* etc., etc., Bologna, 1696.

the beginning of Muratori's [1] book already quoted :
Trevisano treats of it philosophically : Salvini discusses
it in his note upon the *Perfetta Poesia* of Muratori above
mentioned, where the subject of good taste occupies
several pages,[2] and finally it gives its name to the Academy
of Good Taste founded at Palermo in 1718.[3] Scholars of
the day who took up the discussion of the theme, recollect-
ing some passages scattered throughout the ancient
classics, placed the new concept in relation with the
" *tacitus quidam sensus sine ulla ratione et arte* " of Cicero ;
and with the " *iudicium* " which " *nec magis arte traditur
quam gustus aut odor* " of Quintilian.[4] More particularly
Montfaucon de Villars (1671) [5] wrote a book on " Delicacy " ; Ettori strove to find some definition more satisfactory than those current at the time (*e.g.* " it is the
finest invention of wit, the flower of wit and extract of
beauty's self," and similar conceits) ; [6] Orsi made it the
subject of his *Considerazioni* written in reply to Bouhours'
book.

In Italy in the seventeenth century we find imagination or fancy placed on a pinnacle. What do you mean
by talking of probability and historical truth (asks
Cardinal Sforza Pallavicino in 1644), of false or true in
connexion with poetry ; which deals not with fiction,
fact or historical probability but with primary apprehensions which assert neither truth nor falsehood ?
Following this line of argument, imagination takes the
place of that probable, neither true nor false, advocated
by some commentators of Aristotle ; a theory strongly
criticized by Pallavicino, here agreeing with Piccolomini,
whom however he does not name, and in opposition to
Castelvetro whom he explicitly mentions. He who goes
to the play (continues Pallavicino) knows quite well

Fancy or Imagination.

[1] *Delle riflessioni sopra il buon gusto nelle scienze e nell' arti*, 1708 (Venice, 1766).
[2] Muratori, *Della perfetta poesia italiana*, Modena, 1706, bk. ii. ch. 5.
[3] Mazzuchelli, *Scrittori d' Italia*, vol. ii. part iv. p. 2389.
[4] Cicero, *De oratore*, iii. ch. 50 ; Quintilian, *Inst. Orator.* vi. ch. 5.
[5] *De la délicatesse*, Paris, 1671.
[6] *Il buon gusto*, ch. 39, p. 367.

that the scenes acted on the stage are not real ; although
he has no belief in them yet they please him greatly.   For
" if poetry desired to be mistaken for truth, the end she
had in view would be a lie, by the laws of nature and of
God doomed inevitably to perish : for a lie is nothing
but an untruth uttered in the hope that it may be mistaken for truth.   How then should an art so tainted be
allowed to flourish in the best-regulated republics ?   How
should it be commended and used by the very writers
of Holy Scripture ? "   *Ut pictura poësis* : poetry is like
painting, which is a " diligent imitation " aiming at a
close copy of the features, colours, acts, nay, even the
hidden motives, of the objects it represents : and it
" does not pretend that fiction is truth."   The sole aim
of poetic tales is " to adorn our understanding with
imagery, that is to say, with sumptuous, novel, marvellous
and splendid appearances.   And this is known to diffuse
so useful an influence on mankind that humanity insists
on rewarding poets with praise more glorious than is
bestowed on any other men ; their books are protected
from the ravages of time with greater solicitude than is
shown to scientific treatises or productions of any other
art ; in the end the names of poets are crowned with
adoring veneration.   See how the world thirsts for
beautiful first apprehensions, although these are neither
laden with science nor are they vehicles of truth." [1]

Sixty years later these ideas, although expressed by a
Cardinal, seemed all too daring to Muratori, who could
not bring himself to allow poets so much latitude, or to
enfranchize them from their obligations to the probable.
Nevertheless Muratori allows a large space to imagination,
" an inferior apprehensive faculty " which, without caring
whether things be false or true, confines itself to apprehending them, and " represents " the truth merely,
leaving the task of " cognition " to the " superior apprehensive faculty " or intellect.[2]   Even the stony heart

---

[1] *Del bene* (Naples, 1681), bk. i. part i. chs. 49-53. Cf. the same
writer's *Arte della perfezion cristiana*, Rome, 1665, bk. i. ch. 3.

[2] *Perfetta poesia*, bk. i. chs. 14, 21.

of Gravina yields to the charm of imagination : he admits
it occupies a considerable place in the realm of poetry
and suffers his own arid prose to describe it as " a sorceress,
but beneficent," " a delirium which cures madness." [1]

Earlier than either of these, Ettori commended it to
the good rhetorician, " who in order that he may awaken
images " must " familiarize himself with whatever is
subject to bodily feeling " and " encounter the genius
of imagination, which is a sensuous faculty," to these
ends using " species rather than genera (since the latter,
being more universal than the former, are less sensible),
individuals rather than species, effects than causes, the
number of the greater rather than the number of the less." [2]

As far back as 1578 the Spaniard Huarte had maintained that eloquence is the product of imagination rather
than of intellect or reason.[3]   In England Bacon (1605)
ascribed science to intellect, history to memory and
poetry to imagination or fancy : [4] Hobbes inquired into
the procedure of poetry : [5] Addison (1712) devoted several
numbers of his *Spectator* to analysis of the " pleasures of
imagination." [6]   Somewhat later, the importance of imagination was felt in Germany, where it found advocates
in Bodmer, Breitinger and other writers of the Swiss
school, who owed much to the influence of the Italians
(Muratori, Gravina, Calepio) and the English : acting in
their turn as teachers of Klopstock and the new German
critical school.[7]

It was at this same period that opposition became *Feeling.*
clearly marked between those accustomed " *à juger par
le sentiment*" and those used to "*raisonner par principes*." [8]

---

[1] *Ragion poetica*, in *Prose italiane*, ed. De Stefano, Naples, 1839,
i. ch. 7.   [2] *Il buon gusto*, p. 10.

[3] *Esame degl' ingegni degl' huomini per apprender le scienze* (Ital.
trans. by C. Camilli, Venice, 1586), chs. 9-12.

[4] *De dignitate et augmentis scientiarum*, bk. ii. ch. 13.

[5] *De homine* (in *Opera phil.*, ed. Molesworth, vol. iii.), ch. 2.

[6] *Spectator*, Nos. 411-421 (*Works*, London, 1721, pp. 486-519).

[7] *Die Discourse der Mahlern*, 1721–1723 ; *Von dem Einfluss und
Gebrauche der Einbildungskraft*, etc., 1727 ; and other writings of
Bodmer and Breitinger.

[8] Pascal, *Pensées sur l'éloquence et le style*, § 15.

The Frenchman, Du Bos, author of *Réflexions critiques sur la poésie et la peinture* (1719), upholds the theory of feeling ; according to him art is simply a self-abandonment " *aux impressions que les objets étrangers font sur nous,*" setting aside all reflective labour. He laughs at those philosophers who deny the force of imagination, and Malebranche's eloquent discourse founded on this denial draws from Du Bos the remark, " *c'est à notre imagination qu'il parle contre l'abus de l'imagination.*" He refuses to see any intellectual nucleus in the productions of the arts, saying that art consists not in instruction but in style : nor is he too respectful towards the probable : he says he finds himself unable to set limits between it and the marvellous, and leaves to " born poets " the task of thus miraculously uniting opposites. For Du Bos there is no criterion of art save feeling, which he calls a " *sixième sens,*" against which dispute is vain since in such matters popular opinion invariably wins the day over the dogmatic pronouncements of artists and men of letters : all the ingenious conceits of the greatest metaphysicians, though unimpeachable in themselves, will not in the slightest degree diminish the lustre of poetry or despoil it of one single attraction. Attempts to discredit Ariosto and Tasso in the eyes of Italians were as vain as those made against the *Cid* in France. Other people's arguments can never persuade us of the contrary of what we feel.[1]   These notions were adopted by many French writers : for example Cartaut de la Villate [2] observes, " *Le grand talent d'un écrivain qui veut plaire, est de tourner ses réflexions en sentiments* " ; and Trublet, " *C'est un principe sûr, que la poésie doit être une expression de sentiment.*" [2]   Nor were the English slow in emphasizing the concept of " emotion " in their theories of literature.

[1] *Réflexions critiques sur la poésie et la peinture,* 1719 (ed. 7, Paris, 1770), *passim* ; see especially sections 1, 23, 26, 28, 33, 34.
[2] Cartaut de la Villate, *Essais historiques et philosophiques sur le goût,* Aix, 1737 ; Trublet, *Essais sur divers sujets de littérature et de morale,* Amsterdam, 1755.

In the writings of this period *imagination* was often
identified with *wit*, *wit* with *taste*, *taste* with *feeling*,
and *feeling* with first apprehensions or *imagination* ; [1]
we have already noted that taste is sometimes critical
and sometimes productive : this fusion, identification and
subordination of terms apparently distinct shows how they
gravitate round one single concept.

A German critic, one of the very few who have sought
to penetrate the darkness surrounding the origins of
modern Æsthetic, considers the concept of taste (which
we owe, he thinks, to Gracian) " the most important
æsthetic doctrine which remained for modern times to
discover." [2]   But without going so far as to say that taste
is the chief doctrine of the science, and the foundation of
all the rest, instead of only a particular doctrine, and
without recapitulating what we have already said of
Gracian's relation to the theory of taste, it is well to
repeat that taste, wit, imagination, feeling, and so on,
instead of new concepts scientifically grasped, were simply
new words corresponding to vague impressions : at most
they were problems, not concepts : apprehensions of
ground still to be conquered, not yet annexed and brought
into subjection.   It must not be forgotten that the very
men who made use of these terms could scarcely grope
after the ideas they suggested without falling back into
the old traditions, the only ones on which they had an
intellectual grasp.   To them the new words were shades,
not bodies : when they tried to embrace them their arms
returned empty to their own breasts.

Certainly wit differs to a certain extent from intellect.
Yet Pellegrini and Tesauro, with other writers of treatises,
never fail to point out that intellectual truth lies at the
root of wit.   Trevisano defines it as " an internal virtue
of the soul which invents methods for expressing and
executing its own concepts : it is recognizable now in
the arrangement of things we invent, now in the clear
expression of them : sometimes in cunning reconciliations
of matters seemingly opposed, sometimes in tracing

---

[1] Cf. Du Bos, *op. cit.* § 33.   [2] Borinski, *B. Gracian*, p. 39.

analogies but faintly discernible." To sum up, one must
not " allow the actions of wit to go unaccompanied by
those of intellect," or even by those of practical morality.[1]
More ingenuously Muratori says, " Wit is that virtue and
active force with which the intellect is able to assemble,
unite and discover the similarities, relations and reasons
of things." [2] In this manner wit, after having been
distinguished from intellect, eventually becomes a part
or a manifestation of it. By a somewhat different path
the same conclusion is reached by Alexander Pope when
he counsels that wit be reined in like a mettlesome horse,
and observes :

> For wit and judgement often are at strife,
> Though meant each other's aid like man and wife.[3]

Taste and intellectual judgement. Similar vicissitudes befell the word " taste," outcome
of a metaphor (as was noted by Kant) whose effect was
to stand in opposition to intellectualistic principles, as
if to say that the judgement governing the choice of food
destined solely for the delectation of the palate is of the
same nature as that which decides opinions in matters
of art.[4] Nevertheless, the very definition of this anti-
intellectualistic concept contained a reference to intellect
and reason ; the implicit comparison with the palate was
ultimately taken as signifying an anticipation of reflexion :
as Voltaire wrote in the following century : " *De même
que la sensation du palais anticipe la réflexion.*" [5] Intellect
and reason glimmer through all the definitions of taste belonging to·this period. Mme. Dacier wrote in 1684, " *Une
harmonie, un accord de l'esprit et de la raison.*" [6] " *Une
raison éclairée qui, d'intelligence avec le cœur, fait toujours
un juste choix parmi des choses opposées ou semblables,*"
wrote the author of *Entretiens galants.*[7] According to

[1] Trevisano, *op. cit.* pp. 82, 84.
[2] *Perfetta poesia*, bk. ii. ch. 1 (*ed. cit.* i. p. 299).
[3] A. Pope, *An Essay on Criticism*, 1709 (in *Poetical Works*, London, 1827), lines 81, 82.
[4] *Kritik der Urtheilskraft* (ed. Kirchmann), § 33.
[5] *Essai sur le goût* (in appendix to A. Gerard, *Essai sur le goût*, Paris, 1766).
[6] Quoted in Sulzer, *Allg. Th. d. s. K.* ii. p. 377.   [7] *Ibid.*

another writer quoted by Bonhours, "taste" is "a
natural feeling implanted in the soul, independent of
any science that can possibly be acquired"; it is practically "an instinct of right reason."[1] The same Bouhours,
whilst deprecating this interpretation of one metaphor
by another, says, "Taste is more nearly allied to judgement than wit."[2] The Italian Ettori thinks that it
may generally be described as "judgement regulated
by art,"[3] and Baruffaldi (1710) identifies it with "dis-
cernment" reduced from theory to practice.[4] De Crousaz
(1715) observes: "*Le bon goût nous fait d'abord estimer
par sentiment ce que la raison aurait approuvé, après qu'elle
se serait donné le temps de l'examiner assez pour en juger
par des justes idées.*"[5] And somewhat prior to him
Trevisano considered it "a sentiment always willing to
conform to whatsoever reason accepts," and in conjunction with divine grace, a powerful help to man in revealing the true and good, no longer able to circulate freely
among mankind owing to original sin. For König (1727)
in Germany taste was "a power of the intellect, product
of a healthy mind and acute judgement which makes one
able to feel the true, good and beautiful"; and for
Bodmer in 1736 (after lengthy correspondence on the
subject with his Italian friend Calepio) "a practised reflexion, prompt and penetrating into the smallest details,
by which intellect is able to distinguish the true from
the false, the perfect from the imperfect." Calepio and
Bodmer were opponents of pure feeling, and made a
distinction between "taste" and "good taste."[6] Travers-
ing the same intellectualistic path, Muratori speaks of
"good taste" in "erudition" and others of "good taste
in philosophy."

[1] *Manière de bien penser* (Ital. trans. *cit.*), dial. 4.　　[2] *Ibid.*
[3] *Op. cit.* chs. 2-4.
[4] *Osservazioni critiche* (in vol. ii. of Orsi's *Considerazioni*), ch. 8, p. 23.
[5] *Traité du beau* (Amsterdam ed., 1724), i. p. 170.
[6] J. Ulr. König, *Untersuchung von dem guten Geschmack in der
Dicht- und Redekunst*, Leipzig, 1727, and (Calepio-Bodmer) *Briefwechsel
von der Natur des poetischen Geschmackes*, Zürich, 1736; cf. for both
Sulzer, ii. p. 380.

Perhaps those authors were wise who preferred to remain vague and to identify taste with an indefinable Something, a *je ne sais quoi* ; a *nescio quid* : a new expression which expressed nothing new, but at least called attention to the problem. Bouhours (1671) discusses it at length : " *Les Italiens, qui font mystère de tout, emploient en toutes rencontres leur* non so che : *on ne voit rien de plus commune dans leurs poètes,*" and quotes Tasso and others in confirmation.[1] A note upon it is found in Salvini : " This ' good taste ' has but recently come to the front ; it seems a vague term applicable to nothing particular, and is equivalent to the *non so che*, to a happy or successful turn of wit." [2] Father Feijoó, who wrote on the *Razón del gusto* and on *El no se qué* (1733), says very wisely : " *En muchas producciones no solo de la naturaleza, sino del arte, y aun mas del arte que de la naturaleza, encuentran los hombres, fuera di aquellas perfecciones sujetes á su comprehension racional, otro genero de primor misterioso que, lisonjeando el gusto, atormenta el entendemento. Los sentidos le palpan, pero no le puede dissipar la razon, y así, al querer explicarle, no se encuentran voces ni conceptos que cuadren á su idéa, y salimos del paso con decir que hay un non se qué, que agrada, que enamora, que hechiza, sin que pueda encontrarse revelacion mas clara da este natural misterio.*" [3] And President Montesquieu : " *Il y a quelquefois dans les personnes ou dans les choses un charme invisible, une grâce naturelle, qu'on n'a pu définir, et qu'on a été forcé d'appeler le je ne sais quoi. Il me semble que c'est un effet principalement fondé sur la surprise.*" [4] Some writers rebelled against the subterfuge of the *je ne sais quoi*, saying, rightly enough, that it was a confession of ignorance : but they knew not how to escape that ignorance without falling into confusion between taste and intellectual judgement.

[1] *Les Entretiens d'Ariste et d'Eugène*, 1671 (Paris ed., 1734), conversation v. ; " *Le je ne sçai quoi* " ; cf. Gracian, *Oraculo manual*, No. 127, and *El héroe*, ch. 13.

[2] In the notes to Muratori's *Perfetta poesia*.

[3] Feijoó, *Theatro critico*, vol. vi. Nos. 11-12.

[4] *Essai sur le goût dans les choses de la nature et de l'art.* Posthumous fragment (in appendix to A. Gerard, *op. cit.*).

If the attempt to define " wit " and " taste " usually
resulted in intellectualism, it was easy to transform
imagination and feeling into sensationalistic doctrines.
We have seen how earnestly Pallavicino insisted on the
non-intellectuality of the fantasies and inventions of the
imagination. " Nothing presents itself to the admirer of
the beautiful (he writes) to enable him to verify his
cognition and satisfy himself that the object recognized
is or is not that for which he takes it ; if either by vision
or by strong apprehension he is led to think it actually
present by an act of judgement, his taste for beauty as
beauty does not arise from such act of judgement, but
from the vision or lively apprehension which might remain
in ourselves even when the deception of belief was corrected " ; just as happens when we are drowsy and know
ourselves to be but half awake, yet are unwilling to tear
ourselves from sweet dreams. For Pallavicino imagination cannot err ; he assimilates it wholly to the sensations,
which are incapable of truth or falsity. And if imaginative
knowledge pleases, it is not because it holds a special
truth (imaginative truth), but because it creates objects
which " though false are pleasing " : the painter makes
not likenesses but images which, all resemblance apart,
are pleasing to the sight : the poet awakens apprehensions
" sumptuous, novel, marvellous, splendid." [1] His opinion
coincides, if we mistake not, with Marino's sensationalism :
" The poet should aim only at the marvellous . . . he
who cannot amaze his hearers is not worth a straw " : [2]
he applauds the oft-repeated dictum of " Gabriel Chia-
brera, that Pindar of Savona, that poetry should cause
the eyebrows to arch themselves." [3] But in the *Treatise
upon Style* written later (1646) he repents of his youthful achievement and appears willing to return to the
pedagogic theory : " And forasmuch as I theorized concerning poetry in the basest manner, treating it solely
as a minister of that delight which the mind enjoys
in the less noble operation of imagination or apprehension

Imagination and sensationalism. The corrective of Imagination.

---

[1] *Del bene, cap. cit.*

[2] Marino, in one of the sonnets in the *Murtoleide* (1608).

[3] *Del bene*, bk. i. part i. ch. 8.

arising from imagination ; and, therefore, in consequence I somewhat relaxed the strings which bind it to the probable : I now wish to demonstrate that poetry has other functions more exalted and fruitful, while remaining in strict servitude to the probable : which office is to guide our minds in the noble exercise of judgement ; thus it becomes the nurse of philosophy which it nourishes with sweet milk." [1] The Jesuit Ettori, while inculcating the use of imagination and recommending orators to go to school with the " actors," points out that imagination should fulfil the simple office of " interpreter " between intellect and truth, never assuming dominion, otherwise the orator would be treating his audience or readers " not as men, to whom intellect is proper, but as beasts whom imagination satisfies." [2]

The conception of imagination as purely sensuous shows strongly in Muratori, who is so convinced that the faculty, if left to itself, would deteriorate into a riot of dreams and intoxication, that he links it to intellect as to " an authoritative friend " who shall influence the choice and combination of images. [3] The problem of the nature of imagination had strong attraction for Muratori, and, while traducing and vilifying, he returns to it again in his *Della forza della fantasia umana* ; [4] describing it as a material faculty essentially different from the mental or spiritual, and denying it the validity of knowledge. Although he had observed that the aim of poetry is distinct from that of science, in that the latter seeks to " know," and the former to " represent " truth, [5] he persisted in counting Poetry as an " art of delectation " subordinate to Moral Philosophy, of whom she was one of the three servants or ministers. [6] Very similarly Gravina held that along with novelty and delight in the marvellous, poetry should endow the mind of the vulgar with " truth and universal cognitions." [7]

---

[1] *Trattato dello stile* (Rome, 1666), ch. 30.
[2] *Il buon gusto*, pp. 12-13.   [3] *Perf. poesia*, i. ch. 18, pp. 232-233.
[4] Venice, 1745.   [5] *Perf. poesia*, i. ch. 6.
[6] *Op. cit.* i. ch. 4, p. 42.   [7] *Ragion poetica*, i. ch. 7.

Outside Italy the same movement was going on. Bacon, although he assigned poetry to imagination, yet considered it as something intermediary between history and science, approximating epic to history and the most lofty style, the parabolic, to science : (" *poësis parabolica inter reliquas eminet* "). Elsewhere he calls poetry *somnium* or declares absolutely that " *scientias fere non parit*," and that " *pro lusu potius ingenii quam pro scientia est habenda* " : music, painting and sculpture are voluptuous arts.[1] Addison identified the pleasures of the imagination with those produced by visible objects or the ideas to which they give rise : such pleasures are not so strong as those of the senses nor so refined as those of the intellect : he groups together the pleasures experienced respectively in comparing imitations with the objects imitated, and in sharpening by this means the faculty of observation.[2]

The sensationalism of Du Bos and other upholders of feeling appears very clearly. For Du Bos art is a pastime whose pleasantness consists in the fact that it occupies the mind without fatigue, and has affinities with the pleasure provoked by gladiatorial contests, bull-fights and tourneys.[3]

Feeling and Sensationalism.

For these reasons, whilst noting the importance, in the prehistory of Æsthetic, of these new words and the new views they express ; and while recognizing their value as a ferment in the discussion of the æsthetic problem, taken up by thinkers of the Renaissance at the point at which it had been left by the ancients ; we yet cannot discern in their apparition the true origin of our science. By these words and the discussions they aroused, the æsthetic fact clamoured even louder and more insistently for its own philosophical justification ; but this it was not yet to attain either by this means or by any other.

[1] *De dignitate*, ii. ch. 13 ; iii. ch. 1 ; iv. ch. 2 ; v. ch. 1.
[2] *Spectator, loc. cit.* esp. pp. 487, 503.
[3] *Op. cit.* § 2.

ÆSTHETIC IDEAS IN THE CARTESIAN AND LEIBNITIAN SCHOOLS, AND THE "ÆS-THETIC" OF BAUMGARTEN

Cartesianism and Imagination.

THE obscure world of wit, taste, imagination, feeling and the *je ne sais quoi* was not selected for examination or even, so to speak, included in the picture of Cartesian philosophy. The French philosopher abhorred imagination, the outcome, àccording to him, of the agitation of the animal spirits : and though not utterly condemning poetry, he allowed it to exist only in so far as it was guided by intellect, that being the sole faculty able to save men from the caprices of the *folle du logis.* He tolerated it, but that was all ; and went so far as not to deny it anything " *qu'un philosophe lui puisse permettre sans offenser sa conscience.*" [1] It has been observed that the æsthetic parallel with Cartesian intellectualism is to be found in Boileau,[2] slave to rigid *raison* (" *Mais nous que la raison à ses règles engage . . .*") and enthusiastic partisan of allegory. We have already had occasion to draw attention to the diatribe of Male-branche against imagination. The mathematical spirit fostered in France by Descartes forbade all possibility of a serious consideration of poetry and art. The Italian Antonio Conti, living in that country and witness of the literary disputes raging around him, thus describes the French critics (La Motte, Fontenelle and their followers) : " *Ils ont introduit dans les belles lettres l'esprit et la méthode*

---

[1] Letters to Balzac and the Princess Elizabeth.
[2] *Art poétique* (1669–1674).

*de M. Descartes ; et ils jugent de la poésie et de l'éloquence
indépendamment des qualités sensibles. De là vient aussi
qu'ils confondent le progrès de la philosophie avec celui
des arts. Les modernes, dit l'Abbé Terrasson, sont plus
grands géomètres que les anciens : donc ils sont plus
grands orateurs et plus grands poètes."* [1] The fight against
this mathematical spirit in the matters of art and feeling was still going on in France in the day of the encyclopædists ; the din of the battle was heard in Italy, as is
shown by the writings of Bettinelli and others. At the
time when Du Bos published his daring book there was
a counsellor in the parliament of Bordeaux, Jean-Jacques
Bel by name, who composed a dissertation (1726) against
the doctrine that feeling should be the judge of art.[2]

Cartesianism was incapable of an Æsthetic of imagination. The *Traité du beau* by the eclectic Cartesian
J. P. de Crousaz (1715), maintained the dependence of
beauty not upon pleasure or feeling, matters about
which there can be no difference of opinion, but upon that
which can be *approved* and therefore reduced to ideas.
He enumerates five such ideas : variety, unity, regularity,
order and proportion, observing, " *La variété tempérée
par l'unité, la régularité, l'ordre et la proportion, ne sont
pas assurément des chimères ; elles ne sont pas du ressort
de la fantaisie, ce n'est pas le caprice qui en décide* " : for
him, that is to say, they were real qualities of the beautiful
founded in nature and truth. He discovered similar
characteristics of the beautiful in the individual beauties
of the sciences (geometry, algebra, astronomy, physics,
history), of virtue, eloquence and religion, finding in
each the qualities laid down above.[3] Another Cartesian,
the Jesuit André (1742),[4] distinguished between an
essential beauty, independent of every institution, human
and even divine ; a *natural* beauty, independent of the
opinions of mankind ; and, lastly, a beauty to a certain
extent *arbitrary* and of human invention : the first

Crousaz and André.

[1] Letters to Marquis Maffei, about 1720, in *Prose e poesie*, Venice,
1756, ii. p. cxx. [2] Sulzer, *op. cit.* i. p. 50.
[3] *Traité du beau* (2nd ed., Amsterdam, 1724 ; Paris ed., 1810).
[4] *Essai sur le beau*, Paris, 1741.

composed of regularity, order, proportion and symmetry (here André relied upon Plato and also as an afterthought brought in St. Augustine's definition) : the second having its principal measure in the light which generates colours (as a good Cartesian, he took full advantage of Newton's discoveries) : the third belonging to fashion and convention, but never at liberty to violate essential beauty. Each of these three forms of beauty was subdivided into *sensible* beauty pertaining to bodies, and *intelligible* beauty of soul.

The English :
Locke,
Shaftesbury,
Hutcheson
and the
Scottish School.

Like Descartes in France, Locke in England (1690) is an intellectualist, and recognizes no form of spiritual elaboration save reflexion on the senses. None the less he takes over from contemporary literature the distinction between wit and judgement ; according to him the former combines ideas with pleasing variety, discovering their similarities and relations and thus grouping them into beautiful pictures which divert and strike the imagination : the latter (judgement or intellect) seeks dissimilarities, guided by the criterion of truth. " The mind, without looking any further, rests satisfied with the agreeableness of the picture, and the gaiety of the fancy ; and it is a kind of an affront to go about to examine it by the severe rules of truth and good reason ; whereby it appears that it consists in something that is not perfectly conformable to them." [1] England produced philosophers who developed an abstract and transcendent Æsthetic, but one more tinged with sensationalism than that of the French Cartesians. Shaftesbury (1709) raises taste to a sense or instinct for the beautiful ; a sense of order and proportion identical with moral sense and, with its preconceptions or presentations, anticipating the recognition of reason. Bodies, spirits, God are the three degrees of beauty.[2] Lineal descendant of Shaftesbury was Francis Hutcheson (1723), who succeeded in popularizing the idea of an inward sense of beauty as something

[1] *An Essay concerning Human Understanding* (French trans. in *Œuvres*, Paris, 1854), bk. ii. ch. 11, § 2.
[2] *Characteristics of Men, Manners, Opinions, Times*, 1709–1711.

intermediate between sense and reason, and adapted to distinguish unity in variety, concord in the manifold, the true, the beautiful and the good in their substantial identity. Hutcheson maintains that from this sense springs the pleasure we take in art, in imitation and in the likeness between copy and original : the last a relative, as distinct from an absolute, beauty.[1] This view on the whole predominated in England during the eighteenth century and was adopted by Adam Smith as well as by Reid, head of the Scottish school.

Much more thoroughly and with much greater philosophical vigour Leibniz opened the door to that crowd of psychic facts from which Cartesianism recoiled in horror. In his conception of the real, governed by the law of continuity (*natura non facit saltus*), presenting an uninterrupted scale of existence from the lowest beings to God, imagination, taste, wit and the like found ample room for shelter. The facts now called æsthetic were identified by Leibniz with Descartes' *confused* cognition, which might be *clear* without being *distinct* : scholastic terms borrowed, it would appear, from Duns Scotus, whose works were reprinted and widely read in the seventeenth century.[2]

Leibniz. Petites perceptions and confused knowledge.

In his *De cognitione, veritate et ideis* (1684), after dividing *cognitio* into *obscura vel clara*, the *clara* into *confusa vel distincta*, and the *distincta* into *adaequata vel inadaequata*, Leibniz remarks that while painters and other artists are able to judge works of art very fairly they can give no reason for their decisions, and if questioned as to the reason of their condemnation of any work of art, they reply it lacks a *je ne sais quoi* : (" *at iudicii sui rationem reddere saepe non posse, et quaerenti dicere, se in re, quae displicet, desiderare nescio quid* ").[3] They do possess, in fact, clear cognition, but confused and not distinct ; what we should call to-day imaginative, not *ratiocinative*, consciousness : and indeed the latter does not exist in the case of art. There are things impossible to define :

---

[1] *Enquiry into the Original of our Ideas of Beauty and Virtue*, London, 1723.
[2] See above, p. 179.   [3] *Opera philosophica* (ed. Erdmann), p. 78.

*on ne les fait connaître que par des exemples, et, au reste,
il faut dire que c'est un je ne sais quoi, jusqu'à ce qu'on
en déchiffre la contexture.*"[1]   But these *perceptions confuses
ou sentiments* have "*plus grande efficacité que l'on ne pense :
ce sont elles qui forment ce je ne sais quoi, ces goûts, ces
images des qualités des sens.*"[2]   Whence it appears
plainly that in his discussion of these perceptions Leibniz
reposes upon the æsthetic theories we discussed in the
preceding chapter ; indeed at one point[3] he mentions
Bouhours' book.

*Intellectual-
ism of Leibniz.*   It might seem that by according *claritas* and denying
distinctio to æsthetic facts Leibniz recognized that their
peculiar character is neither sensuous nor intellectual.
He might seem to have distinguished them by their
"*claritas*" from pleasure or sense-motions, and from
intellect by their lack of "*distinctio*." But the "*lex
continui*" and the Leibnitian intellectualism forbid this
interpretation.   In this case obscurity and clarity are
quantitative degrees of one single consciousness, distinct
or intellectual, towards which both converge and with
which in the extreme case they unite.

To admit that artists judge with confused perceptions,
clear but not distinct, does not involve denying that these
perceptions may be capable of being connected and
verified by intellectual consciousness.   The self-same
object that is confusedly though clearly recognized by
imagination is recognized clearly and distinctly by the
intellect ; which amounts to saying that a work of art
may be perfected by being determined by thought.   In
the very terminology adopted by Leibniz, who represents
sense and imagination as obscure and confused, there is
a tinge of contempt, as well as the suggestion of a single
form of all cognition.   This will help us to understand
Leibniz' definition of music as "*exercitium arithmeticae
occultum nescientis se numerare animi.*"   Elsewhere he
says : "*Le but principal de l'histoire, aussi bien que de la
poésie, doit être d'enseigner la prudence et la vertu par des*

---

[1] *Nouveaux Essais*, ii. ch. 22.   [2] *Ibid.* preface.
[3] *Op. cit.* ii. ch. 11.

exemples, et puis de montrer le vice d'une manière qui en donne l'aversion et qui porte ou serve à l'éviter." [1]

The " *claritas* " attributed to æsthetic fact is not specifically different from, but rather a partial anticipation of, the "*distinctio*" of intellect. Undoubtedly this distinction of degree marks a great advance : but careful analysis shows that Leibniz does not differ fundamentally from those who, by inventing the new words and empirical distinctions examined above, called attention to the peculiarities of æsthetic facts.

We find the same invincible intellectualism in the speculations on language greatly in vogue at the time. *Speculation on language.* When critics of the Renaissance and sixteenth century tried to rise above merely empirical and practical grammar and strove to reduce grammatical science to a systematic form, they fell into logicism and described grammatical forms by such terms as pleonastic, improper, metaphorical or elliptic. Thus Julius Caesar Scaliger (1540); thus, too, the most learned of all, Francisco Sanchez (Sanctius or Sanzio), called Brocense, who, in his *Minerva* (1587), asserts that names are attached to things by reason, exclusive of interjections which are not parts of speech but merely sounds expressive of joy or sorrow ; he denies the existence of heterogeneous and heteroclitic words, and works out a system of syntax by means of four figures of construction, proclaiming the principle " *doctrinam supplendi esse valde necessarium,*" that is to say, that grammatical diversities must be explained as ellipsis, abbreviation or omission with reference to the typical logical form. [2] Gaspare Scioppio follows him exactly, abusing the old grammar with his accustomed violence and crying up the " Sanctian " method, at that time still almost unknown, in his *Grammatica philosophica* (1628). [3] Amongst critics of the seventeenth century, Jacopo Perizonio

---

[1] *Essais de Théodicée*, part. ii. § 148.

[2] Francisci Sanctii, *Minerva seu de causis linguae latinae commentarius*, 1587 (ed. with add. by Gaspare Scioppio, Padua, 1663) ; cf. bk. i. chs. 2, 9, and bk. iv.

[3] Gasperis Sciopii, *Grammatica philosophica*, Milan, 1628 (Venice, 1728)

must not be forgotten ; he wrote a commentary on
Sanchez' book (1687). Amongst recognized philosophers
who studied the philosophy of grammar and noted the
merits and defects of various tongues, we find Bacon.[1]
In 1660 Claude Lancelot and Arnauld brought out the
Grammaire générale et raisonnée de Port-Royal, a work
applying the intellectualism of Descartes rigorously to
grammatical forms, and dominated by the doctrine of
the artificial nature of language. Locke and Leibniz
both speculated about language,[2] but neither succeeded
in creating a fresh point of view, although the latter did
much to provoke inquiry into the historical origin of
languages. All his life Leibniz cherished the notion of
a universal language and of an " *ars characteristica universalis* " as a combination likely to result in great
scientific discoveries : prior to him, Wilkins had fostered
the same hope, nor indeed, in spite of its utter absurdity,
is it even yet wholly extinct.

J. C. Wolff.   In order to correct the æsthetic ideas of Leibniz it
was necessary to alter the very foundations of his system,
the Cartesianism upon which it rested. This could not
be undertaken by disciples of his own personal school,
in whom we notice rather an increase of intellectualism.
Giving scholastic form to the brilliant observations of the
master, Johann Christian Wolff's system began with the
theory of knowledge conceived as an " organon " or
instrument, followed by systems of natural law, ethics
and politics, together constituting the " organon " of
practical activity : the remainder was theology and
metaphysics, or pneumatology and physics (doctrine of
the soul and doctrine of phenomenal nature). Although
Wolff distinguishes a productive imagination, ruled by
the principle of sufficient reason, from the merely associative and chaotic,[3] yet a science of imagination considered as a new theoretical value could find no niche
in his schematism. Knowledge of a lower order, as such,

---

[1] *De dignitate*, etc., bk. vi. ch. 1.
[2] Locke, *Essay*, etc., bk. iii. ; Leibniz, *Nouveaux Essais*, bk. iii.
[3] *Psychol. empirica* (Frankfurt and Leipzig, 1738), §§ 138-172.

belonged to Pneumatology and was incapable of possessing its own "organon": at most it could be brought under the organon already existing, which corrected and transcended it by means of logical knowledge in the same way in which Ethics treats the "*facultas appetitiva inferior.*" As in France the poetics of Boileau corresponded with the philosophy of Descartes, so in Germany the rationalistic poetics of Gottsched [1] reflect the Cartesian-Leibnitian theories of Wolff (1729).

It was no doubt dimly seen that even in the inferior faculties some distinction was operative between perfect and imperfect, value and non-value. A passage in a book (1725) by the Leibnitian Bülffinger has often been quoted where he says: "*Vellem existerent qui circa facultatem sentiendi, imaginandi, attendendi, abstrahendi et memoriam praestarent quod bonus ille Aristoteles, adeo hodie omnibus sordens, praestitit circa intellectum : hoc est ut in artis formam redigerent quicquid ad illas in suo usu dirigendas et iuvandas pertinet et conducit, quem ad modum Aristoteles in Organo logicam sive facultatem demonstrandi redegit in ordinem.*" [2] But on reading the extract in its context one recognizes at once that the desired organon would have been merely a series of recipes for strengthening the memory, educating the attention, and so forth : a technique, in a word, not an æsthetic. Similar ideas had been spread in Italy by Trevisano (1708), who, by declaring that the senses might be educated through the mind, asserted the possibility of an *art of feeling* which should "endow manners with prudence and judgement with good taste." [3] We notice, moreover, that in his day Bülffinger was counted a depreciator of poetry, so much so that a tract against him was written in order to show that "poetry does not diminish the faculty of clear conception." [4] Bodmer and Breitinger were ready "to

Demand for an organon of inferior knowledge.

---

[1] Joh. Chr. Gottsched, *Versuch einer critischen Dichtkunst*, Leipzig, 1729.

[2] *Dilucidationes philosophicae de Deo, anima humana et mundo*, 1725 (Tübingen, 1768), § 268.

[3] Preface to *Rifless. sul gusto, ed. cit.* p. 75.

[4] Borinski, *Poetik d. Renaiss.* p. 380 note.

deduce all the parts of eloquence with mathematical precision " (1727), and the latter sketched a Logic of the Imagination (1740) to which he would have assigned the study of similitudes and metaphors ; even had he carried out his project, it is difficult to see how it could have differed materially, from a philosophic point of view, from the treatises on the subject written by the Italian rhetoricians of the seventeenth century.

Alexander Baumgarten : his " Æsthetic."

These discussions and experiments filled the boyhood and helped to form the intellect of young Alexander Gottlieb Baumgarten of Berlin, a follower of the philosophy of Wolff and, at the same time, student and teacher of Latin rhetoric and poetry ; these studies led him to reconsider the problem and search for some method by which the precepts of rhetoricians could be reduced to a rigorous philosophical system. On taking his doctor's degree in September 1735, when twenty-one years old, he published a thesis *Meditationes philosophicae de nonnullis ad poëma pertinentibus* :[1] in which the word " Æsthetic " appears for the first time as name of a special science.[2] Baumgarten always remained much attached to his youthful discovery, and in 1742 when called to teach at the university of Frankfort-on-the-Oder, and again in 1749, he gave by request a course of lectures on Æsthetic (*quaedam consilia dirigendarum facultatum inferiorum novam per acroasin exposuit*).[3] In 1750 he printed a voluminous treatise wherein the word " Æsthetic " attained the honours of a title-page ;[4] in 1758 he published a more slender second part : illness and finally death in 1762 prevented him from completing the work.

Æsthetic as science of sensory consciousness.

What was Æsthetic to Baumgarten ? Its objects are sensible facts (αἰσθητά), carefully distinguished by the ancients from mental objects (νοητά) ;[5] hence it becomes *scientia cognitionis sensitivae, theoria liberalium artium,*

---

[1] Halae Magdeburgicae, 1735 (reprinted, ed. B. Croce, Naples, 1900).

[2] *Med.* § 116.   [3] *Aesthetica*, i. pref.

[4] *Aesthetica. Scripsit* Alex. Gottlieb Baumgarten, *Prof. Philosoph., Traiecti cis Viadrum, Impens. Ioannis Christiani Kleyb,* 1750 ; 2nd part, 1758.   [5] *Med.* § 116.

gnoseologia inferior, ars pulcre cogitandi, ars analogi rationis.[1] Rhetoric and Poetry constitute two special and interdependent disciplines which are entrusted by Æsthetic with the distinction between the various styles in literature and other small differences,[2] for the laws she herself investigates are diffused throughout all the arts like guiding-stars for these various subsidiary arts (*quasi cynosura quaedam specialium*)[3] and must be extracted not from isolated cases only, or from incomplete induction empirically, but from the totality of facts (*falsa regula peior est quam nulla*).[4] Nor must Æsthetic be confounded with Psychology, which furnishes its presuppositions only; an independent science, it gives the norm of sensitive cognition (*sensitive quid cognoscendi*) and deals with "*perfectio cognitionis sensitivae, qua talis,*" which is beauty (*pulcritudo*), just as the opposite, imperfection, is ugliness (*deformitas*).[5] From the beauty of sensitive cognition (*pulcritudo cognitionis*) we must exclude the beauty of objects and matter (*pulcritudo obiectorum et materiae*) with which it is often confused owing to habits of language, since it is easy to show that ugly things may be thought of in a beautiful manner and beautiful things in an ugly manner (*quacum ob receptam rei significationem saepe sed male confunditur; possunt turpia pulcre cogitare ut talia, et pulcriora turpiter*).[6] Poetical representations are confused or imaginative: distinctness, that is intellect, is not poetical. The greater the determination, the greater the poetry; individuals "*omnimode determinata*" are highly poetical; poetical also are images or phantasms as well as all that appertains to the senses.[7] That which judges sensible or imaginary presentations is taste, or "*iudicium sensuum.*" These, in brief, are the truths displayed by Baumgarten in his *Meditationes* and, with many distinctions and examples, in his *Æsthetic*.[8]

Nearly all German critics[9] are of opinion that from

[1] *Aesth.* § 1.   [2] *Med.* § 117.   [3] *Aesth.* § 71.   [4] *Ibid.* § 53.
[5] *Med.* § 115.   [6] *Aesth.* § 14.   [7] *Ibid.* § 18.   [8] *Med.* § 92.
[9] Ritter, *Gesch. d. Philos.* (Fr. trans., *Hist. de la phil. mod.* iii. p. 365); Zimmermann, *Gesch. d. Aesth.* p. 168; J. Schmidt, *L. u. B.* p. 48.

his own conception of Æsthetic as the science of sensitive cognition Baumgarten should have evolved a species of inductive Logic.   But he can be cleared of this accusation : a better philosopher, perhaps, than his critics, he held that an inductive Logic must always be intellectual, since it leads to abstractions and the formation of concepts.   The relation existing between " *cognitio confusa* " and the poetical and artistic facts which belong to the realm of taste had been shown before his day, by Leibniz : neither he nor Wolff nor any other oi their school ever dreamed of transforming a treatment of the " *cognitio confusa*" or "*petites perceptions*" into an inductive Logic. On the other hand, as a kind of compensation, these critics attribute to Baumgarten a merit he cannot claim, at least to the extent implied by their praises.   According to them, he effected a revolution by converting [1] Leibniz' differences of degree or quantitative distinctions into a specific difference, and turning confused knowledge into something no longer negative but positive [2] by attributing a " *perfectio* " to sensitive cognition *qua talis* ; and by thus destroying the unity of the Leibnitian monad and breaking up the law of continuity, founded the science of Æsthetic.   Had he really accomplished such a giant stride, his claim to the title of " father of Æsthetic " would have been placed beyond question.   But, in order to win this appellation, Baumgarten ought to have been successful in unravelling all those contradictions in which he was involved no less than Leibniz and all intellectualists. It is not enough to posit a " *perfectio* " ; even Leibniz did that when he attributed *claritas* to confused cognition, which, when devoid of clearness, remains obscure, that is to say, imperfect.   It was imperative that this perfection " *qua talis* " should be upheld against the " *lex continui*," and kept uncontaminated by any intellectualistic admixture.   Otherwise he was bound to fall back into the pathless labyrinth of the " probable " which is and is not false, of the wit which is and is not intellect, of the taste

[1] Danzel, *Gottsched*, p. 218 ; Meyer, *L. u. B.* pp. 35-38.
[2] Schmidt, *op. cit.* p. 44.

which is and is not intellectual judgement, of the imagination and feeling which are and are not sensibility and
material pleasure. And in that case, notwithstanding
the new name : notwithstanding (as we freely admit)
the greater insistence than that of Leibniz upon the
sensible nature of poetry, Æsthetic, as a science, would
not have been born.

Now Baumgarten overcame none of the obstacles above *Intellectualism*
mentioned. Unprejudiced and continued study of his *of*
Baumgarten.
works forces one to this conclusion. Already in his
Meditationes he does not seem able to distinguish clearly
between imagination and intellect, confused and distinct
cognition. The law of continuity leads him to set up a
scale of more and less : amongst cognitions, the obscure
are less poetical than the confused ; the distinct are not
poetical, but even those of the higher kinds (that is the
distinct and intellectual) are to a certain extent poetical
in proportion as they are lower in their nature ; compound concepts are more poetical than simple ; those
of larger comprehension are " *extensive clariores.*" [1] In the
Æsthetic Baumgarten expounds his thought more fully
and thereby exposes its defects. If the introduction of
the book leads one to believe that he sees æsthetic truth
to consist in consciousness of the individual, the belief is
shattered by the explanations which follow. As a good
objectivist he asserts that truth in the metaphysical
sense has its counterpart in the soul, namely, subjective
truth, logical truth in a wide sense, or æsthetico-logical.[2]
And the complete truth lies not in the genus or species,
but in the individual. The genus is true, the species
more true, the individual most true.[3] Formal logical
truth is acquired " *cum iactura,*" by jettisoning much
great material perfection : " *quid enim est abstractio, si
iactura non est ?* " [4] So much being granted, logical truth
differs from æsthetic in this : metaphysical or objective
truth is presented now to the intellect, when it is logical
truth in a narrow sense ; now to the analogy of reason

---

[1] *Med.* §§ 19, 20, 23.　　　　[2] *Aesth.* § 424.
[3] *Op. cit.* § 441.　　　　　　[4] *Op. cit.* § 560.

and the lower cognitive faculties, when it is æsthetic;[1]
a lesser truth in exchange for the greater which man is
not always able to attain, thanks to the " *malum meta-
physicum.*"[2] Thus moral truths are comprehended in
one fashion by a comic poet, in another by a moral philosopher; an eclipse is described in one way by an astronomer
and in another by a shepherd speaking to his friends or
his sweetheart.[3] Universals even are accessible, in part
at least, to the inferior faculty.[4] Take the case of two
philosophers, a dogmatic and a sceptic, arguing, with an
æsthete listening to them. If the arguments of either
party are so balanced that the hearer cannot determine
which is true and which false, this appearance is to him
æsthetic truth : if one adversary succeed in overbearing
the other so that one argument is shown clearly to be
wrong, the error just revealed is likewise æsthetic[5]
falsity. Truths strictly æsthetic are (and this is the
decisive point) those which appear neither entirely true
nor entirely false : probable truths. " *Talia autem de
quibus non complete quidem certi sumus, neque tamen
falsitatem aliquam in iisdem appercipimus, sunt veri-
similia. Est ergo veritas aesthetica, a potiori dicta veri-
similitudo, ille veritatis gradus, qui, etiamsi non evectus
sit ad completam certitudinem, tamen nihil contineat falsi-
tatis observabilis.*"[6] And especially the immediate sequel :
" *Cujus habent spectatores auditoresve intra animum quum
vident audiuntve, quasdam anticipationes, quod plerumque
fit, quod fieri solet, quod in opinione positum est, quod habet
ad haec in se quandam similitudinem, sive id falsum (logice
et latissime), sive verum sit (logice et strictissime), quod non
sit facile a nostris sensibus abhorrens : hoc illud est εἰκός
et verisimile quod, Aristotele et Cicerone assentiente, sectetur
aestheticus.*"[7] The probable embraces that which is true
and certain to the intellect and the senses, that which
is certain to the senses but not to the intellect, that
which is probable logically and æsthetically, or logically

[1] *Aesth.* § 424.   [2] *Op. cit.* § 557.
[3] *Op. cit.* §§ 425, 429.   [4] *Op. cit.* § 443.
[5] *Op. cit.* § 448.   [6] *Op. cit.* § 483.   [7] *Op. cit.* § 484.

improbable but æsthetically probable, or, finally, æsthetically improbable but on the whole probable or that whose improbability is not evident.[1] So we reach the admission of the impossible and absurd, the ἀδύνατον and ἄτοπον of Aristotle.

If after reading these paragraphs, highly important as revealing the true thought of Baumgarten, we turn once more to the Introduction to his work, we notice at once his commonplace and erroneous conception of the poetic faculty. To a friend who suggested that there was no need for him to concern himself with confused or inferior consciousness both because *"confusio mater erroris"* and because *" facultate inferiores, caro, debellandae potius sunt quam excitandae et confirmandae,"* Baumgarten replied that confusion is a condition wherein to find truth : that nature makes no sudden leap from obscurity to clarity : that noonday light is reached from night time through the dawn (*ex nocte per auroram meridies*) : that in the case of the inferior faculties a guide, not a tyrant, is needed (*imperium in facultates inferiores poscitur, non tyrannis*).[2] This is still the attitude of Leibniz, Trevisano and Bülffinger. Baumgarten is terrified lest he should be accused of treating subjects unworthy a philosopher. *" Quousque tandem "* (says he to himself), " dost thou, professor of theoretic and moral philosophy, dare to praise lies and mixtures of true and false as though they were noble works ? "[3] And if there is one thing above all others from which he is anxious to guard himself it is sensualism, unbridled and non-moralized. The sensitive perfection of Cartesianism and Wolffianism was liable to be confused with simple pleasure, with the feeling of the perfection of our organism :[4] but Baumgarten falls into no such confusion. When in 1745 one Quistorp combated his æsthetic theory by saying that if poetry consisted in sensuous perfection it was a thing hurtful to men, Baumgarten answered disdainfully that he did not expect he

---

[1] *Æsth.* §§ 485, 486.   [2] *Op. cit.* §§ 7, 12.   [3] *Op. cit.* § 478.
[4] Cf. Wolff, *Psych. empir.* § 511, and the passage there quoted from Descartes ; also §§ 542, 550.

should ever find time to reply to a critic of such calibre as to mistake his "*oratio perfecta sensitiva*" for an "*oratio perfecte* (that is *omnino*) *sensitiva.*"[1]

New names and old meanings.

Save in its title and its first definitions Baumgarten's *Æsthetic* is covered with the mould of antiquity and commonplace. We have seen that he refers back to Aristotle and Cicero for the first principles of his science ; in another instance he attaches his Æsthetic to the Rhetoric of antiquity, quoting the truth enunciated by Zeno the Stoic, "*esse duo cogitandi genera, alterum perpetuum et latius, quod Rhetorices sit, alterum concisum et contractius, quod Dialectices,*" and identifying the former with the æsthetic horizon, the latter with the logical.[2] In his *Meditationes* he rests upon Scaliger and Vossius ;[3] of modern writers beside the philosophers (Leibniz, Wolff, Bülffinger) he quotes Gottsched, Arnold,[4] Werenfels, Breitinger[5] ; by means of these latter he is able to make acquaintance with discussions upon taste and imagination, even without direct acquaintance with Addison and Du Bos, as well as the Italians, whose writings had immense vogue in Germany in his day, and with whom his resemblances leap to the eye. Baumgarten always feels himself to be in perfect accord with his predecessors ; never at variance with them. He never felt himself to be a revolutionary ; and though some have been revolutionaries without knowing it, Baumgarten was not one of them. Baumgarten's works are but another presentation of the problem of Æsthetic still clamouring for solution in a voice so much the stronger as it uttered a commonplace : he proclaims a new science and presents it in conventional scholastic form ; the babe about to be born receives the name of Æsthetic by premature baptism at his hands : and the name remains. But the new name is devoid of new

---

[1] Th. Joh. Quistorp, in *Neuen Bücher-Saal*, 1745, fasc. 5 ; *Erweis dass die Poesie schon für sie selbst ihre Liebhaber leichtlich unglücklich machen könne* ; and A. G. Baumgarten, *Metaphysica*, 2nd ed., 1748, preface ; cf. Danzel, *Gottsched*, pp. 215, 221.

[2] *Aesth.* § 122.   [3] *Med.* § 9.

[4] *Op. cit.* §§ 111, 113.   [5] *Aesth.* § 11.

matter ; the philosophical armour covers no muscular body.   Our good Baumgarten, full of ardour and conviction, and often curiously brisk and vivacious in his scholastic Latinism, is a most sympathetic and attractive figure in the history of Æsthetic : of the science in formation, that is to say, not of the science brought to completion : of Æsthetic *condenda* not *condita*.

V

GIAMBATTISTA VICO

Vico as inventor of æsthetic science. THE real revolutionary who by putting aside the concept of probability and conceiving imagination in a novel manner actually discovered the true nature of poetry and art and, so to speak, invented the science of Æsthetic, was the Italian Giambattista Vico.

Ten years prior to the publication in Germany of Baumgarten's first treatise, there had appeared in Naples (1725) the first *Scienza nuova*, which developed ideas on the nature of poetry outlined in a former work (1721), *De constantia iurisprudentis*, outcome of "twenty-five years' continuous and harsh meditation." [1] In 1730 Vico republished it with fresh developments which gave rise to two special books (*Della sapienza poetica* and *Della discoperta del vero Omero*) in the second *Scienza Nuova*. Nor did he ever tire of repeating his views and forcing them upon the attention of his hostile contemporaries at every opportunity, seizing such occasion even in prefaces and letters, poems on the occasion of weddings or funerals, and in such press notices as fell to his duty as public censor of literature.

And what were these ideas ? Neither more nor less, we may say, than the solution of the problem stated by Plato, attacked but not solved by Aristotle, and again vainly attacked during the Renaissance and afterwards : is poetry rational or irrational, spiritual or brutal ? and,

---

[1] *Scienza nuova prima*, bk. iii. ch. 5 (*Opere di G. B. Vico*, edited by G. Ferrari, 2nd ed., Milan, 1852–1854).

if spiritual, what is its special nature and what distinguishes it from history and science ?

As we know, Plato confined it within the baser part
of the soul, the animal spirits. Vico re-elevates it and
makes of it a period in the history of humanity : and
since history for him means an ideal history whose periods
consist not of contingent facts but of forms of the spirit,
he makes it a moment in the ideal history of the spirit,
a form of consciousness. Poetry precedes intellect, but
follows sense ; through confusing it with the latter,
Plato failed to grasp the position it should really occupy
and banished it from his Republic. " Men at first feel
without being aware ; next they become aware with a
perturbed and agitated soul ; finally they reflect with
an undisturbed mind. This Aphorism is the Principle of
poetical sentences which are formed by the sense of
passions and affections ; differing thereby from philosophical sentences which are formed by reflexion through
ratiocination ; whence the latter approach more nearly
to truth the more they rise towards the universal, while
the former have more of certainty the more they approach
the individual." [1] An imaginative phase of consciousness,
but one possessed of positive value.

The imaginative phase is altogether independent and *Poetry and*
autonomous with respect to the intellectual, which is not *Philosophy :*
only incapable of endowing it with any fresh perfection *imagination*
but can only destroy it. " The studies of Metaphysics *and intellect.*
and Poetry are in natural opposition one to the other ;
for the former purges the mind of childish prejudice and
the latter immerses and drowns it in the same : the former
offers resistance to the judgement of the senses, while the
latter makes this its chief rule : the former debilitates,
the latter strengthens, imagination : the former prides
itself in not turning spirit into body, the latter does its
utmost to give a body to spirit : hence the thoughts of
the former must necessarily be abstract, while the concepts of the latter show best when most clothed with
matter : to sum up, the former strives that the learned

[1] *Scienza nuova seconda, Elementi,* liii.

may know the truth of things stripped of all passion :
the latter that the vulgar may act truly by means of
intense excitement of the senses, without which stimulant
they assuredly would not act at all. Hence from all
time, in all languages known to man, never has there
been a strong man equally great as metaphysician and
poet : such a poet as Homer, father and prince of poetry."[1]
Poets are the senses, philosophers the intellect, of mankind.[2] Imagination is " stronger in proportion as reason
is weaker." [3]

No doubt " reflexion " may be put in verse ; but it
does not become poetry thereby. " Abstract sentences
belong to philosophers, since they contain universals ;
and reflexions concerning such passions are made by
poets who are false and frigid." [4] Those poets " who
sing of the beauty and virtue of ladies by reflexion
. . . are philosophers arguing in verses or in love-
rhymes." [5] One set of ideas belongs to philosophers,
another to poets : these latter are identical with those
of painters, from which " they differ only in colours and
words." [6] Great poets are born not in epochs of reflexion but in those of imagination, generally called
barbarous : Homer, in the barbarism of antiquity : Dante
in that of the Middle Ages, the " second barbarism of
Italy." [7] Those who have chosen to read philosophic
reason into the verse of the great father of Greek poetry
have transferred the character of a later age into an
earlier, since the era of poets precedes that of philosophers
and countries in infancy were sublime poets. Poetic
locutions arose before prose, " by the necessity of nature "
not " by caprice of pleasure " ; fables or imaginative
universals were conceived before reasoned, *i.e.* philosophical universals.[8]

[1] *Scienza nuova pr.* bk. iii. ch. 26.   [2] *Scienza nuova sec.* bk. ii. introd.
[3] *Op. cit. Elem.* xxxvi.   [4] *Op. cit.* bk. ii. ; *Sentenze eroiche.*
[5] Letter to De Angelis of December 25, 1725.
[6] Letter to De Angelis, *cit.*
[7] *Scienza nuova sec.* bk. iii. ; Letter to De Angelis, *cit.* ; *Giudizio su Dante.*
[8] *Scienza nuova sec.* bk. ii. ; *Logica poetica.*

With these observations Vico justified and at the same
time corrected the opinion of Plato in the *Republic*,
denying to Homer wisdom, every kind of wisdom ; the
legislative of Lycurgus and Solon, the philosophic of
Thales, Anacharsis and Pythagoras, the strategic of military commanders.[1]   To Homer (he says) belongs wisdom,
undoubtedly, but poetic wisdom only : the Homeric
images and comparisons derived from wild beasts and
the elements of savage nature are incomparable ; but
" such success does not spring from talent imbued with
domesticity and civilized with any philosophy." [2]

When anybody takes to writing poetry in an era of
reflexion, it is because he is returning to childhood and
" putting his mind in fetters " ; no longer reflecting with
his intellect, he follows imagination and loses himself in
the particular.   If a true poet dallies with philosophical
ideas, it is not " that he may assimilate them and dismiss
imagination," but merely " that he may have them in
front of him, to examine as though on a stage or public
platform." [3]   The New Comedy which made its appearance after Socrates is undeniably impregnated with
philosophic ideas, with intellectual universals, with " intelligible kinds of human conduct " ; but its authors were
poets in so far only as they knew how to transform logic
into imagination and their ideas into portraits.[4]

The dividing line between art and science, imagination *Poetry and*
and intellect, is here very strongly drawn : the two dis- *History.*
tinct activities are repeatedly contrasted with a sharpness
that leaves no room for confusion.   The line of demarca-
tion between poetry and history is hardly less firm.
While not quoting Aristotle's passage, Vico implicitly
shows why poetry seemed to Aristotle more philosophical
than history, and at the same time he dispels the erroneous
opinion that history concerns the particular and poetry
the universal.   Poetry joins hands with science not because it consists in the contemplation of concepts but
because, like science, it is ideal.   The most beautiful

[1] *Republica*, x.   [2] *Scienza nuova sec.* bk. iii. *ad init.*
[3] Letter to De Angelis, *cit.*   [4] *Scienza nuova sec.* bk. iii. *passim.*

poetic story must be "wholly ideal" : "by means of idea, the poet breathes reality into things otherwise unreal ; masters of poetry claim that their art must be wholly compact of imagination, like a painter of the ideal, not imitative like a portrait-painter : whence, from their likeness to God the Creator, poets and painters alike are called divine." [1] And against those who blame poets for telling stories which, they say, are untrue, Vico protests : " The best stories are those approximating most nearly to ideal truth, the eternal truth of God : it is immeasurably more certain than the truth of historians who often bring into play caprice, necessity or fortune ; but such a Captain as, for instance, Tasso's Godfrey is the type of a captain of all times, of all nations, and so are all personages of poetry, whatever difference there may be in sex, age, temperament, custom, nation, republic, grade, condition or fortune ; they are nothing save the eternal properties of the human soul, rationally discussed by politicians, economists and moral philosophers, and painted as portraits by the poet." [2] Referring to an observation made by Castelvetro, and approving it in part, to the effect that if poetry is a presentiment of the possible it should be preceded by history, imitation of the real, yet finding himself confronted by the difficulty that, nevertheless, poets invariably precede historians, Vico solves the problem by identifying history with poetry : primitive history was poetry, its plot was narration of fact, and Homer was the first historian ; or rather " he was a heroic character amongst Greek men, in so far as they poetically narrated their own history." [3] Poetry and history, therefore, are originally identical ; or rather, undifferentiated. " But inasmuch as it is not possible to give false ideas, since falsity arises from an embroiled combination of ideas, so is it impossible to give a tradition, however fabulous, that has not had, at the beginning, a basis of truth." [4] Hence we gain

---

[1] *Scienza nuova pr.* bk. iii. ch. 4.

[2] Letter to Solla, January 12, 1729 ; cf. *Scienza nuova sec. Elem.* xliii.

[3] *Scienza nuova sec.* bk. iii.   [4] *Scienza nuova pr.* bk. iii. ch. 6.

an entirely new insight into mythology : it is no longer an
arbitrary calculated invention, but a spontaneous vision
of truth as it presented itself to the spirit of primitive
man. Poetry gives an imaginative vision ; science or
philosophy intelligible truth ; history the consciousness
of certitude.

Language and poetry are, in Vico's estimation, sub- *Poetry and*
stantially the same. In refuting the " vulgar error of *language.*
grammarians " who maintain the priority of the birth
of prose over that of verse, he finds " within the origin
of Poetry, so far as it has been herein discovered," the
" origin of languages and the origin of letters." [1] This
discovery was made by Vico after " toil as disagreeable
and overwhelming as we should undergo had we to strip
off our own nature and enter into that of the primæval
men of Hobbes, Grotius, or Puffendorf ; creatures possessing no language at all, by whom were created the languages of the ancient world." [2] But his painful labour
was richly repaid by his refutation of the erroneous
theory that languages sprang from convention or, as he
said, " signified at will," whereas it is evident that " from
their natural origin words must have had natural meanings ; this is plainly seen in common Latin . . . wherein
almost all words have arisen by natural necessity, either
from natural properties or from their sensible effects ;
and in general, metaphor forms the bulk of language in
the case of every people." [3] This argument strikes a
blow at another common error of the grammarians, " that
the language of prose writers is correct, that of poets
incorrect." [4] The poetic tropes grouped under the heading of metonymy seem to Vico to be " born of the nature
of primitive peoples, not of capricious selection by men
skilled in poetic art " ; [5] stories told " by means of simili-

---

[1] *Scienza nuova sec.* bk. ii., *Corollari d' intorno all' origine della
locuzion poetica,* etc.

[2] *Scienza nuova pr.* bk. iii. ch. 22.

[3] *Scienza nuova sec.* bk. ii., *Corollari d' intorno all' origini delle
lingue,* etc.

[4] *Op. cit.* bk. ii., *Corollari d' intorno a' tropi,* etc., § 4.

[5] *Scienza nuova pr.* bk. iii. ch. 22.

tudes, imagery and comparisons," result " from lack of
the genera and species required to define things with
propriety," and " are therefore, by reason of natural
necessities, common to entire peoples." [1] The earliest
languages must have consisted of " dumb gestures and
objects which had natural connexions with the ideas
to be expressed." [2] He observes very acutely that to
these figurate languages belong not only hieroglyphics
but the emblems, knightly bearings, devices and blazons
which he calls " mediæval hieroglyphics." [3] In the
barbarous Middle Ages " Italy was forced to fall back on
the mute language . . . of the earliest gentile nations
in which men, before discovering articulate speech, were
obliged like mutes to use actions or objects having natural
connexions with the ideas, which at that time must have
been exceedingly sensuous, of the things which they
wished to signify ; such expressions, clad in almost vocal
words, must have had all the lively expressiveness of
poetic diction." [4] Hence arise three kinds or phases of
language : dumb show, the language of the gods ; heraldic
language, or that of the heroes ; and spoken language.
Vico also looked forward to a universal system of ety-
mology, a " dictionary of mental words common to all
nations."

Inductive and
formalistic
logic.
A man with ideas of this sort about imagination,
language and poetry could not say he was satisfied with
formalistic and verbal Logic, whether Aristotelian or
scholastic. The human mind (says Vico) " makes use
of intellect when from things which it feels by sense it
gathers something that does not fall under sense : this
is the true meaning of the Latin *intelligere*." [5] In a rapid
outline of the history of Logic, Vico wrote : " Aristotle
came and taught the syllogism, a method more suited
to expound universals in their particulars than to unite
particulars by the discovery of universals : then came
Zeno with his sorites, which corresponds with modern

---

[1] *Scienza nuova sec.* bk. iii., *Pruove filosofiche.*
[2] *Scienza nuova pr.* bk. iii. ch. 22.   [3] *Op. cit.* bk. iii. chs. 27-33.
[4] Letter to De Angelis, *cit.*   [5] *Scienza nuova sec.* bk. ii. introd.

philosophic methods and refines, without sharpening, the wits ; and no advantage whatever was reaped from either by mankind at large. With great reason, therefore, does Verulam, equally eminent as politician and philosopher, propound, commend and illustrate induction in his Organum : he is followed by the English with excellent results to experimental philosophy." [1] From this source is derived his criticism of mathematics, which have always, but especially in his day, been considered as the type of perfect science.

In all this, Vico is not only a thorough revolutionary, but is quite conscious of being so : he knows himself to be in opposition to all previous theories on the subject. *Vico opposed to all former theories of poetry.* He says that his new principles of poetry " are wholly opposed to, and not merely different from, all which have been imagined from the time of Plato and his disciple Aristotle to Patrizzi, Scaliger and Castelvetro among the moderns ; poetry is now discovered to have been the first language used by all nations alike, even the Hebrew." [2] In another passage he says that by his theories " is overthrown all that has ever been said of the origin of poetry, beginning from Plato and Aristotle, right down to our own Patrizzi, Scaliger and Castelvetro ; and it is found that poetry arising through defect of human ratiocination is as sublime as any which owes its being to the later rise of philosophy and the arts of composition and criticism ; indeed, that these later sources never gave rise to any poetry that could equal, far less surpass it." [3] In the Autobiography he boasts of having discovered " other principles of poetry than those found by Greeks and Latins and all others from those times down to the present day ; on these are founded other views on mythology." [4]

These ancient principles of poetry " laid down first by Plato and confirmed by Aristotle " had been the

[1] *Scienza nuova sec.* bk. ii., *Ultimi corollari,* § vi.
[2] *Scienza nuova pr.* bk. iii. ch. 2.
[3] *Scienza nuova sec.* bk. ii., *Della metafisica poetica,* etc.
[4] *Vita scritta da sè medesimo,* in *Opere, ed. cit.* iv. p. 365.

anticipation or prejudice which had misled all writers on
poetic reason (among whom he cites Jacopo Mazzoni).
Statements " even of most serious philosophers such as
Patrizzi and others " upon the origin of song and verse
are so inept that he " blushes even to mention them." [1]
It is curious to see him annotating the *Ars Poetica* of
Horace, with a view to finding some plausible sense in
it by applying the principles of the *Scienza nuova*.[2]

It is probable that he was familiar with the writings
of Muratori among contemporaries, for he quotes him
by name, and of Gravina, who was a personal acquaintance ; but if he read the *Perfetta Poesia* and the *Forza
della fantasia* he could not have been satisfied by the
treatment meted out to the faculty of imagination, so
highly valued and respected by himself ; and if Gravina
influenced him at all it must have been by provoking
him to contradiction. In this latter (if not directly in
such French writers as Le Bossu) he may have met with
the fallacy of regarding Homer as a repository of wisdom,
a fallacy which he combated with vigour and pertinacity.
In his estimation, among the gravest faults of the Cartesians
was their inability to appreciate the world of imagination
and poetry. Of his own times he complained they were
" benumbed by analytical methods and by a philosophy
which sought to deaden every faculty of soul which
reached it through the body, especially that of imagination, now held to be mother of all human error " : times
" of a wisdom which freezes the generous soul of the
best poetry," and prevents all understanding of it.[3]

Vico's judgements of the grammarians and linguists who preceded him.
It is just the same with the theory of language. " The
manner of birth and the nature of languages has been
the cause of much painful toil and meditation : nor,
from the *Cratylus* of Plato, in which in our other works
we have falsely delighted and believed " (he alludes to
the doctrine followed by him in his own first book, *De
antiquissima Italorum sapientia*), " down to Wolfgang

[1] *Scienza nuova pr.* bk. iii. ch. 37.
[2] *Note all' Arte poetica di Orazio*, in *Opere, ed. cit.* vi. pp. 52-79.
[3] Letter to De Angelis, *cit.*

Latius, Julius Caesar Scaliger, Francisco Sanchez and others, can we find anything to satisfy our understanding ; so much that in discussing matters of this kind Signor Giovanni Clerico says there is nothing in philology involved in such a maze of doubt and difficulty." [1] The chief grammarian-philosophers do not escape criticism. Grammar, says he, lays down rules for speaking correctly : Logic for speaking truly ; " and since in the order of nature we must speak truly before learning to speak correctly, Giulio Cesare della Scala, followed by the best grammarians, employs all his magnificent energy to reason to the causes of the Latin language from the principles of logic. But his great design ended in failure for this reason, that he attached himself to the logical principles of a single philosopher, namely Aristotle, whose principles are too universal to explain the almost infinite particulars which naturally beset him who would reason concerning a language. Whence it happened that Francisco Sanchez, who followed him with admirable zeal, attempting in his *Minerva* to explain the innumerable particles which are found in Latin by his famous principle of ellipsis, and trying thereby, though without success, to vindicate the logical principles of Aristotle, fell into the most cumbrous clumsinesses among an almost innumerable host of Latin phrases whereby he meant to make good the slight and subtle omissions employed by Latin in expressing its meaning." [2] The origin of parts of speech and syntax is wholly different from that assigned to them by folk who fancied that " the people who invented language must first have gone to school to Aristotle." [3] The same criticism undoubtedly must have extended to the logico-grammarians of Port-Royal, for Vico remarked that the Logic of Arnauld was built " on the same plan as that of Aristotle." [4]

---

[1] *Scienza nuova pr.* bk. iii. ch. 22 ; cf. the review of Clerico (Le Clerc) in *Opere,* iv. p. 382.

[2] *Giudizio intorno alla gram. d' Antonio d' Aronne,* in *Opere,* vi. pp. 149-150.

[3] *Scienza nuova sec.* bk. ii., *Corollari d' intorno all' origini delle lingue,* etc.   [4] *Vita, cit.* p. 343.

Influence of seventeenth-century writers on Vico.

It may well be granted that Vico was more in sympathy with the seventeenth-century rhetoricians, in whom we have detected a premonition of æsthetic science. For Vico, as for them, wit (referring to imagination and memory) was " the father of all invention " : judgement concerning poetry was for him a " judgement of the senses," a phrase equivalent to " taste " or " good taste," expressions never used by him in this connexion. There is no doubt he was familiar with the writers of treatises on wit and conceits, for, in a dry rhetorical manual written for the use of his school (in which one looks in vain for a shadow of his own personal ideas), he quotes Paolo Beni, Pellegrini, Pallavicino and the Marquis Orsi.[1] He highly esteems Pallavicini's treatise on *Style* and has knowledge of the book *Del bene* by the same author ; [2] perhaps too his mind was not unaffected by the flash of genius which had enabled the Jesuit for one instant to perceive that poetry consists of " first apprehensions." He does not name Tesauro, but there is no doubt he knew him ; indeed the *Scienza nuova* includes a section, besides that on poetry, upon " blazons," " knightly bearings," " military banners," " medals," and so forth, precisely similar in method to that of Tesauro when he treats of " figurate conceits " in his *Cannochiale aristote-lico*.[3] For Tesauro such conceits are merely metaphorical ingenuities, like any other ; for Vico they are wholly the work of imagination, for imagination expresses itself not in words only, but in the " mute language " of lines and colours. He knew something also of Leibniz ; the great German and Newton were by him described as " the greatest wits of the time " [4]; but he seems to have remained in complete ignorance of the æsthetic attempts of the Leibnitian school in Germany. His " Logic of poetry " was a discovery independent of, and earlier than, Bülffinger's Organon of the inferior faculties, the *Gnoseo-*

[1] *Instituzioni oratorie e scritti inediti*, Naples, 1865, pp. 90 *seqq.* : *De sententiis, vulgo del ben parlare in concetti.*

[2] Letter to the Duke of Laurenzana, March 1, 1732 ; and cf. letter to Muzio Gaeta.

[3] Cf. p. 190.   [4] *Scienza nuova sec.* bk. i., *Del metodo.*

logia inferior of Baumgarten, and the *Logik der Einbildungskraft* of Breitinger. In truth, Vico belongs on
one side to the vast Renaissance reaction against formalism and scholastic verbalism, which, beginning with the
reaffirmation of experience and sensation (Telesio, Campanella, Galileo, Bacon), was bound to go on by reasserting the function of imagination in individual and social
life : on the other side he is a precursor of Romanticism.

The importance of Vico's new poetic theory in his
thought as a whole as well as in the organism of his
Scienza nuova has never been fully appreciated, and the
Neapolitan philosopher is still commonly regarded as the
inventor of the Philosophy of History. If by such a
science is meant the attempt to deduce concrete history
by ratiocination and to treat epochs and events as if
they were concepts, the only result of Vico's efforts to
solve the problem could have been failure ; and the same
is true of his many successors. The fact is that his
philosophy of history, his ideal history, his *Scienza nuova
d' intorno alla comune natura delle nazioni*, does not concern
the concrete empirical history which unfolds itself in
time : it is not history, it is a science of the ideal, a
Philosophy of the Spirit. That Vico made many discoveries in history proper which have been to a great
extent confirmed by modern criticism (*e.g.* on the development of the Greek epic and the nature and genesis of
feudal society in antiquity and in the Middle Ages)
certainly deserves all emphasis ; but this side of his work
must be kept distinctly apart from the other, strictly
philosophical, side. And if the philosophical part is a
doctrine expounding the ideal moments of the spirit, or
in his own words " the modifications of our human mind,"
of these moments or modifications Vico undertakes
especially to define and fully describe not the logical,
ethical and economic moments (though on these too he
throws much light), but precisely the imaginative or
poetic. The larger portion of the second *Scienza nuova*
hinges on the discovery of the creative imagination, including the " new principles of Poetry," the observations

Æsthetic in the " Scienza nuova."

on the nature of language, mythology, writing, symbolic figures and so forth. All his " system of civilization, of the Republic, of laws, of poetry, of history, in a word, of humanity at large " is founded upon this discovery, which constitutes the novel point of view at which Vico places himself. The author himself observes that his second book, dedicated to Poetic Wisdom, " wherein is made a discovery totally opposed to Verulam's," forms " nearly the whole body of the work " ; but the first and third books also deal almost exclusively with works of the imagination. It might be maintained, therefore, that Vico's " New Science " was really just Æsthetic ; or at least the Philosophy of the Spirit with special emphasis upon the Philosophy of the Æsthetic Spirit.

Vico's mistakes.   Among so many luminous points, or rather in such a general blaze of light, there are yet dark nooks in his mind ; corners that remain in shadow. By not maintaining a rigid distinction between concrete history and the philosophy of the spirit, Vico allowed himself to suggest historical periods which do not correspond with the real periods, but are rather allegories, the mythological expression of his philosophy of the spirit. From the same source arises the multiplicity of those periods (usually three in number) which Vico finds in the history of civilization in general, in poetry and language and practically every subject. " The first peoples, who were the children of the human race, founded first the world of the arts : next, after a long interval, the philosophers, who were therefore the aged among nations, founded the world of the sciences : with which humanity attained completion." [1] Historically, understood in an approximate sense, this scheme of evolution has some truth ; but only an approximate truth. In consequence of the same confusion of history and philosophy he denied primitive peoples any kind of intellectual logic, and conceived not only their physics, cosmology, astronomy and geography as poetic in character, but their morals, their economy and their politics as well. But not only

[1] *Scienza nuova sec., Ultimi corollari,* § 5.

has there never been a period in concrete human history entirely poetic and ignorant of all abstraction or power of reasoning, but such a state cannot even be conceived. Morals, politics, physics, all presuppose intellectual work, however imperfect they may be. The ideal priority of poetry cannot be materialized into a historical period of civilization.

Linked with this error is another into which Vico often falls when he asserts that " the chief aim of poetry " is to " teach the ignorant vulgar to act virtuously " and to " invent fables adapted with the popular understanding capable of producing strong emotion." [1] Having regard to the clear explanations he himself gave of the inessentiality of abstractions and intellectual artifice in poetry ; when we remember that for him poetry makes her own rules for herself without consulting anybody, and that he clearly established the peculiar theoretical nature of the imagination, such a proposition cannot be taken as a return to the pedagogic and heteronomous theory of poetry which in substance he had left far behind : therefore, without doubt, it follows from his historical hypothesis of a wholly poetical epoch of civilization, in which education, science and morality were administered by poets. Another consequence is that " imaginative universals " are apparently sometimes understood by him as imperfect universals (empirical or representative concepts as they were subsequently called) ; although, on the other hand, individualization is so marked in them and their unphilosophical nature so accentuated that their interpretation as purely imaginative forms may be taken as normal. In conclusion, we remark that fundamental terms are not always used by Vico in the same sense : it is not always clear how far " sensation," " memory," " imagination," " wit " are synonymous or different. Sometimes " sensation " seems outside the spirit, at others one of its chief moments ; poets are sometimes the organ of " imagination," some-

[1] *Scienza nuova pr.* bk. iii. ch. 3 ; *Scienza nuova sec.* bk. ii., *Della metafisica poetica* ; and bk. iii. *ad init.*

times the " sensation " of humanity ; and imagination is described as " dilated memory." These are the aberrations of a thought so virgin and original that it was not easy to regulate.

Progress still to be achieved. To sever the Philosophy of the Spirit from History, the modifications of the human mind from the historic vicissitudes of peoples, and Æsthetic from Homeric civilization, and by continuing Vico's analyses to determine more clearly the truths he uttered, the distinctions he drew and the identities he divined ; in short, to purge Æsthetic of the remains of ancient Rhetoric and Poetics as well as from some over-hasty schematisms imposed upon her by the author of her being : such is the field of labour, such the progress still to be achieved after the discovery of the autonomy of the æsthetic world due to the genius of Giambattista Vico.

VI

MINOR ÆSTHETIC DOCTRINES OF THE
EIGHTEENTH CENTURY

THIS step in advance had no immediate effect. The *The influence* pages in the *Scienza nuova* devoted to æsthetic doctrine *of Vico.* were actually the least read of any in that marvellous book. Not that Vico exercised no influence at all ; we shall see that several Italian authors both of his own time and of the generation immediately following show traces of his æsthetic ideas ; but these traces are all external and material and therefore sterile. Outside Italy the *Scienza nuova* (already announced by a compatriot in 1726 in the *Acta* of Leipzig with the graceful comment that *magis indulget ingenio quam veritati* and the pleasing information that *ab ipsis Italis taedio magis quam applausu excipitur*) [1] was mentioned toward the end of the century, as is well known, by Herder, Goethe, and some few others. [2] In connection with poetry, especially with the Homeric question, Vico's book was quoted by Friedrich August Wolf, to whom it had been recommended by Cesarotti [3] after the publication of the *Prolegomena ad Homerum* (1795), but without any suspicion of the importance of its general doctrine of poetry, of which the Homeric hypothesis was a mere

[1] Vico, *Opere, ed. cit.* iv. p. 305.

[2] Herder, *Briefe zur Beförderung der Humanität*, 1793–1797, Letter 59 ; Goethe, *Italien. Reise*, Mar. 5, 1787.

[3] Letters from Wolf to Cesarotti, June 5, 1802 ; in Cesarotti, *Opere*, vol. xxxviii. pp. 108-112 ; cf. *ibid.* pp. 43-44, and vol. xxxvii. pp. 281, 284, 324 ; cf. on the question of the relations between Wolf and Vico, Croce, *Bibliografia vichiana*, pp. 51, 56-58, and *Supplem.* pp. 12-14.

application.   Wolf (1807) imagined himself in the presence
of a talented forerunner in an isolated problem, instead
of a man of intellectual stature towering above any
philologist, however great.

Italian
writers :
A. Conti.

Neither by reliance on the works of Vico, who founded
no real school, nor, it must be added, by any independent
effort along new lines, did thought succeed in maintaining or
improving upon the position already attained.   A notable
attempt to establish a philosophical theory of poetry and
the arts was made by the Venetian A. Conti, who left
numerous sketches for essays on imagination, the faculties
of the soul, poetic imitation and similar subjects, designed
for inclusion in a large treatise on the Beautiful and Art.
Conti had started by professing ideas very like those of
Du Bos, affirming that the poet must " put everything
in images " ; that taste is as indefinable as feeling, and
that there are persons without taste just as there are
blind and deaf persons ; he also wrote polemical tracts
against the Cartesians.   Later he abandoned his sensationalistic or sentimentalist theories,[1] and, inquiring into
the nature of poetry, declared himself ill-satisfied with
Castelvetro, Patrizzi, and even Gravina.   " Had Castelvetro," he observes, " who writes so subtly of Aristotle's
Poetics, given two or three chapters to a philosophical
explanation of the idea of imitation, he would have solved
many questions raised but not clearly answered by himself
concerning poetic theories.   In his *Poetica* and in his
controversy against Torquato Tasso, Patrizzi never succeeded in clearly defining the philosophical idea of imitation ; he collected much useful information about the
history of poetry, but wilfully lost the Platonic doctrine
by allowing it to mingle with the historical detail instead
of gathering it up without sophistry into a single point,
when it would have appeared in a very different guise.
The *Ragion poetica* of Gravina shadows forth a sort of
philosophical idea of imitation ; but so wholly engrossed
is he in deducing therefrom rules for lyrical, dramatical

[1] Letter in French to Mme. Ferrant (1719), and to the Marquis
Maffei in *Prose e poesie*, vol. ii. (1756), pp. lxxxv.-civ., cviii.-cix.

and epic poetry, and illustrating each with examples
from the most celebrated poets, Greek, Latin and Italian,
that he is too busy to question the sufficiency of the
fertile idea he has propounded." [1] A close follower of
contemporary European thought, Conti was familiar with
Hutcheson, whose theories he vigorously repudiated,
observing, " Why this multiplication of faculties ? " The
soul is one, and for scholastic convenience only has been
divided into three faculties : sense, imagination, intellect ;
the first " concerns herself with objects present before
her ; imagination with those afar into which memory
gradually merges : but the object of sense and imagination is always particular ; it is only the mind, the intellect,
the spirit, that by comparing particulars apprehends the
universal." " Before introducing a new sense for the
pleasure of beauty " Hutcheson should have " assigned
limits to these three faculties of cognition and demonstrated that the pleasure occasioned by beauty does not
arise from the three pleasures of these three faculties,
or from intellectual pleasure alone, to which they all
reduce, if the functions of the soul be carefully analysed."
Thus it would appear that the mistake of the Scotchman [2]
arose from his habit of separating pleasure from the
cognitive faculties, placing the former apart in a special
empty " sense of beauty." [3] On the other hand, when
rewriting the history of the opinions of various critics
upon the Aristotelian doctrine of the universal in poetry,
Conti gave much weight to the dialogue *Naugerius seu
De poëtica* of Fracastoro ; [4] for an instant he seems on
the point of grasping the essence of the poetic universal
and identifying it with the characteristic, which makes
us call even horrible things wholly beautiful. " In all his
journeys Balzac never saw a beautiful old woman : in
the poetic or picturesque sense an old woman is highly

[1] *Prose e poesie*, vol. i., 1739, pref.
[2] Francis Hutcheson (1694–1746) was an Irishman. Croce's mistake
is probably due to the fact that he studied and taught at Glasgow, or
that his family was ultimately of Scottish origin.—TR.
[3] *Prose e poesie*, vol. ii. pp. clxxi.-clxxvii.
[4] See above, pp. 184-185.

beautiful, if depicted as having suffered all the dilapida-
tions of age " : immediately after, however, he identifies
the characteristic with Wolff's concept of perfection :
" It does not differ from being, nor does being differ from
the truth which the schoolmen call transcendental and
which is the object of all arts and all sciences ; we call
it the object of poetry when by means of imaginary
presentations it ravishes the intellect and moves the
will, transporting both these faculties into the ideal
and archetypal world of which, following S. Augustine,
Father Malebranche discourses at length in his *Recherche
de la vérité.*" [1] In the same way Fracastoro's universal
gives place to the universal of science : " Owing to the
infinity of their determinations all we can know of particulars is their common properties, which is merely another
manner of saying that we have no science save of universals. Thus it is precisely the same if we say the object
of poetry is science or the universal ; which is the doctrine
of Navagero, following Aristotle." [2] The " imaginative
universals of Signor Vico " (with whom he had interchanged some letters) opened no new views for him : he
notes that Signor Vico " talks a great deal about them "
and " holds that the most uncivilized men, having framed
them not from any wish to please or serve others, but
from the necessity of expressing their feelings as nature
taught them, spoke in poetical language the elements of
a theology, a physics, and an ethics wholly poetical."
Conti excuses himself from immediate examination of
" this critical question " and only opines that " it can
be shown in many ways that these imaginative universals
are the material or object of poetry, in so far as they
contain within them sciences or things considered in
themselves " [3]—a conclusion diametrically opposed to
that which " Signor Vico " meant to express. Conti is
next obliged to ask himself how it is possible that poetry's
object should be not the true but the probable, when the
universal of poetry is the same as that of science. He

---

[1] *Prose e poesie*, vol. ii. pp. 242-246.   [2] *Op. cit.* ii. p. 249.
[3] *Op. cit.* ii. pp. 252-253.

answers by coming down to the commonplace level of a Baumgarten : " When sciences receive a particular colouring, we pass from the true to the probable." Imitation means giving the impression of truth ; that is done by selecting a few of its features only ; and this is the procedure in which the probable just consists. If you wish to describe the rainbow poetically, a great part of the Newtonian optics must be thrown overboard ; thus " many circumstances of mathematical demonstration " will be neglected in poetical descriptions, and the rest, which is utilized, will form the probable or that particular " which awakens the universal idea, slumbering in the minds of the learned." The great art of poetry consists " in selection of the image containing the greatest number of points of universal doctrine which, by being inserted in the example, may so colour the precept that I may find it without seeking it, or recognize it through its connexion with events described." [1] Hence poetry cannot be content with imitation ; allegory too is needed : " in ancient poetry one thing is read and another is meant." Here follows the inevitable instance of the Homeric poems, in which Conti certainly finds elements which cannot be reduced to instruction and allegory and therefore to some extent deserve the Platonic condemnation.[2] He recognizes a species of imagination differing from passive sensibility, " which Father Malebranche calls active imagination, and Plato the art of imagery ; it comprises all that is meant by wit, sagacity, judgement and good taste, which teach a poet to use or not to use at a given time or place the rules and licences of art, and to control the extravagance of his imagery." [3] On the question of literary taste he follows the opinion of Trevisano and decides that it consists in " setting in mutual harmony, that is to say restraining within limits, the soul's cognitive faculties, memory, imagination and intellect, allowing none to overwhelm another." [4]

By assiduous travail of thought and perpetual search   *Quadrio and Zanotti.*

---

[1] *Prose e poesie*, vol. ii. pp. 233-234.   [2] *Op. cit.* i. pref.
[3] *Op. cit.* ii. p. 127.   [4] *Op. cit.* i. p. xliii.

for the best, Conti kept himself at the highest level
of æsthetic speculation in contemporary Europe (Vico
always excepted) ; at the same level as Baumgarten in
Germany. We pass rapidly over other Italian writers
such as Quadrio (1739), author of the first great encyclopædia of universal literature, in which he defines poetry
as " the science of things human and divine, presented
in pictures to the populace, and written in words connected by measure " ;[1] and Francesco Maria Zanotti
(1768), who describes poetry as " the art of versification
in order to give pleasure " :[2] the first is worthy of a
mediæval anthologist, the second of a no less mediæval
composer of handbooks on rhythm and methods of composition. The only serious student of æsthetic was
Melchior Cesarotti.

M. Cesarotti.   Cesarotti called attention to popular and primitive
poetry : he translated Ossian and illustrated the text
with dissertations ; he unearthed antique Spanish poems
and even the folk-songs of Mexico and Lapland; he studied
Hebrew poetry ; he dedicated the greater part of his
life to the Homeric poems, examining all the theories of
critics past and present, encountering Vico in this connexion and discussing his views. Besides this, he debated
the origin of poetry, the pleasure given by tragedy,
taste, the beautiful, eloquence, style, in short every
problem belonging to æsthetics which had been raised
up to his time.[3] One seems to catch an echo of Vico
as one listens to his words on La Motte : " He had logic,
but knew not that the logic of poetry differs somewhat
from ordinary logic : he was a man of great talent, but
he recognized talent only, and was incapable of feeling
the immeasurable distance between judicious prose and

---

[1] Fr. Sav. Quadrio, *Della storia e della ragione d' ogni poesia*, Bologna,
1739, vol. i. part i. dist. i. ch. 1.
[2] Fr. M. Zanotti, *Dell' arte poetica, ragionamenti cinque*, Bologna,
1768.
[3] On Ossian, *Opere*, vols. ii.-v. ; on Homer, vols. vi.-x. ; *Saggio
sopra il diletto della tragedia*, vol. xxix. pp. 117-167 ; *Saggio sul bello*,
vol. xxx. pp. 13-70 ; on *Filosofia del gusto*, vol. i. ; on *Eloquenza*,
lecture, vol. xxxi.

poetry : the real Homer with his attractive faults will always be more beloved than his reformed Homer with his cold, affected virtue." [1] Cesarotti purposed (1762) bringing out a great theoretico-historical book in whose first part " we shall suppose the non-existence of poetry and poetic art and try to trace by what path a man of illuminated reason can have reached the idea of the possibility of such an art and how he can have attained perfection by these means : every one will be able to see poetry growing up under his eyes, so to speak, and attest the truth of theory by the testimony of his own personal feelings." [2] Although celebrated throughout Italy in his day as one who " with the most pure torch of philosophy has thrown beams of light into the darkest recesses of poetry and eloquence," [3] it does not appear that the distinguished scholar, the pleasing and desultory philosopher, offered any profound or original solutions. In 1797 he defined poetry as " the art of representing and perfecting nature by means of picturesque, animated, imaginative and harmonious discourse." [4]

The fashion of the day in philosophy made men impatient of the ideas found in writers of treatises of former times.   Arteaga praises Cesarotti for " that fine tact, that impartial criticism, that logical spirit derived not from the trickling streamlets of Sperone, Castelvetro, Casa and Bembo, but from the profound and inexhaustible springs of Montesquieu, Hume, Voltaire, d'Alembert, Sulzer, and writers of like temper." [5]   Writing to Saverio Bettinelli, who was preparing a work on *Enthusiasm*, Paradisi hoped it would prove " a metaphysical history of enthusiasm which shall outweigh all those Poetics which are only fit to be burned," and would " make waste paper of Castelvetro, the ' Minturno,' and that stupid

Bettinelli and Pagano.

[1] *Opere*, vol. xl. p. 49.

[2] *Ibid.* p. 55.

[3] Letter from Corniani to Cesarotti, November 21, 1790, in *Opere*, vol. xxxvii. p. 146.

[4] *Saggio sopra le istituzioni scolastiche, private e pubbliche*, in *Opere*, vol. xxix. pp. 1-116.

[5] Letter of March 30, 1764, in *Opere*, vol. xxxv. p. 202.

creature, Quadrio." [1] In spite of these aspirations Betti-nelli's book (1769) contains little beyond vivacious and eloquent empirical observations concerning the psychology of poets, " poetic enthusiasm," to which he assigns six degrees, namely, elevation, vision, rapidity, novelty and surprise, passion and transfusion. Equally empirical was Mario Pagano in his two fragments, *Gusto e le belle arti* and *Origine e natura della poesia* (1783-1785), in which he grotesquely combines some ideas from Vico with the current sensationalism. Theoretico-imaginative form and sensuous pleasure are presented by him as two historical periods of art. " In their cradle the fine arts are directed towards making a true imitation of nature rather than towards loveliness. Their first steps are towards expression rather than charm. . . . In the most ancient poetry, even in the ballads of barbarous ages, there lives a most compelling pathos : passions are expressed naturally, even the sound of the words is alive with the expression of the things described." But " the period of perfection is reached at the moment when exact imitation of nature is coupled with complete beauty, accord and harmony," when " the taste is refined and society reaches its most complete form of culture." Fine arts " precede by a short time the dawn of philosophy, that is to say, the time of the most intense perfection of society " ; indeed, certain modes of art, such as tragedy, must necessarily come later than philosophy whose aid must be invoked to further " the purgation of manners." [2]

German disciples of Baumgarten. G. F. Meier. The compatriots and successors of Baumgarten, like those of Vico, did little by way of understanding or improving upon his work. An enthusiastic admirer and disciple of Baumgarten who had attended his lectures at Frankfort-on-the-Oder, Georg Friedrich Meier, came forward in 1746 to defend the *Meditationes* against the attacks of Quistorp to whom the master had deigned no

[1] Saverio Bettinelli, *Dell' entusiasmo nelle belle arti*, 1769, in *Opere*, iii. pp. xi.-xiii.

[2] Fr. M. Pagano, *De' saggi politici*, Naples, 1783-1785, vol. i. Appendix to § 1, " Sull' origine e natura della poesia "; vol. ii. § 6, " Del gusto e delle belle arti."

reply ; [1] already in 1748, prior to the publication of the *Æsthetic*, he had published the first volume of his *Principles of all the Beautiful Sciences*,[2] followed in 1749 and 1750 by the second and third volumes. This book, which is a complete exposition of Baumgarten's theory, is divided, according to the master's method, into three parts : invention of beautiful thoughts (heuristic), æsthetic method (methodic), and the beautiful signification of thoughts (semiotic) ; the first of these (occupying two and a half volumes) is subdivided into three sections : beauty of sense-apprehension (æsthetic richness, grandeur, verisimilitude, vivacity, certainty, sensitive life and wit), sensitive faculties (attention, abstraction, senses, imagination, subtlety, acumen, memory, poetic power, taste, foresight, conjecture, signification and the minor appetitive faculties), and the diverse kinds of beautiful thought (æsthetic concepts, judgements, and syllogisms). Elsewhere than in this book, which was reprinted many times (in 1757 an epitome was issued [3]), Meier discusses Æsthetic in several of his numerous works, especially in a little tract, *Considerations on the First Principles of all Fine Arts and Sciences*.[4] Who was more tenderly inclined than he towards the science so recently born and baptized ? He was ardent in her defence against those who denied both her possibility and her utility, and against those who admitted these yet complained, not unreasonably, that she was substantially the same as that which in former days had been treated as Poetics and Rhetoric. He parried this accusation, of which he recognized the partial truth, by asserting that it was impossible for one writer to have perfect knowledge of all the arts : another of his excuses was to the effect that Æsthetic was a science too young to show the perfection reached by other sciences after the cultivation of centuries ; in one place he says he has no intention of arguing " with those

---

[1] See above, p. 217.
[2] *Anfangsgründe aller schönen Wissenschaften*, Halle, 1748–1750.
[3] *Auszug aus den Anfangsgründe*, etc., *ibid.* 1758.
[4] *Betrachtungen über den ersten Grundsätzen aller schönen Künste u. Wissenschaften, ibid.* 1757.

enemies of Æsthetic who will not or cannot see the true
nature and aim of this science, but have built for themselves in its place a deformed and miserable image against
which, when they fight, they fight against themselves."
With philosophic resignation he concludes that the same
fate is in store for Æsthetic as for every science : " At
first when almost unknown they encounter enemies and
detractors who ridicule them through ignorance and
prejudice ; but later they meet persons of intellect who,
by working at them conjointly, carry them on to their
proper perfection." [1]

Confusions of Meier.   Students of the new science flocked to Halle University
to hear Meier lecture on Æsthetic whose " chief author "
or " inventor " (*Haupturheber, Erfinder*), as Meier never
tired of repeating, was " Herr Professor Baumgarten " ;
at the same time warning them that his own *Anfangsgründe* were no mere transcription of Baumgarten's
lectures.[2] Still, while recognizing the great gifts of
Meier as publicity-agent, the facility, clarity and wealth
of his eloquence, and his shrewdness in polemic, one
cannot altogether deny the justice of the remark upon
" Professor Baumgarten of Frankfort and his ape (*Affe*)
Professor Meier of Halle." [3] Every defect of Baumgarten's Æsthetic reappears accentuated in Meier ; the
limits of the inferior cognitive faculties, alleged as the
domain of poetry and the arts, are laid down by him
most strangely. It is curious to note how, for example,
he interprets the difference between the confused (æsthetical) and the distinct (logical), and the proposition that
beauty disappears when made the object of distinct
thought. " The cheeks of a beautiful girl whereon bloom
the roses of youth are lovely so long as they are looked
at with the naked eye. But let them be examined with
a magnifying glass. Where is their beauty ? One can
hardly believe that such a disgusting surface, scaly, all

---

[1] Preface to 2nd ed. (1768) of vol. ii. of *Anfangsgründe*, and *Betrachtungen, cit.*, esp. §§ 1, 2, 34.

[2] Preface to vol. i., and cf. § 5.

[3] In a letter to Gottsched, 1747, in Danzel, *Gottsched*, p. 215.

mounts and hollows, the pores full of dirt, with hairs sprouting here and there, can be the seat of that amorous attraction which subdues the heart." [1] That is described as " æsthetically false " whose truth the inferior faculty is unable to grasp : for example, the theory that bodies are composed of monads.[2] Once they have become intelligible to these faculties, general concepts possess great æsthetic richness, since they include infinite consequences and particular cases.[3] Æsthetic also comprehends those things which cannot be thought distinctly or, if so thought, might be capable of upsetting philosophic gravity : a kiss may be an excellent subject for a poet ; but whatever would be thought of a philosopher who sought to demonstrate its necessity by the mathematical method ? [4] Moreover, Meier includes the whole theory of observation and experiment in Æsthetic, to which this theory belongs, he says, by right of its connexion with the senses,[5] and also the whole theory of the appetitive faculties, because " æsthetic requires not only a fine wit but a noble heart as well." [6] He comes near truth sometimes, when, for example, he observes that the logical form presupposes the æsthetic and that our first concepts are sensitive, later becoming distinct by the help of logic ; [7] and when he condemns allegory as " among the most decadent forms of beautiful thinking." [8] But, on the other hand, he thinks that logical distinctions and definitions, although not necessarily sought after by genius, are very useful in poetry ; they are even indispensable as regulators of beautiful thinking and make up, as it were, the skeleton of the body poetic : great care, however, must be taken not to judge æsthetical general concepts, *notiones aestheticae universales*, with the rigorous exactitude demanded by philosophical. And since such concepts, taken singly, may be likened to unstrung jewels, they must be connected by the string of æsthetic judgement and syllogism, the theory of which is identical with

---

[1] *Anfangsgründe*, § 23.   [2] *Op. cit.* § 92.
[3] *Op. cit.* § 49.   [4] *Op. cit.* § 55.   [5] *Op. cit.* §§ 355-370.
[6] *Op. cit.* §§ 529-540.   [7] *Op. cit.* § 5.   [8] *Op. cit.* § 413.

that presented by Logic, setting aside that part which is
of little or no use to genius, but belongs exclusively to
the philosopher.[1] In his *Considerations* of 1757 Meier,
having combated the principle of imitation (which
appeared to him at once too broad, since science and
morals are also imitations of nature, and too narrow,
since art does not imitate natural objects solely nor
should it imitate them all, for the immoral must be
excluded), reaffirmed the thesis that the æsthetic principle
consists in the " greatest possible beauty of sense-perception." [2] He upheld this by condemning as erroneous the
belief that this sense-perception is wholly sensuous and
confused, without any gleam of distinctness or rationality.
The perception of sweet, bitter, red, etc., is wholly
sensuous ; but there is another perception which is both
sensuous and intellectual, confused and distinct, in which
both faculties, the higher and the lower, collaborate.
When intellectuality prevails in this consciousness, then
we have science : when sensibility, then we have poetry.
" From our explanation it will be gathered that the
inferior cognitive faculties must collect all the material
of a poem, and all its parts. Intellect and judgement, on
the other hand, watch and ensure that these materials
are placed side by side in such a way that in their connexion distinction and order may be observed." [3] Here
a plunge into sensationalism, there a fugitive glimpse of
truth : most often, and in conclusion, an adherence to
the old mechanical, ornamental, pedagogic theory of
poetry : this is the impression left on us by the æsthetic
writings of Meier.

M. Mendels-
sohn and
other
followers of
Baumgarten.
Vogue of
Æsthetic.
Another disciple of Baumgarten, Mendelssohn, conceiving beauty as " indistinct image of a perfection,"
deduced that God can have no perception of beauty, as
this is merely a phenomenon of human imperfection.
According to him a primary form of pleasure is that of
the senses, arising from " the bettered state of our bodily
constitution " ; a secondary form is the æsthetic fact of
sensible beauty, that is to say, unity in variety ; a third

[1] *Anfangsgründe*, §§ 541-670.   [2] *Betrachtungen*, § 20.   [3] *Op. cit.* § 21.

form is perfection, or harmony in variety.[1] He too
repudiates Hutcheson's *deus ex machina*, the sense of
beauty. Sensible beauty, perfection such as can be
apprehended by the senses, is independent of the fact
that the object represented is beautiful or ugly, good or
bad by nature; it suffices that it leaves us not indifferent:
whence Mendelssohn agrees with Baumgarten's definition, " a poem is a discourse sensibly perfect." [2] Elias
Schlegel (1742) conceived art as imitation, not so servile
as to seem a copy, but having similarity rather than
identity with nature : he considered the duty of poetry
was first to please and only afterwards to instruct.[3]
Treatises on Æsthetic, university lectures or slender
volumes for use of the public, *Theories of the Fine Arts
and Letters*, *Manuals*, *Sketches*, *Texts*, *Principles*, *Intro-
ductions*, *Lectures*, *Essays*, and *Considerations on Taste*
poured down thick and fast on Germany during the
second half of the eighteenth century. There are at
least thirty full or complete treatises and many dozens
of minor tracts or fragments. After the Protestant
universities, the Catholic took up the new science, which
was taught by Riedel at Vienna, Herwigh at Würzburg,
Ladrone at Mainz, Jacobi at Freiburg, and by others at
Ingolstadt after the expulsion of the Jesuits.[4] A pretty
little volume on the *First Principles of the Fine Arts* [5] was
written (1790) for Catholic schools by the notorious
Franciscan friar Eulogius Schneider, who, after being un-
frocked, terrorised Strasburg in the days of the Convention,
and met his end under the guillotine. The frenzied output
of these German *Æsthetics* resembles that of *Poetics* in

---

[1] *Briefe über die Empfindungen*, 1755 (in *Opere filosofiche*, Ital.
trans., Parma, 1800, vol. ii.), Letters 2, 5, 11.

[2] *Betrachtungen üb. d. Quellen d. sch. Wiss. u. K.*, 1757, later entitled
Über die Hauptgrundsätze, etc., 1761, in *Opere, ed. cit.* ii. pp. 10, 12-15,
21-30.

[3] J. E. Schlegel, *Von der Nachahmung*, 1742 ; cf. Braitmaier, *Gesch.
d. poet. Th.* i. p. 249 *sqq.*

[4] Koller, *Entwurf*, p. 103.

[5] *Die ersten Grundsätze der schönen Kunst überhaupt, und der schönen
Schreibart insbesondere*, Bonn, 1790 ; cf. Sulzer, i. p. 55, and Koller,
pp. 55-56.

Italy in the sixteenth century, after the rise to popularity
of Aristotle's treatise.   Between 1771 and 1774 the Swiss
Sulzer brought out his great æsthetic encyclopædia, *The
General Theory of the Fine Arts*, in alphabetical order,
with historical notes upon each article, which were greatly
enlarged in the second edition of 1792, edited by a retired
Prussian captain, von Blankenburg.[1]   In 1799, one J.
Koller published a first *Sketch of the History of Æsthetic*,[2]
in which he observes not unjustly, " Patriotic youth will
be pleased to recognize that Germany has produced more
literature on this subject than any other country." [3]

Confining ourselves to bare mention of the works of
Riedel (1767), Faber (1767), Schütz (1776–1778), Schubart
(1777–1781), Westenrieder (1777), Szerdahel (1779), König
(1784), Gäng (1785), Meiners (1787), Schott (1789),
Moritz (1788),[4] we will select from the crowd the *Theory
of Fine Arts and Letters* (1783) of Johann August Eberhard, successor to Meier in the Chair at Halle,[5] and the
Sketch of a Theory and Literature of Letters (1783) by Johann
Joachim Eschenburg, one of the most popular books of
the day for students.[6]   Both these authors are followers
of Baumgarten, with inclinations towards sensationalism ;
amongst other things Eberhard considered the beautiful
as " that which pleases the most distinct senses," that is
to say, of sight and hearing.   A word must be accorded
to Sulzer, in whom we find the most curious alternation
of new and old, the romantic influence of the new Swiss
school and the utilitarianism and intellectualism of his
day.   He asserts that beauty exists wherever unity,
variety and order are found : the work of an artist is
strictly in the form, in lively expression (*lebhafte Dar-*

Eberhard and Eschenburg.

J. G. Sulzer.

[1] See Bibliographical Appendix.
[2] *Entwurf zur Geschichte u. Literatur d. Ästhetik*, etc., Regensburg, 1799 ; see Bibl. App.
[3] Koller, *op. cit.* p. 7.
[4] Notices and extracts in Sulzer and Koller, *opp. citt.*
[5] Joh. Aug. Eberhard, *Theorie der schönen Künste u. Wissenschaften*, Halle, 1783 ; reprinted 1789, 1790.
[6] Joh. Joach. Eschenburg, *Entwurf einer Theorie u. Literatur d. s. W.*, Berlin, 1783 ; reprinted 1789.

stellung) : the material is irrelevant to art, but the duty
of every reasonable and sensible man is to make judicious
selection.   The beauty which is used to clothe the good
as well as the bad is not the ineffable, celestial Beauty,
offspring of the alliance between the beautiful, the good
and the perfect, which awakens more than mere pleasure,
a veritable joy which ravishes and beatifies our soul.
Such is the human face when, by filling the eye of the
beholder with the pleasure of form arising from the variety,
proportion and order of the features, it proceeds to
arouse the imagination and intellect by its suggestion of
interior perfection ; of the same nature is the statue of a
great man carved by Phidias, or a patriotic oration by
Cicero.   If truth lie outside art and belong to philosophy,
the most noble use to which art may be put is to make
us feel the important truths which lend her strength and
energy, not to mention that truth itself enters into art in
the shape of truthful imitation or representation.   Sulzer
also repeats (and he is not the last) that orators, historians and poets are intermediaries between speculative
philosophy and the people.[1]   Karl Heinrich Heydenreich *K. H.*
returns to a sounder tradition when he defines art (1790) *Heydenreich.*
as " a representation of a determinate state of sensibility,"
and observes that man, as a cognitive being, is impelled
to enlarge the sphere of his cognitions and impart his
discoveries to his fellows, while as a sensitive being he is
impelled to represent and communicate his sensations ;
whence arise science and art.   But Heydenreich does not
clearly grasp the cognitive character of art ; for in his
opinion sensations become objects of artistic representation either because they are pleasing or, when not pleasing,
because they are useful to further the moral aims of
man as a social being ; the objects of sensibility which
enter into art must be possessed of intrinsic excellence
and value and bear reference not to a single individual
but to the individual as a rational being : hence the
objectivity and necessity of taste.   Like Baumgarten

---

[1] *Allgem. Th. d. sch. Künste*, on words *Schön, Schönheit, Wahrheit,
Werke des Geschmacks*, etc.

and Meier, he divides Æsthetic into three parts : **a** doctrine of *inventio*, another of *methodica*, a third of the *ars significandi*.[1]

J. G. Herder.   Another disciple of Baumgarten is J. G. Herder, who had an unbounded admiration for the old Berlin master, whom he calls " the Aristotle of his day," and defends him warmly against those who think fit to describe him as a "stupid and obtuse syllogizer " (1769). On the other hand he had slight esteem for subsequent Æsthetic, for example Meier's work, which he stigmatized accurately enough as " in part a re-mastication of Logic, in part a patchwork of metaphorical terms, comparisons and examples." " O Æsthetic ! " he cries with emphasis, " O Æsthetic ! the most fertile, the most beautiful and by far the most novel of all abstract sciences, in what cavern of the Muses is sleeping the youth of my philosophic nation destined to bring thee to perfection ? "[2] He denied Baumgarten's claim to have established an *Ars pulchre cogitandi* instead of limiting himself to a simple *Scientia de pulchro et pulchris philosophice cogitans*, and ridiculed the scruple which held Æsthetic to be unworthy of the dignity of Philosophy.[3] To compensate for this, however, he accepted the fundamental definition of poetry as *oratio sensitiva perfecta* : gem of definitions (says he), the best that has ever been invented, that penetrates to the heart of the matter, touches the true poetic principles and opens the most extended view over the entire philosophy of the beautiful, " coupling poetry with her sisters, the fine arts."[4] Like Cesarotti the Italian, but with much less vivacity and brilliance, Herder the German had studied primitive poetry, Ossian and the songs of ancient peoples, Shakespeare (1773), popular love-songs (1778), the spirit of Hebrew poetry

[1] Karl Heinrich Heydenreich, *System der Ästhetik*, vol. i., Leipzig, 1790, esp. pp. 149-154, 367-385, 385-392.

[2] *Kritische Wälder oder Betrachtungen über die Wissenschaft und Kunst des Schönen*, Fourth Forest, 1769, in *Sämmtliche Werke*, ed. B. Suphan, Berlin, 1878, vol. iv. pp. 19, 21, 27.

[3] *Kritische Wälder, loc. cit.* pp. 22-27.

[4] Fragment, *Von Baumgarten Denkart* ; and cf. *op. cit.* pp. 132-133.

(1782), and oriental poetry ; these studies powerfully
impressed upon his mind the sensitive nature of poetry.
His friend Hamann (1762) had written these memorable
words, which read like an extract from one of Vico's
aphorisms : " Poetry is the mother-tongue of mankind :
in the same way that the garden is older than the ploughed
field, painting than writing, song than declamation, barter
than trade. The repose of our most ancient progenitors
was a slumber deeper than ours ; their motion a tumultu-
ous dance. They spent seven days in the silence of
thought or of stupor ; and opened their mouths to
pronounce winged words. Their speech was sensation
and passion, and they understood nothing but images.
Of images is composed all the treasure of human knowledge and felicity." [1] Although Herder, who knew and
admired Vico,[2] does not mention him by name when
treating of language and poetry, one might suppose him
to be influenced by the great Neapolitan at least in the
final consolidation of his theories ; but, on the contrary,
the authors whom he chiefly quotes in this connexion
are Du Bos, Goguet and Condillac, and observes " the
first beginnings of human speech in tone, gesture, expression of sensations and thoughts by means of images
and signs, can only have been a kind of crude poetry,
and so it is among every savage nation in the world."
Not a speech with punctuation and a sense of syllable,
like ours, learning as we do to read and write, but
an unsyllabled melody which gave birth to the primitive epic. " Natural man depicts what he sees and
as he sees it, alive, powerful, monstrous ; in order or
disorder, as he sees and hears, so he reproduces. Not
alone did barbarous tongues thus arrange their images,
but Greek and Latin do the same. As the senses offered
material, so the poets utilized it ; especially in Homer we
see how closely nature is followed in images which glow
and fade perpetually and inimitably. He describes things

---

[1] *Aesthetica in nuce*, in *Kreuzzüge des Philologen*, Königsberg, 1762 ;
quoted in Herder, *Werke*, xii. 145.

[2] See above, p. 235.

252 HISTORY OF ÆSTHETIC VI

and events line by line, scene by scene ; and, in the same way, he paints men in their very bodies, actually as they speak and move." Later we distinguish epic from what we call history ; because the former " not only describes what has happened but describes the event in its entirety, showing how it occurred in the only possible way, having regard to surrounding circumstance of body and spirit " : this is the reason of the more philosophical character of poetry. As for pleasure, no doubt we do find poetry pleasant ; but the idea that the poet's motive is merely to excite pleasure cannot be condemned too strongly. " Homer's gods were as essential and indispensable to the poet's world as the forces of motion are to the world of matter. Without the deliberations and activities of Olympus, none of the necessary events which happen on this earth could take place. Homer's magic island in the western sea belongs to the map of his hero's wanderings by the same necessity which placed it on the map of the world : it was necessary to the plan of his poem. It is the same with the severe Dante and his circles of Hell and Heaven." Art is formative : she disciplines, orders and governs the imagination and every faculty of man : not only did she generate history, " but, earlier yet, she created gods and heroes and purified the uncouth imaginations and fables of peoples with their Titans, monsters and Gorgons, reducing to limit and law the riotous imagination of ignorant men which knows no bounds or rule." [1]

Notwithstanding these intuitions, so like those of Vico early in the same century, Herder as a philosopher is inferior to his Italian predecessor, and in point of fact does not rise superior to Baumgarten. By application of Leibniz' law of continuity, he too arrived at the opinion that the pleasing, the true, the beautiful and the good are degrees of one single activity. For instance, sensible pleasure " is a participation in the true and the good, so far as the senses may comprehend them ; the feeling of pleasure and pain is no other than the feeling of the true

---

[1] *Kaligone*, 1800, in *Werke, ed. cit.*, xii. pp. 145-150.

and the good, that is to say, the consciousness that the
aim of our organism, the conservation of our well-being
and the avoidance of our hurt, has been attained." [1]
Fine arts and letters are all instructive (*bildend*) : hence
the terms *humaniora*, the Greek καλόν, the Latin *pulchrum*, the *gentle* arts of days of chivalry, *les belles lettres
et les beaux arts* of the French. A group of them (gym-
nastic, dance, etc.) educates the body ; a second group
(painting, plastic, music) educates the nobler senses of
man, the eye, the ear, the hand and tongue ; a third
(poetry) touches the intellect, the imagination and the
reason : a fourth group governs human tendencies and inclinations. [2] Herder disapproved of the facile theorists of
art who began straight away with a definition of beauty,
a complex and involved concept. He held that the
theory of fine arts should be subdivided into three theories,
each to be built up from the foundations, the theory of
sight, of hearing and of touch, that is to say of painting,
music and sculpture, *i.e.* into æsthetical Optics, æsthetical
Acoustics and æsthetical Physiology. " Fairly well
elaborated in the psychological and subjective aspects,
Æsthetic is sadly undeveloped in all that belongs to
the object and to the sensation of beauty, without which
there can never be a fertile theory of the Beautiful
capable of influencing all the arts." [3] Taste is not " a
fundamental faculty of the soul but a habitual application
of our judgement (intellectual judgement) to objects of
beauty " ; an acquired facility of the intellect (of which
Herder outlines the genesis). [4] The poet is poet not only
in his imagination but in his intellect. In 1782 he
writes : " The barbarous name Æsthetic of recent invention indicates nothing beyond a section of Logic :
that which we call taste is neither more nor less than a
quick and rapid judgement which does not exclude truth
and profundity, but rather presupposes and promotes
them. All didactic poetry is nothing more than philosophy rendered sensible : the fable as exposition of a

---

[1] *Kaligone*, pp. 34-55.   [2] *Ibid.* pp. 308-317.
[3] *Kritische Wälder, loc. cit.* iv. pp. 47-127.   [4] *Op. cit.* pp. 27-36.

general doctrine is truth in act, in activity. . . . **When**
expounded and applied to human affairs, Philosophy is
not only a fine art in herself (*schöne Wissenschaft*), but
the mother of Beauty : it is only through her that
Rhetoric and Poetry can ever be educational, useful, or
in the truest sense pleasant." [1]

Philosophy of language.
Herder and Hamann deserve our gratitude for having
brought a current of fresh air into the study of the
philosophy of language. The lead given by the Port-
Royal authors had been followed since the beginning of
the century by many writers of logical or general
grammars. According to the French Encyclopædia, " *La
grammaire générale est la science raisonnée des principes
immuables et généraux de la parole prononcée ou écrite
dans toutes les langues*," [2] and d'Alembert spoke of
grammarians of invention and grammarians of memory,
assigning to the former the duty of studying the metaphysics of grammar.[3] General grammars had been
written by Du Marsais, De Beauzée, and Condillac in
France ; Harris in England ; and many others.[4] But
what was the relation between general grammar and
particular grammars ? If logic be one, how comes it
that languages are many ? Is the variety of tongues
but a deviation on their part from one single model ?
And, if there be no such deviation or error, what is the
explanation of the fact ? What is language, and how
was it born ? If language be external to thought, how
can thought exist if not in language ? " *Si les hommes*,"
says Jean-Jacques Rousseau, " *ont eu besoin de la parole
pour apprendre à penser, ils ont eu bien plus besoin encore
de savoir penser pour trouver l'art de la parole* " ; appalled
at the difficulty, he declares his conviction " *de l'im-*

[1] *Sophron*, 1782, § 4.   [2] *Encyclopédie, ad verb.*
[3] *Éloge de Du Marsais*, 1756 (introd. to *Œuvres de Du Marsais*,
Paris, 1797, vol. i.).
[4] Du Marsais, *Méthode raisonnée*, 1722 ; *Traité des tropes*, 1730 ;
Traité de grammaire générale (in *Encyclopédie*) ; De Beauzée, *Grammaire
générale pour servir de fondement à l'étude de toutes les langues*, 1767 ;
Condillac, *Grammaire française*, 1755 ; J. Harris, *Hermes, or a Philosophical Enquiry concerning Language and Universal Grammar*, 1751.

possibilité presque démontrée que les langues aient pu naître et s'établir par des moyens purement humains.'' [1] Such questions became fashionable ; books on the origin and formation of language were written by de Brosses (1765) and Court de Gébelin (1776) in France, by Monboddo (1774) in England, Süssmilch (1766) and Tiedemann in Germany, and Cesarotti (1785) in Italy, and by others who had some slight acquaintance with Vico, but profited little by it.[2] None of the above-named writers was able to free himself of the notion that speech was either natural and mechanical, or else a symbol attached to thought : whereas in fact it was impossible to solve the difficulties under which they were labouring except by dropping the notion of a sign or symbol and attaining the conception of the active and expressive imagination, verbal imagination, language as the expression not of intellect but of intuition. An approach towards this explanation was made by Herder in a brilliant and imaginative thesis in 1770 upon this subject of the origin of language, chosen for discussion by the Berlin Academy. In it he says that language is the reflexion or consciousness (*Besonnenheit*) of man. " Man shows reflexion when he puts forth freely such force of mind as enables him to make selection from amongst the crowd of sensations by which he is assailed : from the ocean of the senses, so to speak, to select a single wave and consciously to watch it. He shows reflexion when, amidst the thronging chaos of images which pass before him as in a dream, he can in a waking moment collect himself and fasten his attention upon a single image, examine it calmly and clearly, and separate it from its neighbours. Once again, man shows reflexion when he is able not merely to grasp vividly and

---

[1] *Discours sur l'origine de l'inégalité parmi les hommes,* 1754.

[2] De Brosses, *Traité de la formation mécanique des langues,* 1765; Court de Gébelin, *Histoire naturelle de la parole,* 1776 ; Monboddo, *Origin and Progress of Language,* 1774 ; Süssmilch, *Beweis dass der Ursprung der menschlichen Sprache göttlich sei,* 1766 ; Tiedemann, *Ursprung der Sprache* ; Cesarotti, *Saggio sulla filosofia delle lingue,* 1785 (in *Opere,* vol. i.) ; D. Colao Agata, *Piano, ovvero ricerche filosofiche sulle lingue,* 1774 ; Soave, *Ricerche intorno all' istituzione naturale d' una società e d' una lingua,* 1774.

clearly all the properties of an image, but also to recognize
one or more of its distinctive properties." The language
of man " does not depend on the organization of the mouth,
for even he who is dumb from birth has, if he reflects,
a language ; it is not a cry of the senses, since it resides
in a reflective creature, not in a breathing machine ; it
is not an affair of imitation, since imitation of nature is
a means, and we are here trying to explain the end : much
less is it an arbitrary convention ; a savage in the depths
of the forest would have had to create a language for
himself even though he never used it. Language is an
understanding of the soul with herself, necessary just in
so far as man is man." [1] Here language begins to show
itself no longer as purely mechanical or as something
derived from arbitrary choice and invention, but as a
creative activity and a primary affirmation of the activity
of the human mind. Herder's essay may not state such
a view unequivocally, but it points forward to such a
conclusion in a striking way for which its author has not
received the credit he deserves. Hamann, in reviewing
his friend's theories, agreed with him in denying the
origin of language by invention or arbitrary choice ;
while dwelling also on the liberty of man, he regarded
language as something which man could only have
learned by means of a mystical *communicatio idiomatum*
from God.[2] That, too, was one way of recognizing that
the mystery of language is not to be solved except by
placing it in the forefront of the problem of the spirit.

[1] *Abhandlung über den Ursprung der Sprache*, in a small book *Zwei
Preisschriften*, etc. (2nd ed., Berlin, 1789), esp. pp. 60-65.
[2] Steinthal, *Ursprung der Sprache*, 4th ed., pp. 39-58.

OTHER ÆSTHETIC DOCTRINES OF THE
SAME PERIOD

A GREAT medley of heterogeneous ideas is noticeable *Other writers* among other writers on Æsthetic during the same period. *of the eighteenth* In 1746 appeared a little volume by Abbé Batteux bear- *century :* ing the attractive title of *The Fine Arts reduced to a* *Batteux.* *Single Principle*, in which the author attempted a unification of all the different rules laid down by the writers of treatises. All such rules (says Batteux) are branches emerging from one trunk ; he who possesses the simple principle will be able to deduce the rules one by one without entangling himself in their mass, which can but involve him in endless coils. The author had passed in review the *Ars Poetica* of Horace and that of Boileau, and the works of Rollin, Dacier, le Bossu and d'Aubignac ; but had found real help only in Aristotle's principle of imitation, which he thought could be easily and strikingly applied to poetry, painting, music and the art of gesture. But suddenly the Aristotelian principle of imitation yields place to a wholly new rendering, namely the " imitation of natural *beauty*." The business of art is to " select the most beautiful parts of nature in order to frame them into an exquisite whole which shall be more beautiful than nature's self, without ceasing to be natural." Now, what may this greater perfection, this beautiful nature, be ? On one occasion Batteux identifies it with truth : but " with the truth which may be ; with beauty-truth, which is represented as though it really existed with all the perfections it could possibly receive," recalling one example from the ancients in the Helen of Zeuxis, and one from the moderns in the *Misanthrope* of Molière. In another place he explains that beautiful nature, " *tum ipsius (obiecti) naturae, tum nostrae convenit,*" *i.e.* that it has the closest connexion with our own perfection, our advantage and our interest, and is, at the same time, perfect in itself. The aim of imitation is " to please, to move, to soften, in one word, to delight " ; so beautiful nature must be interesting and furnished with unity, variety, symmetry and proportion. Embarrassed by the question of artistic imitation of things naturally ugly or objectionable, Batteux falls back on saying, as Castelvetro had said before him, that displeasing objects please when imitated, since imitation, being always imperfect, in comparison with the reality, cannot excite the horror and disgust aroused by the latter. From pleasure he deduces the other aim of utility : if the aim of poetry be to give pleasure, and " pleasure by moving the passions, then in order to give a perfect and enduring pleasure it ought to rouse such passions only as it is well to excite, not those inimical to goodness." [1]

The English :   It is difficult to string together a more insubstantial
W. Hogarth.   mass of contradictions.   But Batteux is rivalled and outdone by the English philosophers or rather scribblers on Æsthetic or rather on things in general which sometimes accidentally include æsthetic facts. Happening to find in Lomazzo some words attributed to Michael Angelo on the beauty of shapes, Hogarth the artist took into his head the idea that the figurative arts can be regulated by a special principle which can be expressed in a particular line.[2] Filled with this discovery, in 1745 he designed a frontispiece for a volume of his engravings ; it depicted a painter's palette scored across with an undulating line and the words *The Line of Beauty*. Public curiosity was immediately aroused by this hieroglyphic, to be satisfied a little later by the publication of his book *The Analysis*

----

[1] *Les Beaux Arts réduits à un même principe*, Paris, 1746; see esp. part i. ch. 3 ; part ii. chs. 4, 5 ; part iii. ch. 3.

[2] See above, p. 110.

of Beauty (1753).[1] In this he combated the mistake of judging pictures either by the subject or the excellence of the imitation instead of by their form, which is the true essential of art and is composed " of symmetry, variety, uniformity, simplicity, intricacy and quantity ; all things which co-operate in the production of beauty, correcting and restraining each other as required." [2] But immediately afterwards Hogarth proclaims that there must also be correspondence and agreement with the thing copied ; for " regularity, uniformity and symmetry give pleasure in so far only as they serve to give the illusion of faithful correspondence." [3] Further on, the reader learns that " amongst the immense variety of undulating lines which may be conceived, there is but one which truly merits the name of the Line of Beauty, and this is a precisely serpentine line which may be called the Line of Grace." [4] Again, we are told that intricacy of lines is beautiful because " the active mind likes to be engaged," and the eye delights in being " guided in a sort of hunt." [5] A straight line has no beauty, and the pig, the bear, the spider and the toad are ugly because devoid of undulating lines.[6] The ancients showed much judgement in the management and grouping of lines, " varying from the precise line of grace only on those occasions when the character or action demanded." [7]

With similar indecision Edmund Burke wavers between *E. Burke.* the principle of imitation and other heterogeneous or imaginary principles in his book, *An Enquiry into the Origin of our Ideas of the Sublime and the Beautiful* (1756). He observes, " Natural properties contained in an object give pleasure or displeasure to the imagination : beyond this, however, imagination may delight in the likeness of a copy to its original " ; he asserts that from " these two reasons " arises the whole pleasure of imagination.[8]

---

[1] *Analysis of Beauty*, London, 1753 (Ital. trans., Leghorn, 1761).
[2] *Op. cit.* p. 47.   [3] *Op. cit.* p. 57.   [4] *Op. cit.* p. 93.
[5] *Op. cit.* pp. 61, 65.   [6] *Analisi della bellezza*, p. 91.
[7] *Op. cit.* p. 176.
[8] *Enquiry into the Origin of our Ideas of the Sublime and the Beautiful*, 1756 (Ital. trans., Milan, 1804) ; cf. the preliminary discourse on " Taste."

Without dwelling further on the second, he proceeds to a lengthy discussion of the natural qualities which should be found in an object of sensible beauty : " Firstly, comparative smallness ; secondly, smooth surface ; thirdly, variety in disposition of the parts ; fourthly, that it have no angularity, all lines fusing one in another ; fifthly, a structure of great delicacy betraying no signs of violence ; sixthly, vivid colouring without glare or harshness ; seventhly, if it have any glaring colour, let it be different from the background." These are the properties of beauty working in harmony with nature and least liable to suffer from caprice and differences of taste.[1]

These books of Hogarth and Burke are generally described as classical ; if so, they belong to the type of classic that fails to convince. To a somewhat higher type *H. Home.* belongs the *Elements of Criticism* (1761) of Henry Home, Lord Kaimes, who seeks " the true principles of the fine arts " with the object of converting criticism into " a rational science," and to this end chooses " the upward path of facts and experiments." Home confines himself to feelings derived from objects of sight and hearing, which, in so far as unaccompanied by desires, are more truly described as simple feelings (emotions, not passions). These occupy a middle position between mere sense-impressions and intellectual or moral ideas, and are therefore akin to both ; and it is from these that the pleasures of beauty are derived. Beauty is divided into beauty of relation and intrinsic beauty.[2] Of the latter, Home's only account is that regularity, simplicity, uniformity, proportion, order and other pleasing qualities have been " so disposed by the Author of nature in order to increase our happiness here on earth which, as is clearly shown in numberless instances, is not foreign to his care." This notion is confirmed when he reflects that " our taste for such details is not accidental, but uniform and universal, being a very part of our nature " ; adding that " regularity, uniformity, order and simplicity help to facilitate

---

[1] *Enquiry into the Origin of our Ideas of the Sublime and the Beautiful,* part iii. § 18.　　[2] *Elements of Criticism,* 1761, vol. i. introd. and chs. 1-3.

perception and make it possible for us to form clearer conception of objects than it would be possible to gain by the most earnest attention were such qualities not present." Proportions are often combined with a view to utility, " as we see that the best proportioned amongst animals are also the strongest ; but there are also many examples in which this conjunction does not hold good " ; wherefore the wisest plan " is to rest content with the final cause just mentioned : that of the increase of our happiness intended by the Author of nature." [1]   In his *Essay on Taste* (1758) and on *Genius* (1774) Alexander Gerard employs by turns, according to the various forms of art, the principles of association, of direct pleasure, of expression, and even of moral sense : the same kind of explanation reappears in another *Essay on Taste* by Alison (1792).

It is impossible to classify works of such calibre, almost wholly lacking as they are in scientific method ; on each page their writers pass from physiological sensationalism to moralism ; from the imitation of nature to mysticism and transcendent finalism without the slightest sense of incongruity.   It would be absurd to take them seriously ; in comparison it is almost refreshing to come across a frank hedonist in the German, Ernst Platner, who interpreted Hogarth's inquiry into lines after a fashion of his own and was unable to see anything in æsthetic facts except a reverberation of sexual pleasure. Where can we find a beauty, he asks, that is not derived from the female figure, the centre of all beauty ?   Undulating lines are beautiful because found in a woman's body ; beautiful are all movements distinctively feminine ; beautiful the tones of music melting one into another ; beautiful the poem where one thought embraces another with tenderness and facility.[2]   Condillac's sensationalism had already shown itself wholly incapable of understanding æsthetic productivity ; the associationism especially promoted by the work of Hume fared no better.

Eclecticism and sensationalism. E. Platner.

[1] *Elements of Criticism*, i. ch. 3, pp. 201-202.
[2] *Neue Anthropologie*, Leipzig, 1790, § 814, and the lectures on Æsthetic published posthumously in 1836 ; cf. Zimmermann, *op. cit.* p. 204.

Fr.
Hemsterhuis.   The Dutchman Hemsterhuis considered beauty as a
phenomenon born of the meeting between sensibility, which
gives multiplicity, and the internal sense, which tends to
unity ; hence the beautiful is " that which exhibits the
greatest number of ideas in the shortest time." Man, to
whom it is not permitted to attain ultimate unity, finds
in beauty an approximate unity which gives him a pleasure
somewhat analogous with the joy of love. This theory
of Hemsterhuis, in which elements of mysticism and
sensationalism mingle with glimpses of truth, developed
later into the sentimentalism of Jacobi, for whom the
totality of Truth and Goodness and even the Supersensible itself are sensibly present to the soul in the form
of beauty.[1]

Neo-
Platonism and
mysticism.
Winckelmann.   Platonism or, more accurately, neo-Platonism was
revived by the creator of the history of figurative art,
Winckelmann (1764). Contemplation of the masterpieces of antique plastic art, and the impression of superhuman loftiness and divine indifference which they create
all the more irresistibly because we cannot reawaken the
life they once possessed or understand their real significance, led Winckelmann, and others with him, to the
conception of a Beauty which, descending from the
seventh heaven of the divine Idea, embodied itself in
works of this description. Baumgarten's follower Mendelssohn had denied the enjoyment of beauty to God :
the neo-Platonist Winckelmann gave it back to him and
lodged it in his bosom.

Beauty and
lack of
significance.   " Wise men who have meditated upon the causes of
universal Beauty, seeking her amongst created things and
trying to gain the contemplation of Supreme Beauty,
have placed it in the perfect harmony of creatures with
their ends and of their parts with one another. But as
this is equivalent to perfection, which man is incapable of
attaining, our concept of universal beauty remains indeterminate, and arises by means of particular cognitions
which, when accurately collected and fitted together,

---

[1] Zimmermann, *op. cit.* pp. 302-309; v. Stein, *Entstehung d. n. Ästh.*
p. 113.

give us the highest idea we can attain of human beauty,
which we elevate in proportion as we raise it above
matter. But, again, since the Creator deals out perfection
to all his creatures in the proportion that befits them, and
since every concept rests on some cause which must be
sought outside the concept itself, the cause of Beauty
which is to be found in every created thing cannot be
sought in anything outside these created things. For
this reason, and because our cognitions are comparative
concepts, whereas Beauty cannot be compared with anything higher, it is difficult to attain a distinct and universal
cognition of Beauty."[1]   The only way out of this difficulty
and others like it is the recognition that " supreme beauty
resides in God " : " the concept of human beauty becomes
the more perfect in proportion as it can be thought more
in conformity and agreement with supreme Being, which
is distinguished from matter by its own unity and indivisibility. This conception of Beauty is as a spirit
which, freed by fire from the prison of matter, strives to
conjure up a creature in the likeness of the first reasonable
creature formed by the divine intelligence. The forms of
such an image are simple and continuous and within this
unity they are varied and for that very reason harmonious." [2]   To these characteristics is added " lack of significance " (Unbezeichnung), since supreme beauty cannot
be described with points or lines different from those
which alone can constitute that beauty ; its form " is not
peculiar to this or that determinate person, neither does
it express any state of feeling or sensation of passion,
things which disturb unity and overcloud beauty."
Winckelmann concludes : " We look upon Beauty as a
purest water drawn from the centre of the spring ; the
less taste it has the higher it is esteemed because free from
all impurities." [3]

To perceive pure beauty, a special faculty is required,
which certainly is not sense, but may perhaps be intellect

[1] *Geschichte der Kunst des Altertums*, 1764 (in *Werke*, Stuttgart,
1847, vol. i.), bk. iv. ch. 2, § 51, p. 131.
[2] *Op. cit.* § 22, pp. 131-132.   [3] *Op. cit.* § 23, p. 132

or even, as Winckelmann says, " a fine internal sense " free from all intentions or passions of instinct, inclination or pleasure. Having asserted beauty to be something supersensible, it is not surprising that Winckelmann should wish, if not wholly to exclude colour, at least to reduce it to a minimum, and treat it not as a constitutive element in beauty but as secondary and ancillary.[1] True beauty is given in form : by which he means line and surface, forgetting that these are only apprehended by the senses, and could not be seen without being in some way coloured.

Winckel-mann's contradictions and compromises.　When error refuses to retire, hermit-like, to the narrow cell of a brief aphorism, it finds itself condemned to self-contradiction in order to live at all in the world of concrete facts and problems. Although composed with a view to stating a theory, the work of Winckelmann always led him among concrete historical facts clamouring to be brought into relation with his formally stated idea of supreme beauty. In his admission of line-drawing and his further admission, on a lower plane, of colour, we have two compromises already ; to which a third is added in his principle of Expression. " Since human nature has no state intermediate between pain and pleasure " and as living creature without such feelings is inconceivable, " the human figure must be represented in a condition of action and passion, which artists call expression." Hence Winckelmann, after dealing with Beauty, goes on to treat of Expression.[2] He then found himself obliged to effect a fourth compromise between the single constant supreme beauty and individual beauties ; for while he preferred the male to the female body as a completer embodiment of perfect beauty, he could not shut his eyes to the obvious fact that we know and admire beautiful women's bodies and even beautiful animals' bodies.

A. R. Mengs.　Friend and, in a sense, collaborator of Winckelmann was Raphael Mengs the artist, no less eager than his archæological fellow-countryman to understand the nature of that beauty which the one studied as a critic while the

---

[1] *Geschichte*, § 19, pp. 130-131.　　　[2] *Op. cit.* bk. iv. ch. ii. § 24.

other produced it as a painter. Remarking, writes
Mengs, that of the two chief duties of a painter, the
imitation of appearances and the selection of the most
beautiful objects, much has been written on the former,
while the latter " has scarcely been touched by the
moderns, who would have been ignorant of the art of
drawing were it not for the statues of ancient Greece " ; [1]
pondering this, " I read, asked and looked at everything
likely to throw light on the subject, but never was I
satisfied ; either they spoke of beautiful things or of
qualities which are the attributes of beauty, or they
pretended to explain, as the saying is, the obscure by the
more obscure, or even confused the beautiful with the
pleasing : so that finally I determined to search for the
nature of beauty on my own account." [2] One of his
works on this subject was published during his lifetime by
the advice and assistance of Winckelmann (1761) ; many
others appeared posthumously (1780), all were reprinted
several times and translated into several languages. In
his *Dreams of Beauty* he says, " I have been sailing a long
time on a vast sea seeking the understanding of beauty,
and still I am far from any shore and in great doubt how to
shape my course : gazing around, my sight is confounded
by the immensity of the subject." [3] In truth it seems as
though Mengs never arrived at a formula satisfactory to
himself, although he conformed more or less to Winckelmann's doctrine that " beauty consists in material perfection according to our ideas ; and since God alone is
perfect, beauty is divine " ; it is the " visible idea of
perfection " and stands in the same relation to it as does
a visible to a mathematical point. Our ideas proceed
from the purposes which the Creator has willed to fulfil
in various things ; hence the multiplicity of beauties.
In general, Mengs finds the types of things in natural
species : *e.g.* " a stone, of which we have the idea that it
should be uniform in colour " ; which " is called ugly if it

---

[1] *Geschichte*, bk. v. chs. ii. and vi.
[2] Letter of January 2, 1778, *Opere*, Rome, 1787 (reprinted Milan,
1836), ii. pp. 315-316.   [3] *Opere*, i. p. 206.

happen to be spotted " ; or a child " would be ugly if he were like a man of mature age, just as a man is ugly when shaped like a woman, and a woman when she is like a man." He adds surprisingly, " As among stones there is but one perfect species, the diamond ; among metals, gold ; and among animated creatures, man only ; so there is difference and distinction in every order, and very rarely is there perfection." [1] In his *Dreams of Beauty* he considers beauty as " a middle disposition, including perfection on the one hand and the pleasing on the other " ; in reality it is a third thing, differing from perfection and the pleasing, and deserving a special name for itself.[2] The art of painting arises from four sources : beauty, significant or expressive character, the pleasing united to harmony, and colouring. Mengs finds the first amongst the ancients, the second in Raphael, the third in Correggio and the fourth in Titian.[3] From this empirical studio-gossip he rouses himself to exclaim, " The force of beauty so transports me that I will tell thee, reader, what I feel. All nature is beautiful, and so is virtue ; beautiful are forms and proportions ; beautiful are appearances and beautiful the causes thereof ; more beautiful is reason, most beautiful of all is the great first cause." [4]

G. E. Lessing.   An attenuated, that is to say, a less metaphysical, echo of Winckelmann's theory is found in Lessing (1766), who infused a new spirit into the literature and social life of the Germany of his time. According to Lessing the aim of art is " delight " ; and since delight is a " superfluous thing " it seems reasonable that the legislator should not allow to art that liberty which is indispensable to science in her search for truth, the soul's necessity. For the Greeks painting was what by its nature it ought to be, " the imitation of beautiful bodies." " Its (Hellenic) cultivator represented nothing but the beautiful : common beauty of a low grade served him as an accidental subject, an exercise, a diversion. The

---

[1] *Riflessioni sulla bellezza e sul gusto della pittura*, in *Opere*, i. pp. 95, 100, 102-103.

[2] *Opere*, i. p. 197.   [3] *Ibid*. p. 161.   [4] *Ibid*. p. 206.

attractiveness of his work must depend simply and solely on the perfection of his subject : he was far too true an artist to wish his audience to content itself with the barren pleasure arising from mere resemblance or from the inspection of skilful workmanship : nothing in his art was dearer to him, nothing seemed more noble, than the end at which it aimed." [1] Pictorial representation must exclude everything unpleasing or ugly ; " painting as imitation may express ugliness : painting as a fine art will refuse to do so : all visible objects belong to art taken under the former title : the latter may claim only such objects as awaken pleasing sensations." If, on the contrary, ugliness may be represented by the poet, the reason is this : poetic description " conveys a less displeasing sense of bodily malformation which, in the end, almost loses its character as such ; unable to use it for itself, the poet uses it as a means to provoke certain mixed feelings (the ridiculous, the terrible), in which we are content to remain, in the absence of any purely pleasant feelings." [2] In his *Dramaturgie* (1767) Lessing takes his stand upon the Aristotelian *Poetics* : . it is well known that not only did he approve of rules in general but he believed those laid down by Aristotle to be as incontrovertible as the theorems of Euclid. His polemic against French writers and critics is waged in the name of probability, not to be confounded with historical accuracy. He understood the universal as a sort of average of what appears in individuals, and catharsis as a conversion of passions into virtuous dispositions, asserting it as beyond doubt that the aim of all poetry is to inspire a love for virtue.[3] He follows the example of Winckelmann in introducing the concept of ideal beauty into the doctrine of figurative art : " expression of corporeal beauty is the aim of painting : therefore supreme beauty of body is the supreme aim of art. But this supreme beauty of body is found in

---

[1] *Laokoon*, § 2.   [2] *Op. cit.* §§ 23, 24.
[3] *Hamburg. Dramaturgie* (ed. Göring, vols. xi. and xii.), *passim*, esp. Nos. 11, 18, 24, 78, 89.

man only, and for him it exists only through the ideal.
This ideal may be found among the brute creation in
inferior degree ; but is entirely absent from vegetable
or inanimate nature." Landscape and flower painters
are not really artists because " they imitate beauties
possessed of no ideal : whereby they work by eye and
hand alone, genius having little or no part in their compositions." Nevertheless, Lessing prefers a landscape
painter to " the painter of historic pieces who, instead of
making beauty his aim, merely depicts a crowd in order
to show his cunning in simple expression, not in expression
subordinate to beauty." [1] The ideal of bodily beauty
then consists " chiefly in the ideal of form, but also in
that of texture of the flesh, and in that of permanent expression. Mere colouring and transitory expression have
no ideal since nature herself has placed no indelible
seal upon them." [2] At the bottom of his heart Lessing
dislikes colour ; and when he finds the pen-sketches of
painters showing " a life, a freedom, a brilliancy never
to be found in their painted pictures," he asks himself
" whether the most marvellous colouring can compensate
so heavy a loss," and whether it is not to be wished
" that painting in oils had never been invented " ? [3]

Theorists of ideal beauty.   Ideal beauty, that curious alliance between God and
the subtle outline traced with pen or graver, that cold
academical mysticism, came into fashion. In Italy (the
home of Winckelmann and Mengs, who published many
of their works in Italian) it was much discussed by
artists, antiquaries and connoisseurs. The architect
Francesco Milizia professed himself a follower of " the
principles of Sulzer and Mengs " ; [4] the Spaniard d'Azara,
living in Italy, edited and annotated Mengs, adding his
own definition of beauty : " The union of the perfect
and the pleasing made visible " ; [5] another Spaniard,

[1] *Laokoon*, appendix, § 31.   [2] *Op. cit.* §§ 22, 23.
[3] *Op. cit. ad fin.* p. 268.
[4] *Dell' arte di vedere nelle belle arti del disegno secondo i principi di Sulzer e di Mengs*, Venice, 1871.
[5] D'Azara, in Mengs, *Opere*, i. p. 168.

Arteaga, one of the many Jesuit refugees in Italy, wrote a treatise on *Ideal Beauty* (1789) ; [1] the Englishman Daniel Webb on coming to Rome and making the acquaintance of Mengs seized upon the ideas he heard him express on beauty, collected them and actually published them in a book anticipating Mengs' own.[2]

The first voice of dissent from this doctrine of ideal beauty was raised in 1764 by a small circle of Italians who asserted the characteristic to be the principle of art. *G. Spalletti and the characteristic.* As such appears to be the necessary interpretation of the little *Essay on Beauty* written by Guiseppe Spalletti in the form of a letter to Mengs, with whom Spalletti had discussed the subject " in the solitudes of Grottaferrata," and who had urged him to put all his thoughts in writing.[3] Its polemical character, though not openly asserted, is discernible in every page. " Truth in general, conscientiously rendered by the artist, is the object of Beauty in general. When the soul finds those characteristics which wholly converge upon the matter which the work of art claims to represent, it judges that work beautiful. The same is true of the works of nature : if the soul perceives a man of fine proportions having the face of a lovely woman, which causes it to doubt whether the object before it be man or woman, it esteems that man ugly rather than the reverse, through deficiency of the characteristic of truth ; if this can be said of natural Beauty, how much more can it be said of the Beauty of art." The pleasure given by Beauty is intellectual, that is to say, it is the pleasure of apprehending truth : when confronted by ugly things represented characteristically, man " delights in having increased his cognitions " : Beauty, " with its property of supplying to the soul likeness, order, proportion, harmony and variety, provides it with an immense field for the construction of

[1] *Investigaciones filosóficas sobre la belleza ideal, considerada como objeto de todas las artes de imitación*, Madrid, 1789.
[2] *Ricerche su le bellezze della pittura* (Ital. trans., Parma, 1804) ; cf. D'Azara, *Vita del Mengs*, in *Opere*, i. p. 27.
[3] *Saggio sopra la bellezza*, dated " Grottaferrata, July 14, 1764," and published at Rome, 1765, anonymously.

innumerable syllogisms, and by reasoning in this manner it will take pleasure in itself, in the object which arouses such pleasure, and in the feeling of its own perfection." Finally, the beautiful may be defined as " the inherent modification of the object under observation which presents it in the inevitably characteristic manner in which it is bound to appear." [1] In contrast to the fallacious profundity of Winckelmann and Mengs we welcome the sound good sense of this obscure Spalletti, upholder of the Aristotelian position against the revived neo-Platonism of the æstheticians.

Beauty and the characteristic : Hirt, Meyer, Goethe.

Many years went by before a similar rebellion arose in Germany ; at length in 1797 the art-historian Ludwig Hirt, basing his case on ancient works of art which depicted all things, even things utterly vulgar and ugly, ventured to deny the view that ideal beauty is the principle of art, and that expression has only a secondary place, above which it must not rise for fear of disturbing ideal beauty.   For the ideal he substituted the characteristic, as a principle to be applied equally to gods, heroes or animals.   Character is " that individuality by which form, movement, signs, physiognomy and expression, local colour, light, shade and chiaroscuro are distinguished and represented in the manner demanded by the object." [2] Another historian of art, Heinrich Meyer, who started from the position of Winckelmann and went on by adopting a series of compromises, finally asserting an ideal of trees and landscape side by side with the ideal of man and various other animals, tried to find an intermediate position between this doctrine and Hirt's, in the course of controversy with the latter.   And Wolfgang von Goethe, forgetful of his youthful days when he chanted the praises of Gothic architecture, returning home from an Italian tour impregnated with Greece and Rome in 1798, also sought a middle term between Beauty and Expression ; dwelling on the thought of certain character-

[1] *Saggio*, esp. §§ 3, 12, 15, 17, 19, 34.
[2] *Über das Kunstschöne*, in the review *Die Horen*, 1797 ; cf. Hegel, *Vorles. ü. Asth.* i. p. 24 ; and Zimmermann, *Gesch. d. Asth.* pp. 356-357.

istic contents which should supply the artist with forms
of beauty to be by him remodelled and developed into
complete beauty.   The characteristic was thus the mere
point of departure, and beauty was simply the result of
the artist's elaboration : " we must start from the characteristic " (says he) " in order to attain the beautiful." [1]

[1] Goethe, *Der Sammler und die Seinigen* (in *Werke*, ed. Goedeke,
vol. xxx.).

IMMANUEL KANT

1. Kant. OF all these writers, Winckelmann and Mengs, Home and Hogarth, Lessing and Goethe, none was a philosopher in the true sense of the word : not even those who like Meier laid claim to the title, nor those who had some gifts for philosophy like Herder or Hamann. After Vico, the next European mind of real speculative genius is Immanuel Kant, who now comes before us in his turn. *Kant and Vico.* That Kant took up the problem of philosophy where Vico laid it down (not, of course, in a directly historical, but in an ideal, sense) has already been noted by others.[1] How far he made an advance upon his predecessor and how far he failed to reach the same level it is not here our business to inquire ; we must confine ourselves strictly to the consideration of Æsthetic questions.

Summarizing the results of such a consideration, we may say at once that though Kant holds an immensely important place in the development of German thought ; though the book containing his examination of æsthetic facts is among his most influential works ; and though in histories of Æsthetic written from the German point of view, which ignore practically the whole development of European thought from the sixteenth to the eighteenth century, Kant can pose as the man who discovered the problem of Æsthetic or solved it or brought it within

---

[1] B. Spaventa, *Prolus. ed introd. alle lezioni di filosofia*, Naples, 1862 pp. 83-102 ; *Scritti filosofici*, ed. Gentile, pp. 139-145, 303-307.

sight of solution ; yet in an unprejudiced and complete history whose aim is to take broad views and to consider not the popularity of a book or the historical importance of a nation but the intrinsic value of ideas, the judgement passed on Kant must be very different. Like Vico in the serious tenacity with which he reflected upon æsthetic facts, more fortunate than he in having a much larger stock of material gathered from preceding discussion and argument, Kant was at once unlike and less successful than Vico in that he was unable to attain a doctrine substantially true, and unable also to give his thoughts the necessary system and unity.

In fact, what was Kant's idea of art ? Strange as *Identity of the* our reply may seem to those who recollect the explicit *concept of art* and insistent war waged by him against the school of *Baumgarten.* Wolff, and the concept of beauty as a perfection confusedly perceived, we must assert that Kant's idea of art was fundamentally the same as that of Baumgarten and the Wolffian school.[1] In that school his mind had been trained ; he always had a great respect for Baumgarten whom in the *Critique of Pure Reason* he calls " that excellent analyst " ; he chose the text of Baumgarten for two of his University lectures on Metaphysics, and that of Meier for his lecture on Logic (*Vernunftlehre*). Kant, like them, therefore considered Logic and Æsthetic (or theory of art) as conjoined sciences. They were thus described by him in his *Scheme of Lectures* in 1765, when he proposed, while expounding the critique of reason, to " throw a glance at that of taste, that is to say, at Æsthetic, since the rules of one apply to the other and each throws light upon the other." In his *Kant's* University lectures he distinguished æsthetic truth from *"Lectures."* logical truth in the style of Meier ; even citing the example of the beautiful rosy face of a girl which, when seen distinctly, *i.e.* through a microscope, ceases to be beautiful.[2] It is æsthetically true (said he) that a man once dead cannot come to life again, although this is

---

[1] *Kritik d. rein. Vernunft* (ed. Kirchmann), i. 1, § 1, note.
[2] See above, p. 244.

in opposition to logic and moral truth : it is æsthetically true that the sun plunges into the sea, but it is false logically and objectively. To what degree it is necessary to combine logical truth with æsthetic the learned have never yet been able to decide ; not even the greatest æstheticians. In order to become accessible, logical concepts must assume æsthetic forms ; a garb to be abandoned only in the rational sciences which seek profundity. Æsthetic certainty is subjective : it is content with authority, *i.e.* the citation of the opinions of great men. On account of our weakness, for we are strongly attached to the sensible, æsthetic perfection often helps us to render our thoughts distinct. In this, examples and images co-operate ; æsthetic perfection is the vehicle for logical perfection ; taste is the analogue of intellect. There are logical truths which are not æsthetic truths : and on the other hand we must exclude from abstract philosophy exclamations and other senti-mental commotions proper to the other truth. Poetry is a harmonious play of thoughts and sensations. Poetry and eloquence differ in this : in the former, thoughts adapt themselves to sensations ; in the latter the contrary is the case. In these lectures Kant sometimes taught that poetry is anterior to eloquence because sensations come before thoughts ; and he observed (perhaps under Herder's influence) that the poetry of Eastern peoples, lacking concepts, is wanting in unity and taste although rich in imaginative detail. Poetry formed out of the pure play of sensibility is doubtless a possibility, *e.g.* love-poems : but true poetry disdains such productions, concerned as they are with sensations which every one knows ought to be expelled from our breasts. True poetry must strive to present virtue and intellectual truth in sensible form, as has been done by Pope in his *Essay on Man*, in which he attempts to vivify poetry by means of reason. On other occasions Kant definitely says that logical perfection is the basis of every other, æsthetic perfection being merely an adornment of the logical ; something of the latter may be omitted in order to appeal to the audience, but it must never be disguised or falsified.[1]

This is Baumgartenism pure and simple ; unless we are prepared to look on these Lectures as representing a pre-critical period of thought, or an exoteric doctrine superseded eventually by Kant's own original esoteric ideas in his *Critique of the Judgment* (1790). Not to open such a controversy, let us put these Lectures on one side (although they often throw no little light on the signification of Kantian phrases and formulæ), and refuse to raise the question what pages of the *Critique of the Judgment* are derived from Baumgarten and Meier ; he who reads the works of these disciples of Wolff and passes immediately to the *Critique of Judgment* often has the impression that the atmosphere surrounding him is unchanged. But if the *Critique of Judgment* itself be examined without prejudice it will be seen that Kant always adhered to Baumgarten's conception of art as the sensible and imaginative vesture of an intellectual concept.

According to Kant, art is not pure beauty wholly detached from the concept, it is adherent beauty, which presupposes and attaches itself to a concept.[2] This is the work of genius, the faculty of representing æsthetic ideas. An æsthetic idea is " a representation of the imagination which accompanies a given concept : a representation conjoined with such truthful representation of particulars as to be unable to find for it any expression that may mark a determinate concept, thereby endowing the given concept with something of the ineffable ; a feeling which stimulates the cognitive faculties and reinforcing the tongue, which is simply the letter, with the spirit." Genius, then, has two constitutive elements, imagination and intellect ; it consists in " that happy disposition, which no science can teach or diligence attain, to find ideas for a

Art in the " Critique of Judgment."

[1] Extract from Kant's lectures of 1764 and later, in O. Schlapp, *Kant's Lehre vom Genie, passim*, esp. pp. 17, 58, 59, 79, 93, 96, 131-134, 136-137, 222, 225, 231-232, etc.
[2] *Kritik d. Urtheilskraft* (ed. Kirchmann), § 16.

given concept and, also, to select the expression by which the subjective commotion it excites as accompaniment to a concept may be communicated to others." No concept is adequate to the æsthetic idea, as no representation of the imagination can ever possibly be adequate to the concept. Examples of æsthetic attributes are found in the eagle of Jupiter with the thunderbolt in its claws, and the peacock of the proud Queen of Heaven : "they do not, like logical attributes, represent that which is contained in our concepts of the sublimity or majesty of creation, but something else which gives occasion to the imagination to run riot over a multitude of kindred representations which make us think more than we can express in a given concept by means of words, and give us an æsthetic idea, which serves to this rational idea instead of a logical representation, precisely with the aim of quickening our feelings by throwing open to them a view over a vast field of kindred representations." There are a *modus logicus* and a *modus aestheticus* of expressing our thoughts : the first consists in following determinate principles : the other in the mere feeling of the unity of the representation.[1] To imagination, to intellect and to spirit (*Geist*) we must add taste, the link between imagination and intellect.[2] Art may therefore represent natural ugliness : artistic beauty "is not a beautiful *thing* but a beautiful representation of a thing " : although the representation of ugliness has limits varying with the individual arts (a reminiscence of Lessing and Winckelmann), and an absolute limit at the disgusting and nauseating, which kill representation itself.[3] In natural things, too, there is adherent beauty which cannot be judged by the æsthetic judgement alone but demands a concept. Nature thus appears as a work of art, though superhuman art : "the teleological judgement is the basis and condition of the æsthetic." When we say "this is a beautiful woman," we merely mean that "nature beautifully represents in the form of this woman her purpose in the construction of the female body " : it is necessary there-

---

[1] *Kritik d. Urth.* § 49. [2] *Op. cit.* § 50. [3] *Op. cit.* § 48.

fore, besides noting simple form, to aim at a concept, " so that the object may be apprehended through an æsthetic judgement logically conditioned." [1] By this means is formed the ideal of beauty in the human face, the expression of moral life.[2] Kant admits that there may also be artistic productions without a concept, comparable with the free beauties of nature, flowers and some birds (parrot, humming-bird, bird of paradise, etc.) : ornamental drawings, cornice-mouldings, musical fantasies without words, represent nothing, no object reducible to a determined concept, and must be reckoned among free beauties.[3] But does not this necessitate their exclusion from true and proper art, from the operation of genius in which fancy and intellect must both, according to Kant, have a place ?

This is Baumgartenism transposed into a higher key, more concentrated, more elaborated, more suggestive, until from moment to moment it seems about to burst into a wholly different conception of art. But it is still Baumgartenism, from whose intellectualistic bonds it never escapes. Nor was escape possible. A profound concept of imagination was entirely lacking to Kant's system and his philosophy of the spirit. Glancing over the table of faculties of the spirit which precedes his *Critique of Judgment*, we see that Kant co-ordinates with it the cognitive faculty, the feeling of pleasure and pain, and the appetitive faculty ; to the first corresponds intellect, to the second, judgement (teleological and æsthetic), to the third, reason ; [4] he finds no place for imagination amongst powers of the spirit but places it among the facts of sensation. He knows a reproductive imagination and an associative, but he knows nothing of a genuinely productive imagination, imagination in the proper sense.[5] We have seen that, in his doctrine, genius is the co-operation of several faculties.

Imagination in Kant's system.

Yet sometimes Kant had an inkling that intellectual

---

[1] *Krit. d. Urth.* § 48. [2] *Op. cit.* § 17. [3] *Op. cit.* § 16.

[4] For the historical genesis of this tripartition, cf. remarks in Schlapp, *op. cit.* pp. 150-153.

[5] See also *Anthropol.* (ed. Kirchmann), §§ 26-31 ; cf. Schlapp, *op. cit.* p. 296.

activity is preceded by something which is not mere sensational material, but is an independent non-intellectual theoretical form.   He obtained a glimpse of this latter form not when he was reflecting on art in the strict sense but when he was examining the process of knowledge : he does not treat of it in his *Critique of Judgment*, but in the first section of his *Critique of Pure Reason*, in the first part of the *Transcendental Doctrine of Elements*.   He says here that sensations only enter the spirit when the latter itself gives them form ; a form not identical with that which intellect gives to sensations, but much simpler, namely pure intuition, the totality of the *a priori* principles of sensibility.   There must therefore be " a science which forms the first part of the transcendental doctrine of elements, distinct from that which contains the principles of pure thought and is named transcendental Logic."   Now, what name does Kant confer upon this science whose existence he has deduced ?   None other than Transcendental Æsthetic (*die transcendentale Ästhetik*).   In a note he even insists that this is the right name for the new science of which he treats, and censures the Germans for their habit of applying it to the Critique of Taste, which, as he thought at that time, could never become a science.   Thus, he concludes, we approach more closely to the usage of the ancients, among whom the distinction between αἰσθητὰ καὶ νοητά [1] was well known.

Nevertheless, after having so rightly postulated the necessity for a science of the forms of sensation or pure intuition, purely intuitive knowledge, Kant went on, simply because he had no exact idea of the nature of the æsthetic faculty and of art, to fall into an intellectualistic error by reducing the form of sensibility or pure intuition into the two categories or functions of space and time, and by asserting that the spirit emerges from the chaos of sensation by organizing its sensations in space and time.[2]   But space and time as such are very far from being primitive categories ; they are relatively late and complex forma-

---

[1] *Kritik d. rein. Vernunft*, i. 1, § 1 and note.
[2] *Op. cit.* §§ 1-8.

tions.[1] As examples of the matter of sensation Kant
quoted hardness, impenetrability, colour and so forth.
But the mind only recognizes colour and hardness in so
far as it has already given form to its sensations ; considered as brute matter, sensations fall outside the cognitive spirit, they are a limit ; colour, hardness, impenetrability and so on, when recognized, are already intuitions,
spiritual elaborations, the æsthetic activity in its rudimentary manifestation. The characterizing or qualifying
imagination which is æsthetic activity ought to have
occupied in the *Critique of Pure Reason* the pages devoted
to the discussion of space and time, and would thus have
constituted a real Transcendental Æsthetic, a real prologue
to the transcendental Logic. In this manner Kant would
have achieved the truth aimed at by Leibniz and Baumgarten and would have joined hands with Vico.

His repeatedly announced opposition to the school of *Theory of*
Wolff concerns not the concept of art but that of Beauty ; *Beauty*
two concepts for Kant entirely distinct. First of all, he *by Kant from*
did not admit that sensation could be called " confused *that of Art.*
knowledge," a confused form, that is, of intellectual
cognition ; rightly judging this to be a false account of
sensibility, since a concept, however confused, is always
a concept or a rough sketch of a concept, never an intuition.[2] But he further denied that pure beauty contained
a concept, and therefore denied that it was a perfection
sensibly apprehended. These reflexions have no doubt
some connexion with those concerning the nature of art in
the *Critique of Judgment* ; but the connexion is far from
close, still less are they actually fused into a single whole.
That Kant was minutely familiar with eighteenth-century
writers who had discussed beauty and taste is shown by
his Lectures, wherein they are all quoted and used.[3] Of
these the greater part, especially the English, were sensationalists, others intellectualists ; some few, as we have
noted, were inclined towards mysticism. Kant began

---

[1] See above, pp. 4-5.
[2] *Krit. d. r. Vern.* § 8, and introd. to § ii. ; cf. *Krit. d. Urth.* § 15.
[3] See catalogue in Schlapp, *op. cit.* pp. 403-404, and *passim*.

by tending towards sensationalism in æsthetic problems, then became the adversary of sensationalists and intellectualists alike. This development can be traced in his *Observations on the Beautiful and Sublime*, as well as in his Lectures ; its final expression is reached in the *Critique of Judgment*.

Of the four moments, as he calls them, *i.e.* the four determinations, he accords to Beauty, the two negative are directed, one against the sensationalists, the other against the intellectualists. "That is beautiful which pleases *without interest*" : " That is beautiful which pleases *without concepts*." [1] Here he asserts the existence of a spiritual region, distinct on one side from the pleasurable, the useful and the good, and on the other from truth. But this region, as we know very well, is not that of art, which Kant attaches to the concept : it is the region of a special activity of feeling which he calls judgement or, more exactly, æsthetic judgement.

Mystical features in Kant's theory of Beauty.

The other two moments give some kind of a definition of this region : " That is beautiful which has the form of finality without the representation of an end " : " That is beautiful which is the object of universal pleasure." [2] What is this mysterious sphere ? What this disinterested pleasure we experience in pure colours and tones, in flowers, and even in adherent beauty when we make abstraction from the concept to which it adheres ?

Our answer is : there is no such sphere ; it does not exist ; the examples given are instances either of pleasure in general or of facts of artistic expression. Kant, who so emphatically criticizes the sensationalists and the intellectualists, does not show the same severity towards the neo-Platonic line of thought whose revival we remarked in the eighteenth century. Winckelmann in particular exercised strong influence over his mind. In one course of his Lectures we find him making a curious distinction between form and matter : in music melody is matter and harmony form : in a flower the scent is material and the shape (*Gestalt*) is form (*Form*). [3] This

[1] *Krit. d. Urth.* §§ 1-9. [2] *Op. cit.* §§ 10-22. [3] Schlapp, *op. cit.* p. 78.

reappears slightly modified in the *Critique of Judgment*. " In painting, statuary and all the figurative arts in architecture and gardening, so far as they are fine arts, the drawing is the essential ; in which the foundation of taste lies not in what gratifies (*vergnügt*) in sensation, but in that which pleases (*gefällt*) by its form. The colours which illuminate the drawing belong to sensuous stimulus (*Reiz*) and may bring the object more vividly before the senses, but do not render it worthy of contemplation as a thing of beauty ; they are, moreover, often limited by the exigencies of the beautiful form, and even where their sensuous stimulus is legitimate, they are ennobled only by the beautiful form." [1] Continuing in pursuit of this phantasm of beauty which is not the beauty of art nor yet the pleasing, and is equally detached from expressiveness and pleasure, Kant loses himself in insoluble contradictions. Little inclined to submit himself to the charm of imagination, abhorring " poetic philosophers " like Herder,[2] he makes statements and refuses to commit himself to them, affirms and immediately criticizes his affirmations, and wraps up Beauty in a mystery which, at bottom, was nothing more than his own individual incertitude and inability to see clearly the existence of an activity of feeling which, in the spirit of his sane philosophy, represented a logical contradiction. " Necessary and universal pleasure " and " finality without the idea of an end " are the organized expression in words of this contradiction.

By way of clearing up the contradiction he arrives at the following thought : " The judgement of taste is founded on a concept (the concept of a general foundation of the subjective teleology of nature through judgement) ; but it is a concept by which it is impossible to know or demonstrate anything of the object, because the object in itself is indeterminable and unsuited to cognition ; on the other hand, it has validity for every one (for every one, I say, in

[1] *Krit. d. Urth.* § 14.
[2] For Kant's judgement of Herder, see Schlapp, *op. cit.* pp. 320-327, note.

so far as it is an individual judgement, immediately accompanying intuition), since its determining reason reposes, perhaps, in the concept of that which may be regarded as the supersensible substrate of mankind." Beauty, then, is a symbol of morality. " The subjective principle alone, that is the indeterminate idea of the supersensible in us, can be considered the only key able to unlock this faculty springing from a source we cannot fathom : excepting by its aid, no comprehension of it can possibly be reached." [1]

These cautious words, and all others here used by Kant to conceal his thoughts, do not hide his tendency to mysticism. A mysticism without conviction or enthusiasm, almost in spite of himself, but very evident nevertheless. His inadequate grasp of the æsthetic activity led him to see double, even triple, and caused the unnecessary multiplication of his explanatory principles. Although he was always ignorant of the genuine nature of the æsthetic activity, he was indebted to it for suggesting to him the pure categories of space and time as the Transcendental Æsthetic ; it caused him to develop the theory of imaginative embellishment of intellectual concepts by the work of genius ; finally it forced him to acknowledge a mysterious faculty of feeling, midway between theoretical and practical activity, cognitive and yet not cognitive, moral and indifferent to morality, pleasing yet wholly detached from the pleasure of the senses. Great use of this power was made by Kant's immediate successors in Germany who were delighted to find their daring speculations supported by that severe critic of experience, the philosopher of Königsberg.

[1] *Kritik d. Urth.* §§ 57-59.

IX

THE ÆSTHETIC OF IDEALISM : SCHILLER, SCHELLING, SOLGER, HEGEL

IT is well known that Schelling held the *Critique of Judgment* to be the most important of the three Kantian *Critiques*, and that Hegel together with the great majority of the followers of metaphysical idealism had a special affection for the book. According to them the third *Critique* was the attempt to bridge the gulf, to resolve the antitheses between liberty and necessity, teleology and mechanism, spirit and nature : it was the correction Kant was preparing for himself, the concrete vision which dispelled the last traces of his abstract subjectivism. *The " Critique of Judgment " and metaphysical idealism.*

The same admiration and an opinion even more *F. Schiller.* favourable were extended by them to Friedrich Schiller, the first to elaborate that part of Kant's philosophy and to study the third sphere which united sensibility to reason. " It was the artistic sense dwelling in his also profoundly philosophical mind," says Hegel, " which, against the abstract infinity of Kant's thought, against his living for duty, against his conception of nature and reality, and of sense and feeling as utterly hostile to intellect, asserted the necessity and enunciated the principle of totality and reconciliation, even before it had been recognized by professed philosophers : to Schiller must be allowed the great merit of having been the first to oppose the subjectivity of Kant, and of having dared try to go beyond it." [1]

Discussion has raged around the true relation between

---

[1] *Vorles. über die Ästhetik* (2nd ed., Berlin, 1842), vol. i. p. 78.

*Relations
between
Schiller and
Kant.* Schiller and Kant, and it has lately been maintained that his Æsthetic was not, as would seem to be the case, derived from Kant, but from the pandynamism which, starting from Leibniz, had propagated itself in Germany through Creuzens, Ploucket and Reimarus down to Herder, who had conceived a wholly animated nature.[1] There can be no doubt that Schiller shared Herder's conception, as may be seen from the theosophical tone of the fragment of correspondence between Julius and Raphael and in other writings. It cannot be denied, however, that whatever personal feelings Kant may have had towards Herder, or Herder towards his former teacher (against whose *Critique of Judgment* he published his *Kaligone,* as he had replied to the *Critique of Pure Reason* with his *Metacritica*), when Kant in a somewhat dubious manner made the first step towards a reconciliation, the breach was at all events partially healed. The dispute is therefore of small importance : we shall find it more useful to observe that Schiller introduced an important correction of Kant's views when he obliterated every trace of the double theory of art and the beautiful, giving no weight to the distinction drawn between pure and adherent beauty, and finally abandoning the mechanical conception of art as consisting in beauty joined to the intellectual concept. It was certainly his own experience of active artistic work that led him to this simplification.

*The æsthetic
sphere as the
sphere of Play.* Schiller defined the æsthetic sphere as the sphere of play (*Spiel*) ; the unfortunate term, suggested to him partly by some phrases of Kant, partly, perhaps, by an article on card-games by one Weisshuhn which he published in his review *The Hours* (*Die Horen*),[2] has given rise to the belief that he anticipated certain modern doctrines of artistic activity as the overflow of exuberant spirits, analogous with the play of children and animals. Schiller did not fail to warn his readers against such a mistaken interpretation (to which, however, he lent himself) when he begged them not to think of " games in

---

[1] Sommer, *Gesch. d. Psych. u. Ästh.* pp. 365-432.
[2] Danzel, *Ges. Aufs.* p. 242.

real life, which are usually concerned with wholly material things," nor yet of the idle dreaming of the imagination left to itself.[1] The activity of the play of which he treated held the mean between the material activity of the senses, of nature, of animal instinct or passion as it is called, and the formal activity of intellect and morality. The man who plays, *i.e.* contemplates nature æsthetically and produces art, sees all natural objects as animated ; in such a phantasmagoria mere natural necessity gives place to the free determination of the faculties ; spirit appears as spontaneously reconciled with nature, form with matter. Beauty is life, the living form (*lebende Gestalt*) ; not life in the physiological sense, since beauty does not extend throughout all physiological life, nor is it restricted to that alone : marble when worked by an artist may have a living form ; and a man, although possessed of life and form, need not be a living form.[2] Wherefore art must conquer nature with form : " in an artistic work of true beauty the content ought to be nil, the form everything : by form man is influenced in his entirety ; by content in his separate faculties only. The true secret of great artists is that they cancel matter through form (*den Stoff durch die Form vertilgt*) ; the more imposing, overwhelming or seductive the matter is in itself, the greater its obstinacy in striving to emphasize its own particular effect, the more the spectator inclines to lose himself immediately in the matter, so much the more triumphant is the art which brings it into subjection and enforces its own sovereign power. The mind of hearer or spectator should remain perfectly free and calm ; from the magic circle of art it should issue as pure and perfect as when it left the hands of the Creator. The most frivolous object should be treated in such a manner as to enable us to pass at once to the most serious matters ; and the most serious in such a way that we may pass from them to the lightest game." There is a fine art of passion ; a passionate fine art would be a

---

[1] *Briefe üb d. ästh. Erzieh.* (in *Werke*, ed. Goedecke), Letters 15, 27.
[2] *Op. cit.* Letter 15.

contradiction in terms.[1] " So long as man in his early physical state passively absorbs the world of senses and simply feels it, he is one with it ; and precisely because he merely is a world there is for him as yet no world at all. Only when in his æsthetic state he places the world outside himself and contemplates it, does he detach his personality from the rest ; then a world appears to him, since he is no longer one with the world." [2]

Æsthetic education.   Schiller ascribed high educational value to art thus conceived as at once sensible and rational, material and formal. Not that it teaches moral precepts or excites to good actions ; if it acted thus, or when it acted thus, it would at once cease, as we have seen, to be art. Determination in whatsoever direction, to the good or the bad, to pleasure or to duty, destroys the character of the æsthetic sphere, which is rather indeterminism. By means of art man frees himself from the yoke of the senses ; but before putting himself spontaneously under that of reason and duty, he takes as it were a little breathing-space by staying in a region of indifference and serene contemplation. " While having no claim to promote exclusively any special human faculty, the æsthetic condition is favourable to each and all without favouritism ; and the reason why it favours none in particular is that it is the foundation of the possibility of all alike. Every other exercise gives some inclination to the soul, and therefore presupposes a special limit ; æsthetic activity alone is unlimited." This indifference, which if not yet pure form is not pure matter, confers its educational value on art ; it opens a way to morality, not by preaching and persuading, that is to say, determining, but by making determination possible. Such is the fundamental concept of his celebrated *Letters on the Æsthetic Education of Man* (1795), in which Schiller took his cue from the conditions of his times and from the necessity of finding a middle way between supine acquiescence in tyranny and savage rebellion as exemplified by the revolution then raging in France.

[1] *Briefe,* Letter 22.   [2] *Op. cit.* Letter 25.

The defects of Schiller's æsthetic doctrine are its lack of precision and its generality.   Who has given a better description of certain aspects of art, the catharsis produced by artistic activity, the serenity and calm resulting from the domination over natural impressions ?   Equally just is his remark that art, although wholly independent of morality, is in some way connected with it.   But what precisely this connexion may be, or what the exact nature of æsthetic activity, Schiller does not succeed in explaining.   Conceiving the moral and intellectual as the only formal activities (*Formtrieb*) and denying as a convinced anti-sensationalist in opposition to Burke and philosophers of his type that art can belong to the passionate and sensuous nature (*Stofftrieb*), he cut himself off from the means of recognizing the general category to which artistic activity belongs.   His own concept of the formal is too narrow : too narrow, also, his concept of the cognitive activity, in which he is able to see the logical or intellectual form, but not that of the imagination. What for him was this art he describes as an activity neither formal nor material, neither cognitive nor moral ? Was it for him, as for Kant, an activity of feeling, a play of several faculties at once ?   It would seem so, since Schiller distinguishes four points of view or relations of man with things : the physical, in which these affect our senses : the logical, in which they excite knowledge : the moral, in which they appear to us as an object of rational volition : and the æsthetic " in which they refer to our powers in entirety without becoming the determinate object of any one faculty."   For example, a man is pleased æsthetically when his feeling depends in no way on the pleasure of the senses and when he is not conscious of thinking about any law or end.[1]   We look in vain for any more conclusive reply.

It must not be overlooked that Schiller delivered a course of lectures on Æsthetic in Jena University in 1792, and that his writings on the subject intended for reviews were couched in a popular style : no less popular,

[1] *Briefe*, Letter 20.

in his own opinion, was the style of the book quoted above, which grew out of a series of letters actually sent to his patron the Duke of Holstein-Augustenburg. But the great work to be entitled *Kallias*, which he intended writing upon Æsthetic, was never completed ; the only fragments which have reached us are contained in the correspondence with Körner (1793-1794). From the discussions between the two friends we gather that Körner was not satisfied with Schiller's formula and desired something objective, something more precise, a positive characteristic of the beautiful : and one day Schiller told him that he had definitely discovered such a characteristic. But what it was that he had discovered we do not know ; no mention of it occurs in any further document, and we are left in doubt as to whether we have lost an integral part of his thought or merely the momentary illusion of a discovery.

Schiller's caution and the rashness of the Romanticists.

The uncertainty and vagueness of Schiller's theory seem almost a merit in contrast with that which followed. He had constituted himself guardian of the teaching of Kant and refused to abandon the realm of criticism ; faithful disciple of his master, he conceived the third sphere not as real but as an ideal, a concept not constitutive but regulative, an imperative. " From transcendental motives, reason here demands that communion be established between formal and material activity ; that is to say, there must be an activity of play, since the concept of humanity can be complete only by the union of reality with form, the accidental with the necessary, passivity with liberty. This demand must be made because reason, in conformity with her essence, aims at perfection and at sweeping away all obstacles ; and every exclusive operation of one or other activity leaves humanity incomplete and confined within limits." [1] Schiller's thought, as it appears in his correspondence with Körner, has been well represented as follows : " The union of sensibility with liberty in the Beautiful, which does not actually take place but is supposed to do

[1] *Briefe*, Letter 15.

so, suggests to man an intuition of the union of these
elements within himself : a union which does not take
place actually but ought to do so." [1] The times which
followed had no such nice scruples. Kant had given new
vigour to the production of works on æsthetic, and, as
in the days following Baumgarten, every new year saw
a number of new treatises. It was the fashion. " Nothing
swarms like æstheticians " (wrote Jean Paul Richter in
1804 when preparing his own book on the subject for
publication) : " it is rare for a youth who has paid his
fees for a course of lectures on Æsthetic not to produce
a book on some point of the science in the hope that the
public may refund him his expenses by buying his book :
some there are indeed who pay their professor's fees
out of their author's royalties." [2] It was hoped, not
unreasonably, that the exploration of the obscure region
of æsthetic might throw some light on metaphysics, and
the procedure of artists seemed to offer a good example
to philosophers seeking to create a world for themselves :
so philosophy modelled itself upon art and, as though to
render the transition easier, the concept of art was brought
as close as possible to that of philosophy. Romanticism,
gaining vogue daily, was a renewal or continuation of
that " age of genius " in which the youth of Goethe and
Schiller had been passed ; and as the period of *Sturm
und Drang* had zealously worshipped the genius who
breaks all rules and oversteps all limitations, so did
Romanticism hail the domination of a faculty called
Fancy, or more frequently Imagination, to which were
attributed the most diverse characteristics and the most
miraculous effects.

The Romantic theorists, artists themselves for the *Ideas on Art :*
most part, abounded in truthful and subtle observations *J. P. Richter.*
concerning artistic procedure. Jean Paul Richter makes
many excellent remarks about productive imagination,
which he distinguishes clearly from the reproductive and

[1] Danzel, *Ges. Aufs.* p. 241.
[2] *Vorschule der Ästh.*, 1804 (French trans., *Poétique ou introduction
à l'Esth.*, Paris, 1862), preface.

asserts to be shared by all men as soon as they are able to say " This is beautiful " ; for " how could a genius be acclaimed or even tolerated for a single month, not to mention thousands of centuries, by the common herd, if he had not a strong connecting-link of relationship with the herd ? " He also describes how imagination is variously divided among individuals : as simple talent, as passive or feminine genius, and in the highest degree as the active or masculine genius, formed by reflexion and instinct, in which " all faculties flourish simultaneously and fancy is no isolated flower, but the goddess Flora herself who, in order to produce new combinations, crosses with each other those blossoms whose conjunction is fertile, and is, so to speak, a faculty full of faculties." [1] This latter sentence betrays a tendency on Richter's part to exaggerate the functions of imagination and to construct

Romantic Æsthetic and idealistic Æsthetic.

upon it a kind of mythology. Contemporary systems of philosophy are partly impregnated with, and partly the source of, such mythologies : the Romantic conception of art may be said to have found its most complete expression in German idealism, where this attained its most coherent and systematic form.

J. G. Fichte.

It did not attain this form with Fichte, the first great pupil of Kant ; for though Fichte regarded imagination as the activity which creates the universe, effects the synthesis of the ego and the non-ego, posits the object and therefore precedes consciousness, he does not connect it with art.[2] In his æsthetic notions Fichte is influenced by Schiller, with the addition of a moralism imposed upon him by the general character of his system ; hence the ethical sphere, midway between the cognitive and the æsthetic, becomes from his point of view a mere appurtenance of morality, as being the representation of, and hence reverence for, the moral ideal.[3] His subjective idealism eventually produced an æsthetic doctrine through

[1] *Vorschule d. Ästh.* chs. 2, 3.
[2] *Grundl. der Wissenschaftslehre*, in *Werke* (Berlin, 1845), vol. i. pp. 214-217.
[3] Danzel, *Ges. Aufs.* pp. 25-30 ; Zimmermann, *G. d. Ä.* pp. 522-572.

the work of Friedrich Schlegel and Ludwig Tieck ; the *Irony :*
doctrine of Irony as the basis of art. The ego which *Schlegel,*
created the universe can also destroy it ; the universe is *Novalis.*
an empty appearance at which the only true reality,
the ego, can smile, holding itself aloof, like an artist or a
creative god, from creatures of its own which it does not
take seriously.[1] Friedrich Schlegel described art as a
perpetual parody of itself and a " transcendental farce."
Tieck defined irony as " a power which allows the poet
to dominate the matter which he handles."   Another
Romantic Fichtian, Novalis, dreamed of a magical
idealism, an art of creation by the instantaneous act of
the ego and of realizing our dreams. But it is only to
the *System of Transcendental Idealism* (1800) of Schelling, *F. Schelling.*
to his *Bruno* (1802), to his celebrated course of lectures
on the *Philosophy of Art* given at Jena in 1802–1803
(repeated at Würzburg, and distributed subsequently in
manuscript notes all over Germany), to the no less celebrated lecture on the *Relation between the Figurative Arts
and Nature* (1807), as well as to other works of this eloquent
and enthusiastic philosopher that we owe the first great
philosophical affirmation of Romanticism, and of a renewed and conscious neo-Platonism in Æsthetic.

   Like all the other idealistic philosophers, Schelling held *Beauty and*
firmly to the fusion of the theories of art and the beautiful *character.*
already effected by Schiller. From this point of view it
is interesting to note his explanation of the condemnation of art by Plato : this condemnation, says Schelling,
was directed against the art of his time, the natural and
realistic art of antiquity in general, with its character of
finitude : Plato could not have uttered such a condemnation (as we moderns are unable to utter it) if he had
known Christian art, whose characteristic is infinity.[2]
The pure abstract beauty of Winckelmann is not enough ;
no less inadequate, false and negative is that concept of
the characteristic which would try to make art some-

---

[1] Hegel, *Vorles. üb. d. Ästh.* introd. vol. i. pp. 82-88.
[2] *Vorles. üb. d. Methode d. akadem. Stud.* (1803), lecture 14 ; in
Werke (Stuttgart, 1856–1861), vol. v. pp. 346-347.

thing dead, hard and ugly by imposing upon it the limitations of the individual. Art is beauty and characteristic in one ; characteristic beauty, character from which beauty is evolved, according to Goethe's saying ; it is therefore not the individual but the living concept of the individual. When the artist's eye recognizes the creative idea of the individual and draws it forth, he transforms the individual into a world in itself, into a species (*Gattung*), an eternal idea (*Urbild*), and fears no more the limitation or hardness which is the condition of life : characteristic beauty is that plenitude of form which kills form ; it does not inflame passion, it regulates it, like the banks of a river which are filled but not overflowed by the waters.[1] In all of this we feel the influence of Schiller, with something added which Schiller could never have expressed. Indeed, whilst gratefully acknowledging the excellent contributions to the theory of art made by the writers who succeeded Kant, Schelling laments that in none of them can he find exact scientific method (*Wissenschaftlichkeit*).[2] The true point of departure in his theory is in the philosophy of nature, *i.e.* in that criticism of the teleological judgement which Kant places directly after that of the æsthetic judgement in his third *Critique*. Teleology is the union of theoretical and practical philosophy ; but the system would be incomplete but for the possibility of demonstrating in the subject itself, in the ego, the identity of the two worlds, theoretical and practical ; an activity which has, and at the same time has not, consciousness ; unconscious as nature, conscious as spirit. This activity is precisely the æsthetic activity : "the general organ of philosophy, keystone of the whole edifice."[3] There are but two ways open to one who is desirous of escaping from common realities : poetry, which transports into the ideal world ; and philosophy which annihilates the real world.[4] Strictly

Art and Philosophy.

[1] *Üb. d. Verhältniss d. bild. Künste, z. d. Natur* in *Werke*, vol. vii. pp. 299-310.

[2] *Philos. d. Kunst*, posthumous, introd. in *Werke*, v. p. 362.

[3] *System d. transcend. Idealismus*, in *Werke*, § i. vol. iii. introd. § 3, p. 349.   [4] *Op. cit.* § 4, p. 351.

speaking, " there is but one sole absolute work of art ; it may exist in various exemplars, but in itself it is one, although it may not yet possess existence in its original form." True art is not the impression of one moment, but the representation of infinite life ; [1] it is transcendental intuition become objective, and is therefore not only the organ but the document of philosophy. A time will come when philosophy will return to poetry, from which she has detached herself ; and from the new philosophy a new mythology will arise.[2] The Absolute is thus the object of art as well as of philosophy (as Schelling insists elsewhere in greater detail) : the first represents it in idea (*Urbild*), the second in its reflexion (*Gegenbild*) : " philosophy portrays ideas, not realities : so is it with art : those same ideas of which real things, as philosophy demonstrates, are imperfect copies, themselves appear in the objective arts as ideas, *i.e.* in all their perfection, and represent the intellectual world in the world of reflexion." [3] Music is the " very ideal rhythm of Nature and the Universe, which by means of this art makes itself felt in the derivative world " ; perfect creations of statuary are " the very ideas of organic nature represented objectively " ; the Homeric epic, " the very identity constituting the foundation of history in the Absolute." [4] But while philosophy gives an immediate representation of the Divine, of absolute Identity, art can but give the immediate representation of Indifference ; and " since the degree of perfection or reality in a thing becomes higher in proportion as it approaches nearer to the absolute Idea and the fulness of infinite affirmation and in proportion as it comprehends within itself other powers, it is clear that art, above everything else, is in closest relation with philosophy, from which it is distinguished merely by the character of its specification : in everything else it may be considered as the highest power in the ideal world." [5] To the three powers

[1] *System d. transcend. Idealismus*, in *Werke*, part vi. § 3, p. 627.
[2] *Op. cit.* §. 3, pp. 627-629.   [3] *Phil. d. Kunst*, pp. 368-369.
[4] *Op. cit.* p. 369.   [5] *Op. cit.* General Part, p. 381.

of the real and ideal world correspond in a rising scale the three ideas of Truth, Goodness and Beauty. Beauty is neither the mere universal (truth), nor mere reality (action), but the perfect interpenetration of both: "beauty exists when the particular (the real) is so adequate to its concept that the latter, as infinite, enters the finite and presents itself to our contemplation in concrete form. With the appearance of the concept, the real becomes truly similar and equal to the idea, wherein the universal and the particular find their absolute identity. Without ceasing to be rational, the rational becomes at the same time apparent and sensible."[1] But as above the three powers is poised God, their point of union, so Philosophy stands supreme over the three ideas; concerning itself not with truth or morality or even beauty alone, but with that which belongs to all the three in common, deduced from one common source. If philosophy assumes the character of science and truth, while yet remaining superior to truth, this is made possible by the fact that science and truth are its formal determination; "philosophy is science in the sense that truth, goodness and beauty, *i.e.* science, virtue and art, interpenetrate each other; therefore it is also not science but is that which is common to science, virtue and art." This interpenetration distinguishes philosophy from all other sciences; for instance, if mathematics can dispense with morality and beauty, philosophy cannot do so.[2]

Ideas and the gods. Art and mythology.
In Beauty are contained truth and goodness, necessity and liberty. When beauty appears to be in conflict with truth, the truth in question is a finite truth with which beauty ought not to agree, because, as we have seen, the art of naturalism and of the merely characteristic is a false art.[3] The individual forms of art, being in themselves representatives of the infinite and the universe, are called Ideas.[4] Considered from the point of view of reality, Ideas are gods; their essence, their "in-itself," is in fact equivalent to God; every idea is an idea so

---

[1] *Phil. d. Kunst*, p. 382.   [2] *Op. cit.* p. 383.
[3] *Op. cit.* p. 385.   [4] *Op. cit.* pp. 389-390.

far as it is God in a particular form ; every idea, therefore, is equal to God, but to a particular god. Characteristic of all the gods is pure limitation and indivisible absoluteness : Minerva is the idea of wisdom united with strength, but she is lacking in womanly tenderness ; Juno is power without wisdom and without the sweet attraction of love, for which she is forced to borrow the cestus of Venus ; Venus again has not the weighty wisdom of Minerva. What would become of these ideas if deprived of their limitations ? They would cease to be objects of Imagination.[1] Imagination is a faculty which has no connexion with pure intellect or with reason (*Vernunft*) and is distinct from fancy (*Einbildungskraft*) which collects and arranges the products of art, whereas imagination intuits them, forms them out of itself, represents them. Imagination is to fancy as intellectual intuition is to reason : it is therefore the intellectual intuition of art.[2] " Reason " no longer suffices in a philosophy such as this : intellectual intuition, which for Kant was a limiting concept, is now asserted as really existing : intellect sinks to a subordinate place : even the genuine imagination which operates in art is overshadowed by this new-fangled Imagination, twin with intellectual Intuition, who sometimes changes places with this sister of hers. Mythology is proclaimed a necessary condition of all art : mythology which is not allegory, for in the latter the particular signifies only the universal, while the former is already itself the universal ; which explains how easy it is to allegorize, and how fascinating are such poems as those of Homer which lend themselves to such interpretations. Christian, as well as Hellenic, art has its mythology : Christ ; the persons of the Trinity ; the Virgin mother of God.[3] The line between mythology and art is as shadowy as that between art and philosophy.

The year 1815 saw the publication of Solger's principal K. W. *Solger.* work, *Erwin*, a long philosophical dialogue on the beautiful;

[1] *Phil. d. Kunst*, pp. 390-393.
[2] *Op. cit.* p. 395.
[3] *Op. cit.* pp. 405-451.

subsequently in 1819 he gave a course of lectures on Æsthetic which were published posthumously. He was one of those who found but a glimpse of truth in Kant and held the post-Kantians in very slight estimation, particularly Fichte ; in Schelling, who begins from the original unity of the subjective and the objective, he detects for the first time a speculative principle not adequately developed, since Schelling had never triumphed dialectically over the difficulties of intellectual intuition.[1]

Fancy and Imagination. Solger was one of those who conceived of Imagination as totally distinct from Fancy : fancy (says he) belongs to common cognition and is none other than " the human consciousness, in so far as it continues, in temporal succession, infinitely reasserting an original intuition " ; it presupposes the distinctions between common cognition, abstraction and judgement, concept and representation, amongst which " it acts as mediator by giving to the general concept the form of individual representation ; and to the latter the form of a general concept ; in this manner it has its being among the antitheses of the ordinary understanding." Imagination is totally different ; proceeding " from the original unity of the antitheses in the Idea, it acts so that the elements in opposition, separated as they are from the idea, find themselves united in the reality ; by its means we are capable of apprehending objects higher than those of common cognition and of recognizing in them the idea itself as real : also, in art, it is the faculty of transforming the idea into reality." It presents itself in three modes or degrees : as Imagination of the Imagination, which conceives the whole as idea, and activity as nothing more than the development of the idea in reality ; as Sensibility of the Imagination, in so far as it expresses the life of the idea in the real and reduces the one to the other ; lastly (and here we have the highest grade of artistic activity, corresponding with Dialectic in philosophy), as Intellect of the Imagination or artistic Dialectic, conceiving idea and reality in such a way that one passes

[1] *Vorles. üb. Ästhetik*, Heyse, Leipzig, 1829, pp. 35-43.

over into the other, that is to say, into reality. Other divisions and subdivisions are made on which it is not necessary to dwell. Imagination is said to produce the Irony essential to true art : this is the Irony of Tieck and Novalis, of whom Solger is in a sense a follower.[1]

Solger joins Schelling in placing beauty in the region of the Idea, inaccessible to common consciousness. It *Art, practice and religion.* is distinct from the idea of Truth, because instead of dissolving the appearances of common consciousness after the manner of truth, art accomplishes the miracle of making appearance dissolve itself while still remaining appearance ; artistic thought, therefore, is practical, not theoretical.   Furthermore, it is distinct from the idea of Goodness, with which at first sight it would seem to be closely related, because in the case of Goodness the union of ideal with real, of the simple with the multiple, of the infinite with the finite, is not real and complete, but remains ideal, a mere ought-to-be.   It is related more closely to Religion, which thinks the Idea as the abyss of life where our individual conscience must lose itself in order to become " essential " (*wesentlich*), while in beauty and art the Idea manifests itself by gathering into itself the world of distinctions between universal and particular and placing itself in their place.   Artistic activity is more than theoretical, it is of a practical nature, but realized and perfected ; art, therefore, belongs not to theoretical philosophy (as Kant thought, according to Solger), but to practical.   Necessarily attached on one side to infinity, it cannot have common nature as its object ; for example, art is absent from a portrait, and the ancients showed their discrimination in selecting gods and heroes for objects in sculpture since every deity —even in limited and particular form—always signifies a determinate modification of the Idea.[2]

The same concept of art appears in the philosophy *G.W.F.Hegel.* of Hegel, whatever may be the minor differences which he felt to separate himself from his predecessors.   Little concerned as we are with the shades and varieties of

[1] *Vorles. üb. Asth.* pp. 186-200.   [2] *Op. cit.* pp. 48-85.

mystical Æsthetic exhibited by each of these thinkers,
we are chiefly concerned to lay bare the substantial
underlying identity, the mysticism of arbitrarism which
gives them their historic place in Æsthetic.   Opening the
Phenomenology and the *Philosophy of Spirit*, one need
not expect to find any discussion of art in the analysis
of the forms of the theoretical Spirit, among definitions
of sensibility and intuition, language and symbolism,
and various grades of imagination and thought.   Hegel
places Art in the sphere of absolute Spirit, together with
Religion and Philosophy,[1] and in this he regards Kant,
Schiller, Schelling and Solger as his precursors, for like
them he strongly denies that art has the function of
representing the abstract concept, but not that it represents the concrete concept or Idea.   Hegel's whole
philosophy consists in the affirmation of a concrete concept,
unknown to ordinary or scientific thought.   " Indeed,"
says he, " no concept has in our day been more mis-
handled than the concept in itself and for itself ; for by
concept is generally meant the abstract determinateness
or one-sidedness of representation and intellectualistic
thought, with which it is naturally impossible to think
either the entirety of truth or concrete beauty." [2]   To
the realm of the concrete concept belongs art, as one of
the three forms wherein the freedom of the spirit is
achieved ; it is the first form, namely that of immediate,
sensible, objective knowledge (the second is religion, a
representative consciousness *plus* worship, an element
extraneous to mere art : the third is philosophy, free
thought of the absolute spirit).[3]   Beauty and truth are
at the same time one yet distinct.   " Truth is Idea as
Idea, according to its being-in-itself and its universal
principle, and so far as it is thought as such.   There is
no sensible or material existence in Truth ; thought
contemplates therein nothing but universal idea.   But
the Idea must also realize itself externally and attain an
actual and determinate existence.   Truth also as such

Art in the
sphere of
absolute spirit.

Beauty as
sensible
appearance
of the Idea.

---

[1] *Encykl. d. phil. Wiss.* §§ 557-563.
[2] *Vorles. üb. Asth.* (*ed. cit.*) i, p. 118.   [3] *Op. cit.* i. pp. 129-133.

has existence ; but when in its determinate external
existence it is immediately for consciousness, and the
concept remains immediately one with the external
appearance, the Idea is not only true but beautiful.   In
this way Beauty may be defined as the sensible appearance of the Idea." [1] The Idea is the content of art :
its sensible and imaginative configuration ; its form : two
elements which must interpenetrate and form a whole,
hence the necessity that a content destined to become a
work of art should show itself capable of such transformation ; otherwise we have but an imperfect union of
poetic form with prosaic and incongruous content.[2]   An
ideal content must gleam through the sensible form ;
the form is spiritualized by this ideal light ; [3] artistic
imagination does not work in the same way as the passive
or receptive fancy, it does not stop at the appearances
of sensible reality but searches for the internal truth
and rationality of the real.   " The rationality of the
object selected by him should not be alone in awakening
the consciousness of the artist : he should have well
meditated upon the essential and the true in all their
extension and profundity, for without reflexion a man
cannot become conscious of that which is within himself,
and all great works of art show that their material has
been thought again and again from every side.   No
successful work of art can issue from light and careless
imagination." [4]   It is a delusion to fancy that poet and
painter need nothing beyond intuitions : " a true poet
must reflect and meditate before and during the execution of his poem." [5]   But it is always understood
that the thought of the poet does not take the form of
abstraction.

Some critics [6] affirm that the æsthetic movement from
Schelling to Hegel is a revived Baumgartenism on the
ground that this movement regarded art as a mediator

*Æsthetic in
metaphysical
idealism and
Baumgarten-
ism.*

[1] *Vorles. üb. Ästh.* i. p. 141.   [2] *Op. cit.* i. p. 89.
[3] *Op. cit.* i. pp. 50-51.   [4] *Op. cit.* i. pp. 354-355.   [5] *Encykl.* § 450.
[6] Danzel, *Ästh. d. hegel. Sch.* p. 62 ; Zimmermann, *G. d. Ä.* pp.
693-697 ; J. Schmidt, *L. u. B.* pp. 103-105 ; Spitzer, *Krit. St.* p. 48.

of philosophical concepts ; they mention the fact that a follower of Schelling, one Ast, was moved by the trend of his system to substitute didactic poetry for drama as the highest form of art.[1] Putting aside some isolated and accidental deviations, there is no truth in this affirmation : these philosophers are hostile to intellectualistic and moralistic views, frequently entering upon definite and explicit polemic against them. Schelling wrote : " Æsthetic production is in its origin an absolutely free production. . . . This independence on any extraneous purpose constitutes the sanctity and purity of art, enabling it to repel all connexion with mere pleasure, a connexion which is a mark of barbarism, or with utility, which cannot be demanded of art save at times when the loftiest form of the human spirit is found in utilitarian discoveries. The same reasons forbid an alliance with morality and hold even science at arm's length, although nearest by reason of her disinterestedness ; having her aim, however, outside herself, she must restrict herself definitely to serve as means to something higher than herself : the arts." [2] Hegel says, " Art contains no universal as such." " If the aim of instruction is treated as an aim, so that the nature of the content represented appears for itself directly, as an abstract proposition, prosaic reflexion, or general theory, and is not merely contained indirectly and implicitly in the concrete artistic form, the result of such a separation is to reduce the sensible and imaginative form, the true constituent of a work of art, to an idle ornament, a covering (*Hülle*) presented simply as a covering, an appearance maintained as mere appearance. The very nature of the work of art is thus completely altered, for a work of art must not present to intuition a content in its universality, but this universal individualized and converted into a sensible individual." [3] It is a bad sign, he adds, when an artist

[1] Fr. Ast, *System der Kunstlehre*, Leipzig, 1805 ; cf. Spitzer, *op. cit.* p. 48.

[2] *System d. transcend. Idealismus* (1800), part vi. § 2 ; in *Werke*, § 1, vol. iii. pp. 622-623.

[3] *Vorles. üb. d. Ästh.* i. pp. 66-67.

sets himself about his work from a motive of abstract
ideas instead of that of the fulness of life (*Überfülle des
Lebens*).[1] The aim of art lies in itself, in presentation
of truth in a sensible form ; any other aim is altogether
extraneous.[2] It would not be hard to prove, certainly,
that by separating art from pure representation and
imagination and making it in some sense the vehicle of
the concept, the universal, the infinite, these philosophers
were facing in the direction of the road opened by Baumgarten.   But to prove this would mean accepting as a
presupposition the dilemma that if art be not pure
imagination, it must be sensuous and subordinate to
reason ; and it is just this presupposition and dilemma
that the metaphysical idealists denied.   The road they
tried to follow was to conceive a faculty which should
be neither imagination nor intellect but should partake
of both ; an intellectual intuition or intuitive intellect, a
mental imagination after the fashion of Plotinus.

In a greater degree than any of his predecessors Hegel
emphasized the cognitive character of art.   But this very
merit brought him into a difficulty more easily avoided
by the rest.   Art being placed in the sphere of absolute
Spirit, in company with Religion and Philosophy, how
will she be able to hold her own in such powerful and
aggressive company, especially in that of Philosophy,
which in the Hegelian system stands at the summit of all
spiritual evolution ?   If Art and Religion fulfilled functions other than the knowledge of the Absolute, they
would be inferior levels of the Spirit, but yet necessary
and indispensable.   But if they have in view the same
end as Philosophy and are allowed to compete with it,
what value can they retain ?   None whatever ; or, at
the very most, they may have that sort of value which
attaches to transitory historical phases in the life of
humanity.   The principles of Hegel's system are at
bottom rationalistic and hostile to religion, and hostile
no less to art.   A strange and painful consequence for a

Mortality and decay of art in Hegel's system.

---

[1] *Vorles. üb. d. Ästh.* i. p. 353.
[2] *Op. cit.* i. p. 72.

man like Hegel, endowed with a warmly æsthetic spirit
and a fervid lover of the arts ; almost a repetition of the
hard fate endured by Plato. But as the Greek philosopher,
in obedience to the presumed command of religion, did
not hesitate to condemn the mimetic art and the Homeric
poetry he loved, so the German refused to evade the
logical exigencies of his system and proclaimed the
mortality, nay, the very death, of art. " We have
assigned," he says, " a very high place to art : but it
must be recollected that neither in content nor in form
can art be considered the most perfect means of bringing
before the consciousness of the mind its true interests.
Precisely by reason of its form, art is limited to a particular content. Only a definite circle or grade of truth
can be made visible in a work of art ; that is to say, such
truth as may be transfused into the sensible and adequately presented in that form, as were the Greek gods.
But there is a deeper conception of truth, by which it
is not so intimately allied to the sensible as to permit
of its being received or expressed suitably in material
fashion. To this class belongs the Christian conception
of truth ; and, furthermore, the spirit of our modern
world, more especially that of our religion and our mental
evolution, seems to have passed the point at which art is
the best road to the apprehension of the Absolute. The
peculiar character of artistic production no longer satisfies our highest aspirations. . . . Thought and reflexion
have superseded fine art." Many reasons have been
adduced in order to account for the moribund condition
of modern art ; in especial, the prevalence of material and
political interests ; the true reason, says Hegel, consists
of the inferiority in grade of art in comparison with
pure thought. " Art in its highest form is and for us
must remain a thing of the past " ; and just because the
thing has vanished, one can reason about it philosophically.[1] The Æsthetic of Hegel is thus a funeral oration :
he passes in review the successive forms of art, shows
the progressive steps of internal consumption and lays

---

[1] *Vorles. üb. d. Asth.* i. pp. 13-16.

the whole in its grave, leaving Philosophy to write its epitaph.

Romanticism and metaphysical idealism had elevated art to such a fantastic height among the clouds that at last they were obliged to admit that it was so far away as to be absolutely useless.

X

SCHOPENHAUER AND HERBART

Æsthetic mysticism in the opponents of Idealism. NOTHING, perhaps, shows more clearly how well this imaginative conception of art suited the spirit of the times (not only a particular fashion in philosophy, but the psychological conditions expressed by the Romantic movement) than the fact that the adversaries of the systems of Schelling, Solger and Hegel either agreed with this conception in general or, while believing themselves to be departing widely from it, actually returned to it involuntarily.

A. Schopen-hauer. Everybody knows with what lack, shall we say, of *phlegma philosophicum* Arthur Schopenhauer fought against Schelling, Hegel and all the " charlatans " and " professors " who had divided amongst themselves the heritage of Kant. But what was the artistic theory *Ideas as the object of art.* accepted and developed by Schopenhauer ? His theory, like Hegel's own, turns upon the distinction between the concept which is abstraction and the concept which is concrete, or Idea ; although Schopenhauer's Ideas are by himself likened to Plato's, and in the particular form in which he presents them more nearly resemble those of Schelling than the Idea of Hegel. They have something in common with intellectual concepts, for like them they are unities representing a plurality of real things : but " the concept is abstract and discursive, entirely indeterminate in its sphere, rigorously precise within its own limits only ; the intellect suffices to conceive and understand it, speech expresses it without need for other intermediary, and its own definition exhausts its whole

nature ; the idea, on the contrary (which may be defined
clearly as the adequate representative of the concept) is
absolutely intuitive, and although it represents an infinite
number of individual things, it is not for that any the
less determined in all its aspects. The individual, as
individual, cannot know it ; in order to conceive it he
must strip himself of all will, of all individuality, and
raise himself to the state of a pure knowing subject.
The idea, therefore, is attained by genius only, or by one
who finds himself in a genial disposition attained by
that elevation of his cognitive powers inspired usually
by genius." " The idea is unity become plurality by
means of space and time, forms of one intuitive apperception ; the concept, on the contrary, is unity extracted
from plurality by means of abstraction, which is the
procedure of our intellect : the concept may be described
as *unitas post rem* : the idea, *unitas ante rem*." [1] Schopenhauer is in the habit of calling ideas the " genera " of
things ; but on one occasion he remarks that ideas are
of species, not genera ; that genera are simply concepts,
and that there are natural species, but only logical genera.[2]
This psychological illusion as to the existence of ideas
for types originates (as we find elsewhere in Schopenhauer) in the habit of converting the empirical classifications of the natural sciences into living realities. " Do
you wish to see ideas ? " he asks ; " look at the clouds
which scud across the sky ; look at a brooklet leaping
over rocks ; look at the crystallization of hoar-frost on
a window-pane with its designs of trees and flowers.
The shapes of the clouds, the ripples of the gushing brook,
the configurations of the crystals exist for us individual
observers, in themselves they are indifferent. The clouds
in themselves are elastic vapour ; the brook is an in-
compressible fluid, mobile, transparent, amorphous ; the
ice obeys the laws of crystallization : and in these determinations their ideas consist." [3] All these are the

[1] *Welt als Wille u. Vorstellung*, 1819 (in *Sämmtl. Werke*, ed. Grisebach, vol. i.), bk. iii. § 49.
[2] *Ergänzungen* (ed. Grisebach, vol. ii.), ch. 29.
[3] *Welt a. W. u. V.* iii. § 35.

immediate objectification of will in its various degrees ;
and it is these, not their pale copies in real things, that
art delineates ; whence Plato was right in one sense
and wrong in another, and is justified and condemned
by Schopenhauer exactly in the same way as by Plotinus
of old, as well as by Schopenhauer's worst enemy, the
modern Schelling.[1] In consequence, each art has a
special category of ideas for its own dominion. Architecture, and in some cases hydraulics, facilitate the clear
intuition of those ideas which constitute the lower degrees
of objectification—weight, cohesion, resistance, hardness,
the general properties of stone and some combinations
of light ; gardening and (most curious association) landscape painting represent the ideas of vegetable nature ;
sculpture and animal painting those of zoology ; historical
painting and the higher forms of sculpture that of the
human body ; poetry the very idea of man himself.[2]
As for music, that (let him who can justify the logical
discontinuity) is outside the hierarchy of the other arts.
We have seen how Schelling considered it to be representative of the very rhythm of the universe ;[3] differing
but slightly from this, Schopenhauer affirms that music
does not express ideas but, parallel with ideas, Will
itself. The analogies between music and the world,
between the fundamental bass and crude matter, between
the scale and the series of species, between melody and
conscious will, led him to the conclusion that music
was not, as Leibniz thought, an arithmetic but a metaphysic : *exercitium metaphysices occultum nescientis se*

*Æsthetic
catharsis.*
philosophari animi.[4] To Schopenhauer, no less than his
idealistic predecessors, art beatifies ; it is the flower of
life ; he who contemplates art is no longer an individual
but a pure knowing subject, at liberty, free from desire,
from pain, from time.[5]

*Signs of a
better theory in
Schopenhauer.*
Schopenhauer's system no doubt contains here and
there premonitions of a better and more profound treatment of art. Schopenhauer, who was capable on occasion

---

[1] See above, p. 291.   [2] *Welt a. W. u. V.* iii. §§ 42-51.
[3] See above, p. 293.   [4] *Welt a. W. u. V.* § 53.   [5] *Op. cit.* § 34.

of clear and keen analysis, constantly insists that the
forms of space and time must not be applied to the idea
or to artistic contemplation, which admits of the general
form of representation only.[1] From this he might have
inferred that art, so far from being a superior and extraordinary level of consciousness, is actually its most
immediate level, namely that which in its primitive
simplicity precedes even common perception with its
reference of objects to a position in the spatial and
temporal series. To free oneself from common perception
and to live in imagination does not mean rising to a
Platonic contemplation of the ideas, but descending once
more into the region of immediate intuition, becoming
children again, as Vico had seen. On the other hand
Schopenhauer had begun to examine the categories of
Kant with an unprejudiced eye ; he was not satisfied
with the two forms of intuition, and wished to add to
them a third, causality.[2] In conclusion, we note that,
like his predecessors, he makes a comparison between
art and history, with this difference and advantage over
the idealist authors of the philosophy of history, that for
him history was irreducible to concepts ; it was contemplation of the individual, and therefore not science.
Had he persevered in his comparison between art and
history, he would have arrived at a better solution than
that at which he stopped ; that is to say, that the matter
of history is the particular in its particularity and contingency, while that of art is that which is, and is always
identical.[3] But instead of pursuing these happy ideas
Schopenhauer preferred to play variations on the themes
fashionable in his day.

Most astounding of all is the fact that a dry in- *J. F. Herbart.*
tellectualist, the avowed enemy of idealism, of dialectic
and of speculative constructions, head of the school
calling itself realistic or the school of exact philosophy,
Johann Friedrich Herbart, when he turns his attention

---

[1] *Welt a. W. u. V.* § 32.
[2] *Kritik d. kantischen Philosophie*, in append. to *op. cit.* pp. 558-576.
[3] *Ergänzungen*, ch. 38.

to Æsthetic, turns mystic too, though in a slightly different way. How weightily he speaks when expounding his philosophical method! Æsthetic must not bear the blame of the faults into which metaphysic has fallen ; we must make it an independent study, and detach it from all hypothesis about the universe. Nor must it be confounded with psychology or asked to describe the emotions awakened by the content of works of art, such as the pathetic or the comic, sadness or joy ; its duty is to determine the essential character of art and beauty. In the analysis of particular cases of beauty and in registering what they reveal lies the way of salvation. These proposals and promises have misled numbers of people as to the nature of Herbart's Æsthetic. But *ce sont là jeux de princes* ; by paying attention we shall see what Herbart meant by analysis of particular cases and how he held himself aloof from metaphysics.

Pure Beauty and relations of form.

Beauty, for him, consisted in relations : relations of tone, colour, line, thought and will ; experience must decide which of these relations are beautiful, and æsthetic science consists solely in enumerating the fundamental concepts (*Musterbegriffe*) in which are summarized the particular cases of beauty. But these relations, Herbart thought, were not like physiological facts ; they could not be empirically observed, *e.g.* in a psycho-physical laboratory. To correct this error it is only necessary to observe that these relations include not only tones, lines and colours, but also thoughts and will, and that they extend to moral facts no less than to objects of external intuition. He declares explicitly " No true beauty is sensible, although it frequently happens that sense-impressions precede and follow the intuition of beauty." [1] There is a profound distinction between the beautiful and the pleasant ; for the pleasant needs no representation, while the beautiful consists in representation of relations, followed immediately in consciousness by a judgment, an appendix (*Zusatz*) which expresses unqualified ap-

---

[1] *Einleitung in die Philosophie*, 1813, in *Werke*, ed. Hartenstein, vol. 1. p. 49.

probation ("*es gefällt!*").   And while the pleasant and the
unpleasant " in the progress of culture gradually become
transient and unimportant, Beauty stands out more and
more as something permanent and possessed of un-
deniable value." [1]   The judgment of taste is universal,
eternal, immutable :   " the complete representation (*vol-
lendete Vorstellung*) of the same relations is always
followed by the same judgment ; just as the same cause
always produces the same effect.   This happens at all
times and in all circumstances, conditions and complications, which gives to the particularity of certain cases
the appearance of a universal rule.   Granted that the
elements of a relation are universal concepts, it is plain
that although in judging we think only of the content
of these concepts, the judgment must have a sphere as
large as that common to the two concepts." [2]   Herbart
considers æsthetic judgements as a general class comprising
ethical judgements as a subdivision :   " amongst other
beauties is to be distinguished morality, as a thing not
only of value in itself but as actually determining the
unconditioned value of persons " ;   within morality in
the narrowest sense is distinguished in turn justice.[3]
The five ethical ideas guiding moral life (internal liberty,
perfection, benevolence, equity and justice) are five
æsthetic ideas or rather æsthetic concepts applied to
relations of will.

Herbart looks on art as a complex fact, the combination of an extra-æsthetic element, content, which may
have logical or psychological or any other kind of value,
and a purely æsthetic element, form, which is an application of the fundamental æsthetic concepts.   Man looks
for that which is diverting, instructive, moving, majestic,
ridiculous ; and " all these are mingled with the beautiful
in order to procure favour and interest for the work.
The beautiful thus assumes various complexions, and
becomes graceful, magnificent, tragic, or comic ; it can

Art as sum of content and form.

---

[1] *Einleitung in die Philosophie*, pp. 125-128.
[2] *Allgemeine praktische Philosophie*, in *Werke*, viii. p. 25.
[3] *Einleitung*, p. 128.

become all these because the æsthetic judgement, in itself
calmly serene, tolerates the company of the most diverse
excitations of the soul which are no part of itself." [1]
But all these things have nothing to do with beauty.
In order to discover the objectively beautiful or ugly,
one must make abstraction from every predicate concerning the content. " In order to recognize the objectively beautiful or ugly in poetry, one must show the
difference between this and that thought, and the discussion will concern itself with thoughts ; to recognize it
in sculpture, one must show the difference between this
and that outline, and the discussion will turn upon
outlines ; to recognize it in music, one should show the
difference between this and that tone, and the discussion
will turn upon tones. Now, such predicates as ' magnificent, charming, graceful ' and so forth contain nothing
whatever about tones, outlines or thoughts, and therefore
tell us nothing about the objectively beautiful in poetry,
sculpture, or music ; indeed they rather lead us to believe
in the existence of an objective beauty to which thought,
outline, or tone are equally accidental, which may be
approached by receiving impressions from poetry, sculpture, music and so forth, obliterating the object and
giving oneself up to the pure emotion of mind." [2] Very
different is the æsthetic judgement, the " cold judgement
of the connoisseur " who considers exclusively form, *i.e.*
objectively pleasant formal relations. This abstraction
from the content in order to contemplate pure form is the
catharsis produced by art. Content is transitory, relative,
subject to moral law and liable to moral judgement :
form is permanent, absolute, free.[3] Concrete art may
be the sum of two or more values ; but the æsthetic
fact is form alone.

Herbart and Kantian thought.

The reader who goes behind appearances and discounts
diversities of terminology will not fail to observe the close
similarity of the æsthetic doctrine of Herbart to that of
Kant. In Herbart we again find the distinction between
free and adherent beauty, and between form and the

[1] *Einleitung,* p. 162.　　[2] *Op. cit.* pp. 129-130.　　[3] *Op. cit.* p. 163.

sensuous stimulus (*Reiz*) attached to form : we find an affirmation of the existence of pure beauty, the object of necessary and universal, but not discursive, judgements; lastly, we find a certain connexion between beauty and morality, between Æsthetic and Ethics.   In these matters Herbart is perhaps the most faithful follower and pro-pagator of the thought of Kant, whose doctrine contains the germ of his own.   In one passage he describes himself as " a Kantian, but of the year 1828 " ; and he is quite right, even in pointing out the exact difference in date. Amidst the errors and uncertainties of his æsthetic thought, Kant is rich in suggestion and scatters fertile seed ; he belongs to a period when philosophy was still young and impressionable.   Herbart, coming later, is dry and one-sided ; he takes whatever is false in Kant's doctrine and hardens it into a system.   If they had done little else, the Romanticists and idealists had at least united the theory of beauty to that of art, and destroyed the rhetorical and mechanical view ; and they had brought into relief (frequently exaggerating, doubt-less) various important characteristics of artistic activity. Herbart restates the mechanical view, restores the duality, and presents a capricious, narrow, barren mysticism, devoid of all breath of artistic feeling.

XI

FRIEDRICH SCHLEIERMACHER

Æsthetic of content and Æsthetic of form : meaning of the contrast.

WE have now reached a point when we are able to give ourselves an exact account of the signification and importance of the celebrated war waged for over a century in Germany between the Æsthetic of content (*Gehaltsästhetik*) and the Æsthetic of form (*Formästhetik*) ; a war which gave birth to vast works on the history of Æsthetic undertaken from one or other point of view, and sprang from Herbart's opposition to the idealism of Schelling, Hegel, and their contemporaries and followers. " Form " and " Content " are among the most equivocal words in the whole philosophical vocabulary, particularly in Æsthetic ; sometimes, indeed, what one calls form, others call content. The Herbartians were specially given to quoting in their own defence Schiller's dictum, that the secret of art consists in " cancelling content by form." But what is there in common between Schiller's concept of " form," which placed the æsthetic activity side by side with the moral and intellectual, and Herbart's " form," which does not penetrate or enliven, but clothes and adorns a content ? Hegel, on the other hand, often gives the name " form " to what Schiller would call " matter " (*Stoff*), that is, the sensible matter which it is the business of spiritual energy to dominate. Hegel's " content " is the idea, the metaphysical truth, the constituent element of beauty : Herbart's " content " is the emotional and intellectual element which falls outside beauty. The Æsthetic of " form " in Italy is an æsthetic of expressive activity ; the form is neither a clothing

312

nor a metaphysical idea nor sensible matter, but a representative or imaginative faculty with the power of framing impressions ; yet there have been attempts to confute this Italian æsthetic formalism with the same arguments that are used against German æsthetic formalism, a totally different thing in every respect. And so forth. Having given a plain account of the thoughts of the post-Kantian æstheticians, we shall be able to appreciate their opponents without seeking light from their obscure terminology or allowing ourselves to be misled by the banners they wave. The antithesis between the Æsthetic of content and that of form, the Æsthetic of idealism and that of realism, the Æsthetic of Schelling, Solger, Hegel and Schopenhauer and that of Herbart, will appear in its true light, as the family quarrel between two conceptions of art united by a common mysticism, although one is destined almost to meet with truth during its long journey, while the other wanders ever further away.

The first half of the nineteenth century was for Germany a period of many fine-sounding philosophical formulæ : subjectivism, objectivism, subjective - objectivism ; abstract, concrete, abstract-concrete ; idealism, realism, idealism - realism ; between pantheism and theism Krause inserted his pan-en-theism. In the midst of this uproar, in which the second-rate men shouted down the first-rate and made good their claim to their only true property, namely words, it is not surprising that a few modest clear thinkers, philosophers who preferred to think about realities, should have the worst of it and remain unheard and unnoticed, lost among the roaring crowd or labelled with a false ticket. This, at least, seems to have been the lot of Friedrich Schleiermacher, whose æsthetic doctrine is amongst the least known although it is perhaps the most noteworthy of the day. *Friedrich Schleiermacher.*

Schleiermacher delivered his first lectures on Æsthetic at Berlin University in 1819, and from that date he began to study the subject seriously with a view to writing *Wrong judgements concerning him.*

a book on it. He repeated his lectures on two occasions, in 1825 and 1832–1833 ; but his death, which occurred in the following year, prevented him from carrying out his plan, and all we know of his thoughts on Æsthetic comes from his lectures, as collected by his pupils and published in 1842.[1] A Herbartian historian of Æsthetic, Zimmermann, attacks the posthumous work of Schleiermacher with real ferocity ; after twenty pages of invective and sarcasm he concludes by asking, how could his pupils so dishonour their great master by publishing such a mass of waste paper, " all play upon words, sophistical conceits and dialectical subtleties " ? [2] Nor was the idealistic historian Hartmann much more benevolent when he describes the work as " a confused mess in which, among much that is merely trivial, many half-truths and exaggerations, one can detect a few acute observations " ; and says that, in order to make bearable " such unctuous afternoon sermons delivered by a preacher in his dotage," it must be shortened by three-quarters ; and that, " as regards fundamental principles," it is simply useless, offering no innovations upon concrete idealism as presented by Hegel and others ; and that, in any case, it seems impossible " to attach it to any line of thought except the Hegelian, to which Schleiermacher's contribution is only of second-rate importance." He further observes that Schleiermacher was primarily a theologian, and in philosophy more or less an amateur.[3] Now it cannot be denied that Schleiermacher's doctrine has reached us in a hazy form, by no means free from uncertainties and contradictions ; and, which is more important, it is here and there affected for the worse by the influence of contemporary metaphysics. But, side by side with these defects, what excellent method, really scientific and philosophical ; what a number of cornerstones well and truly laid ; what wealth of new truths,

[1] *Vorlesungen üb. Ästhetik*, published by Lommatsch, Berlin, 1842 (*Werke*, sect. iii. vol. vii.).
[2] Zimmermann, *G. d. Ä.* pp. 608-634.
[3] E. von Hartmann, *Deutsche Asth. s. Kant*, pp. 156-169.

and of difficulties and problems not suspected or discussed before his day !

Schleiermacher considered Æsthetic as an essentially *Schleier-*
modern line of thought, and drew a sharp distinction *macher con-*
trasted with his
between the *Poetics* of Aristotle, which never shakes itself *predecessors.*
free from the empirical standpoint of the maker of rules,
and what Baumgarten tried to do in the eighteenth
century. He praised Kant for having been the first
truly to include Æsthetic among the philosophical sciences,
and recognized that in Hegel artistic activity had attained
the highest elevation by being brought into connexion
and almost into equality with religion and philosophy.
But he was not satisfied either with the followers of
Baumgarten when they degenerated into the absurd
attempt to construct a science or theory of sensuous
pleasure, or with the Kantian point of view which made
its principal aim the consideration of taste ; or with
the philosophy of Fichte, in which art became a means
of education ; or with the more widely received opinion
which placed at the centre of Æsthetic the vague and
equivocal concept of Beauty. Schiller pleased him by
having called attention to the moment of artistic spontaneity or productiveness, and he praised Schelling for
having laid stress on the importance of the figurative
arts, which lend themselves less easily than poetry to
facile and illusory moralistic interpretations.[1] Having
with the utmost clearness excluded from Æsthetic the
study of practical rules as empirical, and therefore
irreducible to a science, he assigned to Æsthetic the task
of determining the proper position of artistic activity
in the scheme of ethics.[2]

To avoid falling into error over this terminology, we *Place assigned*
to Æsthetic in
must call to mind that the philosophy of Schleiermacher *his Ethics.*
followed the ancient traditions in its tripartite division
into Dialectic, Ethics and Physics. Dialectic corresponds
with ontology ; Physics embraces all the sciences of
natural facts ; Ethics includes the study of all free
activities of mankind (language, thought, art, religion

[1] *Vorles. üb. Ästhetik*, pp. 1-30.   [2] *Op. cit.* pp. 35-51.

and morality). Ethics represented to him not only the
science of morality but what others name Psychology or,
better still, the Science or Philosophy of the Spirit. This
explanation once given, Schleiermacher's point of departure seems to be the only one just and permissible,
and we shall not be surprised when he talks of will, of
voluntary acts and so on, where others would have
simply spoken of activity or spiritual energy ; he even
endows such expressions with a broader meaning than
that conferred upon them by practical philosophy.

*Æsthetic
activity as
immanent and
individual.*
A double distinction may be made amongst human
activities. In the first place, there are activities which
we presume to be constituted in the same manner in
all men (such as the logical activity) and are called
activities of identity ; and others whose diversity is
presumed, which are called activities of difference or
individual activities. Secondly, there are activities which
exhaust themselves in the internal life, and others which
actualize themselves in the external world : immanent
activities and practical activities. To which of the two
classes in each of the two orders does artistic activity
belong ? There can be no doubt of its different modes
of development, if not actually in each individual person,
at least in different peoples and nations ; therefore it
belongs properly to activities of difference or individual
activities.[1] As for the other distinction, it is true that
art does realize itself in the external world, but this fact
is something superadded (" *ein später Hinzukommendes* ")
" which stands to the internal fact as the communication
of thought by means of speech or writing stands to
thought itself " : art's true work is the internal image
(" *das innere Bild ist das eigentliche Kunstwerk* "). Exceptions to this might be adduced, such as mimicry ;
but they would be apparent only. Between a really
angry man and the actor who plays the part of an angry
man on the stage there is this difference : in the second
case anger appears as controlled and therefore beautiful ;
that is, the internal image is in the actor's soul interposed

[1] *Vorles. üb. Ästh.* pp. 51-54.

between the fact of passion and its physical manifestation.[1] Artistic activity "belongs to those human activities in which we presuppose the individual in its differentiation ; it belongs equally to those activities developing essentially within themselves and not completing themselves in any external world. Art, therefore, is an immanent activity in which we presuppose differentiation." Internal, not practical : individual, not universal or logical.

But if art be one form of thought, there must be one *Artistic truth* form of thought in which identity is presupposed, and *and intellectual* another in which difference is presupposed. We do not *truth.* look for truth in poetry ; or, rather, we do look for truth, but for one that is totally different from that objective truth to which there must correspond some being, either universal or individual (scientific and historical truth). " When a character in a poem is said to be devoid of truth, a slur is cast on the given poem ; but if the character is said to be a pure invention, corresponding with no reality, that is quite a different matter." The truth of a poetic character consists in the coherence with which a single person's divers modes of thinking and acting are represented : even in portraits it is not an exact correspondence with an objective reality that makes the thing a work of art. From art and poetry " springs no iota of knowledge " (*das Geringste vom Wissen*) ; " it expresses but the truth of the single consciousness." There are then " productions of thought and of sensible intuitions, opposed to the other productions because they do not presuppose identity, and they express the singular as such." [2]

The domain of art is immediate self-consciousness *Difference of* (*unmittelbare Selbstbewusstsein*), which must be carefully *artistic con-* distinguished from the thought or concept of the ego *sciousness* or of the determinate ego. This latter is the conscious- *and religion.* ness of identity in the diversity of moments ; immediate self-consciousness is " diversity itself, of which one must be aware, since life in its entirety is but the development of consciousness." In this domain art has often been confused with two facts which accompany it : sensuous consciousness (the feeling of pleasure and pain), and religion. A double confusion, of which the sensationalists fall into the first half and Hegel into the second ; Schleiermacher clears it up by proving that art is free productivity, whereas sensuous pleasure and religious feeling, however different in other ways, are both determined by an objective fact (*äussere Sein*).[1]

Dreams and art : inspiration and deliberation.

The better to understand this free productivity, we must further circumscribe the domain of immediate consciousness. In this we can find nothing more helpful than comparing it with the images produced by dreams. The artist has his own dreams : he dreams with open eyes, and from among the thick-thronging images of this dream-state those having sufficient energy alone become works of art, the rest remaining a mere background from which the others stand out. All the essential elements of art are found in the dream-state, which is the production of free thoughts and sensuous intuitions consisting of mere images. Certainly something is lacking in dreams, and they differ from art not only in their absence of technique, which has already been excluded as irrelevant to art, but in another way, viz. that a dream is a chaotic fact, without stability, order, connexion or measure. But when some sort of order is introduced into the chaos the difference at once disappears, and the likeness to art merges in identity. This internal activity which introduces order and measure, fixes and determines the image, is that which distinguishes art from a dream or transforms a dream into art. It often involves struggle, labour, the obligation to stem the involuntary flood of internal images ; in a word, it means reflexion or deliberation. But the dream and the cessation of dreaming are equally indispensable elements of art. There must be production of thoughts and images and, together with such production, there must

[1] *Vorles. üb. Ästh.* pp. 67-77.

be measure, determination and unity, " otherwise each
image would be confused with its neighbour and have no
definiteness." The instant of inspiration (*Begeisterung*)
is as essential as that of deliberation (*Besonnenheit*).[1]

But in order to arrive at artistic truth it is also *Art and the*
necessary (here Schleiermacher's thought becomes less *typical.*
clear and accurate) that the singular be accompanied by
consciousness of the species ; consciousness of the self
as individual man is impossible without consciousness
of mankind ; nor is a single object true unless referred to
its universal. In a pictured landscape " every tree must
possess natural truth, that is to say, it must be contemplated as a specimen of a given kind ; similarly, the
whole complex of natural and individual life must have
effective truth of nature and constitute a single harmony.
Just because in art we do not strive after the production
of individual figures in themselves and for themselves,
but their internal truth as well, we commonly assign to
them a high place as being a free realization of that in
which all cognition has its value, that is to say, in the
principle that all forms of being are inherent in the
human spirit. If this principle fails, truth is no longer
possible ; scepticism only remains." The productions of
art are the ideal or typical figures which real nature
would create were it not impeded by external influences.[2]
" The artist creates a figure on the basis of a general
scheme, rejecting whatever may hinder or impede the
play of the living forces of reality ; such a production,
founded on a general scheme, is what we call the
Ideal." [3]

In spite of all these determinations, Schleiermacher
did not apparently intend to limit the artist's scope.
He remarks, " When an artist represents something
really given, whether portrait, landscape or single human
figure, he renounces the freedom of productivity and
adheres to the real." [4] There is a twofold tendency at
work in the artist : towards perfection of type, and

[1] *Vorles. üb. Ästh.* pp. 79-91.   [2] *Op. cit.* pp. 123, 143-150.
[3] *Op. cit.* p. 505 ; cf. p. 607.   [4] *Op. cit.* p. 505.

towards representation of natural reality. An artist must not fall into the abstractness of the type or into the unmeaningness of empirical reality.[1] If in flower-painting it is necessary to bring out the specific type, a much more complete individualisation is demanded when representing man, owing to the lofty position which he occupies.[2] Representation of the ideal in the real does not exclude " an infinite variety, such as is found in actual reality." " For instance, the human face wavers between the ideal and caricature, in its moral conformation no less than in its physical. Every human face contains elements of disfigurement (*Verbildung*), but it has also something by which it is a determinate modification of human nature ; this does not appear openly, but a practised eye can seize it and ideally complete the face in question." [3] Schleiermacher is keenly aware of the difficulties and perplexities of such problems as the question whether there exists one or many ideals of the human face.[4] He observes that the two views which strive for mastery in the field of poetry may be extended to art as a whole. Some assert that poetry and art should represent the perfect, the ideal, that which would have been produced by nature, had she not been prevented by mechanical forces ; others reject the ideal as incapable of realisation and prefer that the artist should depict man as he really is, with those perturbing elements which in reality belong to him no less than his ideal qualities. Each view is a half-truth : it is the duty of art to represent the ideal as well as the real, the subjective as well as the objective.[5] The comic element, that is the unideal and the faulty ideal, is included in the circle of art.[6]

Independence of art.   In respect to morality, art is free just as philosophical speculation is free : its essence excludes practical and moral effects. This leads to the proposition that " there is no difference between various works of art, except in

[1] *Vorles. üb. Ästh.* pp. 506-508.   [2] *Op. cit.* pp. 156-157.
[3] *Op. cit.* pp. 550-551.   [4] *Op. cit.* p. 608.   [5] *Op. cit.* pp. 684-686.
[6] *Op. cit.* pp. 191-196 ; cf. pp. 364-365.

so far as they can be compared in respect of artistic perfection " (*Vollkommenheit in der Kunst*). " Given an artistic object perfect of its kind, it has an absolute value which cannot be increased or diminished by anything else. If motions of the will could truly be described as consequences of works of art, a different standard of values would apply to works of art : and since the objects which an artist may depict are not all equally adapted to influence volition, a scale of values would exist which did not depend on artistic perfection." Nor must we confound the judgement passed upon the varied and complex personality of the artist himself with the strictly æsthetic judgement passed upon his work. " In this respect the biggest, most complicated canvas is on a level with the smallest arabesque, the longest poem with the shortest: the value of a work of art depends on the perfect manner in which the external corresponds to the internal." [1]

Schleiermacher rejects the doctrine of Schiller because in his opinion it makes art a sort of game or pastime in contrast to the serious affairs of life : a view, he says, for business men to whom their business is the only serious thing. Artistic activity is universally human, a man devoid of it is inconceivable ; although, of course, there are in this respect great differences betwixt man and man, running from the mere desire to enjoy art to real taste, and from this again to productive genius. [2]

The artist makes use of instruments which, by their nature, are framed not for the individual but for the universal ; of this kind is language. But it is the business of poetry to extract the individual from language which is universal without giving to its productions the form of the antithesis between individual and universal which is proper to science. Of the two elements of language, the musical and the logical, the poet claims the first for his own ends and constrains the other to awaken individual images. In comparison with pure science as

Art and language.

---

[1] *Vorles. üb. Ästh.* pp. 209-219 ; cf. pp. 527-528.
[2] *Op. cit.* pp. 98-111.

in comparison with the individual image, there is something irrational about language : but the tendencies of speculation and of poetry are always contrary, even in their use of language ; the former tends to make language approximate to mathematical formulæ ; the latter to imagery (*Bild*).[1]

Schleier-macher's defects.

Leaving out many details which will be touched on in their proper places, the foregoing is a fair summary of the heads of Schleiermacher's æsthetic thought. Adding up the accounts of the whole statement of views, on the side of error and oversight we find : first, ideas or types are not wholly excluded, in spite of all Schleiermacher's care and anxiety to safeguard artistic individualisation and to make the ideas and types superfluous. Secondly, there is still, undefeated and unexpelled, a certain residue of abstract formalism, visible at various points of his theories.[2] Thirdly, the definition of art as an activity of mere difference may be diluted but is not destroyed by making art a difference of complexes of individuals, a national difference. A closer reflexion on the history of art, a recognition of the possibility of appreciating the art of various nations and various times, a more patient investigation into the moment of artistic reproduction, even an examination of the relation between science and art, would have led Schleiermacher to treat this difference as empirical and surmountable, still holding firmly to the distinctive character (individual as opposed to universal) he assigned to art in comparison with science. Fourthly, he did not recognize the identity of æsthetic activity with linguistic, and failed to make it the basis of all other theoretic activity. It would seem, moreover, that Schleiermacher had no clear ideas concerning that artistic element which enters into the constitution of historic narrative and is indispensable as the concrete form of science ; or concerning language, taken not as a complex of abstract means of expression but as expressive activity.

Schleier-macher's services to Æsthetic.

These defects and uncertainties may perhaps be attributable in part to the fact that his thoughts on

---

[1] *Vorles. üb Asth.* pp. 635-648.   [2] Cf. *e.g.* p. 467 *seqq.*

æsthetic have reached us in an inchoate form, very far from a mature development. But if on the other hand we wish to cast up the sum of his very striking merits, it will suffice to run over the list of accusations heaped upon him by the two historians before mentioned, Zimmermann and Hartmann. Schleiermacher has denuded Æsthetic of its imperative character ; he recognizes in it a form of thought differing from logical thought ; he gives this science a non-metaphysical and merely anthropological character ; he denies the concept of beauty, substituting that of artistic perfection, and actually affirms the æsthetic equivalence of small and great works of art, so long as each is perfect in its own sphere ; he considers the æsthetic fact as pure human productivity : and so on and so forth. All these criticisms are meant for blame and are really praise ; for what is blame to the mind of a Zimmermann or a Hartmann, is to ours praise. In the metaphysical orgy of his day, in the perpetual building and pulling down of more or less arbitrary systems, Schleiermacher the theologian, with philosophic acumen, fixed his eye upon what was really characteristic of the æsthetic fact and succeeded in defining its properties and connexions ; when he failed to see clearly and wandered from the track, he never abandoned analysis for fantastic caprice. By his discovery that the obscure region of immediate consciousness is also that of the æsthetic fact, he seems to bid his distracted contemporaries listen to the old adage : *Hic Rhodus, hic salta.*

XII

THE PHILOSOPHY OF LANGUAGE:
HUMBOLDT AND STEINTHAL

Progress of Linguistic.

ABOUT the time when Schleiermacher was meditating on the nature of the æsthetic fact, a movement of thought was gaining ground in Germany which, tending as it did to overthrow the old concept of language, might have proved a powerful aid to æsthetic science. But not only had the æsthetic specialists—if we may so call them—no notion of the existence of this movement, the new philosophers of language never brought their ideas into relation with the æsthetic problem, and their discoveries languished imprisoned within the narrow scope of Linguistic, condemned to sterility.

Linguistic speculation at the beginning of the nineteenth century

Research into the relations between thought and speech, between the unity of logic and the multiplicity of languages, had been promoted, like many other things, by the *Critique of Pure Reason* : the earliest Kantians often tried to apply the Kantian categories of intuition (space and time) and of intellect to language. The first to make the attempt was Roth [1] in 1795 ; the same who wrote an essay twenty years later on *Pure Linguistic.* Many other noteworthy books on this subject appeared in quick succession : those of Vater, Bernhardi, Reinbeck and Koch were published one after another in the first ten years of the nineteenth century. In all these treatises the dominating subject is the difference between language

[1] *Antihermes oder philosophische Untersuchung üb.- d. reine Begriff d. menschl. Sprache und die allgemeine Sprachlehre*, Frankfurt and Leipzig, 1795.

and languages ; between the universal language, corresponding with Logic, and concrete, historical languages
disturbed by feeling and imagination or whatever other
name was applied to the psychological element of differentiation. Vater distinguishes a general Linguistic (*allgemeine Sprachlehre*), constructed *a priori* by means of
the analysis of the concepts contained in the judgement,
from a comparative Linguistic (*vergleichende Sprachlehre*)
which attempts by means of induction to reach probable
laws through the study of a number of languages. Bernhardi considers language to be an " allegory of intellect "
and distinguishes it as functioning either as the organ
of poetry or that of science. Reinbeck speaks of an
Æsthetic Grammar and a Logical. Koch, more energetic
than the others, asserts positively that the character of
language is " *non ad Logices sed ad Psychologiae rationem
revocanda.*" [1] Some few philosophers speculated on language and mythology : for example Schelling considered
them to be the products of a pre-human consciousness
(*vormenschliche Bewusstsein*), presenting them, in a
fantastic allegory, as diabolic suggestions which pre-
cipitate the ego from the infinite to the finite.[2]

Even the famous philologist, Wilhelm von Humboldt, *Wilhelm von*
was unable to detach himself entirely from the prejudice *Humboldt.*
Relics of
of the substantial identity and the purely historical, *intellectualism.*
accidental diversity between logical thought and language.
His celebrated dissertation, *On the Diversity of Structure
of Human Languages* (1836),[3] is based on the notion of a
perfect language split up and distributed amongst particular tongues according to the linguistic or intellectual
capacity of various nations. " For," says he, " since disposition towards speech is general in mankind, and all
men must necessarily carry within themselves the key
to the comprehension of all languages, it follows that the

[1] For these writers, see accounts and quotations in Loewe, *Hist.
crit. gramm. univ.*, *passim*, and Pott, introd. to Humboldt, pp. clxxi.-
ccxii. ; cf. also Benfey, *Gesch. d. Sprachwiss.*, introd.

[2] In *Philos. der Mythologie* : cf. Steinthal, *Urspr.* pp. 81-89.

[3] *Üb. d. Verschiedenheit d. menschl. Sprachbaues*, posthumous work
(2nd ed. by A. F. Pott, Berlin, 1880).

form of all languages must be substantially equal and all must attain the same general end. Diversity can exist solely in the means, and within the bounds permitted by the attainment of the end." Yet this same diversity becomes a real divergence not only in sounds, but in the use of sound made by the linguistic sense in respect to the form of language, or rather, in respect to its own idea of the form of the determinate language. " Languages being merely formal, the operation of the linguistic sense by itself should produce mere uniformity ; the linguistic sense must exact from every tongue the same right and legitimate construction that is found in one of them. In practice, however, the facts are quite otherwise, partly owing to the reaction of sounds, and partly by reason of the individual aspect assumed by the same internal meaning in phenomenal reality." ·Linguistic force " cannot maintain its equality everywhere or show the same intensity, vivacity or regularity ; it cannot be supported by an exactly equal tendency towards the symbolic treatment of thought or by exactly equal pleasure in richness and harmony of sound." These, then, are the causes which produce in human languages that diversity which manifests itself in every branch of the civilization of nations. But reflexion on languages " ought to reveal to us a form which of all possible forms best fits the purpose of language " and approaches most closely to its ideal ; and " the merits and defects of existing languages must be estimated by their nearness or remoteness from this form." Humboldt finds the nearest approximation to such an ideal in the Sanskrit tongues, which can therefore be used as a standard of comparison. Setting Chinese apart in a class by itself, he proceeds to the division of the possible forms of language into inflective, agglutinative and incorporative ; types which are found combined in various proportions in every real language.[1] He also inaugurated the division of languages into inferior and superior, unformed and formed, according to the way in which verbs are

[1] *Verschiedenheit*, etc., pp. 308-310.

treated.   He was never able to rid himself of a second
prejudice connected with the first, namely that language
exists as something objective outside the talking man,
unattached and independent, and waking up when needed
for use.

But Humboldt opposes Humboldt : amongst the old *Language as*
dross we detect the brilliant gleams of a wholly new *activity.*
concept of language.   Certainly his work is for this very *Internal form.*
reason not always free from contradictions and from a
kind of hesitation and awkwardness which appear characteristically in his literary style and make it at times
laboured and obscure.   The new man in Humboldt
criticizes the old man when he says, " Languages must be
considered not as dead products but as an act of production. . . . Language in its reality is something continually
changing and passing away.   Even its preservation in
writing is incomplete, a kind of mummification : it is
always necessary to render the living speech sensible.
Language is not a work, *ergon*, but an activity, *energeia*.
. . . It is an eternally repeated effort of the spirit in
order to make articulated tones capable of expressing
thought."   Language is the act of speaking.   " True
and proper language consists in the very act of producing
it by means of connected utterance ; that is the only
thing that must be thought of as the starting-point or
the truth in any inquiry which aims at penetrating into
the living essence of language.   Division into words and
rules is a lifeless artifice of scientific analysis." [1]   Language is not a thing arising out of the need of external
communication ; on the contrary, it springs from the
wholly internal thirst for knowledge and the struggle to
reach an intuition of things.   " From its earliest commencement it is entirely human, and extends without
intention to all objects of sensory perception or internal
elaboration. . . . Words gush spontaneously from the
breast without constraint or intention : there is no
nomad tribe in any desert without its songs.   Taken as a
zoological species, man is a singing animal which connects

[1] *Verschiedenheit*, etc., pp. 54-56.

its thoughts with its utterances." [1]   The new man leads Humboldt to discover a fact hidden from the authors of logico-universal grammars : namely the internal form of language (*innere Sprachform*), which is neither logical concept nor physical sound, but the subjective view of things formed by man, the product of imagination and feeling, the individualization of the concept.   Conjunction of the internal form of language with physical sound is the work of an internal synthesis ; " and here, more than anywhere else, language by its profound and mysterious operation recalls art.   Sculptor and painter also unite the idea with matter, and their efforts are judged praise-worthy or not according as this union, this intimate interpenetration, is the work of true genius, or as the idea is something separate, painfully and laboriously imposed upon the matter by sheer force of brush or chisel." [2]

Language and art in Humboldt.   But Humboldt was content to regard the procedure of artist and speaker as comparable by analogy, without proceeding to identify them.   On the one hand, he was too one-sided in his view of language as a means for the development of thought (logical thought) ; on the other, his own æsthetic ideas, always vague and not always true, prevented his perception of the identity.   Of his two principal writings on Æsthetic, that on *Beauty Masculine and Feminine* (1795) seems to be wholly under the influence of Winckelmann, whose antithesis between beauty and expression is revived, and the opinion ex-pressed that specific sexual characters diminish the beauty of the human body and that beauty asserts itself only by triumphing over differences of sex.   His other work, which is inspired by Goethe's *Hermann und Doro-thee*, defines art as " representation of nature by means of fancy ; the representation being beautiful, just because it is the work of fancy," a metamorphosis of nature carried to a higher sphere.   The poet reflects the pictures of language, itself a complex of abstractions.[3]   In his

[1] *Verschiedenheit*, etc., pp. 25, 73-74, 79.   [2] *Op. cit.* pp. 105-118.
[3] Zimmermann, *G. d. Ä.* pp. 533-544.

dissertation on Linguistic, Humboldt distinguishes poetry and prose, treating the two concepts philosophically, not by the empirical distinction between free and measured or periodic and metric language. " Poetry gives us reality in its sensible appearance, as it is felt internally and externally ; but is indifferent to the character which makes it real, and even deliberately ignores that character. It presents the sensuous appearance to fancy and, by this means, leads towards the contemplation of an artistically ideal whole. Prose, on the contrary, looks in reality for the roots which attach it to existence, the cords which bind her to it : hence it fastens fact to fact and concept to concept according to the methods of the intellect, and strives towards the objective union of them all in an idea." [1] Poetry precedes prose : before producing prose, the spirit necessarily forms itself in poetry. [2] But, beside these views, some of which are profoundly true, Humboldt looks on poets as perfecters of language, and on poetry as belonging only to certain exceptional moments, [3] and makes us suspect that after all he never recognized clearly or maintained firmly that language is always poetry, and that prose (science) is a distinction not of æsthetic form but of content, that is, of logical form.

Humboldt's contradictions about the concept of language lost him his principal follower, Steinthal. With the help of his master, Steinthal restated the position that language belongs not to Logic but to Psychology, [4] and in 1855 waged a gallant war against the Hegelian Becker, author of *The Organisms of Language*, one of the last logical grammarians, who pledged himself to deduce the entire body of the Sanskrit languages from twelve cardinal concepts. Steinthal declares it is not true that one cannot think without words : the deaf-mute thinks in signs ; the mathematician in formulæ. In

H. Steinthal. The linguistic function independent of the logical.

---

[1] *Verschiedenheit*, etc., pp. 326-328.

[2] *Op. cit.* pp. 239-240.

[3] *Op. cit.* pp. 205-206, 547, etc.

[4] *Grammatik, Logik und Psychologie, ihre Principien u. ihr Verhältn. z. einand.*, Berlin, 1855.

some languages, as in Chinese, the visual element is as necessary to thought as the phonetic, if not more so.[1] In this he may have overshot the mark, and failed to establish the autonomy of expression with regard to logical thought ; for his examples only confirm the fact that if we can think without words, we cannot think without expressions.[2] But he successfully demonstrates that concept and word, logical judgement and proposition, are incommensurable. The proposition is not the judgement but the representation (*Darstellung*) of a judgement ; and all propositions do not represent logical judgements. It is possible to express several judgements in a single proposition. The logical divisions of judgements (the relations of concepts) find no counterpart in the grammatical divisions of propositions. " A logical form of the proposition is just as much a contradiction as the angle of a circle or the circumference of a triangle." He who talks, in so far as he talks, possesses not thoughts but language.[3]

Identity of the problems of the origin and the nature of language.

Having thus freed language from all dependence on Logic, having repeatedly proclaimed the principle that language produces its forms independently of Logic and in the fullest autonomy,[4] and having purified Humboldt's theory from the taint of the logical grammar of Port Royal, Steinthal seeks the origin of language, recognizing, with his master, that the question of its origin is identical with that of nature of language, its psychological genesis or rather the position it occupies in evolution of the spirit. " In the matter of language there is no difference between its original creation (*Urschöpfung*) and the creation which is daily repeated."[5] Language belongs to the vast class of reflex movements ; but to say that is to look at it from one side only and to omit its own essential peculiarity. Animals have reflex movements

---

[1] *Gramm., Log. u. Psych.* pp. 153-158.

[2] See above, pp. 28-30.

[3] *Gramm., Log. u. Psych.* pp. 183, 195.

[4] *Einleitung i. d. Psych. u. Sprachwissenschaft* (2nd ed., Berlin, 1881), p. 62.

[5] *Gramm., Log. u. Psych.* p. 231.

and sensations like man ; but in animals the senses " are
wide gates through which external nature rushes to the
assault with such impetus as to overwhelm the mind
and deprive it of all independence and freedom of movement." In man, however, language can arise because
man is resistance to nature, conqueror of his own body,
freedom incarnate : " language is liberation : even to-day
we feel our mind lightened and freed from a weight when
we speak." In the situation immediately preceding the
production of speech man must be conceived as " accompanying all his sensations and all the intuitions
received by his mind with the most lively contortions of
body, attitudes of mimicry, gestures, and above all tones,
articulate tones." What element of speech did he lack ?
One only, but a most important one : the conscious
conjunction of reflex bodily movements with the excitations of his mind. If sensuous consciousness is
already consciousness, it lacks the consciousness of being
conscious ; if it is already intuition, it is not intuition
of intuition ; what it lacks is in a word the internal form
of speech. When that arises, there arises too its inseparable accompaniment, words. Man does not select
sound : it is given him, and he takes it of necessity,
instinctively, without intention or choice.[1]

This is not the place for detailed examination of the *Steinthal's
mistaken ideas
on art : his
failure to
unite Linguis-
tic and
Æsthetic.*
whole of Steinthal's theory and the various phases, not
always progressive, through which he travelled, especially
after the beginning of his spiritual collaboration with
Lazarus, with whom he studied ethnopsychology (*Völkerpsychologie*), of which they both took Linguistic to be a part.[2]
But, while giving him full credit for bringing Humboldt's ideas into coherent order, and for clearly differentiating, as had never before been done, between
linguistic activity and the activity of logical thought, it
must be noted that Steinthal never recognized the identity

[1] *Op. cit.* pp. 285, 292, 295-306.
[2] Steinthal, *Ursprung d. Sprache* (4th ed. Berlin, 1888), pp. 120-124.
M. Lazarus, *Das Leben der Seele,* 1855 (Berlin, 1876–1878), vol. ii.
Zeitschrift f. Völkerpsych. u. Sprachwiss. from 1860 onwards, edited by
Steinthal and Lazarus together.

of the internal form of language (which he also called
the intuition of intuition, or apperception) with the
æsthetic imagination. The Herbartian psychology to
which he clung afforded him no clue to such a discovery.
Herbart and his followers divorced psychology from logic
as a normative science and never succeeded in discerning
the true connection between feeling and spiritual formation, soul and spirit ; they never understood that logical
thought is one of these spiritual formations : an activity,
not a code of external laws. The domain allotted by
them to Æsthetic we already know ; for them Æsthetic
too was only another code of beautiful formal relations.
Under the influence of these doctrines Steinthal was led
to regard Art as the embellishment of thoughts, Linguistic
as the science of speech, and Rhetoric or Æsthetic as a
thing differing from Linguistic since it is science of fine
or beautiful speaking.[1]   In one of his innumerable tracts
he says, " Poetics and Rhetoric both differ from Linguistic,
since they are obliged to touch on many important topics
before reaching language.   These sciences therefore have
but one section devoted to Linguistic, which is the
concluding section of Syntax.   Moreover Syntax has a
character entirely different from Rhetoric and from
Poetics ; the former is occupied solely with correctness
(*Richtigkeit*) of language ; the latter two sciences study
beauty or grace of expression (*Schönheit oder Angemessen-
heit des Ausdrucks*) : the principles of the first are merely
grammatical, the others must consider matters outside
language ; for example, the disposition of the orator
and so forth.   To speak plainly, Syntax is to Stylistic
as is the grammatical measure of the quantity of vowels
to the theory of metre." [2]   That speaking invariably
means good or beautiful speaking, since speech that is
neither good nor beautiful is not really speech,[3] and that
the radical renewal of the concept of language inaugurated
by Humboldt and himself must produce far-reaching
effects on the cognate sciences of Poetics, Rhetoric and

[1] *Gramm., Log. u. Psych.* pp. 139-140, 146.
[2] *Einleit.* pp. 34-35.   [3] See above, pp. 78-79.

Æsthetic and, by transforming, unify them, never entered Steinthal's head. After all this labour and all this minute analysis, the identification of language and poetry, and of the science of language with the science of poetry, the identification of Linguistic with Æsthetic, still found its least faulty expression in the prophetic aphorisms of Giambattista Vico.

XIII

MINOR GERMAN ÆSTHETICIANS

Minor
æstheticians
in the
metaphysical
school.

WHEN we turn from the pages of methodical and serious thinkers such as Schleiermacher, Humboldt and Steinthal, we are filled with distaste by the books written in enormous quantities during the first half of the nineteenth century by disciples of Schelling and Hegel. We are fatigued and almost disgusted as we pass from this illuminating and scientific study to something which oscillates between vapid fancies and charlatanism ; between the vanity of empty formulæ and the attempt, not always free from dishonesty, to employ them in order to amaze and overwhelm the reader or student.

Krause,
Trahndorff,
Weisse and
others.

Why should we encumber a general History of Æsthetic (which ought, certainly, to take account of aberrations from the truth, but only in so far as they indicate the general trend of contemporary thought) with the theories of such men as Krause, Trahndorff, Weisse, Deutinger, Oersted, Zeising, Eckardt and the crowd of manipulators of manuals and systems ? The only one who obtained a hearing outside his native Germany was Krause, who was imported into Spain ; we are justified, therefore, in leaving them to the memory or forgetfulness of their compatriots. For Krause,[1] the humanitarian, the free-thinker, the theosophist, everything is organism, everything is beauty ; beauty is organism, and organism is beauty : Essence, that is to say God, is one, free and entire ; one, free and entire is Beauty. There is but

---

[1] *Abriss der Ästhetik*, post. 1837 ; *Vorlesung üb. Ästh.* (1828–1829), post. 1882.

one artist, God ; but one art, the divine. The beauty of finite things is the Divinity, or rather the likeness of Divinity manifested in the finite. Beauty brings into play reason, intellect and imagination in a mode conforming to their laws, and awakens disinterested pleasure and inclination in the soul. Trahndorff,[1] describing the various degrees by which the individual seeks to grasp the essence or form of the universe (the degrees of feeling, intuition, reflexion and presentiment), and noting the insufficiency of simple theoretical knowledge till supplemented by the Will, the Will which is power (Können), in its three degrees of Aspiration, Faith and Love, places the Beautiful in the highest grade, in Love : it would seem, therefore, that Beauty is Love which comprehends itself. Christian Weisse [2] attempted, like Trahndorff, to reconcile the God of Christianity with the Hegelian philosophy : in his estimation the æsthetic Idea is superior to the logical, and leads to religion, to God ; the idea of beauty, existing outside the sensible universe, is the reality of the concept of beauty, and, as the idea of divinity is absolute Love, so must that of Beauty be found truly in Love. The same reconciliation was attempted by the Catholic theologian Deutinger ; [3] beauty, for him, is born of power (Können), an activity parallel with those of the knowledge of truth and the doing of good but (differing in this from knowledge, which is receptive) realizing itself in an outward movement from within, mastering the world of matter and imprinting upon it the seal of personality. An internal ideal intuition, the Idea : an external shapable matter : the power of interpenetrating internal with external, invisible with visible, ideal with real : such is Beauty. Oersted [4] (the celebrated Danish naturalist whose works

[1] *Ästhetik*, Berlin, 1827.

[2] *Ästhetik*, Leipzig, 1830 ; *System di Ästh.*, lectures, post. Leipzig, 1872.

[3] *Kunstlehre*, Ratisbon, 1845–1846 (*Grundlinien einer positiven Philosophie*, vols. iv. v.).

[4] *Der Geist in der Natur*, 1850–1851 ; *Neue Beiträge z. d. Geist i. d. Natur*, post. 1855.

were translated into German and gained him a considerable reputation in Germany) defines beauty as the objective Idea in the moment of subjective contemplation : the Idea expressed in things in so far as it reveals itself to intuition. Zeising [1] turned his attention partly to exploration of the mysteries of the golden section, and partly to speculations on Beauty, which he considered as one of the three forms of the Idea ; first, the Idea which expresses itself in object and subject ; secondly, the Idea as intuition ; and thirdly, the Absolute which appears in the world and is conceived intuitively by the spirit. Eckardt,[2] intent on creating a theistic Æsthetic which should avoid the one-sided transcendence of deism on the one hand and the one-sided immanence of pantheism on the other, maintained that its principles must be sought not in the feelings of the contemplator, not in works of art, not in the idea of the beautiful, not in the concept of art, but in the creative spirit of the artist, the original fount of beauty ; and since a creative artist cannot be conceived except as derived from the highest creative genius which is God, Eckardt invokes aid from a psychology of God (*eine Psychologie des Weltkünstlers*).

Fried. Theodor Vischer.   If quantity is as important as quality, we must devote some space to Friedrich Theodor Vischer, the bulkiest of all German æstheticians, indeed the German æsthetician *par excellence* : after publishing a book on *The Sublime and the Comic, a contribution to the Philosophy of the Beautiful*,[3] in 1837, he produced four huge tomes on *Æsthetic as Science of the Beautiful* between 1846 and 1857,[4] where, in hundreds of paragraphs and long observations and sub-observations, is massed a stupendous amount of æsthetic material, of matter foreign to Æsthetic, and of subjects taken haphazard from the whole thinkable

[1] *Ästhetische Forschungen*, Frankfurt a. M. 1855.
[2] *Die theistische Begründung d. Ästhetik im Gegensatz z. d. pantheistichen*, Jena, 1857 ; same author, *Vorschule d. Asth.*, Karlsruhe, 1864-1865.
[3] *Üb. d. Erhabene u. Komische*, Stuttgart, 1837.
[4] *Ästhetik oder Wissenschaft d. Schönen*, Reutlingen, Leipzig and Stuttgart, 1846-1857. 3 parts in 4 vols.

XIII   MINOR GERMAN ÆSTHETICIANS   337

universe. Vischer's work is divided into three parts :
a Metaphysic of the Beautiful, which investigates the
concept of Beauty in itself, no matter where and how it
is realized : a treatise on concrete Beauty, which inquires
into the two one-sided modes of realization, Beauty of
nature and Beauty of imagination, one lacking subjective,
the other lacking objective, existence : lastly, a theory of
the arts, which studies the synthesis in art of the two
artistic moments, the physical and psychical, the objective
and subjective. It is easy to sum up Vischer's concept
of æsthetic activity ; it is Hegel's concept, debased. For
Vischer, Beauty belongs neither to the theoretical nor
to the practical activity, but is placed in a serene sphere,
superior to these antitheses ; that is to say in the sphere
of absolute Spirit, in company with Religion and Philosophy ; [1] but, in contradistinction to Hegel, Vischer
assigns the first place in this sphere to Religion, the second
to Art, and the third to Philosophy. Much ingenuity
was devoted in those days to moving these words about
like pieces on a chess-board ; it has been observed that
of the six possible combinations of the three terms Art,
Religion and Philosophy, four were actually adopted :
by Schelling, *P.R.A.* ; by Hegel, *A.R.P.* ; by Weisse,
P.A.R. ; and by Vischer, *R.A.P.*[2] But Vischer himself[3]
states that Wirth, author of a *System of Ethics,*[4] opted for
the fifth combination, *R.P.A.*, which leaves us but the
sixth, *A.P.R.*, unclaimed, unless (as is not improbable)
some unrecognized genius seized upon it and made it
the text of his system. Beauty, therefore, as the second
form of the absolute Spirit, is the realization of the Idea,
not as abstract concept but as union of concept and
reality ; and the Idea determines itself as species (*Gattung*),
and every idea of a species, even on the lowest degree, is
beautiful as being an integral part in the totality of
Ideas ; although the higher the degree of the idea the

[1] *Ästh.* introd. §§ 2-5.
[2] Hartmann, *Dtsch. Ästh. s. Kant*, p. 217, note.
[3] *Ästh.* introd. § 5.
[4] *System der spekulativen Ethik*, Heilbronn, 1841-1842.

greater is its beauty.[1] Highest of all degrees is that of
human personality : " in this spiritual world the Idea
attains its true significance ; the name of idea is given to
the great moral motive powers to which the concept of
species may also be applied in the sense that they stand
to their restricted spheres in the same relation in which
the genus stands to its species and individuals." At the
head of all is the Idea of morality : " the world of moral
and autonomous ends is destined to furnish the most
important, the most worthy content of the Beautiful " ;
with the warning, however, that Beauty, in actualizing
this world through intuition, excludes art having a moral
tendency.[2] So Vischer proceeds now to degrade Hegel's
Idea to the simple class-concept, now to couple it with
the idea of the Good ; now, in accord with the teaching
of his master, to make it different from, yet superior to,
intellect and morality.

Other tendencies. From the first, the Herbartian formalism was little
studied and less followed : two writers, Griepenkerl in
1827 and Bobrik in 1834, made some attempt to develop
and apply the cursory notes with which Herbart contented himself.[3] Schleiermacher's lectures, even before
their appearance in book form, had served as basis for a
series of elegant dissertations by Erich Ritter (1840) [4]
(better known as a historian of philosophy) ; his work is
of little value, for instead of dwelling on the important
points of the master's doctrine Ritter brings into promin-
ence secondary matters relating to sociability and the
æsthetic life. A penetrating critic of German Æsthetic
from Baumgarten to the post-Kantian school was Wilhelm
Theodor Danzel, who lived about this time and very
properly rebelled against the claim to find " thought " in
works of art : " Artistic thought : " he writes ; " un-
happy phrase, which helped to condemn an entire epoch
to the Sisyphean labour of trying to reduce art to intel-

[1] *Ästh.* §§ 15-17.   [2] *Op. cit.* §§ 19-24.
[3] Griepenkerl, *Lehrb. d. Ästh.*, Brunswick, 1827. Bobrik, *Freie
Verträge üb. Ästh.*, Zürich, 1834.
[4] *Üb. d. Principien d. Ästh.*, Kiel, 1840.

lectual and rational thinking! The thought of a work of art is nothing save that which is contemplated in a definite way; it is not represented, as is commonly asserted, in a work of art, it is the work of art itself. Artistic thought can never be expressed by concepts and words." [1] By his early death Danzel ended the hopes he raised by his original views on the science and history of Æsthetic.

The post-Hegelian metaphysical Æsthetic is chiefly noteworthy for the fuller development of two theories or, to speak more accurately, of two very curious combinations of arbitrary assertion and fanciful caprice : the so-called theory of Natural Beauty, and the theory of Modifications of the Beautiful. Neither of the two had any intimate or necessary connexion with this philosophical movement, to which they are rather linked by historical or psychological causes ; by the relationship between facts of pleasure and pain and the inclination towards mysticism ; by the confusion arising from the really æsthetic (imaginative) quality of some representations wrongly described as observation of natural beauties ; or by the scholastic and literary tradition of discussing these cases of pleasure and pain and extra-æsthetic natural beauties in books devoted to the discussion of art.[2] These metaphysicians were sometimes rather grotesque and remind one of the story told of Paisiello, that in the fury of composition he set even the stage directions of his libretto to music ; bitten with the rage for construction and dialectic, they did not spare even the indexes of chaotic old books, but seized on them as suitable material for a dialectical exercise.

Theory of the Beautiful in nature, and that of the Modifications of Beauty.

Beginning with the theory of Natural Beauty, observations on beautiful natural objects are found among the inquiries of the ancient philosophers on beauty, and especially among the mystical effusions of neo-Platonists and their followers in the Middle Ages and the Renaissance.[3] Less frequently such questions were introduced into treatises on Poetics: Tesauro (1654) is among the first

Development of the first theory. Herder.

---

[1] *Ges. Aufs.* pp. 216-221.   [2] See above, pp. 87-93.
[3] See above, pp. 179-180.

who, in his *Cannochiale aristotelico*, discusses not only the conceits of men, but also of God, the angels, nature and animals ; and somewhat later (1707) Muratori speaks of "the beauty of matter," of which examples are "the gods, a flower, the sun, a rivulet."[1] Observations on that which is outside art and is merely natural, are made by Crousaz, by André, and especially by those authors of the eighteenth century who wrote on Beauty and Art in an empirical and gallant style.[2] It was the influence of these persons that led Kant, as we have seen, to sever the theory of beauty from that of art, specially connecting free beauty with objects of nature and those productions of man which reproduce natural beauties.[3] When the adversary of Kant's theory of Æsthetic, Herder (1800), in his sketch of an ethical system united spirit and nature, pleasure and value, feeling and intellect, he inevitably made much of natural beauty, and affirmed that everything in nature has its own beauty, the expression of its own greatest content, and that this accounts for the ascending scale of beautiful objects : beginning with outlines, colours and tones, light and sound, and proceeding by way of flowers, water and sea, to birds, terrestrial animals, and man himself. For instance " a bird is the sum of the properties and perfections of its element, a representation of its potency, a creature of light, song and air " ; amongst terrestrial animals, the ugliest are those resembling man, as the melancholy moping monkey ; the most beautiful, those of perfect build, well proportioned, noble, free in action ; those which express sweetness ; those, in fine, which live in harmony and happiness, endowed with a perfection of their own, *Schelling,* harmless to man.[4] Schelling, on the contrary, utterly *Solger, Hegel.* denies the concept of beauty in nature, and considers that such beauty is purely accidental and that art alone supplies the norm by which it can be discovered and judged.[5] Solger also excludes natural beauty ;[6] so does

---

[1] *Cannochiale arist.* ch. 3 : *Perfetta poesia*, bk. I. chs. 6, 8.
[2] See above, pp. 205-206, 258-261.
[3] See above, pp. 275-277.   [4] *Kaligone, op. cit.* pp. 55-90.
[5] *System d. transcend. Ideal.* part vi. § 2.   [6] *Vorles. üb. Ästh.* p. 4.

Hegel, who distinguishes himself not by denying it but by proceeding with the utmost inconsequence to deal at length with the beautiful in nature. It is in fact not clear whether he means that really no beauty exists in nature and that man introduces it in his vision of things, or whether natural beauty really exists though inferior in degree to the beauty of art. " The beauty of art," he says, " stands higher than that of nature ; it is beauty born and reborn by the work of the spirit, and spirit alone is truth and reality ; hence beauty is truly beauty only when it participates in spirit and is produced therefrom. Taken in this sense, the beauty of nature appears as a mere reflexion of the beauty appertaining to spirit, as an imperfect and incomplete mode, which substantially is contained within the spirit itself." In confirmation, he adds that nobody has attempted a systematic exposition of natural beauties, whereas there actually is, from the point of view of the utility of natural objects, a *materia medica*.[1] But the second chapter of the first part of his Æsthetic is devoted precisely to natural Beauty on the ground that, in order to grasp the idea of artistic beauty in its entirety, three stages must be traversed : beauty in general, natural beauty (whose defects show the necessity for art), and, lastly, the Idea ; " the first existence of the Idea is nature, and its first beauty is natural beauty." This beauty, which is beauty for us and not for itself, has several phases, from that in which the concept is immersed in matter to the point of disappearing, such as physical facts and isolated mechanisms, to that higher phase in which physical facts are united in systems (*e.g.* the solar system) ; but the Idea first reaches a true and real existence in organic facts, in the living creature. And even the living creature is liable to the distinction between beautiful and ugly ; for example, among animals, the sloth, trailing itself laboriously and incapable of animation or activity, displeases us by its apathetic somnolence ; nor can beauty be found in amphibians or in many kinds of fish, or in crocodiles, or

[1] *Vorles. üb. Æsth.* I. pp. 4-5.

toads, as well as in many insects and especially in those equivocal creatures which express a transition from one class to another, such as the ornithorhyncus, a mixture of bird and beast.[1] These samples may suffice to show the general trend of Hegel's doctrine of natural beauty ; elsewhere he discusses the external beauty of abstract form, regularity, symmetry, harmony, etc., which are precisely the concepts which the formalism of Herbart placed in the heaven of the Ideas of the Beautiful.

Schleier-macher. Schleiermacher, who praised Hegel for his attempt to exclude natural beauty from his Æsthetic, excluded it from his own not verbally but actually, by confining his attention to the artistic perfection of the internal image formed by the energy of the human spirit.[2] But the so-called Feeling for Nature which came in with Romanticism, and the *Cosmos* and other descriptive works of

Alexander von Humboldt. Humboldt,[3] directed attention increasingly to the impressions awakened by natural facts. This led to the compilation of those systematic lists of natural beauties whose impossibility had been proclaimed by Hegel, though he himself had furnished an example of them ; amongst others, Bratranek published an *Æsthetic of the Vegetable World.*[4]

Vischer's " Æsthetic Physics." The best-known and most widely circulated treatment of the subject was contained in this very work of Vischer's ; who following Hegel's example devoted a section of his *Æsthetic,* as we have seen, to the objective existence of Beauty, *i.e.* to the Beauty of nature, and entitled it by the perhaps new and certainly characteristic name of Æsthetic Physics (*ästhetische Physik*). This Æsthetic Physics comprised the beauty of inorganic nature (light, heat, air, water, earth) ; organic nature, with its four vegetable types and its animals vertebrate and invertebrate ; and beauty of human beings, divided into generic and historic. The generic was subdivided into

[1] *Vorles. üb. Ästh.* I. pp. 148-180.
[2] *Op. cit.* introd.
[3] *Ansichten der Natur,* 1088 ; *Kosmos,* 1845-1858.
[4] *Ästhetik d. Pflanzenwelt,* Leipzig, 1853.

sections on the beauty of general forms (age, sex, conditions, love, marriage, family) ; of special forms (races,
peoples, culture, political life) ; and of individual forms
(temperament and character). Historical beauty included that of ancient history (Oriental, Greek, Roman),
of Mediæval or Germanic, and of modern times ; because,
according to Vischer, it was the duty of Æsthetic to
cast a glance over universal history before summing up
the different degrees of the beautiful according to the
varying phases of the struggle for freedom against
nature.[1]

As regards the Modifications of Beauty, it should be
remembered that the ancient manuals of Poetics, and
more frequently those of Rhetoric, contained more or
less scientific definitions of psychological states and facts ;
Aristotle attempted in his *Poetics* to determine the nature
of a tragic action or personality, and sketched a definition
of the comic ; in his Rhetoric he writes at considerable
length of wit ; [2] sections of the *De oratore* of Cicero and
the *Institutions* of Quintilian [3] are devoted to wit and the
comic ; the lofty style was the subject of a lost treatise
of Caecilius, which anticipated that attributed to Longinus,
whose title was translated in modern times as *De sublimitate* or *On the Sublime*. Following the example of
the ancients, this kind of medley was perpetuated by
writers of the sixteenth and seventeenth centuries ; whole
treatises on the comic are incorporated in, for instance,
the *Argutezza* of Matteo Pellegrini (1639) and the *Cannoc-
chiale* of Tesauro. La Bruyère treated of the sublime [4]
and Boileau by his translation gave a fresh vogue to
Longinus : the following century saw Burke inquiring
into the origin of our ideas of the beautiful and the
sublime, and deriving the former from the instinct for
sociability, the latter from that of self-preservation ; he
also tried to define ugliness, grace, elegance and extraordinary beauty ; Home, in his celebrated *Elements of
Criticism*, discussed grandeur, sublimity, the ridiculous,

*The Theory of
the Modifica-
tions of
Beauty.
From anti-
quity to the
eighteenth
century.*

---

[1] *Æsth.* § 341.   [2] *Poet.* 5. 13-14 ; *Rhet.* iii. 10, 18.
[3] *De orat.* ii. 54-71 ; *Inst. orat.* vi. 3.   [4] *Caractères*, I.

wit, dignity and grace : Mendelssohn discussed sublimity, dignity and grace in fine art, and described some of these facts as due to mixed feelings, in' which he was followed by Lessing[1] and others : Sulzer welcomed all these various concepts into his æsthetic encyclopædia and collected round them an elaborate bibliography. A new and curious meaning of the word humour reached the continent from England at this time. Its original meaning was simply " temperament," and sometimes " spirit," or " wit " (" *belli umori* " in Italy ; in the seventeenth century there was in Rome an Academy of *Umoristi*). Voltaire introduced it into France and wrote in 1761, " *Les Anglais ont un terme pour signifier cette plaisanterie, ce vrai comique, cette gaieté, cette urbanité, ces saillies, qui échappent à un homme sans qu'il s'en doute ; et ils rendent cette idée par le mot* humour . . ." ; [2] in 1767 Lessing distinguishes humour from the German *Laune* (caprice, whim),[3] a distinction maintained by Herder in 1769 in opposition to Riedel who had confused the terms.[4]

Kant and the post-Kantians. Accustomed to find all these subjects treated in the same book, philosophers at first theorized about them all without attempting to link them up together by introducing an artificial logical connexion. Kant, who had already in imitation of Burke written in 1764 a dissertation on the beautiful and the sublime, ingenuously remarked in the course of his lectures on Logic in 1771 that the beautiful and the æsthetic are not identical, because " the sublime also belongs to Æsthetic " ; [5] and in his *Critique of Judgment*, while treating of the comic in a mere digression (a magnificent piece of psychological analysis) [6] places side by side with and as if on an equality with the " Analytic of Beauty," an " Analytic of the Sublime." [7] We may note in passing that, before the publication of the third Critique, Heydenreich arrived at

[1] *Hamb. Dramat.* Nos. 74-75.
[2] Letter to abbé d'Olivet, August 20, 1761.
[3] *Hamb. Dramat.* No. 93 ; in *Werke, ed. cit.* xii. pp. 170-171, note.
[4] *Kritische Wälder*, in *Werke, ed. cit.* iv. pp. 182-186.
[5] Schlapp, *op. cit.* p. 55.
[6] *Kr. d. Urth., Anmerkung*, § 54.   [7] *Op. cit.* bk. ii. §§ 23-29.

the same doctrine of the sublime which is contained in
Kant's book.[1]   Did Kant ever think of uniting the beautiful and the sublime and deducing them from a single
concept ? Apparently not.   By his declaration that the
principle of beauty must be sought outside ourselves,
and that of the sublime within us, he tacitly assumes
that the two objects are wholly disparate.   In 1805 Ast,
a follower of Schelling, declared the necessity of overcoming what he called the Kantian dualism of the beautiful and the sublime : [2]   others reproached Kant with
having treated the comic by the psychological, not the
metaphysical, method.   Schiller wrote a series of dissertations on the tragic, the sentimental, the ingenuous, the
sublime, the pathetic, the trivial, the low, the dignified
and the graceful, and their varieties, the fascinating, the
majestic, the grave, and the solemn.   Another artist,
Jean Paul Richter, discoursed at great length on wit and
humour, described by him as the romantic comic, or the
sublime reversed (*umgekehrte Erhabene*).[3]

Herbart, in virtue of his formalistic principle, asserts
that all these concepts are irrelevant to Æsthetic ; he
attributes them to the work of art, not to pure beauty ; [4]
Schleiermacher comes to the same conclusion, but for
much better reasons, as a result of his sane conception
of art.   Amongst other things he observes : " It is usual
to describe the beautiful and the sublime as two kinds
of artistic perfection ; and so accustomed have we grown
to the union of these two concepts that we must make
an effort to convince ourselves how very far they are
from being co-ordinate or from together exhausting the
concept of artistic perfection " ; he regrets that even
the best æstheticians should give rhetorical descriptions
of them instead of demonstrating them.   " The thing,"
says he, " is not right and just " (*hat keine Richtigkeit*),
and he proceeds to exclude the whole subject from his
Æsthetic,[5] as he had done previously in the case of

[1] *System d. Ästh.* introd. p. xxxvi *n.*
[2] *System der Kunstlehre* : cf. Hartmann, *op. cit.* p. 387.
[3] *Vorschule d. Ästh.* chs. 6-9.
[4] See above, pp. 309-310.   [5] *Vorles. üb. Ästh.* p. 240 *seqq.*

natural beauty. Other philosophers, however, clung persistently to their search for a connexion between these various concepts, and called in dialectic to help them. The habit of applying dialectic to empirical concepts affected everybody at that time ; even the great enemy of dialectic, Herbart, showed the cloven hoof, when in order to explain the union of different æsthetic ideas in the beautiful he appealed to the formula " they lose regularity in order to regain it." [1] Schelling asserted that the sublime is the infinite in the finite, and the beautiful the finite in the infinite, adding that the absolutely sublime includes the beautiful, and the beautiful the sublime ; [2] and Ast, whom we have mentioned already, spoke of a masculine, positive element, which is the sublime, and a feminine, negative element which is the graceful and pleasing : between which there is a contrast and a struggle. These exercises in dialectical system-building developed and increased till about the middle of the nineteenth century they assumed two distinct forms whose history must here be shortly outlined.

Culmination of the development.

Double form of the theory. The overcoming of the ugly. Solger, Weisse and others.

The first form may be called the Overcoming of the Ugly. This theory conceives the comic, the sublime, the tragic, the humorous, and so forth, as so many engagements in the war between the Ugly and the Beautiful, wherein the latter was invariably victorious, and arose by means of this war to more and more lofty and complex manifestations. The second form of the theory may be described as the Passage from Abstract to Concrete ; it held that Beauty cannot emerge from the abstract, cannot become this or that concrete beauty, except by particularizing itself in the comic, tragic, sublime, humorous, or some other modification. The first form was already well developed in Solger, an adherent of the romantic theory of Irony : but historically it presupposes the æsthetic theory of the Ugly, first sketched by Friedrich Schlegel in 1797. We have

[1] Cf. Zimmermann, *G. d. Asth.* p. 788.
[2] *Philos. d. Kunst,* §§ 65-66.

already noted that Schlegel considered the characteristic
or interesting, not the beautiful, to be the principle of
modern art ; hence the importance attached by him to
the piquant, the striking (*frappant*), the daring, the cruel,
the ugly.[1] Solger found here the basis for his dialectic :
amongst other things he maintains that the finite, earthly
element may be dissolved and absorbed in the divine,
which constitutes the tragic : or else the divine element
may be entirely corrupted by the earthly, producing the
comic.[2] These methods of Solger were followed by Weisse
(1830), and by Ruge (1837) ; for the former, ugliness is
"the immediate existence of beauty " which is overcome
in the sublime and the comic ; for the latter, the effort
to achieve the Idea, or the Idea searching for itself,
generates the sublime ; when the Idea loses instead of
discovering itself, ugliness is produced ; when the Idea
rediscovers itself and rises out of ugliness to new life,
the comic.[3] A whole treatise entitled *The Æsthetic of
the Ugly*[4] was published by Rosenkranz in 1853, presenting
this concept as intermediate between the beautiful and
the comic, and tracing it from its first origin to that
" sort of perfection " it attains in the satanic. Passing
from the common (*Gemeine*) which is the petty, the weak,
the low, and the sub-species of the low, viz. the usual,
the casual, the arbitrary and the crude, Rosenkranz goes
on to describe the repugnant, trisected into the awkward,
the dead and empty, and the horrible : thus he proceeds
from tripartition to tripartition, dividing the horrible
into the absurd, the nauseating and the wicked : the
wicked into criminal, spectral and diabolical : the
diabolical into demoniac, magical and satanic. He
opposes the childish notion that ugliness acts as a foil
to beauty in art, and justifies its introduction by the
necessity for art to represent the entire appearance of
the Idea ; on the other hand he admits that the ugly

[1] Cf. Hartmann, *Deutsch. Ästh. s. Kant*, pp. 363-364.
[2] *Vorles üb. Ästh.* p. 85.
[3] *Neue Vorschule d. Ästh.* Halle, 1837.
[4] K. Rosenkranz, *Ästhetik des Hässlichen*, Königsberg, 1853.

is not on the same level as the beautiful, for, if the beautiful can stand by itself alone, the other cannot do so and
must always be reflected by and in the beautiful.[1]

*Passage from
abstract to
concrete:
Vischer.*

The second form prevailed with Vischer. The following extract will serve as an illustration of his manner :
" The Idea arouses itself from the tranquil unity in
which it was fused with the appearance and pushes onward, affirming, in face of its own finitude, its infinity " ;
this rebellion and transcendence is the sublime. " But
Beauty demands full satisfaction for this disruption of
its harmony : the violated right of the image must be
reasserted : this can be accomplished only by means of
a fresh contradiction, that is to say by the negative
position now taken up by the image towards the Idea
by rejecting all interpenetration with it and by affirming
its own separate existence as the whole " ; this second
moment is the comic, negation of a negation.[2] The same
process is further enriched and complicated by Zeising,
who compares the modifications of Beauty to the re-
fraction of colours : the three primary modifications, the
sublime, the attractive and the humorous, correspond with
the primary colours violet, orange and green ; the three
secondary, pure beauty, comic and tragic, to the colours
red, yellow and blue. Each of these six modifications
(exactly like the degrees of the Ugly in Rosenkranz)
branches out, like fireworks, into three rays : pure beauty
into the decorous, noble and pleasing : the attractive
into graceful, interesting and piquant : the comic into
buffoonery, the diverting and burlesque : the humorous
into the quaint, capricious and melancholy : the tragic
into the moving, pathetic and demoniac : the sublime
into the glorious, majestic and imposing.[3]

*The Legend
of Sir
Purebeauty.*

All the works of this period on Æsthetic are filled in
this way with the *gest, chanson* or romaunt of the knight
Sir Purebeauty (*Reinschön*) and his extraordinary ad-
ventures, recounted in two conflicting versions. According to one story, Sir Purebeauty is constrained to abandon

[1] *Ästh. d. Hässl.* pp. 36-40.   [2] *Ästh.* §§ 83-84, 154-155.
[3] *Ästh. Forsch.* p. 413.

his beloved leisure by the Mephistophelean devices of the temptress Ugliness, who leads him into countless dangers from which he invariably emerges victorious; his victories and successes (his Marengo, Austerlitz and Jena) are called the Sublime, the Comic, the Humorous and so forth. The other story tells how the knight, bored by his life of loneliness, sallies forth purposely to seek adversaries and occasions for fighting; he is always vanquished, but even in his overthrow *ferum victorem capit*, he transforms and irradiates the enemy. Beyond this artificial mythology, this legend composed without the least imagination or literary skill, this miserably dull tale, it is vain to look for anything whatever in the much elaborated theory of German æstheticians known as the Modifications of Beauty.

XIV

ÆSTHETIC IN FRANCE, ENGLAND AND ITALY DURING THE FIRST HALF OF THE NINE-TEENTH CENTURY

Æsthetic movement in France : Cousin, Jouffroy. IN the last quarter of the eighteenth century and the first half of the nineteenth century German thought, notwith-standing the glaring errors which vitiated it, and were soon to bring about a violent and indeed exaggerated reaction, must on the whole be awarded the foremost place in the general history of European thought as well as in the individual study of Æsthetic, the contemporary philosophy of other countries standing on an inferior level of the second and third degree. France still lay under the dominion of the sensationalism of Condillac and, at the opening of the century, was quite incapable of grasping the spiritual activity of art. A faint gleam of Winckelmann's abstract spiritualism just appears in the theories of Quatremère de Quincy, who, in criticism of Émeric-David (in his turn a critic of ideal beauty and an adherent of the imitation of nature),[1] maintained that the arts of design have pure beauty, devoid of individual character, as their objective ; they depict man and not men.[2] Some sensationalists, such as Bonstetten, vainly endeavoured to trace the peculiar processes of imagina-tion in life and in art.[3] Followers of the orthodox

[1] Émeric-David, *Recherches sur l'art du statuaire chez les anciens*, Paris, 1805 (Ital. trans., Florence, 1857).

[2] Quatremère de Quincy, *Essai sur l'imitation dans les beaux arts*, 1823.

[3] *Recherches sur la nature et les lois de l'imagination*, 1807.

spiritualism of the French universities date the beginning
of a new era, and the foundation of Æsthetic in France, to
1818, the year when Victor Cousin first delivered at the
Sorbonne his lectures on the True, the Beautiful and the
Good, which later formed his book with the same name,
frequently reprinted.[1] These lectures of Cousin are but
poor stuff, although some scraps of Kant are to be found
in them here and there ; he denies the identity of the
beautiful with the pleasant or useful, and substitutes the
affirmation of a threefold beauty, physical, intellectual
and moral, the last being the true ideal beauty, having
its foundations in God ; he says that art expresses ideal
Beauty, the infinite, God, that genius is the power of
creation, and that taste is a mixture of fancy, sentiment
and reason.[2]   Academic phrases all of them ; pompous
and void and, for that very reason, well received.   Of
much greater value were the lectures on Æsthetic delivered
by Théodore Jouffroy in 1822, before a small audience,
and published posthumously in 1843.[3]   Jouffroy allowed
a beauty of expression, to be found alike in art and
nature : a beauty of imitation, consisting in the perfect
accuracy with which a model is reproduced : a beauty
of idealisation, which reproduces the model, accentuating
a particular quality in order to give it greater significance :
and, finally, a beauty of the invisible or of content,
reducible to force (physical, sensible, intellectual, moral),
which, as force, awakens sympathy.   Ugliness is the
negation of this sympathetic beauty ; its species or
modifications are the sublime and the graceful.   One sees
that Jouffroy did not succeed in isolating the strictly
æsthetic fact in his analysis and gave, instead of a scientific
system, little beyond explanations of the use of words.
He could not see or understand that expression, imitation
and idealization are identical with each other and with
artistic activity.   Moreover he had many curious ideas,
chiefly concerning expression.   He said that if we were

---

[1] Du vrai, du beau et du bien, 1818, many lines revised (23rd ed.
Paris, 1881).   [2] Op. cit. lectures 6-8.

[3] Cours d'esthétique, ed. Damiron, Paris, 1843.

to see a drunkard with all the most disgusting symptoms
of intoxication on a road where there was also an unhewn
rock, we should be pleased by the drunken man, since
he had expression, and not by the rock, since it had none.
Beside Jouffroy, whose theories, crude and immature
though they be, reveal an inquiring mind, it is hardly
worth while to cite Lamennais,[1] who like Cousin regarded
art as the manifestation of the infinite through the finite,
of the absolute through the relative.   French Romanticism in de Bonald, de Barante and Mme. de Staël had
defined literature as " the expression of society," had
honoured, under German influence, the characteristic and
the grotesque,[2] and had proclaimed the independence
of art by means of the formula " art for art's sake " ; but
these vague affirmations or aphorisms did not supersede,
philosophically speaking, the old doctrine of the " imitation of nature."

*English
Æsthetic.*
In England associationistic psychology still flourished
(and has continued to flourish uninterruptedly), unable
to emancipate itself wholly from sensationalism or to
understand imagination.   Dugald Stewart [3] had recourse
to the wretched expedient of establishing two forms of
association : one of accidental associations, the other of
associations innate in human nature and therefore common
to all mankind.   England did not escape German influence, as appears, for example, in Coleridge, to whom
we owe a saner concept of poetry and the difference
between it and science [4] (in collaboration with the poet
Wordsworth), and in Carlyle, who placed intellect lower
than imagination, " organ of the Divine."   The most
noteworthy English æsthetic essay of this period is the
Defence of Poetry by Shelley (1821),[5] containing profound,
if not very systematic, views on the distinctions between
reason and imagination, prose and poetry ; on primitive

[1] *De l'art et du beau*, 1843-1846.

[2] Victor Hugo, Preface to *Cromwell*, 1827.

[3] Dugald Stewart, *Elements of the Philosophy of the Human Mind*,
1837.

[4] Gayley-Scott, *An Introd.* pp. 305-306.

[5] P. B. Shelley, *A Defence of Poetry* (in *Works*, London, 1880, vol. vii.)

language and the faculty of poetic objectification which
enshrines and preserves " the record of the best and
happiest moments of the happiest and best minds."

In Italy, where neither Parini nor Foscolo [1] had been *Italian*
able to shake off the fetters of the old doctrines (although *Æsthetic.*
the latter, in his later writings, was in several ways an
innovator in literary criticism), many treatises and essays
on Æsthetic were published during the earlier decades
of the century, the greater part showing the influence of
Condillac's sensationalism, which had a great vogue in
Italy. Such authors as Delfico, Malaspina, Cicognara,
Talia, Pasquali, Visconti and Bonacci belong more exclusively to the special, or rather, the anecdotal, history
of Italian philosophy. Now and then, however, one
comes across remarks that are not wholly contemptible,
as in Melchiorre Delfico (1818) who, after wandering
aimlessly hither and thither, fixes on the principle of
expression, observing, " If it were possible to establish
that expression is always an element in the beautiful, it
would be a legitimate inference to regard it as the real
characteristic of beauty, *i.e.* a condition without which
the beautiful could not exist, and the pleasing modification which arouses the sentiment of beauty could not
take place in us " ; he tries to develop this principle by
asserting that all other characters (order, harmony,
proportion, symmetry, simplicity, unity and variety) have
significance only by their subordination to the principle
of expression.[2]   In opposition to Malaspina's definition of
beauty as " pleasure born of a representation " ; and in
opposition to the then fashionable threefold division of
beauty into sensible, moral and intellectual, a critic of
Malaspina observed that if beauty be representation, it
is inconceivable that there should be intellectual beauty,
which would be intelligible but not presentable.[3]   Nor
must Pasquale Balestrieri be forgotten ; he was a student

[1] Parini, *Principî delle belle lettere applicati alle belle arti*, from 1773
onward ; Foscolo, *Dell' origine e dell' uffizio della letteratura*, 1809, and
Saggi di critica, composed in England.
[2] M. Delfico, *Nuove ricerche sul bello*, Naples, 1818, ch. 9.
[3] Malaspina, *Delle leggi del bello*, Milan, 1828, pp. 26, 233.

of medicine who in 1847 tried to construct an Æsthetic
of an exact or mathematical kind, with neither better
nor worse result than many famous authors in other
countries. He noticed, while turning his algebraical
expressions into numerals, that such general formulæ
" fulfil their object with an infinite number of systems of
different ciphers " ; and that in art there is an element
" not arbitrary, but unknown." [1] Works by German
authors were frequently translated at this time, some of
them, for example the writings of the two Schlegels,
being reprinted several times ; the *Æsthetic* of Bouterweck,
deriving from Kant and Schiller,[2] was read and discussed ;
Colecchi gave an excellent statement of the æsthetic
doctrines of Kant ; [3] and in 1831 a certain Lichtenthal
adapted the *Æsthetic* of Franz Ficker [4] to the use of
Italian readers ; later the same book was fully translated by another hand ; some of Schelling's writings
were translated, *e.g.* his discourses on the relation between
figurative art and nature.

Rosmini and Gioberti.   It must be admitted that in Italy Æsthetic received
but inadequate treatment in the revival of philosophical
speculation effected by the work of Galluppi, Rosmini
and Gioberti. It is treated in a merely incidental and
popular manner by the first named.[5] Rosmini devotes
a section of his philosophical system to the deonto-
logical sciences, which " treat of the perfection of being,
and the method of acquiring or producing such perfection
or losing it " ; among these sciences is that of " beauty
in the universal " under the name of Callology, of which
a special part is Æsthetic, the science of " beauty in the
sensible," establishing the " archetypes of beings." [6] In his
longest literary work, considered by him as his Æsthetic,[7]

[1] P. Balestrieri, *Fondamenti di estetica*, Naples, 1847.

[2] Friedrich Bouterweck, *Ästhetik*, 1806, 1815 (3rd ed., Göttingen, 1824–1825).

[3] O. Colecchi, *Questioni filosofiche*, vol. iii., Naples, 1843.

[4] P. Lichtenthal, *Estetica ossia dottrina del bello e delle arti belle*, Milan, 1831.

[5] *Elementi di filosofia* (5th ed., Naples, 1846), vol. ii. pp. 427-476.

[6] *Sistema filosofico*, by A. Rosmini-Serbati, Turin, 1886, § 210.

[7] Cf. *Nuovo saggio sopra l' orig. delle idee*, § v. part iv. ch. 5.

his essay on *The Idyl*,[1] Rosmini declares the aim of art
to be neither imitation of nature nor direct intuition of
the archetypes, but the reduction of natural things to
their archetypes, which are arranged in a hierarchy of
three ideals, natural, intellectual and moral. Gioberti [2]
is clearly under the influence of German idealism, especially
of Schelling's ; for him the beautiful is " the individual
union of an intelligible type with an imaginative element
called into being by fancy " ; the phantasm gives material,
while the intelligible type (concept) gives form, in the
Aristotelian sense,[3] and since the ideal element predominates over the sensible or fantastic, art is a propædeutic
to the true and the good. Gioberti is of opinion that
Hegel was wrong in detaching natural beauty from
Æsthetic, for perfect beauty of nature is " the full correspondence of sensible reality with the Idea which informs
and represents it," and as such " makes its appearance
in the sensible universe during the second period of the
primordial age described in detail by Moses in the six
days of creation " ; it is only through original sin that
imperfection and ugliness arose in nature.[4] Art is
nothing but a supplement to natural beauty, whose
decadence it presupposes, and thus art is at once record
and prophecy, referring to the first and last ages of the
world. The Last Judgement will reintroduce perfect
beauty : " organic restitution, by empowering the
faculties to contemplate the intelligible in the sensible,
and by refining their capabilities, will greatly intensify
and purify æsthetic enjoyment. The contemplation of
perfect beauty will be the beatitude of imagination, of
which Christ gave an ineffable foretaste by appearing to
his disciples visibly transfigured and shining with celestial
radiance." [5] Gioberti agrees with Schelling's division of
art into pagan and Christian, a " heterodox beauty "
(Oriental and Græco-Italian art), imperfect when compared with " orthodox beauty " ; and between the two,

[1] *Sull' idillio e sulla nuova letteratura italiana* (*opuscoli filosofici*, vol. i.).
[2] V. Gioberti, *Del buono e del bello* (Florence ed., 1857).
[3] *Del bello*, ch. i.   [4] *Op. cit.* ch. 7.   [5] *Op. cit.* ch. 7.

a " semi-orthodox " beauty,[1] transitional to Christian art ;
he also attempted a doctrine of modifications of the
beautiful, wherein he held the sublime to be creator of the
beautiful.   Beauty is the relative intelligibility of created
things apprehended by fancy : the sublime is the absolute
intelligibility of time, space and infinite power as presented to itself by the faculty of imagination : " The
ideal formula : the Being creates the Existing, translated
into æsthetic language, gives the following formula : by
means of the dynamical sublime Being creates the
beautiful ; and by means of the mathematical sublime
contains it : this shows the ontological and psychological connexions of Æsthetic in First Science."   Ugliness enters into the beautiful either as relief and counter-
poise, or to open a way to the comic, or to depict the
struggle between good and evil.   The Christian ideal of
artistic beauty is the figure of the God-Man, absolute
union of the two forms of beauty, the sublime and the
beautiful, a transfigured and divinely illuminated expression of man.[2]   However carefully we sift the thoughts
of Gioberti from their mythological Judaico-Christian
husk, we find nothing of the least value to science.

*Italian
Romantics.
Dependence
of Art.*
On the other hand, if Italian literature of the day
chose to revive and refurbish certain antiquated critical
ideas, a much wider field was opened by social and
political upheavals which tended to make use of literature
as a practical instrument for spreading abroad the truths
of history, science, religion and morality.   In 1816
Giovanni Berchet wrote that " poetry . . . is intended
to improve the habits of man and satisfy the cravings of
his imagination and heart, since the tendency towards
poetry, like every other desire, awakens in us moral
needs " ; [3] and Ermes Visconti in his *Conciliatore* of 1818
says that æsthetic aims must be subordinated " to the
improvement of mankind and public and private weal,
the eminent aim of all studies."   Manzoni, who subsequently took to philosophizing on art on the principles

---

[1] *Del bello*, chs. 8-10.   [2] *Op. cit.* ch. 4.
[3] G. Berchet, *Opere*, ed. Cusani, Milan, 1863, p. 227.

of Rosmini, declared in his letter on Romanticism (1823)
that " poetry or literature in general should have utility
as its objective, truth as its subject and interest as its
means " ;[1] and though noticing the vagueness of the
concept of truth in poetry, he inclined always (as is
seen also in his discourse on the historical novel) to its
identification with historical and scientific truth.[2] Pietro
Maroncelli proposed as a substitute for the classic formula
of art, " founded on imitation of the real and having
pleasure as its object," a formula of art as " founded on
inspiration, having the beautiful as means and good as
end " ; this doctrine he baptized " cormentalism," contrasting it with the doctrine of art for art's sake found
in the writings of August Wilhelm Schlegel and Victor
Hugo.[3] Tommaseo defined beauty as " the union of
many truths in one concept " effected by the power of
feeling.[4] Giuseppe Mazzini, too, always conceived literature as the mediator of the universal idea or intellectual
concept.[5] Attempting to restore serious content to a
literature grown weak and frivolous, the Italian Romantics
found themselves forced on the theoretical side, by a
natural reaction, into constant and perpetual opposition
to every tendency of thought likely to affirm the independence of art.

[1] Words suppressed in ed. of 1870.

[2] *Epistolario*, ed. Sforza, i. pp. 285, 306, 308 ; *Discorso sul romanzo
storico*, 1845 ; *Dell' invenzione*, dialogue.

[3] *Addizioni alle Miei Prigioni*, 1831 (in Pellico, *Prose*, Florence,
1858) ; see pp. about the *Conciliatore*.

[4] *Del bello e del sublime*, 1827 ; *Studi filosofici* (Venice, 1840), vol. ii.
part v.

[5] Cf. De Sanctis, *Lett. ital. nel s. XIX*, ed. Croce, Naples 1896,
pp. 427-431.

FRANCESCO DE SANCTIS

ON the other hand, the autonomy of art found a strong
supporter in Italy in the critical work of Francesco de
Sanctis, who held private classes in literature at Naples
from 1838 to 1848, taught at Turin and Zürich from 1852
to 1860 and in 1870 became professor in the University
of Naples. He expressed his doctrines in critical essays,
in monographs on Italian writers and in his classic
History of Italian Literature. Receiving his first elements
of old Italian culture in Puoti's school, his natural bent
towards speculation led him to investigate grammatical
and rhetorical doctrines with the view of reducing them
to a system ; but he soon began to criticize and to grow
out of this phase. He pronounced Fortunio, Alunno,
Accarisio and Corso " empirics " ; he had a slightly
better opinion of Bembo, Varchi, Castelvetro and Salviati,
who introduced " method " into grammar, a process
completed subsequently by Buonmattei, Corticelli and
Bartoli ; and he proclaimed Francisco Sanchez, author
of the *Minerva,* " the Descartes of grammarians." From
these his admiration spread to the French writers of the
eighteenth century and the philosophical grammars of
Du Marsais, Beauzée, Condillac and Gérard ; following
in their wake and pursuing the ideal of Leibniz, he conceived a " logical grammar " ; in this effort, however,
he soon began to recognize the impossibility of reducing
the differences of languages to fixed logical principles.
If he found the French theorists admirable in their ability
to reconstitute the simple and primitive forms ; from

" I love " to " I am loving," something disquieted him ;
" Such decomposition of ' I love ' into ' I am loving ' "
(said he) " deadens the word by depriving it of the
movement proceeding from active will." [1]   In the same
way he read and criticized the writers of treatises on
Rhetoric and Poetics from sixteenth-century men such
as Castelvetro and Torquato Tasso (whom he dared to
describe as an " indifferent critic," to the great scandal
of Neapolitan men of letters) to Muratori and Gravina,
" more acute than accurate " ; and eighteenth-century
Italians, Bettinelli, Algarotti and Cesarotti. Coldly
rational rules found no favour with him : he urged the
young to confront literary works boldly and freely
absorb impressions, the only possible foundation for
taste.[2]

Philosophical study had not been abandoned and had   *Influence of*
not even fallen into entire decadence in Southern Italy ;   *Hegelism.*
in these days of renewed interest in philosophy the
theories on Beauty from over the Alps and the new
ideas of Gioberti and other Italians [3] aroused enthusiastic
discussion.   Vico was read again, and Bénard's French
translation of Hegel's *Æsthetic* appeared and was canvassed
in Naples volume by volume (the first in 1840, the second
in 1843, and the rest between 1848 and 1852).   In its
desire for new intellectual food Italian youth set itself
to learn German : De Sanctis himself had to translate
the greater *Logic* of Hegel and Rosenkranz's *History of
Literature* in the dungeon of the Bourbon prison where
he was incarcerated on account of his liberal opinions.
The new critical tendency was named " philosophism "
to distinguish it from the old grammatical criticism and
from the vague, incoherent, exaggerated Romanticism.
Philosophism attracted De Sanctis ; to show how deeply
he was imbued with the Hegelian spirit a tale was told
that, having devoured the first volumes of Bénard's

---

[1] *Frammenti di scuola*, in *Nuovi saggi critici*, pp. 321-333 ; *La
giovinezza di Fr. de S.* (autobiography), pp. 62, 101, 163-166 (works
cited are those of De S. in stereotyped Naples ed. by Morano, 12 vols.).

[2] *La giovinezza di Fr. de S.* pp. 260-261, 315-316.

[3] *Saggi critici*, p. 534.

translation, he guessed the contents of the remaining volumes and, before they could appear, was expounding them publicly in his classroom.[1]

His first writings show traces of metaphysical idealism and Hegelism ; and they still linger here and there in the terminology of his later works. In a lecture prior to 1848 he placed the safety of criticism in the philosophic school which, in works of literature, fixed its eyes upon " that absolute part . . . that uncertain idea which moves within the mind of great writers, till it appears abroad clothed in fine raiment only less beautiful than itself." [2] In a preface to Schiller's plays (1850) he wrote, " The Idea is not thought, nor is poetry reason in song, as a poet of our time is pleased to assert ; the idea is at once necessity and freedom, reason and passion, and its perfect form in drama is action." [3] Elsewhere he calls attention to the death of faith and poetry, absorbed by the development of philosophy : a thesis, he remarked some years later, " imposed on our generation by Hegel with his omnipotent thought." [4] In 1856 he attempted a definition of humour as " an artistic form having for signification the destruction of limit, with consciousness of such destruction." [5] Not to dwell too long on other particulars, in the distinction to which De Sanctis always held firm throughout his critical work, that between Fancy and Imagination, the latter considered as the true and only faculty of poetry, arises undoubtedly from suggestions of Schelling and Hegel (*Einbildungskraft, Phantasie*) ; from the same philosophers come the phrases " prosaic content," " prosaic world," sometimes used by him.

Unconscious criticism of Hegelism. For De Sanctis the Hegelian Æsthetic was but a lever wherewith to lift himself clear of the discussions and views of the old Italian schools. A fresh, clear spirit

[1] De Meis, *Comm. di Fr. de S.* (in vol. *In Memoria*, Naples, 1884, p. 116).
[2] *Scritti vari*, ed. Croce, vol. ii. pp. 153-154.
[3] *Saggi critici*, p 18.
[4] *Op. cit.* pp. 226-228 ; *Scritti vari*, ii. pp. 185-187 ; cf. vol. ii. p. 70.
[5] *Saggi critici*, ed. Imbriani, p. 91.

such as his could not escape the arbitrary shackles of grammarians and rhetoricians only to fall into those of metaphysicians, the torturers of art. He absorbed the vital part of Hegel's teaching and re-expressed the Hegelian theories in correct or somewhat attenuated interpretations ; but he only maintained with hesitation, and in the end openly rebelled against, all that was artificial, formalistic and pedantic in Hegel.

The following examples of such reductions and attenuations show how substantial and radical was the change he effected. " Faith has vanished and poetry is dead " (he wrote in 1856, echoing Hegel) ; " or it were better to say " (here is De Sanctis' own correction) " faith and poetry are immortal : what has disappeared is but one particular mode of their being. To-day faith springs from conviction and poetry is the spark struck from meditation ; they are not dead, they are transformed." [1]   Certainly he distinguished between imagination and fancy ; but for him imagination was never the mystic faculty of transcendental apperception, the intellectual intuition of German metaphysicians, but simply the poet's faculty of synthesis and creation, contrasting with fancy as the faculty of collecting particulars and materials in a somewhat mechanical fashion.[2]   When students of Vico and Hegel understood and expounded their master's theories as emphasizing the importance of concepts in art, De Sanctis replied, " The concept does not exist in art, nature or history : the poet works unconsciously and sees no concept but only form, in which he is involved and wellnigh lost. If the philosopher, by means of abstraction, can extract the concept thence and contemplate it in all its purity, he acts in a way entirely contrary to that of art, nature and history." He warned his hearers not to misunderstand Vico, who, when he extracts concepts and exemplary types from the Homeric poems, is not writing as an art critic but as a historian of civilization : Achilles

---

[1] Saggi critici, p. 228 ; cf. Scritti vari, vol. ii. p. 70.
[2] Storia della letteratura, i. pp. 66-67 ; Saggi critici, pp. 98-99 ; Scritti vari, vol. i. pp. 276-278, 384.

is artistically Achilles, not strength or any other abstraction.[1] Thus his polemic is directed in the first instance against misunderstanding what he called the true Hegelian thought, which was in fact usually a correction made upon Hegel more or less consciously by himself. He was able to boast in his latter years that even at the time when all Naples went wild over Hegel, " at the time when Hegel was master of the field," he had always " made certain reservations and refused to accept his apriorism, his triad or his formulæ." [2]

Criticisms of German Æsthetic.

De Sanctis also took up an independent attitude towards the other German æstheticians. The views of Wilhelm Schlegel, very advanced for the day in which they had been promulgated, seemed to him to have been already superseded. In 1856 he wrote that Schlegel strives to " transcend ordinary criticism, which leads a humdrum existence among phraseology, versification and elocution, but loses its way and never comes face to face with art : whereas Schlegel throws himself headlong into the probable, the decorous and the moral ; into everything save art." [3] Thrown by the hazards of life into German territory, he found himself at the Zürich Polytechnic, and found among his colleagues (only imagine such a thing !) Theodor Vischer. What opinion can he have formed of the ponderous Hegelian scholastic who emerged dusty and panting from the systematic labours so well known to us, and smiled disdainfully at the poetry and music of the decadent Italian race ? De Sanctis writes, " I went there with my opinions and my prejudices and ridiculed their ridicule. Richard Wagner seemed to me a corrupter of music, and nothing could be more inæsthetic than the Æsthetic of Vischer." [4] His desire to correct the distorted views of Vischer, Adolf Wagner, Valentin Schmidt and other German critics and philosophers led him to undertake in 1858–59 a course of lectures before an international

---

[1] *La giovinezza di Fr. de S.* pp. 279, 313-314, 321-324.
[2] *Scritti varî*, vol. ii. p. 83 ; cf. p. 274.
[3] *Op. cit.* vol. i. pp. 228-236.
[4] *Saggio sul Petrarca*, new ed. by B. Croce, p. 309 *seqq.*

audience at Zürich upon Ariosto and Petrarch, the two
Italian poets worst maltreated by these judges because
hardest to reduce to philosophical allegory. He sketched
a typical German critic and contrasted him with a French
one, each with his own characteristic defects. " The
Frenchman does not indulge in theories ; he goes straight
to the subject : his argument palpitates with warmth of
impression and sagacity of observation : he never leaves
the concrete : he estimates the quality of the talent and
the work, studying the man in order to understand the
writer." He makes the mistake of substituting reflexion
on the psychology of the author and history of his time
for reflexion upon art. "Quite otherwise is your German:
be a thing never so plain, he makes it his business to
manipulate, distort and embroil : he accumulates a mass
of darkness from whose centre rays of dazzling light now
and again shoot forth : truth is there at bottom, in griev-
ous pangs of parturition. Confronted with a work of art,
he labours to fasten down and fix the quality which is
most evanescent and impalpable. While nobody is more
given to talk of life and the world of the living, nobody on
earth takes more pains to decompose and disembody it in
generalities : as consequence of this last process (last in
appearance, that is to say ; in reality preconceived and
a priori), he is able to fit you the same boot on every foot
and the same coat on every back." " The German school
is dominated by metaphysic, the French by history." [1]
About this time (1858) a Piedmontese review published
his exhaustive critical survey of the philosophy of Schopenhauer,[2] which was then beginning to attract disciples
among his friends and companions in exile in Switzerland ;
the criticism provoked the philosopher himself to confess
that " this Italian " had " absorbed him *in succum et
sanguinem*." [3] What value did De Sanctis attach to all
Schopenhauer's subtleties concerning art ? Having fully

[1] *Saggi critici*, pp. 361-363, 413-414 ; cf. as touching Klein, *Scritti
vari*, vol. i. pp. 32-34.

[2] *Op. cit.*, *Schopenhauer e Leopardi*, pp. 246, 299.

[3] Schopenhauer, *Briefe*, ed. Grisebach, pp. 405-406 ; cf. pp. 381-383,
403-404, 438-439.

stated his doctrine of ideas, he contents himself with the merest reference to the third book " wherein is found an exaggerated theoıy of Æsthetic." [1]

Final rebellion against metaphysical Æsthetic.

This moderate resistance and opposition to the partisans of the concept and to the romantic Italian mystics and moralists (he directed criticisms equally against Manzoni, Mazzini, Tommaseo and Cantú [2]) turned to open rebellion in one of his critical writings on Petrarch (1868) in which this false tendency is characterized with biting sarcasm. " According to this school " (he says, meaning the school of Hegel and Gioberti), " according to this school the real and living is art only in so far as it surpasses its form and reveals its concept or the pure idea. The beautiful is the manifestation of the idea. Art is the ideal, a particular idea. Under the gaze of the artist the body becomes subtilized until it is nothing but the shadow of the soul, a beautiful veil. The world of poetry is peopled with phantasms ; and the poet, eternal dreamer, with the eyes of one slightly intoxicated sees bodies float unsteadily around him and change their shapes. Nor do bodies merely become attenuated into forms and phantasms ; these forms and phantasms themselves become free manifestations of every idea and every concept. The theory of the ideal has been driven to its last victorious limit, to the destruction of the very phantasms themselves, to concept as concept, form becoming a mere accessory." " Thus the vague, the undecided, the undulating, the vaporous, the celestial, the aerial, the veiled, the angelic, have now a high position among artistic forms : whilst criticism revels in the beautiful, the ideal, the infinite, genius, the concept, the idea, truth, the superintelligible, the supersensible, the being and the existent, and many more generalities cast into barbarous formulæ just like those of the scholastics from whose influence we had so much difficulty in escaping." All these things, instead of determining the character of art, do nothing

---

[1] *Saggi critici*, p. 269, note.
[2] Cf. *Scritti vari*, i. pp. 39-45, and *Letterat. ital. nel sec. XIX*, lectures, ed. Croce, pp. 241-243, 427-432.

save illustrate the contrary of art : its feebleness and
impotence, preventing it from slaying abstractions and
laying hold of life.   If beauty and the ideal have actually
the meaning given them by these philosophers " the
essence of art is neither the beautiful nor the ideal, but the
living, the form ; the ugly too belongs to art since ugliness
lives also in nature ; outside the domain of art lies nothing
but the formless and the deformed.   Thais in Malebolge is
more living and poetical than Beatrice, who is pure allegory
representing abstract combinations.   The Beautiful ?
Tell me of anything as beautiful as Iago, a form uprisen
from the profundity of real life ; so rich, so concrete ; in
every part, in each finest gradation, one of the most
beautiful creations in the world of poetry."   If in the
course of " wrangling about the idea or the concept or real,
moral, or intellectual beauty, and confusing philosophical
or moral truths with æsthetic " you choose to call " a
great part of the poetic world ugly, granting it a permit
merely that it may act as contrast, antagonist or foil to
beauty, accepting Mephistopheles as a foil to Faust, or
Iago as foil to Othello," you are imitating " those good
folk who thought, *in illo tempore*, that the stars shone in
the firmament in order to give light to this earth." [1]

The æsthetic theory of De Sanctis himself arises entirely *De Sanctis'*
from the criticism of the highest manifestations of Euro- *own theory.*
pean æsthetic as known to him.   Its nature is revealed by the
contrast.   " If you desire a statue in the vestibule of art,"
says he, " let it be that of Form ; gaze upon this, question
this, begin with this.   Before form is attained, that exists
which existed before the creation : chaos.   Chaos is no
doubt a respectable thing, with a most interesting history :
science has not yet uttered its last word about this pre-
world of fermenting elements.   Art also has its pre-world :
art also has its geology, born but yesterday and as yet
scarcely stretched, a science *sui generis*, which is neither
Criticism nor Æsthetic.   Æsthetic appears when form
appears, in which this pre-world is sunk, fused, forgotten
and lost.   Form is itself as the individual is himself ; and

[1] *Saggio sul Petrarca*, introd. pp. 17-29.

no theory is so destructive to art as the continual harping upon the beautiful as manifestation, clothing, light, or veil of truth or the idea.   The æsthetic world is not appearance, it is substance ;   to it indeed belongs everything substantial and living : its criterion, its *raison d'être*, lies nowhere save in this motto : I live." [1]

The concept of form.   For De Sanctis, form did not mean form " in the pedantic sense attached to it until the end of the eighteenth century," that is to say, that which first strikes a superficial observer, the words, the period, the sense, the individual image ; [2] or form in the Herbartian sense, the metaphysical hypostatization of the former.   " Form is not *a priori*, it is not something existing of itself and distinct from the content as though it were a kind of ornament or vesture or appearance or adjunct of the content : it is generated by the content acting in the mind of the artist : such as the content is, such is the form." [3]   Between form and content there is at the same time identity and diversity.   In a work of art the content, which had been lying in a chaotic state in the mind of the artist, appears " not as it was originally, but as it has become ; the whole of it, with its own value, its own importance, its own natural beauty enriched, not weakened, by the process."   Therefore content is essential for the production of concrete form ; but the abstract quality of the content does not determine that of artistic form."   If the content, though beautiful and important, remain inoperative or lifeless or waste within the mind of the artist, if it have not sufficient generative power and reveal itself in the form as weak or false or vitiated, why trouble to sing its praises ?   In such cases the content may be important in itself, but as literature or art it is worthless.   On the other hand the content may be immoral, absurd, false or frivolous : but if at certain times or in certain circumstances it has worked powerfully on in the brain of the artist, and taken form, such content is immortal.   The gods of Homer are dead ;

[1] *Saggio sul Petrarca*, p. 29 seqq.
[2] *Scritti vari*, vol. i. pp. 276-277, 317.
[3] *Nuovi saggi critici*, pp. 239-240, note.

the *Iliad* remains. Italy may die and, with her, every memory of Guelf and Ghibelline ; the *Divina Commedia* will remain. The content is subject to all the hazards of history ; it is born and it dies ; the form is immortal." [1] He held firmly to the independence of art, without which there can be no Æsthetic ; but he objected to the exaggeration of the formula of art for art's sake in that it tended to the separation of the artist from life, to the mutilation of the content and to the conversion of art into a proof of mere cleverness. [2]

For De Sanctis, the concept of form was identical with that of imagination, the faculty of expression or representation, artistic vision. *De Sanctis as art-critic.* So much must be said by any one anxious to express clearly the direction which his thought was taking. But De Sanctis himself never succeeded in defining his own theory with scientific exactitude ; and his æsthetic ideas remained the mere sketch of a system never properly interrelated and deduced. The speculative tendency shared his attention with many other lively interests, the desire to understand the concrete, to enjoy art and rewrite its actual history, to plunge into practical and political life ; so that by turns he was professor, conspirator, journalist and statesman. " My mind inclines to the concrete," he was wont to say. He philosophized just so much as was necessary to the acquisition of a point of view in problems of art, history and life ; and, having procured light for his intellect, found his bearings, derived some satisfaction from the consciousness of his own activity, he plunged as quickly as possible into the particular and the determinate. To immense power of seizing the truth in the highest general principles was joined a no less intense abhorrence for the pale region of ideas in which the philosopher takes an almost ascetic delight. As critic and historian of literature he is unrivalled. Those who have compared him with Lessing, Macaulay, Sainte-Beuve or Taine are making rhetorical comparisons.

[1] *Nuovi saggi critici, loc. cit.*
[2] *Ibid.* and cf. *Saggio sul Petrarca*, p. 182 ; also *Scritti vari*, i. pp. 209-212, 226.

Gustave Flaubert wrote to George Sand : " In your last letter you speak of criticism, and say you expect it soon to disappear. I think, on the contrary, that it is just appearing over the horizon. Criticism to-day is the exact opposite of what it was, but that is all. In the days of Laharpe the critic was a grammarian ; to-day he is a historian like Sainte-Beuve and Taine. When will he be an artist, a mere artist, but a real artist ? Do you know a critic who interests himself whole-heartedly in the work itself ? They analyse with the greatest delicacy the historical surroundings of the work and the causes which produced it : but the underlying poetry and its causes ? the composition ? the style ? the author's own point of view ? Never. Such a critic must have great imagination and a great goodness of heart ; I mean an ever-ready faculty of enthusiasm ; and then, taste ; but this last is so rare, even among the best, that it is never mentioned nowadays." [1] Flaubert's ideal has been worthily reached by one critic only (that is to say, amongst critics who have given themselves to the interpretation of great writers and entire periods of literature) and that one is De Sanctis.[2] No literature of any country possesses so perfect a mirror as that possessed by Italy in the *History* and the other critical essays of Francesco de Sanctis.

De Sanctis as philosopher. But the philosopher of art, the æsthetician in De Sanctis is less great than the critic and historian of literature. The critic is primary, the philosopher a mere accessory. The æsthetic observations scattered in aphorisms up and down his essays and monographs take various colours from various occasions, and are expressed in uncertain and often metaphorical language ; this has led to his being accused of contradictions and inexactitudes which had no existence in his inmost thought and whose very appearance vanishes as soon as one takes into account the particular cases with which he was dealing. But form, forms, content, the living, the beautiful, natural beauty, ugliness, fancy, feeling, imagination, the real,

---

[1] *Lettres à George Sand*, Paris, 1884 (Letter of Feb. 2, 1869), p. 81.
[2] See above, p. 363, the judgement of De S. on French criticism.

the ideal, and all the other terms which he used with
varying signification, demand a science both on which to
rest and from which to derive. Meditation on these
words stirs up doubts and problems on every side and
reveals everywhere gaps and discontinuities. Compared
with the few philosophical æstheticians, De Sanctis seems
wanting in analysis, in order and in system, and vague
in his definitions. But these defects are outweighed by
the contact he establishes between the reader and real
concrete works of art, and by the feeling for truth which
never leaves him. He has, too, the attraction possessed
by those writers who lead one on to suspect and to divine
new treasures in store beyond what they themselves reveal
—living thought, which stimulates living men to pursue
and prolong it.

XVI

ÆSTHETIC OF THE EPIGONI

Revival of Herbartian Æsthetic. WHEN the cry " Away with metaphysic ! " was raised in Germany, and a furious reaction began against the kind of Walpurgis-night to which the later Hegelians had reduced the life of science and history, the disciples of Herbart came to the front and seemed to ask, with an insinuating air : " What is all this ? a rebellion against Idealism and Metaphysic? why, it is exactly what Herbart wished and undertook all by himself half a century ago ! Here we stand, his legitimate descendants, and we offer you our services as allies. We shall not find it hard to agree. Our Metaphysic accords with the atomic theory, our Psychology with mechanism, and our Ethics and Æsthetic with hedonism." Herbart himself (had he not died in 1841) would most likely have spurned these disciples of his who pandered to popularity, cheapened metaphysics and gave naturalistic interpretations to his reals, his representations, his ideas, and all his highest conceptions.

With the school thus coming into fashion, the Herbartian Æsthetic too tried to put on flesh and acquire a pleasing plumpness so as not to cut too miserable a figure beside the well-nourished *corpora* of science launched upon the world by idealists. The feeding-up process was accomplished by Robert Zimmermann, professor of philosophy at Prague and later at Vienna, who, after years of laborious effort and an introductory sample in the shape of an ample history of Æsthetic (1858), at length produced his *General Æsthetic as Science of Form* in 1865.[1]

This formalistic Æsthetic, born under bad auspices, is a curious example of servile fidelity in externals combined with internal infidelity. Starting from unity, or rather from subordination of Ethics and Æsthetic to a general Æsthetic defined as " a science which treats of the modes by which any given content may acquire the right to arouse approval or disapproval " (thereby differing from Metaphysic, science of the real, and from Logic, science of right thinking), Zimmermann places such modes in form, that is to say, in the reciprocal relation of elements. A simple mathematical point in space, a simple impression of hearing or sight, a simple note, is in fact neither pleasing nor displeasing : music shows that the judgement of beauty or ugliness always depends on the relation between two notes at least. Now these relations, *i.e.* forms universally pleasing, cannot be empirically collected by induction ; they must be developed by deduction. By the deductive method it can be demonstrated that the elements of an image, which in themselves are representations, may enter into relations either according to their force (quantity), or according to their nature (quality) ; whence we have two groups—æsthetic forms of quantity, and æsthetic forms of quality. According to the first, the strong (large) is pleasing in comparison with the weak (small), and these latter are displeasing when set beside the former ; according to the other form, that pleases which is substantially identical in quality (the harmonious), and that displeases which is on the whole diverse (the discordant).

But the substantial identity must not be pushed to the point of absolute identity, for in that case the harmony itself would cease to be. From harmonious form is deduced the pleasure of the characteristic or expression ; for what is the characteristic but a relation of prevalent

Robert Zimmermann.

---

[1] *Allgemeine Ästhetik als Formwissenschaft*, Vienna, 1865 ; see also Meyer's *Konversations - Lexikon* (4th ed.), art. *Ästhetik*, by Zimmermann.

identity between the thing itself and its model ? But while similarity prevailing in the distinction produces accord (*Einklang*), qualitative disharmony is as such disagreeable, and demands a resolution. (It is easy to detect the sleight of hand with which Zimmermann first slips the characteristic into the relations of pure form, thereby entirely altering Herbart's original thought ; and how, by a second trick, he here introduces into pure beauty the variations and modifications of the beautiful, by the help of the despised Hegelian dialectic.) If such resolution is effected by the skilful substitution of something other than the unpleasant image, we shall certainly have removed the cause of offence and established quietude (not accord : *Eintracht, nicht Einklang*), but we shall have gained the mere form of correctness : it is better, then, to supersede this by means of the true image so as to reach the form of compensation (*Ausgleichung*) ; and, when the true image is also pleasing in itself, the final form of definitive compensation (*abschliessende Ausgleich*), with which we exhaust the series of possible forms. And, in conclusion, what is Beauty ? It is a conjunction of all these forms : a model (*Vorbild*) which has grandeur, plenitude, order, accord, correctness, definitive compensation ; all this appears in a copy (*Nachbild*) in the form of the characteristic.

Putting on one side the artificial connexion Zimmermann makes between the sublime, the comic, the tragic, the ironic, the humorous and the æsthetic forms, notice must be taken (so that we may recognize into which of the seven heavens he is wafting us) that these general æsthetic forms concern art equally with nature and morality, whose individual spheres are differentiated solely by the application of the general æsthetic forms to particular contents. These forms, applied to nature, give us natural beauty, the cosmos ; applied to representation, beauty of wit (*Schöngeist*) or imagination ; applied to feeling, the beautiful soul (*schöne Seele*) or taste ; applied to the will, character or virtue. On one side, then, is natural beauty, on the other human beauty, in which

(latter), on one hand, we have the beauty of representation, that is to say æsthetic fact in the strict sense (art) ;
on the other, we have the beauty of will, or morality ; and
between the two, lastly, we have taste, common to Ethics
and Æsthetic. Æsthetic in the narrow sense, as the theory
of beautiful representation, determines the beauty of representations, divided into the three classes of the beauty
of temporal and spatial connexion (figurative arts) ; the
beauty of sensitive representation (music) ; and the beauty
of thoughts (poetry). This tripartition of beauty into figurative, musical and poetical brings to a conclusion theoretical
Æsthetic, the only section developed by Zimmermann.

Zimmermann's work was a polemic against the prin- *Vischer versus*
cipal representative of Hegelian Æsthetic, Vischer, who *Zimmermann.*
had little difficulty in defending his own position and
counter-attacking that of his assailant. He held Zimmermann up to ridicule, for example, in connexion with
his view of symbolism. Zimmermann defined a symbol
as the object " round which beautiful forms adhere." A
painter depicts a fox simply for the sake of painting a
part of animal nature. Nothing of the sort : this is a
symbol, because the painter " makes use of lines and
colours to express things other than lines and colours."
" You think I'm a fox," says the animal in the picture,
" but you make a great mistake : I'm a clothes-peg :
I'm an appearance created by the painter with gradations
of grey, white, yellow and red." Even easier was it to
make game of Zimmermann's enthusiastic praises of the
æsthetic quality of the sense of touch. It was a pity, the
latter had written, that the pleasures of this sense were
so difficult to attain ; since " to touch the back of the
Resting Hercules and the sinuous limbs of the Venus of
Melos or the Barberini Faun would give to the hand a
delight comparable only with that felt by the ear when
listening to the majestic fugues of Bach or the suave
melodies of Mozart." Vischer does not seem to be far
wrong in declaring formalistic Æsthetic to be " a grotesque
union of mysticism and mathematics." [1]

---

[1] *Kritische Gänge*, vi., Stuttgart, 1873, pp. 6, 21, 32.

The works of Zimmermann seem to have given satisfaction to nobody save himself. Even Lotze, by no
means an adversary of Herbartianism, blames him severely
in his *History of Æsthetic in Germany* (1868) and other
writings. Still, Lotze was unable to offer any better
substitute for æsthetic formalism than of a variant of the
old idealism. " Can any one persuade us," he wrote in
criticism of the formalists, " that a spiritual discord
expressed by a corresponding discord in external appearances may have a value equal to that of the harmonious
expression of a harmonious content solely because, in
both cases, the formal relation of accord is respected ?
Can any one persuade us that the human form is pleasing
solely for its formal stereometric relations, irrespective of
the spiritual life by which it is animated ? In empirical
reality the three domains of laws, facts and values invariably appear as divided ; and although they are united
in the Highest Good, in Goodness in itself, in the living
Love of a Personal God, in the Ought which is the basis
of Being, our reason is unable to attain or to know such
union. Beauty alone can reveal it to us : it is in close
connexion with the Good and the Holy and reproduces
the rhythm of the divine ordinance and the moral govern-
ment of the universe. Æsthetic fact is neither intuition
nor concept ; it is idea, which presents the essential of
an object in the form of an end referred to the ultimate
end. Art, like beauty, must include the world of values
in the world of forms." [1] The war between the Æsthetic
of content and that of form, having Zimmermann, Vischer
and Lotze as protagonists, reached its culminating point
between 1860 and 1870.

*Efforts to
reconcile
Æsthetic of
form and
Æsthetic of
content.*

Several people were in favour of a reconciliation. But
the reconciliations they offered were not the right one,
which was at least glimpsed by a certain young Johann

---

[1] *Geschichte d. Ästh. i. Deutschl., passim,* esp. pp. 27, 97, 100, 125,
147, 232, 234, 265, 286, 293, 487 ; *Grundzüge der Ästh.* (posth., Leipzig,
1884), §§ 8-13 ; and two juvenile works, *Üb. d. Begriff d. Schönheit,*
Göttingen, 1845, and *Üb. d. Bedingungen d. Kunstschönheit,* Göttingen,
1847.

Schmidt, who in his thesis for doctorate observed (1875)
that, with all respect for Zimmermann and Lotze, it
seemed to him they were both wrong in confusing the
various meanings of the word " beauty," and discussed
such an absurdity as a beauty or ugliness of natural
objects, that is to say, of things external to the spirit ;
that Lotze, following Hegel, added the second absurdity of
an intuitive concept or conceptual intuition : lastly, that
neither of them grasped the fact that the æsthetic problem
does not turn upon the beauty or ugliness of the abstract
content or of form understood as a system of mathematical
relations, but with the beauty or ugliness of representation.   Form undoubtedly must exist, but " concrete form,
full of content." [1]   These utterances of Schmidt met with
a hostile reception : it is easy (he was told in reply) to
identify beauty with artistic perfection, but the whole
crux of the matter lies in finding whether, beside this
perfection, there exists another beauty dependent on a
supreme cosmic or metaphysical principle : otherwise one
is guilty of a naïve *petitio principii*.[2]   It was thought
better, therefore, to seek other modes of reconciliation,
which consisted in cooking up an appetizing dish in which
a little formalism and a little contentism were mixed to
taste, the latter as a rule giving the predominant flavour.

Some Herbartians were found in the ranks of the medi-
ating or conciliatory party.   Hardly had Zimmermann's
rigid formalism appeared, when Nahlowsky jumped up to
protest that it had never entered the master's head to
exclude content from Æsthetic ; [3] but even the ablest of
the school, men such as Volkmann and Lazarus, chose a
middle course.[4]   In the opposite camp Carriere,[5] and even
Vischer himself (in a criticism of his own old *Æsthetic*),
began to concede a larger part to the consideration of

[1] *Leibniz u. Baumgarten*, Halle, 1875, pp. 76-102.
[2] G. Neudecker, *Studien z. Gesch. d. dtschn. Ästh. s. Kant*, pp. 54-55.
[3] Polemic in *Zeitschr. f. exacte Philos.* (Herbartian organ) for 1862–
1863, ii. p. 309 *seqq.*, ii. p. 384 *seqq.*, iv. pp. 26 *seqq.*, 199 *seqq.*, 300 *seqq.*
[4] Volkmann, *Lehrbuch der Psychologie*, 3rd ed., Cöthen, 1884-1885.
Lazarus, *Das Leben der Seele*, 1856-1858.
[5] Moriz Carriere, *Ästhetik*, 1859 (3rd ed., Leipzig, 1885).

form ; thus for Vischer beauty became " life appearing harmoniously," which when it appears in space is called form, and must always possess form, *i.e.* limitation (*Begrenzung*) in space and time, measure, regularity, symmetry, proportion, propriety (these characters constituting its quantitative moments) and harmony (qualitative moment), which includes variety and contrast and is therefore the most important characteristic.[1]

K. Köstlin. A conciliatory Æsthetic in which formalism prevailed was attempted by Karl Köstlin, a professor at Tübingen and formerly collaborator in the musical section of the works of Vischer. Köstlin[2] had been influenced by Schleiermacher, Hegel, Vischer and Herbart, but, truth to tell, does not seem to have perfectly understood the teaching of any one of his predecessors. According to him, the æsthetic object presented three requirements : richness and variety of imagery (*anregende Gestaltenfülle*), interesting content and beautiful form. Under the first we recognize, with no little difficulty, a distorted reflexion of Schleiermacher's " inspiration " (*Begeisterung*). Interesting content he defined as that which concerns man ; that which he knows or does not know ; that which he loves or hates (it is thus always relative to the individual and the conditions in which he exists) ; and he asserted that interest of content is joined to value of form, that is, he conceived content as a second value, the same of which we have heard Herbart speak. He also agreed with Herbart that form is absolute, and that its general character is determined as being easily perceptible by intuition (*anschaulich*), and by its power of giving satisfaction, pleasure and delight, in fact, as being beautiful. Its particular characteristics for Köstlin were, according to quantity, circumscription, simplicity (*Einheitlichkeit*), extensive and intensive size, and equilibrium (*Gleichmass*) ; according to quality, determination (*Bestimmtheit*), unity (*Einheit*), importance (*Bedeutung*) extensive and intensive, and harmony. But when Köstlin sets himself to the

[1] *Kritische Gänge*, v., Stuttgart, 1866, p. 59.
[2] *Ästhetik*, Tübingen, 1869.

empirical verification of his categories, he falls into hopeless confusion. Greatness is pleasing, but so is smallness ;
unity is pleasing, but so is variety ; regularity is pleasing,
but so, confound it, is irregularity : uncertainties and
contradictions at every step ; he was aware of them and
made no effort to conceal them ; but they should have
convinced him that the abstraction of " beautiful form,"
whose qualities and quantities he had so laboriously
collected, is a ghostly shape without body, since that
alone gives æsthetic pleasure which fulfils an expressive
function. But having illustrated the three demands of
the æsthetic object, Köstlin wasted all his remaining
breath in constructing a kingdom of intuitive imagination
in the manner of Vischer, *i.e.* beauty of organic and
inorganic nature ; of civil life ; of morality ; of religion ;
of science ; of games ; of conversations ; of feasts and
banquets ; and lastly of history, reviewing and passing
æsthetic comment on its three periods, patriarchal, heroic
and historical.

Schasler, who had written as vast a history on Æsthetic
as Zimmermann's own, found a starting-point for a movement toward formalism in absolute idealism, or realism-
idealism, as he called it.   He began by defining Æsthetic
as " the science of the beautiful and of art " (a single
science ill defined as having two different objects), and
proceeded to justify his unmethodical definition by saying
that beauty does not exist in art alone, nor does art concern itself solely with beauty.   The sphere of Æsthetic he
defines as that of intuition (*Anschauung*) in which knowledge assumes a practical character and will a theoretical :
the sphere of indivisible unity and absolute reconciliation
of the theoretical and practical spirit, in which in a certain sense the highest human activities are developed.
Beauty is the ideal, but the concrete ideal ; this is why
there is no ideal of a human body in abstraction from sex,
no ideal of a mammal in general, but only of such and such
species, as of horse or dog, and then only of determinate
kind of horse or dog.   Thus by descending from the more
to the less abstract genus Schasler vainly attempted to

*Æsthetic of
content.
M. Schasler.*

reach the concrete, which inevitably escaped his grasp.　In art we pass from the typical, which is natural beauty, to the characteristic, which is the typical of human feeling ; hence we can frame the ideal of an old woman, a beggar or a ruffian.　The characteristic of art is in closer relation-ship to the ugly than to the beautiful in nature.　On this head (passing over the remainder, which is on familiar lines) it is well to notice that Schasler has a bias towards that version of the romaunt of Sir Purebeauty which ascribes the birth of the " modifications of Beauty " to the influence of the Ugly.[1]　" Although," he writes, " the thought may disturb our minds, it must not be forgotten that were there no world of ugliness there could be no world of beauty ;　for it is only when the Ugly stirs up empty abstract Beauty, that it begins to combat the enemy and thus to produce concrete Beauty." [2]　He even succeeded in converting Vischer himself, the chief supporter of the other version :　" Formerly I had been accustomed to think in the old-fashioned Hegelian style," Vischer con-fesses, " that unrest, fermentation and strife dwelt in the essence of Beauty ;　that the Idea prevails and thrusts the image forth into the infinite ;　so arises the Sublime ;　that the image, offended in its finitude, makes war on the Idea ;　whence arises the Comic ;　this finished the struggle ;　Beauty returned to itself from the conflict of the two moments, and was created."　But now, he continues, " I must acknowledge that Schasler is right, and so are his predecessors Weisse and Ruge :　the Ugly has a hand in the matter ;　this is the principle of movement, the ferment of differentiation :　without such leaven we never reach the special forms of Beauty, for each single one presupposes the Ugly." [3]

Ed. von Hartmann.　Closely allied to that of Schasler is the Æsthetic of Eduard von Hartmann (1890), preceded by a historical treatise on *German Æsthetic since Kant*,[4] wherein with

---

[1] See above, pp. 348-349.
[2] *Ästhetik*, Leipzig, 1886, i. pp. 1-16, 19-24, 70 ; ii. p. 52 : cf. *Kritische Gesch. der Ästhetik*, pp. 795, 963, 1041-1044, 1028, 1036-1038.
[3] *Kritische Gänge*, v. pp. 112-115.
[4] *Die dtsche. Ästh. s. Kant*, 1886 (Part i. of *Ästh.*).

meticulous, critical and polemical study he upholds the definition of Beauty as " the appearance of the Idea " (*das Scheinen der Idee*). Inasmuch as he insisted on appearance (*Schein*) as the necessary characteristic of Beauty, Hartmann held himself justified in naming his Æsthetic the " Æsthetic of Concrete Idealism," and in ranging himself alongside Hegel, Trahndorff, Schleiermacher, Deutinger, Oersted, Vischer, Meising, Carriere and Schasler, against the abstract idealism of Schelling, Solger, Schopenhauer, Krause, Weisse and Lotze, all of whom, by placing beauty in the supersensible idea, overlooked the sensory element and reduced it to the rank of a mere accessory.[1] By his insistence on the idea as the other indispensable and determining element, Hartmann proclaimed himself as opposed to the Herbartian formalism. Beauty is truth ; neither historical, scientific nor reflective, but metaphysical or idealistic, the very truth of Philosophy : " in proportion as Beauty is in opposition to every science and to realistic truth, so much nearer is it to Philosophy and metaphysical truth " : " Beauty, with its own peculiar efficacy, remains the prophet of idealistic truth in an unbelieving age that abhors Metaphysic and recognizes no value in anything but realistic truth." Æsthetic truth, which leaps immediately from subjective appearance to ideal essence, is lacking in the control and method possessed by philosophical truth ; in compensation, however, she possesses the fascinating power of conviction, the sole property of sensible intuition, and unattainable by gradual or reflected mediation. The higher Philosophy soars, the less does it need the gradual passage through the world of the senses and of science, and the slighter becomes the distance separating Philosophy and Art. The latter, for its part, will be well advised to start on its journey towards the ideal world as Baedeker's handbooks counsel the intending traveller, " with as little luggage as possible " ; " not overloading herself with a weight which paralyses the wings and is

[1] *Philosophie des Schönen* (Part ii. of *Asth.*), Leipzig, 1890, pp. 463-464 ; cf. *Deutsche Asth. s. K.* pp. 357-362.

made up of unnecessary and indifferent trifles." [1]   Logical
character, the microcosmic idea, the unconscious are
immanent in beauty ; by means of the unconscious,
intellectual intuition operates in it,[2] and, from its being
rooted in the unconscious, it is a Mystery.[3]

Hartmann and the theory of Modifications.   In his employment of the exciting or reactionary
influence of the Ugly, Hartmann exceeded Schasler him-
self. Lowest among the degrees of Beauty, indeed
forming the lower limit of æsthetic fact, lies sensuous
pleasure, which is unconscious formal beauty ; its first
true degree is formal beauty of the first order, or the
mathematically pleasing (unity, variety, symmetry, proportion, the golden section, etc.) ; its second degree is
formal beauty of the second order, the dynamically pleasing ; its third is formal beauty of the third order, the
passive teleological, as in the case of utensils or machinery.
Indeed it may here be noted that among machines and
utensils, on a level with jars, plates and cups, Hartmann
placed language : it is a dead thing, said he ; receiving
the appearances of life (*Scheinleben*) [4] only at the very
instant of utterance. Language a " dead thing," an
" utensil " for the philosopher of the Unconscious, in the
land of Humboldt, with a Steinthal still living ! There
follow, as formal beauty of the fourth order, the active
teleological or living, and as formal beauty of the fifth
order, conformity to species (*das Gattungsmässige*) : lastly
and above all, since the individual idea is superior to the
specific, is beauty concrete beauty or the microcosmic
individual, which is no longer formal, but beauty of
content. As is to be expected, the passage from lower to
higher degrees is made by means of the Ugly : nobody has
laboured like Hartmann to recount in detail the services
rendered by Ugliness to Beauty. From ugliness, in the
form of the destruction of the beauty of equality, arises
symmetry : from ugliness in the case of the circle arises
the ellipse ; the beauty of a waterfall tumbling over rocks
is caused by the mathematically ugly ; destruction, that

[1] *Phil. d. Sch.* pp. 434-437.   [2] *Op. cit.* pp. 115-116.
[3] *Op. cit.* pp. 197-198.   [4] *Op. cit.* pp. 150-152.

is to say, of a fall in a parabolic curve ; beauty of spiritual expression is achieved through the introduction of an ugliness relative to fleshly perfection. Beauty of a higher degree is founded on ugliness at a lower degree. When the highest degree is reached, that of individual beauty beyond which there can be nothing, even then elemental ugliness continues its work of beneficent irritation. The later phases thus produced are well known to us as the famous Modifications of the Beautiful : in this section also, nobody is so copious or detailed as Hartmann. He certainly does admit, side by side with simple or pure beauty, certain modifications free from conflict, such as the sublime or graceful ; but the more important modifications can arise only through conflict. There are four cases, because the resolution must be either immanent, logical, transcendent or combined : immanent in the idyllic, the melancholy, the sad, the cheerful, the moving, the elegiac ; logical in the comic in all its varieties ; transcendent in the tragic ; combined in the humorous with the tragi-comic and its other varieties. When none of these resolutions is possible, there arises ugliness ; when an ugliness of content is expressed by an ugliness of form, we have the maximum of ugliness, the real æsthetic devil.

Hartmann is the last considerable representative of the old æsthetic school in Germany ; he inspires terror by the mass of his literary production, like many others of the school, who seem to accept it as a dogma that art cannot be dealt with except in several volumes a thousand pages long. Those who are not afraid of giants and are able to attack this sort of Æsthetic, will find it a fat good-humoured Magog full of vulgar prejudices, and so constituted that, despite his apparent strength, a little blow will kill him. *Metaphysical Æsthetic in France. C. Levêque.*

In other countries metaphysical Æsthetic had few followers. In France the celebrated competition of the Academy of Moral and Political Sciences in 1857 crowned with their approval and presented to the world the *Science of Beauty* by Levêque ; [1] of which nobody now thinks or

[1] Ch. Levêque, *La Science du beau*, Paris, 1862.

speaks, only remembering the author (who attitudinized as
a disciple of Plato) by his eight characteristics of Beauty,
derived by him from examination of a lily. The eight
characteristics were as follows :—sufficient size of form,
unity, variety, harmony, proportion, normal vivacity of
colour, grace and propriety ; ultimately reducible to two,
size and order. As supplementary proof of the truth of his
theory, Levêque applied it to three beautiful things : a
child playing with its mother, a symphony of Beethoven
and the life of a philosopher (Socrates). Really, it is
somewhat difficult (says one of his fellow-spiritualists,
venturing to comment on this doctrine though speaking
with the utmost deference) to imagine what may be the
normal vivacity of colour in the life of a philosópher.[1]
Translations and explanatory articles by Charles Bénard [2]
and books by various writers belonging to French Switzerland (Töpffer, Pictet, Cherbuliez) were not successful in
popularizing the German systems of Æsthetic in France.

In England.
J. Ruskin.
England showed even less disposition to interest herself, although John Ruskin may have some claim to be
considered a metaphysical æsthetician with a distinctive
national stamp. But it is difficult to treat of Ruskin in
a history of science, for his temperament was wholly
opposed to the scientific. His disposition was that of the
artist, impressionable, excitable, voluble, rich in feeling ;
a dogmatic tone and the appearance of theoretical form
veil, in his exquisite and enthusiastic pages, a texture of
dreams and fancies. The reader who recalls those pages
will regard as irreverent any detailed and prosaic review
of Ruskin's æsthetic thought, which must incvitably
reveal its poverty and incoherence. Suffice it to say that,
following a finalistic, mystical intuition of nature, he
considered beauty as a revelation of divine intentions, the
seal " God sets on his works, even upon the smallest."
For him the faculty which perceives the beautiful is
neither intellect nor sensibility, but a particular feeling

---

[1] E. Saisset, *L'Esthétique française* (in app. to vol. *L'Âme et la vie*,
Paris, 1864), pp. 118-120.

[2] In *Revue philosophique*, vols. i. ii. x. xii. xvi.

which he names the theoretic faculty. Natural beauty, which reveals itself to a pure heart when contemplating any object untouched and unspoiled by the hand of man, asserts itself for this reason as immeasurably superior to any work of art. Ruskin was too hasty in analysis to understand the complicated psychological and æsthetic process which went on in his mind when he was moved to an artist's ecstasy by contemplating some humble natural object such as a bird's nest or a flowing rivulet.[1]

In Italy the Abate Tornasi wrote a half-Hegelian, half- *Æsthetic in* Catholic Æsthetic, wherein the beautiful is identified with *Italy.* the second person of the Trinity, the Word made man ; [2] by this means he hoped to raise a bank of opposition against the liberal criticism of De Sanctis, whom he considered, from the sublime height of his own philosophy, as " a subtle grammarian." Combined Giobertian and German, especially Hegelian, influence produced several works of secondary importance ; De Meis developed at length the thesis of the death of Art in the historical world.[3] Somewhat later Gallo also treated Æsthetic from the Hegelian point of view,[4] and others repeated, nearly word for word, the doctrines of Schasler and Hartmann on the overcoming of the Ugly.[5] The only genuine Italian teacher of metaphysical Æsthetic according to the Ger- mans was Antonio Tari, who lectured on this very subject *Antonio Tari* in Naples University from 1861 to 1884. He had a *and his lectures.* meticulous and superstitiously minute knowledge of every- thing that issued from German printing-presses, and was the author of an *Ideal Æsthetic* as well as essays on style, taste, serious work and play (*Spiel*), music and archi- tecture, wherein he tried to keep the mean between the idealism of Hegel and the formalism of Herbart : [6] his

[1] J. Ruskin, *Modern Painters* (4th ed., London, 1891) ; cf. De la Sizeranne, pp. 112-278.

[2] Vito Fornari, *Arte del dire*, Naples, 1866–1872 ; cf. vol. iv.

[3] A. C. De Meis, *Dopo la laurea*, Bologna, 1868–1869.

[4] Nic. Gallo, *L' idealismo e la letteratura*, Rome, 1880; *La scienza dell' arte*, Turin, 1887.

[5] *E.g.* F. Masci, *Psicologia del comico*, Naples, 1888.

[6] *Estetica ideale*, Naples, 1863 ; *Saggi di critica* (collected post-humously), Trani, 1886.

lectures on Æsthetic attracted huge throngs and were one of the regular sights in the noisy, crowded Neapolitan university. Tari divided his treatment under three heads, Æsthesinomy, Æsthesigraphy and Æsthesipraxis, corresponding to the Metaphysic of the beautiful, to the doctrine of beauty in nature, and to that of beauty in art ; like the German idealists, he defined the æsthetic sphere as intermediate between the theoretical and practical : he says emphatically that " in the world of spirit the temperate zone is equidistant from the glacial, peopled by the Esquimaux of thought, and from the torrid, peopled by the giants of action." He pulled Beauty from her throne, substituting in her stead the Æsthetic, of which Beauty is but an initial moment, the simple " beginning of æsthetic life, eternal mortality, flower and fruit in one," whose successive moments are represented by the Sublime, the Comic, the Humorous, and the Dramatic. But the most attractive part of Tari's lectures was *Æsthesigraphy.* that devoted to Æsthesigraphy, subdivided into Cosmography, Physiography and Psychography, in the course of which he frequently quoted Vischer with great devotion ; " the great Vischer " as he called him, in imitation of whom he constructed his own " æsthetic physics," brightening it with much varied erudition and enlivening it with quaint comparisons. Is he speaking of beauty in inorganic nature—water, for example ? He says in his fanciful manner, " When water ripples in the sunshine, in that act it has its smile ; it has its frown in the breaking wave, its caprice in the fountain, its majestic fury in the foam." Is he speaking of geological configuration ? " The vale, cradle perchance of the human race, is idyllic ; the plain, monotonous but fat, is didactic." Of metals ? " Gold is born great ; iron, the apotheosis of human toil, achieves greatness ; the former boasts of its cradle when it does not bring it to dishonour ; the latter causes it to be forgotten." He looked on vegetable life as a dream, repeating Herder's fine saying that the plant is " the new-born babe that hangs sucking upon the breast of mother nature." He divided vegetables into three types :

foliaceous, ramified and umbelliferous : " the foliaceous type," he says, " attains gigantic proportions in the tropics, where the queen of monocotyledons, the Palm-tree, represents despotism, the human scourge of those desert regions. Of that solitary pinnacle, all crown, the negro may well be identified as the reptile that crawls round its base." Amongst flowers, the carnation is " symbol of betrayal, by reason of the variegation of its colours and its deeply-dissected petals " ; the celebrated comparison by Ariosto of a rose with a young girl is permissible only when the flower is still in bud, because " when it has unfolded its petals, disdaining the protection of thorns, displaying itself in all the pomp of its full colour, and boldly asking to be plucked by any hand, then it is woman, all woman, to call it by no harsher name, giving pleasure without feeling it, simulating love by its perfume and modesty by the crimson of its petals." He searches for and comments upon analogies between certain fruits and certain flowers ; between the strawberry, for instance, and the violet ; between the orange and the rose ; he admired " the luxuriant spirals and the delicate architecture of a bunch of grapes " : the mandarin-orange reminded him of the nobleman *qui s'est donné la peine de naître* ; the fig, on the contrary, was the great country bumpkin, " rough, rude, but profitable." In the animal kingdom, the spider symbolized primitive isolation ; the bee, monasticism ; the ant, republicanism. He noted, with Michelet, that the spider is a living paralogism ; it cannot feed itself without its web, and it cannot spin its web without feeding. Fish he condemns as unæsthetic : " they are of stupid appearance with their wide - open eyes and incessant gaping, which makes them look voraciously gluttonous." Not so with amphibians, for which he entertains a sympathy : the frog and the crocodile, " alpha and omega of the family, start from the comical, or even the scurrilous, and attain the sublimity of the horrid." Birds are especially æsthetic by nature, " possessing the three most genial attributes of a living being : love, song, and flight " ; moreover, they present contrasts and antitheses : " opposite to the eagle, queen of the skies, stands the swan, the mild king of the marshes ; the libertine vainglorious cock has its contrast in the humble uxorious turtle-dove ; the magnificent peacock is balanced by the rude and rustic turkey." Amongst mammals, nature compensates for defects of pure beauty by dramatic value ; if they cannot throw their song into the air, they have the rudiments of speech ; if they have no variegated, myriad-hued plumage, they have dark, heavily-marked colouring, instinct with life ; if they cannot fly, they have many other modes of powerful progression ; and, the higher they go, the more do they attain individuality in appearance and life. "The epic of animal life is comedy in the donkey, *iniquae mentis asellus* ; idyl in the great wild beasts ; downright tragedy in the Kaffir bull, that cloven-hoofed Codrus, who gives himself voluntarily to the lion in order to save the herd." As amongst birds, so amongst beasts attractive contrasts are to be made :—the lamb and the kid seem to typify Jesus and the devil ; dog and cat, abnegation and egoism ; hare and fox, the foolish simpleton and crafty villain. Many quaint and subtle observations does Tari let fall on human beauty and the relative beauty of the sexes, allowing the female to have charm, not beauty : " bodily beauty is poise, and woman's body is so ill-poised that she falls easily when running ; made for child-bearing, she has knock-kneed legs, adapted to support the large pelvis ; her shoulders have a curve compensating the convexity of the chest." He describes the various parts of the body : " curly hair expresses physical force ; straight hair, moral " ; " blue, napoleonic eyes have sometimes a depth like the sea ; green eyes have a melancholy fascination ; grey eyes are wanting in individuality ; black eyes are the most intensely individual " ; " a lovely mouth has been best described by Heine ; two lips evenly matched ; to lovers the mouth will rather seem a shell whose pearl is the kiss." [1]

---

[1] A. Tari, *Lezioni di estetica generale*, collected by C. Scamaccia-Luvarà, Naples, 1884 ; *Elementi di estetica*, compiled by G. Tommasuolo, Naples, 1885.

How could we better take a smiling leave of metaphysical Æsthetic in the German manner than by recording this quaint vernacular version of it made by Tari, that
kindly little old man, " the last jovial high-priest of an
arbitrary and confused Æsthetic " ? [1]

[1] V. Pica, *L'Arte dell' Estremo Oriente*, Turin, 1894, p. 13.

XVII

ÆSTHETIC POSITIVISM AND NATURALISM

Positivism and Evolutionism.

THE ground lost by idealistic metaphysic was conquered in the latter half of the nineteenth century by positivistic and evolutionary metaphysic, a confused substitution of natural for philosophical sciences, and a hotch-potch of materialistic and idealistic, mechanical and theological theories, the whole crowned with scepticism and agnosticism. Characteristic of this trend of opinion was its contempt of history, especially the history of philosophy ; which prevented its ever making that contact with the unbroken and age-long efforts of thinkers without which it is idle to hope for fertile work and true progress.

Æsthetic of H. Spencer.

Spencer (the greatest positivist of his day), whilst discussing Æsthetic, actually did not know that he was dealing with problems for all, or almost all, of which solutions had been already proposed and discussed. At the beginning of his essay on the *Philosophy of Style*, he remarks innocently : "I believe nobody has ever sketched a general theory of the art of writing " (in 1852 !) ; and in his *Principles of Psychology* (1855), touching the æsthetic feelings he remarks that he has some recollection of observations concerning the relation of art and play made " by some German author whose name I cannot recall " (Schiller !). Had his pages on Æsthetic been written in the seventeenth century, they would have won a low position amongst the early crude attempts at æsthetic speculation ; in the nineteenth century, one knows not how to judge them. In his essay on *The*

Useful and the Beautiful (1852–1854), he shows how the useful becomes beautiful when it ceases to be useful, illustrating this by a ruined castle useless for the purposes of modern life, but a suitable scene for picnic parties and a good subject for a picture to hang on a parlour wall ; which leads him to identify the principle of evolution from the useful to the beautiful as contrast. In another essay on the *Beauty of the Human Face* (1852) he explains this beauty as a sign and effect of moral goodness ; in that on *Grace* (1852) he considers the sentiment of the graceful as sympathy for power in conjunction with agility. In the *Origin of Architectural Styles* (1852–1854) he discovers the beauty of architecture as consisting in uniformity and symmetry, an idea which is aroused in a man looking at the bodily equilibrium of the higher animals or, as in Gothic architecture, by analogy with the vegetable kingdom ; in his essay on *Style*, he places the cause of stylistic beauty in economy of effort ; in his *Origin and Function of Music* (1857) he theorizes on music as the natural language of the passions, adapted to increase sympathy between men.[1] In his *Principles of Psychology*, he maintains that the æsthetic feelings arise from the overflow of exuberant energy in the organism, and distinguishes various degrees of them, from simple sensation to that accompanied by representative elements, and so on until perception is reached, with more complex elements of representation, then emotion, and, last of all, that state of consciousness which transcends sensation and perception. The most perfect form of æsthetic feeling is attained by the coincidence of the three orders of pleasures, a coincidence produced by the full action of their respective faculties with the least possible subtraction due to the painful effect of excessive activity. But it is very rarely that we experience æsthetic excitement of this kind and strength ; almost all works of art are imperfect because they contain a mixture of artistic with anti-artistic effects ; now the technique is unsatisfactory, now the emotion is of a low order. These

---

[1] *Essays, Scientific, Political, and Speculative, 1858–1862.*

works of art which are universally admired, are found
when measured by this criterion to deserve a lower place
than that accorded them by popular taste. " Beginning
with the Greek epic and the representations of analogous
legends given by their sculptors, tending to excite egoistic
or ego-altruistic sentiments, and passing through the
literature of the Middle Ages, equally impregnated with
inferior sentiments, then through the works of the old
masters, whose ideas and sentiments seldom compensate
for the displeasing effect they inflict on our senses over-
refined in study of appearances ; and coming at last to
the vaunted works of modern art, excellent for technical
execution in many cases but deplorable for the emotions
they arouse and express, such as Gérôme's battle-pieces,
alternately sensual and sanguinary ;—they are all far off
indeed from the qualities deemed desirable, from the
artistic forms corresponding to the highest forms of
æsthetic feeling." [1]   These last critical denunciations, like
the theories noticed above, are mere substitutions of one
word for another ; " facility " for " grace " ; " economy "
for "beauty," and so on.   Indeed, when one tries to define
the exact philosophical position of Spencer, one can only
possibly say that he wavers between sensationalism and
moralism, and is never for a moment conscious of art as
art.

*Physiologists
of Æsthetic.
Grant Allen,
Helmholtz,
and others.*   The same oscillation is noticeable in other English
writers such as Sully and Bain, in whom, however, we
find more familiarity with works of art.[2]   In his numerous
essays and in *Physiological Æsthetics* (1877), Grant Allen
collected a great many records of physiological experiments, all of which may be of supreme value to physiology,
for aught we know to the contrary, but most assuredly
are worthless from the point of view of Æsthetic.   He
keeps to the distinction between necessary or vital activity

---

[1] *Principles of Psychology*, 1855 ; 2nd ed. 1870, part viii. ch. 9,
§§ 533-540.

[2] J. Sully, *Outlines of Psychology*, London, 1884 ; *Sensation and
Intuition, Studies in Psychology and Æsthetics*, London, 1874 ; cf.
Encycl. Britannica, ed. 9, art. " Æsthetics"; Alex. Bain, *The Emotions
and the Will*, London, 1859, ch. 14.

and the superfluous or that of play, and defines æsthetic
pleasure as "the subjective concomitant of the normal
sum of activity, not connected directly with the vital
functions, in the terminal peripheric organs of the cerebro-
spinal nervous system." [1] Physiological processes considered as causes of pleasure in art are presented under
other aspects by later investigators, who assert that such
pleasure arises not only "from the activity of the visual
organs and the muscular systems associated with them,
but also from the participation of some of the more important functions of the organism, as for instance breathing, circulation of the blood, equilibrium and internal
muscular accommodation." Art, then, indubitably origi-
nated in "a prehistoric man who was habitually a deep-
breather, having no call to rearrange his natural habits
when scratching lines on bones or in mud and taking
pains to draw them regularly spaced." [2] Physical-Æsthetic
researches were pursued in Germany by Helmholtz, Brücke
and Stumpf, [3] who generally confined themselves to the
narrower field of optics and acoustics, giving descriptions
of the physical processes of artistic technique and the
conditions to which pleasurable visual and auditive impressions must conform, without claiming to merge
Æsthetic in Physics, but even pointing out the divergences
between them. Degenerate Herbartians hastened to disguise in physiological terms the metaphysical forms and
relations of which their master had spoken, and to
coquet with the hedonism of the naturalists.

The superstitious cult of natural sciences was often
accompanied (as is frequently the fate of superstition) by

Method of the natural sciences in Æsthetic.

---

[1] *Physiological Æsthetics*, London, 1877; various arts. in *Mind*,
vols. iii. iv. v. (o.s.).

[2] Vernon Lee and C. Anstruther-Thomson, "Beauty and Ugliness,"
in *Contemp. Review*, October-November, 1897: (abstract in Arréat, *Dix
années de philosophie*, pp. 80-85); same author's *Le Rôle de l'élément
moteur dans la perception esthétique visuelle*, *Mémoire et questionnaire
soumis au 4ᵐᵉ Congrès de Psychologie*, reprinted Imola, 1901.

[3] H. Helmholtz, *Die Lehre von der Tonempfindungen als physiolo-
gische Grundlage für die Theorie der Musik*, 1863, 4th ed., 1877; Brücke-
Helmholtz, *Principes scientifiques des beaux arts*, Fr. ed., Paris, 1881;
C. Stumpf, *Tonpsychologie*, Leipzig, 1883.

a sort of hypocrisy. Chemical, physical and physiological laboratories became Sybilline grottoes, resounding with the questions of credulous inquirers concerning the profoundest problems of the human spirit ; and many of those who were really conducting their inquiries on inherently philosophic principles pretended or deluded themselves into believing that they followed the Method of Natural Science. A proof of this illusion or pretence is Hippolyte Taine's *Philosophy of Art*.[1] " If by studying the art of various peoples and various epochs," says Taine, " we could define the nature and establish the conditions of the existence of each art, we should have arrived at a complete explanation of the fine arts and of art in general, *i.e.* at what is called an Æsthetic." A historical Æsthetic, not a dogmatic, which fixes characters and indicates laws " like Botany, and studies with equal attention orange and ivy, pine and birch ; indeed it is a sort of botanical science applied to the works of man instead of to plants " ; an Æsthetic which shall follow " the general movement which tends daily more and more to join the moral to the natural sciences and by extending to the former the principles, the safeguards and the rules of the latter, enables both to attain the same security and maintain the same progress." [2] The naturalistic prelude is followed by definitions and doctrines indistinguishable from those offered by philosophers whose infallibility is not guaranteed by scientific methods, indeed, from those of the wildest of such philosophers. For, says Taine, art is imitation, an imitation so carried out as to render sensible the essential character of objects ; the essential character being " a quality from which all other qualities, or many others, are derived and follow unalterably from it." The essential character of a lion, for example, is to be " a great carnivore " ; this determines the formation of all its limbs ; the essential character of Holland is to be " a country formed by alluvial soil." This is why art is not restricted to objects existing in

H. Taine's
Æsthetic.

---

[1] *Philosophie de l'art*, 1866–1869 (4th ed. Paris, 1885).
[2] *Op. cit.* i. pp. 13-15.

reality, but is able, as in architecture or in music, to represent essential characters without natural objects to correspond.[1] Now, in what do these essential characters, this carnivorosity and this alluviality differ, save perhaps in extravagance of example, from the " types " and " ideas " which intellectualistic or metaphysical Æsthetic had always considered as the proper content of art ? Taine himself clears away every doubt in the matter by explicitly stating that " this character is what philosophers call the ' essence of things,' in virtue of which they affirm that the aim and end of art is to make manifest the essence of things " ; he adds that, for his part, he " refuses to make use of the word ' essence ' as being a technical term " : [2] of the word itself, maybe ; not of the concept for which it stands. There are two ways (says Taine, for all the world as though he were a Schelling) leading to the higher life of man, to contemplation : the way of science and the way of art : " the former investigates the causes and fundamental laws of reality, and expresses them in exact formulæ and abstract terms : the latter makes manifest these causes and laws, not in dry definitions inaccessible to the vulgar, and intelligible only to the select few, but in a sensible manner, appealing not merely to the reason but to the heart and senses of the most commonplace man ; it has the power of being both elevated and popular, of manifesting what is most noble and elevated, and of manifesting it to every one." [3]

Taine's metaphysic and moralism.

For Taine, as for the Hegelian æstheticians, works of art are arranged in a scale of values ; so that, having begun by condemning as absurd every judgement of taste (every one to his taste [4]), he ends by asserting that " personal taste has no value whatever," and that some common measure should be abstracted and set up as a standard of progress and retrogression, ornamentation and degeneracy ; a standard by which to approve and disapprove, praise and blame.[5] The scale of values set up by him is twofold or threefold, in the first instance

[1] *Philosophie de l'art*, i. pp. 17-54.   [2] *Op. cit.* i. p. 37.
[3] *Op. cit.* i. p. 54.   [4] *Op. cit.* i. p. 15.   [5] *Op. cit.* ii. p. 277.

it turns on the degree of importance of the character,
i.e. the greater or less generality in idea, and the degree
of beneficent effect (*degré de bienfaisance*), *i.e.* the greater
or less moral value of the representation (two grades
which are aspects of one single quality, viz. power, considered first for its own sake and then in its connexion
with others) : in the second instance upon the degree of
convergence of effects, *i.e.* the fulness of expression, the
harmony between idea and form.[1] This intellectualistic,
moralistic, rhetorical doctrine is interrupted now and
then by the usual naturalistic protests : " We shall,
according to our custom, study this question in the manner
of the natural scientist ; that is to say methodically, by
analysis ; hoping to raise not merely a song of praise,
but a code of laws," etc. ;[2] as though that sufficed to alter
the substance of the method adopted and the doctrine
expounded.   Taine finally gave himself over to dialectical
treatments and solutions, and asserted that in the primitive
period of Italian art, in the pictures of Giotto, we have
soul without body (thesis) ; under the Renaissance, in
Verrocchio's pictures, body without soul (antithesis) ; in
the sixteenth century, in Raphael, there is harmony of
expression and anatomy, soul and body (synthesis).[3]

G. T. Fechner.   The same protests and similar methods are to be found
Inductive   in the works of Gustav Theodor Fechner.   In his *Introduc-*
Æsthetic.   *tion to Æsthetic* (1876), Fechner claims to " abandon the
attempt at conceptual determination of the objective
essence of beauty," since he desires to compose not a
metaphysical Æsthetic from above (*von oben*), but an
inductive Æsthetic from below (*von unten*) and to achieve
clearness, not sublimity ; metaphysical Æsthetic should
bear the same relation to inductive, as the Philosophy of
Nature to Physics.[4] Proceeding on inductive lines, he
discovers a long series of æsthetic laws or principles : the
æsthetic threshold ; assistance or increment ; unity in
variety ; absence of contradictions ; clarity ; association ;

---

[1] *Philos. de l'art*, ii. pp. 257-400.
[2] *Op. cit.* ii. pp. 257-258.   [3] *Op. cit.* ii. p. 393.
[4] *Vorschule der Ästhetik*, 1876 (2nd ed. Leipzig, 1897–1898).

contrast ; consequence ; conciliation ; the correct mean ; economic use ; persistency ; change ; measure ; and so on without end. This chaos of concepts he expounds with a chapter apiece, pleased and proud to show himself so highly scientific and so wholly inconclusive. *Experiments.* Next he describes the experiments he can recommend to his readers. They are of this type. Take ten rectangular pieces of white cardboard of fairly equal area (say ten square inches), but with sides variously proportioned from a ratio of 1 : 1 to one of 2 : 5, including the ratio of the golden section, 21 : 34 ; mix all these together on a black table and collect persons of every kind and character, but all belonging to the educated classes, and applying the method of choice ask these people first to free their minds of all questions as to a particular use and then to pick out the pieces of cardboard which give them the highest sensation of pleasure and those which inspire them with the strongest feelings of disgust ; the answers to be most carefully noted, keeping male and female subjects apart, and tabulated. Then see what follows. Fechner admits that the chosen cardboard-pickers often made reservations when questioned by himself, not knowing (very naturally) how to tell whether they liked a shape or disliked it without referring it to a definite use ; sometimes they refused point-blank to make any selection at all ; and they almost always seemed vague and perplexed in mind and generally, when submitted to a second test, answered in a way totally different from the first. Still, we all know that errors cancel out ; and anyhow the tabulations showed that the highest sensations of delight were aroused not by the square, but by rectangular forms most nearly approaching the square, an enthusiastic rush being made for the proportion 21 : 34.[1] This method of selection received an extraordinarily felicitous definition ; it was known as " an average of arbitrary judgements by an arbitrary number of persons arbitrarily selected." [2] Fechner also informs us (always

---

[1] *Vorschule der Ästhetik*, i. ch. 19.

[2] Schasler, *Krit. Geschichte d. Ästh.* p. 1117.

Trivial nature of his ideas on Beauty and Art.

in tabular form) of the result of a statistical inquiry of his own, by means of countless heaps of catalogues and gallery-guides, as to the dimensions and shapes of pictures in relation to the subjects they depict.[1] Nevertheless, when he tries to tell us what beauty is, he falls back on using— whether well or ill—the old speculative method, which he prefaces with the remark that for him the concept of beauty is " merely an expedient in conformity with linguistic usage for indicating briefly the link which unites the prevailing conditions of immediate pleasure." [2] He distinguishes three meanings of the word " beauty " : first, in a broad sense, the pleasing in general : secondly, in a narrow sense, a higher pleasure, but still sensuous : thirdly, in the narrowest sense, true beauty, which " not only pleases, but has the right of pleasing, possesses value in pleasing " ; in it are united the concepts of beauty (the pleasing) and of goodness.[3] Beauty, in fact, is that which must please objectively and as such it corresponds with the good of action. " The Good," says Fechner, " is like a serious man, the capable organiser of his whole domestic life, sagaciously weighing the present and future, setting himself to extract the greatest benefit from both. Beauty is his florid spouse, careful of the present and mindful of her husband's wishes. The Pleasing is the baby, all senses and play : the Useful is the servant who puts his hands at his master's disposal and is given bread solely in accordance with his deserts. Truth, lastly, is the preacher and teacher to the household ; preacher in matters of faith, teacher in those of learning : he gives an eye to the Good and a helping hand to the Useful, and holds up a looking-glass to Beauty." [4] When speaking of art, he sums up all essential laws or rules into the following : (1) art chooses a valuable or, at any rate, an interesting, idea for representation : (2) it expresses the idea in sensible material in the manner most suitable to its contents : (3) from amongst the various means at its disposal, it selects those which in themselves are more pleasing than

[1] *Vorschule der Ästh.* ii. pp. 273-314.　　[2] *Op. cit.* pref. p. iv.
[3] *Op. cit.* i. pp. 15-30.　　[4] *Op. cit.* i. p. 32.

the others : (4) the same procedure is observed in all
particulars : (5) in the event of conflict between these
rules, one is made to give way to another in such a way
that the greatest possible pleasure and that of highest
value is attained (*das grösstmögliche und werthvollste
Gefallen*).[1] But why should Fechner, who had this
eudemonistic theory of beauty and art (as he calls it) all
ready made in advance,[2] take the trouble to enumerate
principles and laws and conduct experiments and tabulate
statistics wholly incapable of illustrating or proving it ?
One is tempted to believe that these pseudo-scientific
operations were to him, and still are to his followers, a
pastime or hobby neither more nor less important than
playing Patience or collecting stamps.

Another example of the superstitious cult of the *Ernst Grosse.*
natural sciences is to be found in Professor Ernst Grosse's *Speculative*
Origins of Art.[3] Contemner of all philosophical research *Æsthetic*
into art, which he dismisses under the title of " Specula- *science of art.*
tive Æsthetic," Grosse invokes a Science of art (*Kunstwissenschaft*) whose mission is to dig out all the laws lying
hidden in the mass of historical facts collected to date.
It is his opinion that all ethnographic and prehistoric
material should be united to historical matter proper,
there being no possibility, according to him, of framing
general laws when study is restricted to the art of cultured
peoples " just as a theory of generation must necessarily
be imperfect if founded exclusively on the form of that
function predominant among mammals." [4] But immediately after his declaration of abhorrence for philosophy,
and of faith in scientific methods, Grosse finds himself in
the same difficulty as Taine and Fechner. Indeed, there
is no escape ; in order to examine the artistic productions
of primitive and savage peoples, a start must be made
from some sort of concept of art. All the scientific metaphors, all the verbal emollients employed by Grosse
cannot hide the nature of the plan he is forced to adopt,
or its striking resemblance to the despised speculative

---

[1] *Vorschule der Ästh.* ii. pp. 12-13.   [2] *Op. cit.* i. p. 38.
[3] *Die Anfänge der Kunst*, Freiburg i. B. 1894.   [4] *Op. cit.* p. 19.

Æsthetic. " As a traveller who desires to explore an unknown land must provide himself with a general outline of the country and have some knowledge of the direction in which his path should lie, if he does not wish to lose his way entirely ; so we, before beginning our enquiry, need a general preliminary orientation concerning the essence of the phenomena (*über das Wesen der Erscheinungen*) about to engage our attention." Most certainly " we may count upon having an exact and exhaustive answer, at earliest, when our enquiry is finished ; and it is not yet begun. That characteristic which we seek to determine at the outset . . . may be most radically modified by the time we reach the end : " there is no question, fie on the suggestion ! of imitating the old æstheticians : the only question is how " to give a definition which may serve as provisional scaffolding, to be broken away on completion of the edifice." [1] Words, words, words : the mite of general ideas and artistic laws to be found in his book has been quarried by Grosse not from study of the reports brought back by travellers in savage lands, but from speculation on the forms of the spirit ; and (inevitably) his interpretation of the former is reached by the light thrown on it by the latter. In his final definition, Grosse concludes by considering art as an activity which in its development or as its result, possesses immediate feeling-value (*Gefühlswerth*), and is an end to itself ; practical and æsthetic activity are in direct mutual opposition between which as a middle term lies the activity of play, which like the practical activity has its end outside itself, but, like the æsthetic, finds its enjoyment not in its external end, which is more or less insignificant, but in its own activity.[2] At the end of his book he remarks that the artistic activity of primitive peoples is hardly ever unaccompanied by the practical ; and that art began by being social and became individual only in civilized times.[3]

The Æsthetics of Taine and Grosse have also been

[1] *Die Anfänge der Kunst*, pp. 45-46.   [2] *Op. cit.* pp. 46-48.
[3] *Op. cit.* pp. 293-301.

described by the epithet sociological. But since no one *Sociological* knows what the science of Sociology is, we must deal with *Æsthetic.* the sociological superstition as we dealt with the naturalistic ; that is to say, by skipping the preface with its proposals that can never be carried out, and seeing what it is that the objective necessities of the case have forced the author to assert, and which of the possible alternative views he accepts, or between what selection of them his allegiance wavers. During this examination we shall ignore the fairly common case of an author who while pretending to construct an Æsthetic simply compiles a list of facts connected with the history of art or civilization.

Some social reformers of our day, like Proudhon, have revived the condemnations of Plato, or the mitigated moralism of antiquity and the Middle Ages. Proudhon *Proudhon.* denied the formula Art for Art's sake ; he looked on art as a mere purveyor of sensuous pleasure, something which must be subordinated to legal and economical ends ; poetry, sculpture, painting, music, romance, history, comedy, tragedy had for him no aim save exhortation to virtue and dissuasion from vice.[1] Development of social sympathy is the whole duty of art in the estimation of J. M. Guyau, who became famous as the founder of Social *J. M. Guyau.* Æsthetic and was, according to certain French critics, inaugurator of the third epoch in the history of Æsthetic, the first being the æsthetic of the ideal (Plato), the second that of perception (Kant), and the third that of " Social Sympathy " (Guyau). In his *Problems of Contemporary Æsthetic* (1884) Guyau combats the theory of play, and substitutes that of Life ; in a posthumous publication *Art in Its Sociological Aspect* (1889) he explains more clearly that the life of which he speaks is social life.[2] If the beautiful be the intellectually pleasing, certainly it cannot be identified with the useful which is only searching for what is pleasing ; but the useful (says Guyau, in the

[1] *Du principe de l'art et de sa destination sociale*, Paris, 1875.

[2] M. Guyau, *L'Art au point de vue sociologique*, 1889 (3rd ed. Paris, 1895) ; *Les Problèmes de l'esthétique contemporaine*, Paris, 1884 ; cf. Fouilleé, pref. to the former work, pp. xli-xliii.

belief that he is correcting both Kant and the evolutionists)
does not always exclude the beautiful, of which indeed it
often forms the lowest degree. The study of art is embraced partly,[1] not wholly, by Sociology : for art fulfils
two ends, firstly and primarily that of provoking pleasant
sensations (of colour, sound, etc.) and in this sense finds
itself in the presence of practically incontestable scientific
laws which connect Æsthetic with the physics (optics,
acoustics, etc.), mathematics, physiology and psycho-
physics. Sculpture, in fact, rests especially on anatomy
and physiology : painting on anatomy, physiology and
optics : architecture on optics (golden section, etc.) :
music on physiology and acoustics : poetry on metrics,
whose most general laws are acoustical and physiological.
The second function of art is to produce the phenomena
of " psychological induction," which bring to a head ideas
and sentiments of most complex nature (sympathy with
personages represented, interest, pity, indignation, etc.),
in short all the social feelings, which constitute it " the
expression of life." Whence are derived the two tendencies recognised in art ; one inclining towards harmony,
consonance, and everything delightful to ear and eye :
the other towards the transfusion of life into the domain
of art. Genius, true genius is destined to preserve the
balance of the two tendencies : decadents and degenerates
deprive art of its social sympathetic aim by setting
æsthetic sympathy at war against human sympathy.[2]
Translating all this into familiar terms, we may say that
Guyau asserts one purely hedonistic art, above which he
superimposes another art, also hedonistic, but serviceable
to the cause of morality.

M. Nordau. The same polemic against decadents, degenerates and
individualists is carried on by another writer, Max
Nordau, who gives art the task of re-establishing the
wholeness of life amongst the fragmentary specialisation
characteristic of industrial society ; he asserts that art for
art's sake, art as the simple expression of internal states

[1] *L'Art au point de vue sociologique,* pref. p. xlvii.
[2] *Op. cit., passim,* esp. ch. 4 ; cf. pp. 64, 85, 380.

or the objectification of the artist's feelings, no doubt exists, but is merely " the art of Quaternary man, the art of the cave-dweller." [1]

Naturalistic is the best term with which to qualify the Æsthetic derived from that identification of genius with degeneracy which made the fortune of Lombroso and his school. This identification derives its chief strength from the following piece of reasoning. Great mental efforts, total absorption in one dominating thought, often bring about physiological disorders in the bodily organism and weakness or atrophy of various vital functions. But such derangements come under the head of the pathological concept of illness, degeneration, madness. Therefore genius is identical with illness, degeneration and madness. A syllogism from particular to general, in which case, according to traditional Logic, *non est consequentia*. But with sociologists such as Nordau, Lombroso and company, we almost overstep the line separating respectable error from that grosser form which we call a blunder.

A mere confusion between scientific analysis and historical inquiry or description is visible in the works of certain sociologists and anthropologists. Thus one of them, Carl Bücher, in studying the life of primitive peoples, asserts that poetry, music and work were originally fused in one single act ; that poetry and music were used to regulate the rhythms of labour.[2] This may be historically true or false, important or no : it has nothing whatever to do with æsthetic science. In the same way Andrew Lang maintains that the doctrine concerning the origin of art as disinterested expression of the mimetic faculty finds no confirmation from what we know of primitive art, which is decorative rather than expressive : [3] as though primitive art, which is a mere fact awaiting interpretation, could ever be converted into a criterion for the interpretation of art in general.

The same vague naturalism exercised a baneful in-

Naturalism.
C. Lombroso.

Decline of
Linguistic.

[1] Max Nordau, *Social Function of Art*, 2nd ed., Turin, 1897.
[2] Karl Bücher, *Arbeit u. Rhythmus*, 2nd ed., Leipzig, 1899.
[3] *Custom and Myth*, p. 276 ; quoted by Knight, *The Philosophy of the Beautiful*, vol. i. pp. 9-10.

fluence on Linguistic, which of late years has been wholly
lacking in such profound research as that inaugurated by
Humboldt and followed up by Steinthal. But Steinthal
never succeeded in founding a school. Max Müller, popular and inaccurate, maintained the indivisibility of speech
and thought, confounding, or at least not distinguishing,
æsthetic and logical thought ; although at one time he
had noted that the formation of names had a closer
connexion with wit, in the sense of Locke, than with
judgement. He maintained, moreover, that the science
of language is not a historical but a natural science,
because language is not the invention of man :. the
dilemma of " historical " and " natural " was canvassed
and resolved over and over again with little result.[1]
Another philologist, Whitney, attacked the " miraculous "
theory of Müller and denied that thought is indivisible
from speech : " The deaf-mute does not speak, but he
can think," he observes ; " thought is not function of the
acoustic nerve." By this means Whitney relapsed into
the ancient doctrine that speech is a symbol or means
of expression, of human thought, subject to the will,
the result of a synthesis of faculties and of a capacity
for intelligent adaptation of means to end.[2]

Signs of revival. H. Paul.
Philosophical spirit reappeared in Paul's *Principles of
the History of Language* (1880),[3] though the author's
efforts to defend himself from the terrifying accusation
of being a philosopher led him to hunt out a fresh title
to replace the scandalous " Philosophy of Language."
But if Paul is vague about the relation of Logic to
Grammar, he must be given every credit for identifying,
as Humboldt had already done, the question of the origin
of language with that of its nature ; and reasserting that
language is created afresh whenever we speak. He must
also be given credit for having conclusively criticized the

[1] *Lectures on the Science of Language*, 1861 and 1864 (Fr. tr., Paris, 1867).

[2] William Dwight Whitney, *The Life and Growth of Language*, London, 1875 (It. tr., Milan, 1876).

[3] Hermann Paul, *Principien der Sprachgeschichte*, 1880 (2nd ed., Halle, 1886).

Ethnopsychology (*Völkerpsychologie*) of Steinthal and Lazarus, showing that there is no such thing as collective psyche and that there can be no language other than of the individual.   Wundt [1] on the other hand attached the study of language, mythology and customs to this non-existent science of Ethnopsychology ; in his latest work, on this very subject of language,[2] he foolishly echoes Whitney's gibes and denounces as a " miracle theory " (*Wundertheorie*) that glorious doctrine inaugurated by Herder and Humboldt, whom he accuses of " mystical obscurity " (*mystiche Dunkel*) : he observes that this view may have had some justification before the principle of evolution had reached its triumphant application to organic nature in general and to man in particular.   He has not the faintest notion of the function of imagination, or of the true relation between thought and expression ; he finds no substantial difference between expression in the naturalistic, and expression in the spiritual and linguistic sense ; he considers language as a special highly developed form of the vital psychophysical manifestations and of the expressive movements of animals.   Out of these facts language is developed by imperceptible grada-tions ; so that, beyond the general concept of expressive movement (*Ausdrucksbewegung*) " there is no specific mark by which language can be distinguished in any but an arbitrary manner."[3]   The philosophy of Wundt betrays its own weakness by showing its inability to master the problem of language and art.   In his *Ethics* æsthetic facts are presented as a complex of logical and ethical elements ; the existence of æsthetic as a special normative science is denied, not for the good and sufficient reason that there are no such things as " normative sciences," but because this special science is said by him to be absorbed by the two sciences of Logic and Ethics,[4] which amounts to deny-ing the existence of Æsthetic and the originality of art.

The linguistic of Wundt.

[1] Wilh. Wundt, *Über Wege u. Ziele d. Völkerpsychologie*, Leipzig, 1886.

[2] *Die Sprache*, Leipzig, 1900, 2 vols. (part i. of *Völkerpsychologie, eine Untersuchung der Entwicklungsgesetze von Sprache, Mythus und Sitte*).

[3] *Die Sprache, passim* ; cf. i. p. 31 *seqq.*, ii. pp. 599, 603-609.

[4] *Ethik*, ed. 2, Stuttgart, 1892, p. 6.

XVIII

ÆSTHETIC PSYCHOLOGISM AND OTHER
RECENT TENDENCIES

Neo-criticism and empiricism. THE neo-critical or neo-Kantian movement was power-less to make headway against hedonistic, psychological and moralistic views of the æsthetic fact, although it made every effort to save the concept of spirit from the invading rush of naturalism and materialism.[1] Kant bequeathed to neo-criticism his own failure to under-stand creative imagination, and the neo-Kantians do not seem to have had the faintest notion of any form of cognition other than the intellectual.

Kirchmann. Amongst German philosophers of any renown who clung to æsthetic sensationalism and psychologism was Kirchmann, promoter of a so-called realism, and author of *Æsthetic on a Realistic Basis* (1868).[2] In his doctrine the æsthetic fact is an image (*Bild*) of a real ; an animated (*seelenvolles*) image, purified and strengthened, that is, idealized, and divided into the image of pleasure, which is the beautiful, and that of pain, which is the ugly. Beauty admits of a threefold series of varieties or modifi-cations, being determined according to the content as sublime, comic, tragic, etc. ; according to the image, as beauty of nature or of art ; and according to the idealiza-tion as idealistic or naturalistic, formal or spiritual,

[1] A. F. Lange, *Geschichte des Materialismus, u. Kritik seiner Bedeu-tung i. d. Gegenwart*, 1866.
[2] J. F. v. Kirchmann, *Ästhetik auf realistischer Grundlage*, Berlin, 1868.

symbolical or classical. Not having grasped the nature
of æsthetic objectification, Kirchmann takes the trouble
to draw up a new psychological category of ideal or
apparent feelings, arising from artistic images and being
attenuations of the feelings of real life.[1]

To the evolution or involution of the Herbartians into
physiologists of æsthetic pleasure corresponds a similar
evolution or involution of the idealists into adherents of
psychologism. The first place must be given to the
veteran Theodor Vischer, who in a criticism of his own
work pronounced Æsthetic to be " the union of mimics
and harmonics " (vereinte Mimik und Harmonik), and
Beauty the " harmony of the universe," never actually
realized because realized only at infinity, so that when
we think to seize it in the Beautiful, we are under an
illusion : a transcendent illusion, which is the very essence
of the æsthetic fact.[2] His son Robert Vischer coined the
word Einfühlung to express the life with which man
endows natural objects by means of the æsthetic process.[3]
Volkelt, when treating of the Symbol [4] and joining symbolism to pantheism, opposed associationism and favoured
a natural teleology immanent in Beauty. The Herbartian
Siebeck (1875) abandoned the formalistic theory and tried
to explain the fact of beauty by the concept of the appearance of personality.[5] He distinguishes between objects
which please by their content alone (sensuous pleasures),
those which please by form alone (moral facts), and those
which please by the connexion of content with form
(organic and æsthetic facts). In organic facts the form
is not outside the content, but is the expression of the
reciprocal action and conjunction of the constitutive
elements : whereas in æsthetic facts the form is outside
the content, and as it were its mere surface ; not a means
to the end, but an end in itself. Æsthetic intuition is a

Metaphysic translated into Psychology. Vischer.

Siebeck.

[1] Ästh. auf real. Grund. vol. i. pp. 54-57 ; see above, pp. 80-81.
[2] Kritische Gänge, vol. v. pp. 25-26, 131.
[3] R. Vischer, Über das optische Formgefühl, Leipzig, 1873.
[4] Der Symbol-Begriff in der neuesten Ästh., Jena, 1876.
[5] Das Wesen d. ästh. Anschauung, Psychologische Untersuchungen z.
Theorie d. Schönen u. d. Kunst, Berlin, 1875.

relation between the sensible and the spiritual, matter
and spirit, and is thus form regarded as the appearance
of personality. Æsthetic pleasure arises from the spirit's
consciousness of discovering itself in the sensible. Siebeck
borrows the theory of modifications of the beautiful from
the metaphysical idealists, who held that only in such
modifications can beauty be found in the concrete, just
as humanity can only exist as a man of determinate race
and nationality. The sublime is that species of beauty
wherein the formal moment of circumscription is lost, and
is therefore the unlimited, which is a kind of extensive
or intensive infinity ; the tragic arises when the harmony
is not given but is the result of conflict and development ;
the comic is a relation of the small to the great ; and so
on. These traces of idealism, together with his firm hold
on the Kantian and Herbartian absoluteness of the judgement of taste, make it impossible to regard Siebeck's
Æsthetic as purely psychological and empirical and wholly
devoid of philosophical elements. It is the same with
M. Diez. Diez, who, in his *Theory of Feeling as Foundation of
Æsthetic* (1892),[1] tries to explain the artistic activity as a
return to the ideal of feeling (*Ideal des fühlenden Geistes*),
parallel with science (ideal of thought), morality (ideal
of will) and religion (ideal of personality). But whatever
is this so-called feeling ? is it the empirical feeling of the
psychologists, irreducible to an ideal, or the mystic faculty
of communication and conjunction with the Infinite and
the Absolute ? the absurd " pleasure-value " of Fechner,
or the " judgement " of Kant ? One is inclined to say
that these writers, and others like them, still under the
influence of metaphysical views, lack the courage of their
opinions : they feel themselves to be in an atmosphere of
hostility and speak under reservations or compromises.
The psychologist Jodl asserts the existence of elementary
æsthetic feelings, as discovered by Herbart, and defines
them as " immediate excitations not resting upon associative or reproductive activity or on the fancy," although

[1] Max Diez, *Theorie des Gefühls z. Begründung d. Ästhetik*, Stuttgart,
1892.

" in ultimate analysis they must be reduced to the same principles." [1]

The purely psychological and associationistic tendency becomes clearly defined in Professor Teodor Lipps and his school. Lipps criticizes and rejects a whole series of æsthetic theories : (a) of play ; (b) of pleasure ; (c) of art as recognition of real life, even if displeasing ; (d) of emotion and passional excitation ; (e) syncretism, attributing to art beside the primary purpose of play and pleasure the further ends of recognition of life, in its reality, revelation of individuality, commotion, freedom from a weight, or free play of the imagination. His theory differs little at bottom from that of Jouffroy, for in his thesis he assumes artistic beauty to be the sympathetic. " The object of sympathy is our objectified ego, transposed into others and therefore discovered in them. We feel ourselves in others and we feel others in ourselves. In others, or by means of them, we feel ourselves happy, free, enlarged, elevated, or the contrary of all these. The æsthetic feeling of sympathy is not a mere mode of æsthetic enjoyment, it is that enjoyment itself. All æsthetic enjoyment is founded, in the last analysis, singly and wholly upon sympathy ; even that caused by geometrical, architectonic, tectonic, ceramic, etc., lines and forms." " Whenever in a work of art we find a personality (not a defect of the man, but something positively human) which harmonizes with and awakes an echo in the possibilities and tendencies of our own life and vital activities : whenever we find positive, objective humanity, pure and free from all real interests lying outside the work of art, as art only can reproduce it and æsthetic contemplation alone can demand ; the harmony, the resonance, fills us with joy. The value of personality is ethical value : outside it there is no possibility or determination of ethical character. All artistic and in general æsthetic enjoyment is, therefore, the enjoyment of something which has ethical value (eines ethische

Psychological tendency. Teodor Lipps.

[1] Friedr. Jodl, *Lehrb. der Psychologie*, Stuttgart, 1896, § 53, pp. 404-414.

Werthvollen) ; not as element of a complex, but as object of æsthetic intuition.[1]

The æsthetic fact is thus deprived of all its own value and allowed merely a reflexion from the value of morality.

K. Groos.   Without lingering over Lipps's pupils (such as Stern and others [2]) and writers of similar tendency (such as Biese, with his theory of anthropomorphism and universal metaphor ; [3] or Konrad Lange, who propounds a thesis that art is conscious self-deception),[4] we will call attention to Professor Karl Groos (1892), who comes within measurable distance of the concept of æsthetic activity as a theoretic value.[5]   Between the two poles of consciousness, sensibility and intellect, are several intermediate grades, amongst which lies intuition or fancy, whose product, the image or appearance (*Schein*), is midway between sensation and concept.   The image is full like sensation, but regulated like the concept ; it has neither the inexhaustible richness of the former, or the barren nudity of the latter.   Of the nature of image or appearance is the æsthetic fact ; which is distinguished from the simple, ordinary image not by its quality, but by its intensity alone :   the æsthetic image is merely a simple image occupying the summit of consciousness.   Representations pass through consciousness like a crowd of people hurrying over a bridge, each bent on his own business ; but when a passer-by halts on the bridge and looks at the scene, then is it holiday, then arises the æsthetic fact.   This is therefore not passivity but activity ; according to the formula adopted by Groos it is internal imitation (*innere Nachahnung*).[6]   It may be objected against the theory

[1] *Komik und Humor, eine psychol. ästhet. Untersuch.*, Hamburg-Leipzig, pp. 223-227.

[2] Paul Stern, *Einfühling u. Association i. d. neueren Åsth.*, 1898, in *Beiträge z. Åsth.*, ed. Lipps and R. M. Werner (Hamburg-Leipzig).

[3] Alfr. Biese, *Das Associationsprincip u. d. Anthropomorphismus i. d. Åsth.*, 1890 ; *Die Philosophie des Metaphorischen*, Hamburg-Leipzig, 1893.

[4] Konrad Lange, *Die bewusste Selbsttäuschung als Kern des künstlerischen Genusses*, Leipzig, 1895.

[5] Karl Groos, *Einleitung i. d. Asthetik*, Giessen, 1892.

[6] *Op. cit.* pp. 6-46, 83-100.

that every image, so far as it is an image at all, must occupy the summit of consciousness if only for an instant ; and that the mere image is either the product of an activity just as is the æsthetic image, or it is not a real image at all. It may also be objected that the definition of the image as something sharing in the nature of sensation and concept may lead back to intellectual intuition and the other mysterious faculties of the metaphysical school, for which Groos professes abhorrence. His division of the æsthetic fact into form and content is even less happy. He recognizes four classes of content : associative (in the strict sense), symbolic, typical, individual : [1] and into his inquiries he introduces, quite unnecessarily, the concepts of infusion of personality and of play. In connexion with the latter he remarks that " internal imitation is the noblest game of man," [2] and adds that " the concept of play applies fully to contemplation, but not to æsthetic production, save in the case of primitive peoples." [3]

Groos does however free himself from the " modifications of Beauty," because, æsthetic activity having been identified with internal imitation, it is clear that whatever is not internal imitation is excluded from that activity as something different. " All Beauty (beauty understood in the sense of ' sympathetic ') belongs to the æsthetic activity, but not every æsthetic fact is beautiful." Beauty, then, is the representation of the sensuously pleasant ; ugliness, the representation of the unpleasant ; the sublime, that of a mighty thing (*Gewaltiges*) in a simple form ; the comic, that of an inferiority which arouses in us a pleasing sense of our own superiority. And so forth.[4] With great good sense Groos holds up to derision the office assigned to the ugly by Schasler and Hartmann with their superficial dialectic. To say that an ellipse contains an element of ugliness in comparison with the circle because it is symmetrical about its two axes only and not about infinite diameters is like saying " wine has a relatively unpleasant taste because in it is lacking

The modifications of the Beautiful in Groos and Lipps.

---

[1] *Einleitung i. d. Ästh.* pp. 100-147.   [2] *Op. cit.* pp. 168-170.
[3] *Op. cit.* pp. 175-176.   [4] *Op. cit.* pp. 46-50, and all part iii.

(*ist aufgehoben*) the pleasant taste of beer." [1] Lipps too, in his writings upon Æsthetic, recognizes that the comic (of which he gives an accurate psychological analysis) [2] has in itself no æsthetic value ; but his moralistic views lead him to outline a theory of it not unlike that of the over-coming of the ugly ; he explains it as a process leading to a higher æsthetic value (*i.e.* sympathy).[3]

E. Véron and the double form of Æsthetic.

Work such as that of Groos and, occasionally, of Lipps is of some value towards the elimination of errors, as well as confining æsthetic research to the field of internal analysis. Merit of the same kind belongs to the work of a Frenchman, Véron,[4] who controverts the Absolute Beauty of academical Æsthetic and, after accusing Taine of confounding Art with Science and Æsthetic with Logic, remarks that if it be the duty of art to make manifest the essence of things, their one dominating quality, then " the greatest artists would be those who have best succeeded in exhibiting this essence . . . and the greatest works would resemble each other more closely than any others and would clearly demonstrate their common identity, whereas the exact opposite happens." [5] But one looks in vain for scientific method in Véron ; a pre-cursor of Guyau,[6] he asserts that art is at bottom two different things ; there are two arts : one decorative, whose end is beauty, that is to say the pleasure of eye and ear resulting from determinate dispositions of lines, forms, colours, sounds, rhythms, movements, light and shade, without necessary interventions of ideas and feel-ings, and capable of being studied by Optics and Acoustics : the other, expressive, which gives " the agitated expres-sion of human personality." He considers that decorative art prevails in the ancient world, and expressive art in the modern.[7]

We cannot here examine in detail the æsthetic theories

---

[1] *Einleitung i. d. Ästh.* p. 292, note.   [2] See above, pp. 91-92.

[3] *Komik und Humor*, p. 199 *seqq.*

[4] Eug. Véron, *L'Esthétique*, 2nd ed., Paris, 1883.

[5] *Op. cit.* p. 89.   [6] See above, pp. 399-400.

[7] *Esthétique*, pp. 38, 109, 123 *seqq.*

of artists and men of letters ; the scientific and historicist prejudices, the theory of experiment and human document, which underlie the realism of Zola, or the moralism which underlies the problem-art of Ibsen and the Scandinavian school. Gustave Flaubert wrote of art profoundly, better perhaps than any other Frenchman has ever written, not in special treatises but throughout his letters, which were published after his death.[1] Under the influence of Véron and his hatred for the concept of beauty, Leo Tolstoy wrote his book on art,[2] *L. Tolstoy.* which, according to the great Russian artist, communicates feelings in the same way in which words communicate thoughts. The meaning of this theory is made clear by the parallel he drew between Art and Science, and his conclusion that " the mission of art is to render sensible and capable of assimilation that which could not be assimilated under the form of argumentation " ; and that " true science examines truths considered as important for a certain society at a given epoch and fixes them in the consciousness of man, whereas art transports them from the domain of knowledge to that of feeling." [3] There is therefore no such thing as art for art's sake, any more than science for science' sake. Every human function should be directed to increase morality and to suppress violence. This amounts to saying that nearly all art, from the beginning of the world, is false. Aeschylus, Sophocles, Euripides, Aristophanes, Dante, Tasso, Milton, Shakespeare, Raphael, Michael Angelo, Bach, Beethoven are (according to Tolstoy) " artificial reputations created by critics." [4]

Amongst artists rather than amongst philosophers must *F. Nietzsche.* be reckoned Friedrich Nietzsche, whom we should wrong (as we said of Ruskin) by trying to expound his æsthetic doctrines in scientific language and then holding them up to the facile criticism which, so translated, they would draw upon themselves. In none of his books, not even in

---

[1] *Correspondance*, 1830–1880, 4 vols., new ed., Paris, 1902-1904.
[2] *What is Art ?* Eng. tr. [3] *Op. cit.* pp. 171-172, 308.
[4] *Op. cit.* pp. 201-202.

his first, *The Birth of Tragedy*,[1] in spite of the title, does he offer us a real theory of art ; what appears to be theory is the mere expression of the author's feelings and tendencies. He shows a kind of anxiety concerning the value and aim of art and the problem of its inferiority or superiority to science and philosophy, a state of mind characteristic of the Romantic period of which Nietzsche was, in many respects, a belated but magnificent representative. To Romanticism, as well as to Schopenhauer, belong the elements of thought which issued in the distinction between Apollinesque art (that of serene contemplation, to which belong the epic and sculpture) and Dionysiac art (the art of agitation and tumult, such as music and the drama). The thought is vague and does not bear criticism ; but it is supported by a flight of inspiration which lifts the mind to a spiritual region seldom if ever reached again in the second half of the nineteenth century.

The most notable æsthetic students of that time were perhaps a group of persons engaged in constructing theories of particular arts. And since—as we have seen [2]—philosophical laws or theories of individual arts are inconceivable, it was inevitable that the ideas presented by such thinkers should be (as indeed they are) nothing more than general æsthetic conclusions. First may be mentioned the *An æsthetician of music: E. Hanslick.* acute Bohemian critic Eduard Hanslick, who published his work *On Musical Beauty* in 1854 ; it was often reprinted and was translated into various languages.[3] Hanslick waged war against Richard Wagner and in general against the pretension of finding concepts, feelings and other definite contents in music. " In the most insignificant musical works, where the most powerful microscope can discover nothing, we are now asked to recognize a *Night Before the Battle*, a *Summer Night in Norway*, a *Longing for the Sea*, or some such absurdity,

[1] *Die Geburt der Tragödie oder Griechenthum und Pessimismus*, 1872 (Ital. trans., Bari, 1907).

[2] See above, p. 114.

[3] *Vom Musikalisch-Schönen*, Leipzig, 1854 ; 7th ed. 1885 (French trans., *Du beau dans la musique*, Paris, 1877).

should the cover have the audacity to affirm that this is the subject of the piece." [1] With equal vivacity he protests against the sentimental hearers who, instead of enjoying the work of art, set themselves to extract pathological effects of passionate excitement and practical activity. If it be true that Greek music produced effects of this kind, " if it needed but a few Phrygian strains to animate troops with courage in the face of the enemy, or a melody in the Dorian mode to ensure the fidelity of a wife whose husband was far away, then the loss of Greek music is a melancholy thing for generals and husbands ; but æstheticians and composers need not regret it." [2] " If every senseless *Requiem*, every noisy funeral march, every wailing *Adagio* had the power of depressing us, who could put up with existence under such conditions ? But let a real musical work confront us, clear-eyed and glowing with beauty, and we feel ourselves enslaved by its invincible fascination even if its material is all the sorrows of the age." [3] Hanslick maintained that the sole aim of music is form, musical beauty. This affirmation won him the goodwill of the Herbartians, who hastened to welcome such a vigorous and unexpected ally ; by way of returning the compliment, Hanslick felt obliged in later editions of his work to mention Herbart himself and his faithful disciple Robert Zimmermann who had given (so he said) " full development to the great æsthetic principle of Form." [4] The praises of the Herbartians and the courteous declarations of Hanslick both arose from a misunderstanding : for the words " beauty " and " form " have one meaning for the former and quite another for the latter. Hanslick never thought that symmetry, purely acoustical relations and pleasures of the ear constituted musical beauty ; [5] mathematics, he held, are utterly useless to musical Æsthetic. [6] Musical beauty is spiritual and significative : it has thoughts, undoubtedly ; but those thoughts are musical. " Sonorous forms are not empty, but perfectly

Hanslick's concept of form.

---

[1] *Vom Musikalisch-Schönen*, p. 20.　　　[2] *Op. cit.* p. 98.
[3] *Op. cit.* p. 101.　　[4] *Op. cit.* p. 119, note.　　[5] *Op. cit.* p. 50.
[6] *Op. cit.* p. 65.

filled; they cannot be compared with simple lines delimiting a space; they are the spirit assuming body and extracting from itself the stuff of its own incarnation. Rather than an arabesque, music is a picture; but a picture whose subject can neither be expressed in words nor enclosed in precise concept. There are in music both meaning and connexion, but these are of a specifically musical nature; music is a language we understand and speak, but which it is not possible to translate."[1] Hanslick asserts that though music does not portray the quality of feelings, it does portray their dynamic aspect or tone: if not the substantives, then the adjectives: it depicts not "murmuring tenderness" or "impetuous courage," but the "murmuring" and the "impetuous."[2] The backbone of the book is the denial that form and content can ever be separated in music. "In music there can be no content in opposition to the form, since there can be no form outside the content." "Take a motive, the first that comes into your head; what is its content, what its form? where does this begin, and that end? . . . What do you wish to call content? The sounds? Very well: but they have already received a form. What will you call form? Also the sounds? but they are form already filled; form supplied with content."[3] Such observations denote acute penetration of the nature of art, though not scientifically formulated or framed into a system. Hanslick thought he was dealing with peculiarities of music,[4] instead of with the universal and constitutive character of every form of art, and this prevented him from taking larger views.

Æstheticians of the figurative arts. C. Fiedler. Another specialist æsthetician is Conrad Fiedler, author of many essays on the figurative arts, the most important being his *Origin of Artistic Activity* (1887).[5] No one, perhaps, has better or more eloquently emphasized the activistic character of art, which he compares with

[1] *Vom Musikalisch-Schönen*, pp. 50-51.   [2] *Op. cit.* pp. 25-39.
[3] *Op. cit.* p. 122.   [4] *Op. cit.* pp. 52, 67, 113, etc.
[5] Conrad Fiedler, *Der Ursprung der künstlerischen Thätigkeit*, Leipzig, 1887. Collected with others of same author in *Schriften über die Kunst*, ed. H. Marbach, Leipzig, 1896.

language. " Art begins exactly where intuition (perception) ends. The artist is not differentiated from other
people by any special perceptive attitude enabling him
to perceive more or with greater intensity, or endowing his
eye with any special power of selecting, collecting, transforming, ennobling or illuminating ; but rather by his
peculiar gift of being able to pass immediately from perception to intuitive expression ; his relation with nature
is not perceptive, but expressive." " A man standing
passively at gaze may well imagine himself in possession
of the visible world as an immense, rich, varied whole :
the entire absence of fatigue with which he traverses the
infinite mass of visual impressions, the rapidity with
which representations dart across his consciousness,
convince him that he stands in the midst of an immense
visible world, although he may quite well be unable at
any one instant to represent it to himself as a whole. But
this world, so great, so rich, so immeasurable, disappears
the moment art seeks to become its master. The very
first effort to emerge from this twilight and arrive at clear
vision restricts the circle of things to be seen. Artistic
activity may be conceived as continuation of that concentration by which consciousness makes the first step
towards clear vision, which it reaches only by self-limita-
tion." Spiritual process and bodily process are here an
indivisible whole, which is expression. " This activity, *Intuition and*
simply because it is spiritual, must consist of forms *Expression.*
wholly determinate, tangible, sensibly demonstrative."
Art is not in a state of subjection to science. Like the
man of science, the artist desires to escape from the
natural perceptive state and to make the world his own ;
but there are regions to which we can penetrate not by the
forms of thought and science but only through art. Art
is, strictly speaking, not imitation of nature ; for what is
nature save this confused mass of perceptions and representations, whose real poverty has been demonstrated
already ? In another sense, however, art may be called
imitation of nature inasmuch as its aim is not to expound
concepts or to arouse emotions, that is to create values of

intellect and feeling. Art does create both these values,
if you like to say so ; but only in one quite peculiar
quality, which consists in complete visibility (*Sichtbar-
keit*). Here we have the same sane conception, the
same lively comprehension of the true nature of art which
we found in Hanslick, only expressed in a more rigorous
and philosophical manner. With Fiedler is connected
his friend Adolf Hildebrand, who brought into high relief
the activistic, or architectonic as opposed to imitative,
character of art, illustrating his theoretical discussions
especially from sculpture, the art which he himself
followed.[1]

*Narrow limits
of these
theories.*

What we chiefly miss in Fiedler and others of the same
tendency is the conception of the æsthetic fact not as
something exceptional, produced by exceptionally gifted
men, but as a ceaseless activity of man as such ; for man
possesses the world, so far as he does possess it, only in
the form of representation-expressions, and only knows
in so far as he creates.[2] Nor are these writers justified in
treating language as parallel with art, or art with language ;
for comparisons are drawn between things at least partially
different, whereas art and language are identical. The
same criticism can be made in the case of the French

H. Bergson.

philosopher Bergson, who in his book on *Laughter*[3] states
a theory of art very similar to that of Fiedler and makes
the same mistake of conceiving the artistic faculty as
something distinct and exceptional in comparison with
the language of everyday use. In ordinary life, says
Bergson, the individuality of things escapes us ; we see
only as much of them as our practical needs demand.
Language helps this simplification ; since all names, proper
names excepted, are names of kinds or classes. Now and
then, however, nature, as if in a fit of absence of mind,
creates souls of a more divisible and detached kind
(artists), who discover and reveal the riches hidden under

[1] *Das Problem der Form in der bildunden Kunst*, 2nd ed. 1898 (4th
ed., Strassburg, 1903).

[2] See above, pp. 12-18.

[3] H. Bergson, *Le Rire, essai sur la signification du comique*, Paris,
1900, pp. 153-161 (Eng. tr., London).

the colourless signs and labels of everyday life, and help
others (non-artists) to catch a glimpse of what they themselves see, employing for this purpose colours, forms,
rhythmic connexions of words, and those rhythms of life
and breath even more intimate to man, the sounds and
notes of music.

A healthy return to Baumgarten, a revival and correc- *Attempts to*
tion of the old philosopher's theories in the light of later *return to*
Baumgarten.
discoveries, might perhaps have given Æsthetic some *C. Hermann.*
assistance, after the collapse of the old idealistic metaphysic, towards thinking the concept of art in its universality and discovering its identity with pure and
true intuitive knowledge. But Conrad Hermann, who
preached the return to Baumgarten [1] in 1876, did bad
service to what might have been a good cause. According
to him Æsthetic and Logic are normative sciences ; but
Logic does not contain, as does Æsthetic, " a definite
category of external objects exclusively and specifically
adequate to the faculty of thought " ; and on the other
hand " the products and results of scientific thought are
not so external and sensibly intuitive as those of artistic
invention." Logic and Æsthetic alike refer not to the
empirical thinking and feeling of the soul, but to pure and
absolute sensation and thought. Art constructs a representation standing midway between the individual and
the universal. Beauty expresses specific perfection, the
essential or, so to speak, the rightful (*seinsollend*) character
of things. Form is " the external sensible limit, or mode
of appearance of a thing, in opposition to the kernel of
the thing itself and to its essential and substantial content."
Content and form are both æsthetic, and the æsthetic
interest concerns the entirety of the beautiful object.
The artistic activity has no special organ such as thought
possesses in speech. The æsthetician, like the lexico-
grapher, has the task of compiling a dictionary of tones
and colours and of the different meanings which may
possibly be attached to them.[2] We can see that Hermann

[1] Conrad Hermann, *Die Ästhetik in ihrer Geschichte und als wissen-
schaftliches System*, Leipzig, 1876. [2] *Die Ästhetik*, etc., *passim*.

accepted side by side the most inconsistent propositions. He welcomes even the æsthetic law of the golden section, and applies it to tragedy ; the longer segment of the line is the tragic hero ; the punishment which overtakes him (the entire line) exceeds his crime in the same proportion in which he oversteps the common measure (the shorter segment of the line).[1]   It reads almost like a joke.

Without direct reference to Baumgarten, a proposal that Æsthetic be reformed and treated as the " science of intuitive knowledge " was made in a miserable little work by one Willy Nef (1898),[2] who makes the dumb animals share his " intuitive knowledge," in which he distinguishes a formal side (intuition) and a material side or content (knowledge), and considers the everyday relations between men, their games and their art, as belonging to intuitive knowledge.

Eclecticism.
B. Bosanquet.   The English historian of Æsthetic, Bosanquet (1892) tried to find a reconciliation between content and form in unity of expression. " Beauty," says Bosanquet in the Introduction to his *History*, " is that which has character- istic and individual expressiveness for sensuous perception or imagination, subject to the conditions of general or abstract expressiveness by the same means."   In another passage he observes : " The difficulty of real Æsthetic is to show how the combination of decorative forms in characteristic representations, by intensifying the essential character immanent in them from the beginning, subor- dinates them to a central signification which stands to their complex combination as their abstract signification stands to each one of them taken singly." [3] But the problem, as propounded in a way suggested by the antithesis between the two schools (contentism and formalism) of German Æsthetic, is in our opinion insoluble.

Æsthetic of
expression :
present state.   De Sanctis founded no school of æsthetic science in Italy. His thought was quickly misunderstood and

---

[1] *Die Ästhetik*, § 56.

[2] Willy Nef, *Die Ästhetik als Wissenschaft der anschaulichen Erkennt- niss*, Leipzig, 1898.

[3] *A History of Æsthetics*, pp. 4-6, 372, 391, 447, 458, 466.

mutilated by those who presumed to correct it, and, in fact, only returned to the outworn rhetorical conception of art as consisting of a little content and a little form. Only within the last ten years has there been a renewal of philosophical studies, arising out of discussions concerning the nature of history [1] and the relation in which it stands to art and science, and nourished by the controversy excited by the publication of De Sanctis' posthumous works.[2] The same problem of the relation between history and science, and their difference or antithesis, reappeared also in Germany, but without being put in its true connexion with the problem of Æsthetic.[3] These inquiries and discussions, and the revival of a Linguistic impregnated by philosophy in the work of Paul and some others, appear to us to offer much more favourable ground for the scientific development of Æsthetic than can be found on the summits of mysticism or the low plains of positivism and sensationalism.

[1] B. Croce, *La storia ridotta sotto il concetto generale dell' arte*, 1893 (2nd ed. entitled *Il concetto della storia nelle sue relazioni col concetto dell' arte*, Rome, 1896) ; P. R. Trojano, *La storia come scienza sociale*, vol. i., Naples, 1897 ; G. Gentile, *Il concetto della storia* (in Crivellucci's *Studi storici*, 1889) ; see also F. de Sarlo, *Il problema estetico*, in *Saggi di filosofia*, vol. ii., Turin, 1897 ; and by same author, *I dati dell' esperienza psichica*, Florence, 1903, concluding chapter.

[2] *La letteratura italiana nel secolo XIX*, edited by B. Croce, Naples, 1896 ; also *Scritti vari*, ed. Croce, Naples, 1898, 2 vols.

[3] H. Rickert, *Die Grenzen der naturwissenschaftlichen Begriffsbildung*, Freiburg i. B., 1896-1902.

HISTORICAL SKETCHES OF SOME PARTICULAR
DOCTRINES

Result of the history of Æsthetic. WE have reached the end of our history. Having passed in review the travail and doubt through which the discovery of the æsthetic concept was achieved, the vicissitudes first of neglect, then of revival and rediscovery to which it was exposed, the various oscillations and failures in its exact determination, the resurrection, triumphant and overwhelming, of ancient errors supposed to be dead and buried ; we may now conclude, without appearing to assert anything unproven, that of Æsthetic in the proper sense of the word we have seen very little, even including the last two centuries' active research. Exceptional intellects have hit the mark and have supported their views with energy, with logic, and with consciousness of what they were doing. It would no doubt be possible to extract many true affirmations leading to the same point of view from the works of non-philosophical writers, art-critics and artists, from commonly received opinions and proverbial sayings ; such a collection would show that this handful of philosophers does not stand alone, but is surrounded by a throng of supporters and is in perfect agreement with the general mind and universal common sense. But if Schiller was right in saying that the rhythm of philosophy is to diverge from common opinion in order to return with redoubled vigour, it is evident that such divergence is necessary, and constitutes the growth of science, which is science itself. During this tedious process Æsthetic made mistakes which were

at once deviations from the truth and attempts to reach
it : such were the hedonism of the sophists and rhetoricians
of antiquity and of the sensationalists of the eighteenth
and second half of the nineteenth century ; the moralistic
hedonism of Aristophanes, of the Stoics, of the Roman
eclectics, of the mediæval and Renaissance writers ; the
ascetic and logical hedonism of Plato and the Fathers of
the Church, of some mediæval and even some quite
modern rigorists ; and finally, the æsthetic mysticism
which first appeared in Plotinus and reappeared again
and again until its last and great triumph in the classical
period of German philosophy.   In the midst of these
variously erroneous tendencies, ploughing the field of
thought in every direction, a tenuous golden rivulet seems
to flow, formed by the acute empiricism of Aristotle, the
forceful penetration of Vico, the analytical work of
Schleiermacher, Humboldt, De Sanctis and others who
echoed them with weaker voice.   This series of thinkers
suffices to remind us that æsthetic science no longer
remains to be discovered ; but at the same time the fact
that they are so few and so often despised, ignored or
controverted, proves that it is in its infancy.

The birth of a science is like that of a living being :
its later development consists, like every life, in fighting
the difficulties and errors, general and particular, which
lurk in its path on every side.   The forms of error are
numerous in the extreme and mingle with each other and
with the truth in complications equally numerous : root
out one, another appears in its stead ; the uprooted ones
also reappear, though never in the same shape.   Hence
the necessity for perpetual scientific criticism and the
impossibility of repose or finality in a science and of an
end to further discussion.   The errors which may be
described as general, negations of the concept of art itself,
have been touched on from time to time in the course
of this History ; whence it may be gathered a simple
affirmation of the truth has not always been accompanied
by any considerable recapture of enemy territory.   As to
what we have called particular errors, it is clear that

History of science and history of the scientific criticism of particular errors.

when freed from confusing admixture of other forms and divested of fanciful expression, they reduce themselves to three heads, under which they have already been criticized in the first or theoretical part of this work. That is to say, errors may be directed (*a*) against the characteristic quality of the æsthetic fact; (*b*) against the specific; (*c*) against the generic: they may involve denial of the character of intuition, of theoretic contemplation, or of spiritual activity, which together constitute the æsthetic fact. Among the errors which fall into these three categories we are now to sketch in outline the history of those which have had, or have to-day, the greatest importance. Rather than a history it will be a historical essay, sufficient to show that, even in the criticism of individual errors, æsthetic science is in its infancy. If among these errors some appear to be decadent and nearly forgotten, they are not dead; they have not accomplished a legal demise at the hands of scientific criticism. Oblivion or instinctive rejection is not the same thing as scientific denial.

I

RHETORIC : OR THE THEORY OF ORNATE FORM

Rhetoric in the ancient sense. Proceeding according to rank in importance, we inevitably head the list of theories for examination with the theory of Rhetoric, or Ornate Form.

It will not be superfluous to observe that the meaning given in modern times to the word Rhetoric, namely, the doctrine of ornate form, differs from that which it had for the ancients. Rhetoric in the modern sense is above all a theory of elocution, while elocution (λέξις, φράσις, ἑρμηνεία, *elocutio*) was but one portion, and not the principal one, of ancient Rhetoric. Taken as a whole, it consisted strictly of a manual or *vade-mecum* for advocates and politicians; it concerned itself with the two or the three " styles " (judicial, deliberative, demonstrative), and gave advice or furnished models to those striving to produce certain effects by means of speech.

No definition of the art is more accurate than that given by its inventors the earliest Sicilian rhetoricians, scholars of Empedocles (Corax, Tisias, Gorgias) : Rhetoric is the creator of persuasion ($\pi\epsilon\iota\theta o\hat{v}s$ $\delta\eta\mu\iota o\nu\rho\gamma\acute{o}s$). It devoted itself to showing the method of using language so as to create a certain belief, a certain state of mind, in the hearer ; hence the phrase " making the weaker case stronger " ($\tau\grave{o}$ $\tau\grave{o}\nu$ $\mathring{\eta}\tau\tau\omega$ $\lambda\acute{o}\gamma o\nu$ $\kappa\rho\epsilon\acute{\iota}\tau\tau\omega$ $\pi o\iota\epsilon\hat{\iota}\nu$) ; the " increase or diminution according to circumstances " (*eloquentia in augendo minuendoque consistit*) ; the advice of Gorgias to " turn a thing to a jest if the adversary takes it seriously, or to a serious matter if he takes it as a jest," [1] and many similar well-known maxims. He who acts in this manner is not only æsthetically accomplished, as saying beautifully that which he wishes to say ; he is also and especially a practical man with a practical end in view. As a practical man, however, he cannot evade moral responsibility for his actions ; this point was fastened upon by Plato's polemic against Rhetoric, that is to say against fluent political charlatans and un-scrupulous lawyers and journalists. Plato was quite right to condemn Rhetoric (when dissociated from a good pur-pose) as blameworthy and discreditable, directed to arouse the passions, a diet ruinous to health, a paint disastrous to beauty. Even had Rhetoric allied herself to Ethics, becoming a true guide of the soul ($\psi\nu\chi\alpha\gamma\omega\gamma\acute{\iota}\alpha$ $\tau\iota s$ $\delta\iota\grave{\alpha}$ $\tau\hat{\omega}\nu$ $\lambda\acute{o}\gamma\omega\nu$) ; had Plato's criticism been directed solely against her abusers (everything being liable to abuse save virtue itself, says Aristotle) ; had Rhetoric been purified, pro-ducing such an orator as Cicero desired, *non ex rhetorum officinis sed ex academiae spatiis*,[2] and imposing on him, with Quintilian, the duty of being *vir bonus dicendi peritus* ; [3] yet the unalterable fact remains that Rhetoric can never be considered a regular science, being formed of a congeries of widely dissimilar cognitions. It included descriptions of passions and affections, comparisons of political and judicial institutions, theories of the abbrevi-

Criticism from moral point of view.

Accumulation without system.

---

[1] For Gorgias' saying see Aristotle, *Rhet.* iii. ch. 18.
[2] Cicero, *Orat. ad Brut.*, introd.   [3] Quintilian, *Inst. orat.* xii. ch. 1.

ated syllogism or enthymeme and of proof leading to a probable conclusion, pedagogic and popular exposition, literary elocution, declamation and mimicry, mnemonic, and so forth.

Its fortunes in the Middle Ages and Renaissance.
The rich and heterogeneous content of this ancient Rhetoric (which reached its highest development in the hands of Hermagoras of Temnos in the second century B.C.) gradually diminished in volume with the decadence of the ancient world and the change in political conditions. This is not the place to dwell on its fortunes in the Middle Ages or its partial replacement by formularies and *Artes dictandi* (and later by treatises upon the art of preaching), or to quote the reasons given by such writers as Patrizzi and Tassoni for its disappearance from the world of their day ; [1] such history would be well worth writing, but would be out of place here. We will merely state that whilst conditions were at work on every side corroding this complex of cognitions, Louis Vives, Peter Ramus and Patrizzi himself were busy criticizing it from the point of view of systematic science.

Criticisms by Vives, Ramus and Patrizzi.
Vives emphasized the confused methods of the ancient treatise-writers, who embraced *omnia*, united eloquence with morality, and insisted that the orator must be *vir bonus*. He rejected four-fifths of ancient Rhetoric as extraneous : namely, memory, which is necessary in all arts ; invention, which is the matter of each individual art ; recitation, which is external ; and disposition, which belongs to invention. He retained elocution only, not that which treats of *quid dicendum*, but of *quem ad modum*, extending it beyond the three styles or kinds to include history, apologue, epistles, novels and poetry.[2] Antiquity furnishes us with few and faint attempts at such extension ; now and then a Rhetorician ventures to suggest that the γένος ἱστορικόν and ἐπιστολικόν be included in Rhetoric, and even (in spite of opposition) " infinite "

---

[1] Fran. Patrizzi, *Della rhetorica*, ten dialogues, Venice, 1582, dial. 7 ; Tassoni, *Pensieri diversi*, bk. x. ch. 15.

[2] *De causis corruptarum artium*, 1531, bk. iv. ; *De ratione dicendi*, 1533.

questions, that is to say merely theoretical questions with
no practical application, which amounts to a scientific or
philosophical genus ; [1] others agreed with Cicero [2] that
when one had mastered the most difficult of all arts,
forensic eloquence, all else seemed child's-play (ludus est
homini non hebeti . . .). Ramus and his pupil Omer
Talon reproached Aristotle, Cicero and Quintilian with
having confused Dialectic and Rhetoric ; and they assigned
invention and disposition to the former, agreeing with
Vives that " elocution " alone should be allowed to
Rhetoric.[3] Patrizzi, on the other hand, refused the name
of science to either, recognizing them as simple " faculties,"
containing no individual matter (not even the three
genera), and differentiating them only by attaching the
term Dialectic to the dialogue form and proof of the
necessary, and Rhetoric to connected discourse directed
to persuasion in matters of opinion. Patrizzi observes
that " conjoined speech " is used by historians, poets and
philosophers, no less than by orators ; and thus approaches
the view of Vives.[4]

In spite of these opinions the body of rhetorical *Survival into*
doctrine continued to flourish in the schools. Patrizzi *modern times.*
was forgotten ; if Ramus and Vives had some followers
(such as Francisco Sanchez and Keckermann), they were
generally held up to odium by the traditionalists. In
the end, Rhetoric found a supporter in philosophy when
Campanella made the following declaration in his *Rational
Philosophy* : " *quodammodo Magiae portiuncula, quae
affectus animi moderatur et per ipsos voluntatem ciet ad
quaecumque vult sequenda vel fugienda.*" [5] Baumgarten
owed to it his tripartition of Æsthetic into heuristic,
methodology and semeiotic (invention, disposition and
elocution), adopted later by Meier. Among Meier's

---

[1] Cicero, *De orat.* i. chs. 10-11 ; Quintil. *Inst. orat.* iii. ch. 5.

[2] *De orat.* ii. chs. 16-17.

[3] P. Ramus, *Instit. dialecticae*, 1543 ; *Scholae in artes liberales*,
1555, etc. ; Talaeus, *Instit. orator.*, 1545.

[4] *Della rhetorica*, dial. 10, and *passim*.

[5] *Ration. Philos.*, part iii. *Rhetoricorum liber unus juxta propria dog-
mata* (Paris, 1636), ch. 3.

numerous works is a little book entitled *Theoretic Doctrine of Emotional Disturbances in General*,[1] considered by him to be a psychological introduction to æsthetic doctrine. On the other hand, Immanuel Kant in his *Critique of Judgment* observes that eloquence, in the sense of *ars oratoria* or art of persuasion by means of beautiful appearance and dialectical form, must be distinguished from beautiful speaking (*Wohlredenheit*) ; and that the art of oratory, playing upon the weakness of men to gain its own ends, "is worthy of no esteem" (*gar keiner Achtung würdig*).[2] But in the schools it flourished in many celebrated compilations, including one by the French Jesuit Father Dominique de Colonne, which was in use until some few decades ago. Even to-day, in so-called Literary Institutions, we come across survivals of ancient Rhetoric, notably in chapters devoted to the art of oratory ; and fresh manuals on judicial or sacred eloquence (Ortloff, Whately, etc.[3]) are actually appearing, though rarely, to-day. Still, Rhetoric in the ancient sense may be said to have disappeared from the system of the sciences ; to-day no philosopher would dream of following Campanella in dedicating a special section of rational philosophy to Rhetoric.

Modern sig-
nification of
Rhetoric.
Theory of
literary form.

In compensation for this process, the theory of elocution and beautiful speech has been in modern times progressively emphasized and thrown into scientific form. But the idea of such a science is ancient, as we have seen ; and equally ancient is the style of exposition, consisting in the doctrine of a double form and the concept of ornate form.

Concept of
ornament.

The concept of "ornament" must have occurred spontaneously to the mind as soon as attention was directed to the values of speech by listening to poets reciting [4] or to oratorical contests in public gatherings. It must very early have been thought that the difference

[1] *Theoretische Lehre von den Gemüthsbewegungen überhaupt*, Halle, 1744.
[2] *Kritik d. Urtheilskraft*, § 53 and *n*.
[3] H. F. Ortloff, *Die gerichtliche Redekunst*, Neuwied, 1887 ; R. Whately, *Rhetoric*, 1828 (for *Encycl. Brit.*) ; Ital. trans., Pistoia, 1889.
[4] Aristotle, *Rhet.* iii. ch. 1.

between good speaking and bad, or between that which
gave more pleasure and that which gave less, between
grave or solemn, and commonplace or colloquial, consisted
in something additional superimposed upon the canvas of
ordinary speech like an embroidery by a skilful orator.
These considerations led the Græco-Roman rhetoricians
to adopt the practice, like the Indians, who arrived at
the distinction independently, to distinguish the bare
(ψιλή) or purely grammatical form from another form
containing an addition which they called ornament,
κόσμος : *ornatum est* (Quintilian will serve, as typical of
all the rest) *quod perspicuo ac probabili plus est.*[1]

The notion of ornament as something added on from
outside forms the basis of the theory which Aristotle, the
philosopher of Rhetoric, gave of the queen of ornaments,
Metaphor. According to him the high pleasure aroused
by metaphor arises from the collocation of different terms
and the discovery of relations between species and genera,
producing " learning and knowledge by means of the
genus " (μάθησιν καὶ γνῶσιν διὰ τοῦ γένους), and that
easy learning which is the greatest of human pleasures,[2]
which amounts to saying that metaphor adds to the
concept under consideration a group of minor incidental
cognitions, as a kind of diversion and relief and pleasant
instruction for the mind.

Ornaments were divided and subdivided in a number *Classes of*
of different ways. Aristotle (and previously Isocrates, *ornament.*
rather differently) classified the ornaments which diversify
bare or nude form, under the heads of dialect forms,
substitutions and epithets, prolongations, truncations and
abbreviations of words, and other departures from common
usage, and, finally, rhythm and harmony. Substitutions
were of four classes : species for genus ; genus for species ;
species for species ; and proportionate.[3] After Aristotle,
elocution was especially studied by Theophrastus and
Demetrius Phalereus ; these rhetoricians and their
followers further solidified the classification of ornament

---

[1] Quintil. *Inst. orat.* viii. ch. 3.   [2] *Rhet.* iii. ch. 10.
[3] *Poet.* chs. 19-22 ; cf. *Rhet.* iii. cc. 2, 10.

by distinguishing tropes from figures (σχήματα) and dividing figures into figures of speech (σχήματα τῆς λέξεως) and of thought (τῆς διανοίας), figures of speech into grammatical and rhetorical, and figures of thought into pathetic and ethic. Substitutions were divided into fourteen principal forms,—metaphor, synecdoche, metonymy, antonomasia, onomatopeia, catachresis, metalepsis, epithet, allegory, enigma, irony, periphrase, hyperbaton and hyperbole ; each divided into subspecies and contrasted with its relative vice. Figures of speech amounted to a score or so (repetition, anaphora, antistrophe, climax, asyndeton, assonance, etc.) ; figures of thought to about the same number (interrogation, prosopopœia, ætiopœia, hypotyposis, commotion, simulation, exclamation, apostrophe, aposiopesis, etc.). If these divisions have any value as aids to memory in relation to particular literary forms, considered rationally they are simply capricious, as is evidenced by the fact that many classes of the ornate appear now under the heading of tropes, now of figures ; sometimes under figures of speech, then as those of thought ; no reason for the alteration is given except the arbitrary caprice of an individual rhetorician which so decrees and disposes. And since one function which may be fulfilled by the rhetorical categories is to point out the divergence between two ways of expressing the same thing, one of which is arbitrarily selected as " proper," [1] it is easy to see why the ancients defined metaphor as " *verbi vel sermonis a propria significatione in aliam cum virtute mutatio,*" and figure as " *conformatio quaedam orationis remota a communi et primum se offerenti ratione.*" [2]

The concept of the Fitting.   So far as we know, antiquity raised no revolt against the theory of ornament or of double form. We do sometimes hear Cicero, Quintilian, Seneca and others saying, *Ipsae res verba rapiunt, Pectus est quod disertos facit et vis mentis, Rem tene, verba sequentur, Curam verborum rerum volo esse sollicitudinem,* or *Nulla est verborum nisi rei cohaerentium virtus.* But these maxims did not bear the weighty meanings which we moderns might attach to

---

[1] See above, pp. 68-69.   [2] Quintilian, *Inst. orat.* viii. ch. 6 ; ix. ch. 1.

them ; they were perhaps in contradiction with the theory
of ornament, but as the contradiction was unheeded, it
was ineffective : they were the protests of common sense,
powerless to combat the fallacies of school doctrine.
Moreover, the latter was fitted with a safety-valve, a sage
contrivance to disguise its inherent absurdity. If the
ornate consisted of a *plus*, in what degree should it be
used ? if it gave pleasure, must we not conclude that the
more it were used, the greater the pleasure derived ?
would its extravagant use be attended by extravagant
pleasure ?   Herein was peril : instinctively the rhetoricians hastened to the defence, snatching up the first
weapon that came to hand, namely, the fitting (πρέπον).
Ornament must be used carefully ; neither too much nor
too little ; *in medio virtus* ; as much as is fitting (ἀλλὰ
πρέπον).   Aristotle recommends a style seasoned with
" a certain dose " (δεῖ ἄρα κεκρᾶσθαί πως τούτοις) ; for
ornament should be a condiment, not a food (ἥδυσμα,
οὐκ ἔδεσμα).[1]   The fitting was a concept quite inconsistent
with that of ornament ; it was a rival, and enemy,
destined to destroy it.   Fitting to what ? to expression,
of course ; but that which is fitting to expression cannot
be called an ornament, an external addition ; it coincides
with expression itself.   But the rhetoricians contented
themselves with maintaining peaceful relations between
the ornate and the fitting, without troubling to mediate
them through a third concept.   The pseudo-Longinus
alone, in answer to an observation of his predecessor
Caecilius that more than two or three metaphors must not
be used in the same place, remarked that a larger number
ought to be used where passion (τὰ πάθη) rushes headlong
like a torrent, carrying with it as necessaries (ὡς
ἀναγκαῖον) a multitude of such substitutions.[2]

Preserved in the compilations of later antiquity (such
as the works of Donatus and Priscian and the celebrated
allegorical tract of Marcianus Capella), and in the com-
pendia of Bede, Rhabanus Maurus and others, the theory

The theory of ornament in the Middle Ages and Renaissance.

[1] Aristotle, *Rhet.* iii. ch. 2 ; *Poet.* ch. 22.
[2] *De sublimitate* (in *Rhet. graeci*, ed. Spengel, vol. i. § 32).

of ornament passed to the Middle Ages.   Throughout this
period Rhetoric, Grammar and Logic continued to form
the *trivium* of the schools.   The theory was to some extent
favoured in mediæval times by the fact that writers and
scholars made use of a dead language ; this helped to
reinforce the idea that beautiful form was not a spontaneous thing but consisted in an addition or embroidery.
Under the Renaissance the theory continued to flourish
and was revived by study of the best classical sources ;
to the works of Cicero were added the *Institutiones* of
Quintilian and the *Rhetoric* of Aristotle, with the host of
minor Latin and Greek rhetoricians, amongst whom was
Hermogenes with his celebrated *Ideas,* brought into
fashion by Giulio Camillo.[1]

Even those writers who dared to criticize the organism of ancient Rhetoric left the theory of ornament
unassailed.   Vives lamented over the " exaggerated
subtlety of the Greeks " which had multiplied distinctions
to infinity in this matter without diffusing light,[2] but he
never took up a definite stand against the theory of
ornament.   Patrizzi was dissatisfied with the insufficient
definition of ornament given by the ancients ; but he
asserted the existence of ornaments and metaphors as well
as seven different modes of " conjoined speech,"—narrative, proof, amplification, diminution, ornament with its
contrary, elevation and depression.[3]   The school of Ramus
continued to entrust Rhetoric with the " embellishment "
of thought.   Owing to the vast extension and intensifica-
tion of life and literature in the sixteenth century, it would
be easy to quote phrases, as we have done from ancient
authors, asserting the strict dependence of speech upon
the things it wishes to express, and lively attacks on
pedants and pedantic forms and rules for beautiful speech.
But what would be the use ?   The theory of ornament
was always in the background, tacitly admitted as

---

[1] Giulio Camillo Delminio, *Discorso sopra le Idee di Ermogene* (in
Opere, Venice, 1560) ; and trans. of Hermogenes (Udine, 1594).

[2] *De causis corruptarum artium, loc. cit.*

[3] *Della rhetorica,* dial. 6.

indisputable by all. Juan de Valdés, for instance, makes the following confession of stylistic faith : " *Escribo como hablo ; solamente tengo cuidado de usar de vocablos que sinifiquen bien lo que quiero decir, y dígolo cuanto más llanamente me es posible, porqué, á mi parecer, en ninguna lengua está bien la afectación.*" But Valdés also says that beautiful language consists " *en que digais lo que quereis con las menos palabras que pudiéredes, de tal manera que . . . no se pueda quitar ninguna sin ofender á la sentencia, ó al encarescimiento, ó á la elegancia.*" [1] Here it seems that amplification and elegance are conceived as extraneous to the meaning or content.—A gleam of truth is visible in Montaigne, who, confronted by the laboured categories into which rhetoricians divide ornament, observes : " *Oyez dire Métonymie, Métaphore, Allégorie et aultres tels noms de la Grammaire ; semble il pas qu'on signifie quelque forme de langage rare et pellegrin ? Ce sont tiltres qui touchent le babil de vostre chambrière.*" [2] That is to say, they are anything but language remote from the *primum se offerens ratio.*

The impossibility of upholding the theory of ornament was first noticed during the decadence of Italian literature in the seventeenth century, when literary production became but a play of empty forms, and the " convenient," long violated in practice, was abandoned and forgotten even in theory, and came to be looked on as a limit arbitrarily imposed on the fundamental principle of ornamentation. The opponents of that style loaded with conceits which is known as " secentismo " from its prevalence in the seventeenth century (Matteo Pellegrini, Orsi and others) felt the viciousness of the literary production of their day ; they were aware that decadence was due to the fact that literature was no longer the serious expression of a content ; but they were embarrassed by the reasoning of the champions of bad taste, who were able to demon-

Reductio ad absurdum in the seventeenth century.

---

[1] *Diálogo de las lenguas* (ed. Mayans y Siscar, *Origines de la lengua española*, Madrid, 1873), pp. 115, 119.

[2] *Essais*, i. ch. 52 (ed. Garnier, i. 285) ; cf. *ibid.* chs. 10, 25, 39 ; ii. ch. 10.

strate that the whole business conformed in every particular with the literary theory of ornament, the common ground of both parties. In vain did the former appeal to the " convenient," the " moderate," the " avoidance of affectation," to ornament as " condiment, not food," and all the other weapons which had sufficed in times when healthy literary production and sound æsthetic taste had automatically corrected faulty theory : the other party replied, there was no reason to be sparing in use of ornament when it lay in masses ready to hand, or to avoid an ostentatious display of wit when one had an inexhaustible supply.[1]

Polemic concerning the theory of ornament.

The same reaction against the abuse of ornament, against " Spanish and Italian conceits " (whose supporters had been Gracian in Spain and Tesauro in Italy), took place in France. " . . . *Laissez à l'Italie De tous ces faux brillants l'éclatante folie* " ; " *Ce que l'on conçoit bien s'énonce clairement. Et les mots, pour le dire, arrivent aisément.* " [2] Among the sharpest critics of conceits was the Jesuit Bouhours, already quoted, author of the *Manière de bien penser dans les œuvres d'esprit.* The rhetorical forms were the subject of warm controversy. Orsi, on national grounds the opponent of Bouhours (1703), asserted that all the ornamental devices of wit rested on a middle term and could be reduced to a rhetorical syllogism, and that wit consists of a truth which appears false or a falsehood which appears true.[3] If this controversy produced no great scientific result at the time, at least it prepared the mind for greater liberty ; and, as we have remarked elsewhere,[4] it may have influenced Vico, who, in framing his new concept of poetical imagination, recognized that it necessitated a wholesale reconstruction of the theory of rhetoric and the conclusion that its figures and tropes are not " caprices of pleasure " but " necessities of the human mind." [5]

[1] Croce, *I trattatisti italiani del concettismo*, pp. 8-22.
[2] Boileau, *Art poétique*, i. ll. 43-44, 153-154.
[3] G. G. Orsi, *Considerazioni sopra la maniera di ben pensare*, etc., 1703 (reprinted Modena, 1735, with all polemics relating thereto).
[4] See above, pp. 230-231.   [5] See above, pp. 225-226.

We find the theory of rhetorical ornament jealously *Du Marsais* kept intact by Baumgarten and Meier, while in France it *and metaphor.* was as vigorously assailed by César Chesneau du Marsais, who published in 1730 a treatise on *Tropes* (the seventh part of his *General Grammar*),[1] wherein he develops, on the subject of metaphor, the observation already made by Montaigne : indeed he was perhaps inspired by Montaigne, although he does not mention his name. Du Marsais remarks that it is said that figures are modes of speech and turns of expression removed from the ordinary and common ; which is an empty phrase, as good as saying " the figured differs from the non-figured and figures are figures and not non-figures." On the other hand it is wholly untrue that figures are removed from ordinary speech, for " nothing is more natural, ordinary and common than figures : more figures of speech are used in the town square on a market-day than in many days of academical discussion " ; and no speech, however short, can be composed entirely of non-figurative expressions. And Du Marsais gives instances of quite obvious and spontaneous expressions in which Rhetoric cannot refuse to recognize the figures of apostrophe, congeries, interrogation, ellipsis, prosopopœia : " The apostles were persecuted and suffered their persecutions with patience. What can be more natural than the description given by St. Paul ? *Maledicimur et benedicimus ; persecutionem patimur et sustinemus ; blasphemamur et obsecramus.* Yet the apostle makes use of a fine figure of antithesis ; cursing is the opposite to blessing ; persecution to endurance ; blasphemy to prayer." But further, the very language of the figure is figured, since it is a metaphor.— But after such acute observations, Du Marsais ends by himself becoming confused and defines figures as " manners of speech differing from others in a particular modification by which it is possible to reduce each one to a species apart, and give a more lively, noble or pleasing effect than

---

[1] *Des tropes ou des différens sens dans lesquels on peut prendre un même mot dans une même langue*, Paris, 1730 (*Œuvres de Du Marsais*, Paris, 1797, vol. i.).

can be gained by a manner of speech expressing the same content of thought without such particular modification." [1]

Psychological interpretation.   But the psychological interpretation of figures of speech, the first stage towards their æsthetic criticism, was not allowed to drop here.   In his *Elements of Criticism*, Home says that he had long questioned whether that part of Rhetoric concerning figures might not be reduced to rational principles, and had finally discovered that figures consist in the passional element ; [2] he set himself therefore to analyse prosopopœia, apostrophe and hyperbole in the light of the passional faculty.   From Du Marsais and Home is derived everything of value in the *Lectures on Rhetoric and belles lettres* of Hugh Blair, professor at Edinburgh University from 1759 onwards ; [3] published in book form, these lectures had an immense vogue in all the schools of Europe including those of Italy, and replaced advantageously, by their " reason and good sense," works of a much cruder type.   Blair defined figures in general as " language suggested by imagination or passion." [4] Similar ideas were promulgated in France by Marmontel in his *Elements of Literature*.[5]   In Italy Cesarotti was contrasting the logical element or " cypher-terms " of language with the rhetorical element or " figure-terms," and rational eloquence with imaginative eloquence.[6] Beccaria, though a shrewd psychological analyst, held to the view of literary style as " accessory ideas or feelings added to the principal in any discourse " ; that is, he failed to free himself from the distinction between the intellectual form intended for the expression of the principal ideas, and the literary form, modifying the first by the addition of accessory ideas.[7]   In Germany an effort was made by Herder to interpret tropes and meta-

---

[1] *Des tropes ou des différens sens dans lesquels on peut prendre un même mot dans une même langue*, part i. art. 1 ; cf. art. 4.

[2] *Elem. of Criticism*, iii. ch. 20.

[3] Hugh Blair, *Lectures on Rhetoric and belles lettres* (London, 1823).

[4] *Lect. on Rhet. and belles lettres*, lecture 14.

[5] Marmontel, *Éléments de littérat.* (in *Œuvres*, Paris, 1819), iv. p. 559.

[6] Cesarotti, *Saggio sulla filos. del linguaggio*, part ii.

[7] *Ricerche intorno alla natura dello stile* (Turin, 1853), ch. 1.

phors as Vico had done, that is to say as essential to
primitive language and poetry.

Romanticism was the ruin of the theory of ornament, *Romanticism*
and caused it practically to be thrown on the scrap-heap ; *and Rhetoric.*
Present day.
but it cannot be said to have gone under for good or to
have been superseded by a new and accurately stated
theory. The chief philosophers of Æsthetic (not only
Kant, who as we know remained in bondage to the
mechanical and ornamental theory ; not only Herder,
whose knowledge of art seems to have been confined to
a little music and a great deal of rhetoric ; but such
romantic philosophers as Schelling, Solger and Hegel)
still retained the sections devoted to metaphor, trope and
allegory for tradition's sake, without severe scrutiny.
Italian Romanticism with Manzoni at its head destroyed
the belief in beautiful and elegant words, and dealt a
blow at Rhetoric : but was it killed by the stroke ?
Apparently not, judging by the concessions unconsciously
made by the scholastic treatise-writer Ruggero Bonghi,
whose *Critical Letters* assert the existence of two styles
or forms, which at bottom are nothing else than the
plain and the ornate.[1] German schools of philology
have pretty generally accepted the stylistic theory of
Gröber, who divides style into logical (objective) and
affective (subjective) :[2] an ancient error masked by terminology borrowed from the psychological philosophy in
fashion at modern universities. In the same spirit a recent
writer rechristens the rhetorical doctrine of tropes and
figures by the title " Doctrine of the Forms of Æsthetic
Apperception," and divides them into the four categories
(the ancient wealth of categories reduced to a paltry four !)
of personification, metaphor, antithesis, and symbol.[3]

[1] R. Bonghi, *Lettere critiche*, 1856 (4th ed., Naples, 1884), pp. 37,
65-67, 90, 103.

[2] Gustav Gröber, *Grundiss d. romanischen Philologie*, vol. i. pp.
209-250 ; K. Vossler, *B. Cellinis Stil in seiner Vita, Versuch einer psychol.
Stilbetrachtung*, Halle a. S., 1899 ; cf. the self-criticism of Vossler,
Positivismus u. Idealismus in der Sprachwissenschaft, Heidelberg, 1904
(It. trans., Bari, Laterza, 1908).

[3] Ernst Elsteb, *Principien d. Literaturwissenschaft*, Halle a. S., 1897,
vol. i. pp. 359-413.

Biese has devoted an entire book to metaphor ; but one searches it in vain for a serious æsthetic analysis of this category.[1]

The best scientific criticism of the theory of ornament is found scattered throughout the writings of De Sanctis, who when lecturing on rhetoric preached what he called anti-rhetoric.[2]   But even here the criticism is not conducted from a strictly systematic point of view.   It seems to us that the true criticism should be deduced negatively from the very nature of æsthetic activity, which does not lend itself to partition ;   there is no such thing as activity of type *a* or type *b*, nor can the same concept be expressed now in one way, now in another.   Such is the only way of abolishing the double monster of bare form which is, no one knows how, deprived of imagination, and ornate form which contains, no one knows how, an addition on the side of imagination.[3]

II

HISTORY OF THE ARTISTIC AND LITERARY KINDS

The kinds in antiquity. Aristotle.

The theory of artistic and literary kinds and of the laws or rules proper to each separate kind has almost always followed the fortunes of the rhetorical theory.

Traces of the threefold division into epic, lyric and dramatic are found in Plato ;   and Aristophanes gives an example of criticism according to the canon of the kinds, particularly that of tragedy.[4]   But the most conspicuous theoretical treatment of the kinds bequeathed us by antiquity is precisely the doctrine of Tragedy which forms a large part of the Aristotelian fragment known as the Poetics.   Aristotle defines such a composition as an imitation of a serious and complete action, having size,

---

[1] Biese, *Philos. des Metaphorischen*, Hamburg-Leipzig, 1893.

[2] *La Giovinezza di Fr. de S.* chs. 23, 25 ; *Scritti vari*, ii. pp. 272-274.

[3] See above, pp. 67-73.

[4] *Republic*, iii. 394 ;   see also E. Muller, *Gesch. d. Th. d. Kunst*, i. pp. 134-206 ; ii. pp. 238-239, note.

in language adorned in accordance with the requirements
of the different parts, its exposition to be by action and
not by narration, and using pity or terror as means to
free or purify us from these same passions ; [1] he gives
minute details as to the six parts of which it is composed,
especially the plot and the tragic character.   It has been
often said, ever since the days of Vincenzo Maggio in the
sixteenth century, that Aristotle treated of the nature of
poetry, or particular forms of poetry, without claiming to
give precepts.   But Piccolomini answered that " all these
things and other similar ones are shown or asserted with
no other purpose but that we may see in what way their
precepts and laws must be obeyed and carried out," just
as, to make a hammer or saw, one begins by describing
the parts of which they are composed.[2] The error of
which we take Aristotle as representative lies in trans-
muting abstractions and empirical partitions into rational
concepts : this was almost inevitable at the beginnings
of æsthetic reflexion, and the Sanskrit theory of poetry
employed the same method independently when, for
example, it defines and legislates for ten principal and
eighteen secondary styles of drama ; forty-eight varieties
of hero ; and we know not how many kinds of heroines.[3]

After Aristotle, the theory of poetic kinds does not *In the Middle*
seem to have been completely or elaborately developed *Ages and*
in antiquity.   The Middle Ages may be said to have *Renaissance*
expressed the doctrine in treatises of the kind known
as " rhythmic arts " or " methods of composition."   When
the Aristotelian fragment was first noticed, it is curious
to see the way in which the paraphrase of Averroes distorted the theory of kinds.   Averroes conceives tragedy
as the art of praise, comedy as that of blame, which
amounts to identifying the former with panegyric, the
latter with satire ; and he believes the *peripeteia* to be
the same thing as antithesis, or the artifice of beginning
the description of a thing by describing its opposite.[4]

---

[1] *Poet.* ch. 6.   [2] *Annotazioni*, introd.
[3] Cf. for Sanskrit poetry S. Levi, *Le Théâtre indien*, pp. 11-152.
[4] Cf. Menendez y Pelayo, *op. cit.* I., i. pp. 126-154, 2nd ed.

This distortion demonstrates afresh the merely historical character of these kinds and their unintelligibility by the methods of pure logic to a thinker living in times and under customs different from those of the Hellenic world. The Renaissance seized upon Aristotle's text, partly expounded it, partly distorted it and partly thought it out afresh, and thus succeeded in establishing a long list of kinds and sub-kinds rigidly defined and subjected to inexorable laws.   Controversy now began over the correct understanding of the unities of epic or dramatic poetry ; over the moral quality and social standing proper to the characters in this kind of poem and in that ; over the nature of the plot, and whether it includes passions and thoughts, and whether lyrics should or should not be received as true poetry ; whether the material of tragedy should be historical ; whether the dialogue of comedy may be in prose ; whether a happy ending may be allowed in tragedy ; whether the tragic character may be a perfect gentleman ; what kind and number of episodes is admissible in the poem, and how they should be incorporated in the main plot ; and so on.   Great anguish was caused by the mysterious rule of catharsis found in black and white in Aristotle's text, and Segni naïvely predicted that tragic poetry would be revived in its perfect spectacular entirety for the sake of experiencing the effect spoken of by Aristotle, that " purgation " which causes " the birth of tranquillity in the soul and of freedom of all perturbation." [1]

The doctrine of the three unities.   Amongst the many undertakings brought to a glorious end by the critics and treatise-writers of the sixteenth century, the best known is the establishment of the three unities of time, place and action.   One cannot indeed see why they are called unities, for in strictness they could at most be spoken of as shortness of time, straitness of space and limitation of tragic subjects to a certain class of action.   It is well known that Aristotle prescribed unity of action only, and reminded his hearers that theatrical custom alone imposed on the action a time-

[1] Introd. to his tr. of the *Poetics*.

limit of one day. On this last point the critics of the sixteenth century accorded six, eight, or twelve hours according to individual taste or humour : some of them (amongst them Segni) allowed twenty-four hours, including the night as particularly propitious to assassinations and the other acts of violence which usually form the plot of tragedies ; others extended the limit to thirty-six or forty-eight hours. The last, and most curious, unity, that of place, was slowly developed by Castelvetro, Riccoboni and Scaliger until the Frenchman Jean de la Taille joined it as a third to the existing two in 1572, and in 1598 Angelo Ingegneri finally formulated it more explicitly.

The Italian treatises were widely read and regarded *Poetics of the* as authoritative all over Europe, and awakened the first *kinds and* effort towards a learned theory of poetry in France, Spain. *Scaliger.* England and Germany. A good representative of his class is Julius Cæsar Scaliger, who has been considered, with some exaggeration, as the true founder of French pseudo-classicism or neo-classicism ; as one who (it has been said) " laid the first stone of the classical Bastille." But if he was neither the first nor the only one, he certainly helped greatly to reduce " to a system of doctrines the principal consequences of the sovranty of Reason in works of literature," with his minute distinctions and classifications of kinds, the insurmountable barriers he erected between them, and his distrust of free inspiration and imagination.[1] Scaliger numbers among his descendants (beside Daniel Heinsius) d'Aubignac, Rapin, Dacier and other tyrants of French literature and drama : Boileau turned the rules of neo-classicism into neat verses. It has been noticed that Lessing entered the same field ; *Lessing.* his opposition to the French rules (which was an opposition of rule to rule, in which he had been forestalled by Italian writers, for example by Calepio in 1732) is anything but radical. Lessing maintained that Corneille and other authors had misinterpreted Aristotle, to whose laws even the Shakespearian drama could be shown to con-

[1] Lintilhac, *Un Coup d'État*, etc., p. 543.

form ;[1] but on the other hand he strongly opposed the abolition of all rules and those who shouted " genius, genius," placing genius above the law and saying that genius makes the law. For the very reason that genius is law, replied Lessing, laws have their value and can be determined : negation of them would entail the confinement of genius to its first trial flights, making example or practice useless.[2]

Compromises and extensions.

But the " kinds " and their " limits " could be maintained for centuries solely by means of infinitely subtle interpretations, analogical extensions and more or less concealed compromises. The Italian Renaissance critics, while working at their Poetics in the style of Aristotle, found themselves confronted with chivalric poetry, and had to make the best of it ; this they did by assigning it to a kind of poem not foreseen by antiquity (Giraldi Cintio).[3] Here and there indeed a rigorist was heard protesting that romances were in no way different from heroic poetry, and were only " badly written heroics " (Salviati). And since it was impossible to deny a place in Italian literature to Dante's poem, Iacopo Mazzoni, in his *Defence of Dante*, overhauled once more the categories of Poetics in order to find a niche for the sacred poem.[4] Farces made their appearance at this time, and Cecchi (1585) declares " Farce is a third novelty, occupying a place between tragedy and comedy . . ."[5] The *Pastor fido* of Guarini was published, neither tragedy nor comedy, but tragicomedy ; and discovering no heading among the kinds deduced from moral or civil philosophy suitable for the intruder, Jason de Nores proceeded to rule it out of existence ; Guarini made a valiant defence and claimed special protection for his beloved *Pastor* under a third, or mixed, style, representative of real life.[6] Another

[1] *Hamburg. Dramat.* Nos. 81, 101-104. [2] *Op. cit.* Nos. 96, 101-104.
[3] G. B. Giraldi Cintio, *De' romanzi, delle comedie e delle tragedie*, 1554 (ed. Daelli, 1864).
[4] Iacopo Mazzoni, *Difesa della commedia di Dante*, Cesena, 1587.
[5] G. M. Cecchi, prologue to *Romanesca*, 1585.
[6] Cf. besides the two *Veratti*, the *Compendio della poesia tragicomica*, Venice, 1601.

rigorist, Fioretti (Udeno Nisieli) proclaimed the poem " a poetic monster, so huge and deformed that centaurs, hippogriffs and chimæras are comparatively graceful and charming . . ., fit to bring a blush to the cheek of the muse, a disgrace to poetry, a mixture of ingredients in themselves discordant, inimical and incompatible " ; [1] but will this bluster drive the delicious *Pastor fido* from the hands of lovers of poetry ?   The same thing occurred in the case of Marino's *Adone,* described by Chapelain as " a poem of peace " for want of a better definition, though other supporters called it " a new form of epic poem " ; [2] and the same thing happened again in the case of the comedy of art and musical drama.   Corneille, who had called down a furious tempest from Scudéry and the Academicians on the head of his *Cid,* remarked in his discourse on Tragedy, though basing his position on that of Aristotle, that there was necessity for "*quelque modéra-tion, quelque favorable interprétation, . . . pour n'être pas obligés de condamner beaucoup de poèmes, que nous avons vu réussir sur nos théâtres.*" "*Il est aisé de nous accommoder avec Aristote . . .*" [3] he says in another place : a piece of literary hypocrisy which startles by its verbal resemblance to "*les accommodements avec le Ciel*" of the Tartuffian ethics. The following century saw the accepted kinds augmented by " bourgeois tragedy " and pathetic comedy, nick-named " lachrymose " by its enemies ; de Chassiron [4] attacked, and Diderot, Gellert and Lessing [5] defended the new arrival.   In this way the schematism of the kinds continued to suffer violence and to cut a very poor figure ; nevertheless, in spite of adversity, it made every effort to retain power even at the sacrifice of dignity : just as an absolute king turns constitutional by force of

---

[1] *Proginn. poet.,* Florence, 1627, iii. p. 130.

[2] Cf. A. Belloni, *Il seicento,* Milan, 1898, pp. 162-164.

[3] *Examens,* and *Discours du poème dramatique, de la tragédie, des trois unités,* etc.

[4] *Réflexions sur le comique larmoyant,* 1749 (trans. by Lessing, *Werke, vol. cit.*).

[5] Gellert, *De comaedia commovente,* 1751 ; Lessing, *Abhandlungen von den weinerlichen oder rührenden Lustspiele,* 1754 (in *Werke,* vol. **vii.**).

circumstance, and chooses the lesser evil of squaring his
divine right with the will of the nation.

*Rebellion
against rules
in general.*

This retention of power would have been more difficult
had any success attended the attempts at rebellion against
all laws, against law in general, which broke out in varying degrees at the end of the sixteenth century. Pietro
Aretino made mock of the most sacred precepts : in a
prologue to one of his comedies he remarks derisively, " If
you see more than five characters on the stage at once,
do not laugh ; for chains which would fasten water-mills
to the river could not hold the fools of to-day." [1] A

*G. Bruno.
Guarini.*

philosopher, Giordano Bruno, entered the lists against
the " regulators of poetry " : rules, said he, are derived
from poetry : " there are as many genera and species of
true rules as there are genera and species of true poets " ;
such an individualization of kinds dealt them a death-
blow. " How then " (asks the interlocutory opponent)
" shall veritable poets be recognized ? "   " By their singing of verse " (answers Bruno) ; " of that which, being
sung, either delights or instructs, or delights and instructs
at the same time." [2] In much the same way Guarini
defended his *Pastor fido* in 1588, declaring " the world is
the judge of poets ; against its sentence there is no
appeal." [3]

*Spanish
critics.*

Amongst European countries, Spain was perhaps the
sturdiest in her resistance to the pedantic theories of the
writers of treatises ; Spain was the land of freedom in
criticism from Vives to Feijóo, from the sixteenth to the
middle of the eighteenth century when decadence of the
old Spanish spirit allowed Luzán, with others, to introduce
neo-classical poetry of Italian and French origin. [4] That
rules must change with the times and with actual conditions ; that modern literature demands modern poetics ;
that work carried out contrary to established rule does not
signify that it is contrary to all rule or unwilling to submit

---

[1] Prologue to the *Cortigiana*, 1534.
[2] *Degli eroici furori* in *Opere italiane*, ed. Gentile, ii. pp. 310-311.
[3] *Il Veratto* (against Jason de Nores), Ferrara, 1588.
[4] Menendez y Pelayo, *op. cit.* iii. pp. 174-175 (1st ed.), i.

itself to a higher law ; that nature should give, not receive, laws ; that the laws of the three unities are as ridiculous as it would be to forbid a painter to paint a large land-scape in a small picture ; that the pleasure, taste, appro-bation of readers and spectators are the deciding element in the long run ; that notwithstanding the laws of counter-point, the ear is the true judge of music ; these affirma-tions and many like them are frequent in Spanish criticism of the period.   One critic, Francisco de la Barreda (1622), went so far as to compassionate the strong wits of Italy bound by fear and cowardice (*temerosos y acobardados*) to rules that hampered them on every side ; [1] he may have been thinking of Tasso, a memorable case of such degrada-tion.   Lope de Vega wavered between neglect of rules in practice, and obsequious acceptance of them in theory, alleging in excuse for his conduct that he was forced to yield to the demands of the public who paid money to see his plays ; he said, " when I write my comedies, I lock and double-lock the door against the precept-mongers, that they may not rise up and bear witness against me " ; " Art (that is, Poetics) speaks truth which is contradicted by the vulgar ignorant " ; " may the rules forgive us when we are induced to violate them." [2]   But a contem-porary admirer of Lope's work writes of him that " *en muchas partes de sus escritos dice que el no guardar el arte antiguo lo hace por conformarse con el gusto de la plebe . . . dicelo por su natural modestia, y porqué no atribuya la malicia ignorante á arrogancia lo que es politica perfeccion.*" [3]

Giambattista Marino also protested " I assert that I   G. B. *Marino.* have a more thorough knowledge of the rules than have all the pedants in the world ; but the only true rule is to know how to break the rules at the right place and time, and to conform with the custom and taste of the day." [4] The drama of Spain, the comedy of art, and other literary novelties of the seventeenth century caused Minturno,

---

[1] Menendez y Pelayo, *op. cit.* iii. p. 468 (2nd ed.).

[2] *Arte nuevo de hacer comedias* (1609), ed. Morel Fatio, ll. 40-41, 138-140, 157-158.

[3] Menendez y Pelayo, *op. cit.* iii. p. 459.

[4] Marino, letter to G. Preti, in *Lettere*, Venice, 1627, p. 127.

Castelvetro and other rigid treatise-writers of the preceding
century to be looked at with contemptuous pity as
"antiquaries"; this may be seen in Andrea Perucci
(1699), the theorist of improvised comedy.[1] Pallavicino
criticized the writers on "the disciplines of beautiful
speech" on the ground that they "generally base their
precepts on observing by experience what things in
writers give pleasure, rather than pointing out what
would naturally conform to the particular affections and
instincts implanted by the Creator in the souls of men."[2]
A note of distrust towards the fixed kinds may be heard
in the *Discorso sull' Endimione* (1691), wherein Gravina
severely blames the "ambitious and miserly precepts"
of rhetoricians, and makes the penetrating comment:
"No work can see the light without finding itself confronted by a tribunal of critics specially convened to
examine it, and questioned firstly as to its name and
nature. Next begins the action which lawyers call
prejudicial, and controversy arises as to its status,
whether it is a poem, a romance, a tragedy, a comedy, or
another of the prescribed kinds. And if the said work
have ignored the slightest precept . . . they decree
forthwith its exile and perpetual banishment. And yet,
however they recast and expand their aphorisms, they
will never be able to include all the different kinds that
can be freshly created by the varied and ceaseless motion
of human wit. For this reason I cannot see why we should
not free ourselves from this insolent curb on the soaring
grandeur of our imaginations, and allow them to follow an
open road amongst those immeasurable spaces they are
fitted to explore." He remarks on the work of Guidi
which forms the subject of his discourse, "I know not
whether it be tragedy, comedy, tragicomedy, or anything
else invented by rhetoricians. It is a representation of
the loves of Endymion and Diana. If those terms have
sufficient breadth of extension, they will comprehend this

G. V. Gravina.

---

[1] *Dell' arte rappresentiva meditata e all' improvviso*, Naples, 1699;
cf. pp. 47, 48, 65.

[2] *Trattato dello stile e del dialogo*, 1646, preface.

work ; if they have not, let another be framed (a power which may be granted to any one in so unimportant a matter) ; if no such term can be invented, let us not, for want of a word, deprive ourselves of a thing so beautiful." [1] These remarks have quite a modern ring, but Gravina can hardly have thought out their implications very deeply, for later on he wrote a special treatise on the rules of the tragic kind.[2] Antonio Conti too declared at times his antagonism towards the rules, but he referred to the Aristotelian rules only.[3] More courage was displayed by Count Francesco Montani of Pesaro in the polemic roused *Fr. Montani.* by Orsi's book against Bouhours ; in 1705 he wrote : " I know that there are immutable and eternal rules, founded on such sound good sense and solid reason as will remain unshaken as long as mankind lives. But these rules, whose incorruptibility gives them authority to guide our spirits to the end of time, are rare enough to be counted with the nose, and it seems to me somewhat arbitrary to claim to test and regulate our new works by old laws now wholly abrogated and annulled." [4]

In France the rigorism of Boileau was followed by the *Critics of the* rebellion of Du Bos, who unhesitatingly declared that *eighteenth* *century.* " men will always prefer poetry which moves them to that composed according to rule," [5] and the like heresies. In 1730, De la Motte made war against the unities of time and place, asserting as the most general, and even superior to that of action, the unity of interest.[6] Batteux tended to make free with the rules ; and Voltaire, though he opposed De la Motte and declared the three unities to be the " three great laws of good sense," uttered some bold senti- ments in his *Essay on Epic Poetry*, and it was he who remarked that " *tous les genres sont bons hors le genre ennuyeux*," and that the best kind is " *celui qui est le mieux traité*." Diderot was in certain respects a fore- runner of Romanticism, and with him must be mentioned

[1] *Discorso su l' Endimione* (in *Opere italiane, ed. cit.*), ii. pp. 15-16.
[2] *Della tragedia*, 1715 (*ibid.* vol. i.).
[3] *Prose e poesie, cit.*, pref. and *passim*.
[4] In Orsi, *Considerazioni, ed. cit.* ii. pp. 8, 9.
[5] *Réflexions, cit.* sect. 34. [6] *Discours sur la tragédie*, 1730.

Friedrich Melchior Grimm, who was influenced by him. A breath of liberty was wafted into Italy by Metastasio, Bettinelli, Baretti and Cesarotti : in 1766 Buonafede notes in his *Epistola della libertà poetica* that when erudite persons " define epic poetry, or comedy, or odes, they ought to frame as many definitions as there are compositions and authors." [1] In Germany the first to rise in rebellion against the rules (opposing Gottsched and his disciples) were the representatives of the Swiss school.[2] In England, after examining the definitions by which critics endeavoured to distinguish epic poetry from other compositions, Home wrote, " It affords no little diversion to watch so many profound critics hunting after that which does not exist. They presuppose—without shadow of proof—that there exists a precise criterion by which to distinguish epic poetry from all other kinds of composition. But literary compositions melt one into another like colours : and if in their stronger shades it is easy to recognize them, they are susceptible of such variety and of so many different forms that it is impossible to say where one ends and another begins." [3]

Romanticism and the "strict kinds" : Berchet, V. Hugo.

Literary thought between the late eighteenth and the first decades of the nineteenth century, that is to say from " the period of genius " to that of romanticism properly so called, rose in rebellion against separate individual rules and against all rules as such. But to describe the battles fought, and their more important episodes ; to recount the names of captains victorious or discomfited, or to deplore the excesses committed by the conquerors, is no part of our present task. Upon the ruins of the strict kinds, the " *genres tranchés* " beloved by Napoleon [4] (a Romanticist in the art of war, but a Classicist in poetry), flourished the drama, the romance and every other mixed kind : upon the ruins of the three unities, flourished the unity of *ensemble*. Italy made her protest

---

[1] *Opuscoli* of Agatopisto Cromaziano, Venice, 1797.

[2] Danzel, *Gottsched*, p. 206 seqq.

[3] *Elements of Criticism*, iii. pp. 144-145, note.

[4] See conversation of Napoleon with Goethe, in Lewes, *The Life and Works of Goethe*, ii. p. 441.

against rules of style in Berchet's famous *Lettera semiseria di Grisostomo* (1816) ; and France made hers somewhat later in Victor Hugo's preface to *Cromwell* (1827). Henceforth men discussed not the kinds, but Art. What is the unity of *ensemble* but the demand of art itself, which is always an *ensemble*, a synthesis ? What else is the principle, introduced by August Wilhelm Schlegel and adopted by Manzoni and other Italian romanticists, to the effect that form of component parts must be " organic not mechanical, resulting from the nature of the subject and its interior development . . . not from the impress of an external and extraneous stamp " ? [1]

But it would be quite wrong to suppose that this victory over the rhetoric of kinds was either the cause or the consequence of a final victory over its philosophical presuppositions. In pure theory, none of the critics above named wholly abandoned the kinds and the rules. Berchet admitted four elementary forms, that is four fundamental kinds, in poetry ; lyrical, didactic, epic and dramatic, claiming for the poet only the right of "uniting and fusing together the elementary forms in a thousand fashions." [2] Manzoni's only real quarrel was with those rules " founded on special facts instead of on general principles ; on the authority of rhetoricians instead of reason." [3] Even De Sanctis was satisfied with a concept somewhat vague, though true enough at bottom : " the most important rules are not those capable of being applied to every content, but those which draw their force *ex visceribus caussae*, from the very heart of the content itself." [4] Even more diverting than the spectacle which had delighted Home, is the sight of German philosophy according the honour of a dialectical deduction to the empirical classification of kinds. We shall give two examples, each representing one extreme end of the chain : Schelling at the beginning of the century (1803), and Hart-

Their persistence in philosophical theories.

Fr. Schelling.

[1] Manzoni, *Epistol.* i. pp. 355-356 ; cf. *Lettera sul romanticismo, ibid.* pp. 293-299.

[2] *Lettera di Grisostomo, opere,* ed. Cusani, p. 227.

[3] *Lettera sul romanticismo, ibid.* p. 280.

[4] *La giovinezza di F. de S.* chs. 26-28.

mann at the end (1890). One section of Schelling's *Philosophy of Art* is devoted to "the construction of individual poetic kinds "; in it he remarks that were he to follow the historical order, Epic would come first; whereas in the scientific order the Lyric occupies the first place : indeed, if poetry is the representation of the infinite in the finite, the Lyric, in which difference prevails (the finite, the subject), is its first moment, corresponding with the first power of the ideal series, reflexion, knowledge, consciousness, whereas Epic corresponds with the second power, action.[1] From Epic, which is *par excellence* the objective kind (as being the identity of subjective and objective), derive the Elegy and the Idyl if subjectivity be placed in the object and objectivity in the poet : if objectivity be placed in the object and subjectivity in the poet, didactic poetry results.[2] To these differentiations of the Epic, Schelling adds the romantic or modern Epic, the poem of chivalry ; the novel ; and the experiments in an epic of ordinary life such as the *Luisa* of Voss and the *Hermann and Dorothea* of Goethe ; and, co-ordinate with all the foregoing, the *Comedia* of Dante, " an epic kind in itself " (*eine epische Gattung für sich*). Finally, from the union on a higher plane of Lyric with Epic, liberty with necessity, arises the third form, the Drama, the reconciliation of antitheses in a totality, " supreme incarnation of the essence and the in-itself of all art." [3] In Hartmann's *Philosophy of the Beautiful*, poetry is divided into spoken poetry and read poetry. The former is subdivided into Epic, Lyric and Dramatic, with further subdivisions of Epic into plastic Epic, or strictly epic Epic, and pictorial or lyrical Epic ; of Lyric into epical Lyric, lyrical Lyric and dramatic Lyric ; of Dramatic into lyrical Drama, epic Drama and dramatic Drama. Read poetry (*Lesepoesie*) is again subdivided into predominantly epical, lyrical or dramatic form with tertiary partitions of the affecting, the comic, the tragic and humorous ; and into poems " to be read at a sitting " (like the short story) or

E. von Hartmann.

---

[1] *Philos. d. Kunst*, pp. 639-645.
[2] *Op. cit.* pp. 657-659.   [3] *Op. cit.* p. 687.

to be taken up again and again (like the novel).[1] Without *The kinds in*
these highly philosophical trivialities the divisions of *the schools.*
kinds still wander through the books called *Institutions of
Literature*, written by philologists and men of letters, and
the ordinary school-books of Italy, France and Germany ;
and psychologists and philosophers still persist in writing
about the Æsthetic of the tragic, of the comic and of the
humorous.[2] The objectivity of literary kinds is frankly
maintained by Ferdinand Brunetière, who looks on literary
history as " the evolution of kinds," [3] and gives sharply
defined form to a superstition which, seldom confessed so
truthfully or applied so rigorously, survives to contaminate
modern literary history.[4]

<h1 style="text-align:center">III</h1>

THE THEORY OF THE LIMITS OF THE ARTS

To Lessing must be ascribed the merit and the sole
glory of having discovered that every art has its special
character and inviolable limits. But his merit lies not
in his own theory, which, in itself, is scarcely tenable,[5]
but in having, though by an error, aroused discussion of
a highly important æsthetical point till then wholly overlooked. After some slight notice from Du Bos and
Batteux, some preparation of the field by Diderot [6] and
Mendelssohn,[7] and long disquisitions by Meier and other
Wolffians upon natural and conventional symbols,[8] Lessing

[1] *Philosophie d. Schönen*, ch. 2, § 2.
[2] See, *e.g.*, Volkelt, *Ästh. d. Tragischen*, Munich, 1897 ; Lipps, *Der Streit über Tragödie*, etc.
[3] See his other works, *L'Évolution des genres dans l'histoire de la littérature*, Paris, 1890 seqq., and *Manuel de l'hist. de la littér. française, ibid.*, 1898.
[4] Croce, *Per la storia della critica e storiografia letter.* pp. 23-25.
[5] See above, pp. 113-115.
[6] D. Diderot, *Lettre sur les aveugles*, 1749 ; *Lettre sur les sourds et muets*, 1751 ; *Essai sur la peinture*, 1765.
[7] M. Mendelssohn, *Briefe über Empfind.*, 1755 ; *Betrachtungen, cit.*, 1757.
[8] J. Chr. Wolff, *Psychol. empirica*, §§ 272-312 ; Meier, *Anfangs-gründe*, §§ 513-528, 708-735 ; *Betrachtungen*, § 126.

was the first to raise clearly the question of the value attaching to the distinction between the various arts. Antiquity, the Middle Ages and the Renaissance had enumerated the arts according to denominations of current phraseology, and had composed numbers of technical hand-books distinguishing major and minor arts ; but in Aristoxenus or Vitruvius, Marchetto da Padova or Cennino Cennini, Leonardo da Vinci or Leon Battista Alberti, Palladio or Scamozzi, it would be vain to look for the problem proposed by Lessing, for the spirit of these technical treatise-writers is entirely different. Some rudiments of the question may be detected in the comparisons made, and the questions of precedence raised, between poetry and painting or painting and sculpture, to be found now and then in stray paragraphs of their books (Leonardo da Vinci pressed the claims of painting, Michael Angelo those of sculpture) : the theme eventually became a favourite one for academic discussion, and was not despised by Galileo himself.[1]

The limits of the arts in Lessing. Arts of space and arts of time.

Lessing was induced to raise the question in the attempt to controvert the strange views of Spence concerning the close union between painting and poetry among the ancients, and of Count Caylus, who held that the excellence of a poem must be judged by the number of subjects it offers to the brush of the painter. He was further instigated by the comparisons between poetry and painting upon which were commonly founded the most ridiculous rules for tragedy : the maxim *Ut pictura poësis*, whose original motive was to emphasize the representative or imaginative character of poetry, and the community of nature among the arts, had been converted by superficial interpretation into a defence of the most vicious intellectualistic and realistic prejudices. Lessing argued in this wise : " If painting in its imitations employs precisely a medium or symbol different from that of poetry (the former employing spatial forms and colours, the latter temporal articulated sounds), since the symbol must certainly be in close relation with that

[1] Letter to Lodovico Cardi da Cigoli, June 26, 1612.

which is signified, coexistent symbols can only express
coexistent objects or parts of objects, and consecutive
symbols can only express consecutive objects or parts of
objects. Objects mutually coexistent, or having mutually
coexistent parts, are called bodies. Bodies, then, through
their quality of visibility, are the true objects of painting.
Objects successively consecutive amongst themselves, or
whose parts are consecutive, are called in general actions.
Actions, then, are the suitable objects of poetry." Painting, undoubtedly, may represent action, but only by
means of bodies which indicate it ; and poetry may represent bodies, but only by indicating them by means
of actions. When a poet using language, *i.e.* arbitrary
symbols, sets himself to describe bodies, he is no longer
a poet but a prose-writer, since a true poet only describes
bodies by the effect they produce on the soul.[1] Retouching and developing this distinction, Lessing described
action or movement in a picture as an addition made by
the imagination of the beholder ; so true is this, says he,
that animals perceive nothing save immobility in a picture.
He further studied the various unions of arbitrary with
natural symbols, such as that of poetry with music (in
which the former is subordinate to the latter), of music
with dancing, of poetry with dancing, and of music and
poetry with dancing (union of arbitrary consecutive audible symbols with natural visible symbols) : of the pantomime of antiquity (union of arbitrary consecutive visible
symbols with natural consecutive visible symbols) : of
the language of the dumb (the only art that employs
arbitrary consecutive visible symbols) : and, lastly, of imperfect unions, such as that of painting with poetry. If
not every use to which language is put is poetic, Lessing
holds that not every use of natural coexistent signs is
pictorial : painting, like language, has its prose. Prosaic
painters are those who represent consecutive objects notwithstanding the character of coexistence in their signs,
allegorical painters those who make arbitrary use of natural
signs, and those who pretend to represent the invisible or

[1] *Laokoon*, §§ 16-20.

the audible by means of the visible.   Desirous of preserving the naturalness of symbolism, Lessing ended by condemning the custom of painting objects on a diminished
scale, and concludes: " I think that the aim of an art
should be that only to which it is specially adapted, not
that which can be performed equally well by other arts.
I find in Plutarch a comparison which illustrates this
admirably : he who would split wood with a key and
open the door with an axe not only spoils both utensils
but deprives himself of the unity of each alike." [1]

Limits and classifications of the arts in later philosophy.

The principle of limitations or of the specific character
of individual arts, as laid down by Lessing, occupied the
attention of philosophers in later days, who, without discussing the principle itself, employed it in classifying the
arts and arranging them in series.

Herder and Kant.

Herder here and
there continued Lessing's examination in his fragment on
Plastic (1769) ; [2] Heydenreich wrote a treatise (1790) on
the limits of the six arts (music, dance, figurative arts,
gardening, poetry and representative art), and criticized
the *clavecin oculaire* of Father Castel, a contrivance for
the combination of colours which should act in the same
way as the series of musical notes in harmony and melody; [3]
Kant appealed to the analogy of a speaking man, and
classified the arts according to speech, gesture and tone as
arts of speech, figurative arts, and arts producing a mere

Schelling.

play of sensations (mimicry and colouring).[4]   Schelling
differentiated the artistic identity according as it consisted
in the infusion of the infinite into the finite, or of the
finite into the infinite (ideal art or real art) : into poetry
and art proper.   Under the heading of real arts he included the figurative arts, music, painting, plastic (which
comprehended architecture, bas-relief and sculpture) : in
the ideal series were the three corresponding forms of

Solger.

poetry, lyrical, epical and dramatic.[5]   With a similar

[1] *Laokoon*, appendix, § 43.
[2] *Plastik, einige Wahrnehmungen über Form und Gestalt aus Pyg-
malions bildenden Traume*, 1778 (Select Works of Herder in the collection *Deutsche Nationlitteratur*, vol. 76, part iii. § 2).
[3] *System der Ästhetik*, pp. 154-236.
[4] *Kritik d. Urtheilskr.* § 51.   [5] *Phil. d. Kunst*, pp. 370-371.

method, Solger placed poetry, the universal art, side by
side with art strictly so called, which is either symbolical
(sculpture) or allegorical (painting), and, in either case, is
a union of concepts and bodies : if you take corporality
without concept, you have architecture ; if concept without matter, music.[1] Hegel makes poetry the bond of
union between the two extremes of figurative art and of
music.[2] We have already seen how Schopenhauer de- *Schopenhauer.*
stroyed the accepted limitations of art and built them
up again, following the order of the ideas which they
represent.[3]   Herbart clung to Lessing's two groups, *Herbart.*
simultaneous arts and successive arts, and defined the
former as " permitting themselves to be inspected from
every side," the latter as " rejecting complete investigation and remaining in semi-darkness " : in the first group
he placed architecture, plastic, church music and classical
poetry ; in the second ornamental gardening, painting,
secular music and romantic poetry.[4] Herbart was im-
placable against those who look in one art for the perfections of another ; who " look on music as a sort of
painting, painting as poetry, poetry as an elevated plastic
and plastic as a species of æsthetic philosophy," [5] while
admitting that a concrete work of art, such as a picture,
may contain elements of the picturesque, the poetic and
other kinds, held together by the skill of the artist.[6]
Weisse divided the arts into three triads, intended to *Weisse.*
recall the nine Muses.[7] Zeising invented·a cross-division *Zeising.*
into figurative arts (architecture, sculpture, painting),
musical arts (instrumental music, song, poetry), and arts
of mimicry (dance, musical mimicry, representative art),
and into macrocosmic arts (architecture, instrumental
music, dance), microcosmic arts (sculpture, song, musical
mimicry) and historical arts (painting, poetry and representative art).[8] Vischer classified them according to *Vischer.*

---

[1] *Vorles. üb. Ästh.* pp. 257-262.   [2] *Op. cit.* ii. p. 222.
[3] See above, pp. 305-306.   [4] *Einleitung*, § 115, pp. 170-171.
[5] *Schriften z. prakt. Phil.* in *Werke*, viii. p. 2.
[6] *Einleitung*, § 110, pp. 164-165.
[7] Cf. Hartmann, *Dtsche. Ästh. s. Kant*, pp. 539-540.
[8] *Ästh. Forsch.* pp. 547-549.

the three forms of imagination (figurative, sensuous and poetic), into objective arts (architecture, plastic and painting), a subjective art (music) and an objective-subjective art [1] (poetry). Gerber proposed to recognize a special "art of language" (*Sprachkunst*), distinguishable alike from prose and poetry and consisting in the expression of simple movements of the soul. Such an art would correspond with plastic in the following scheme : arts of the eye—(*a*) architecture, (*b*) plastic, (*c*) painting ; arts of the ear—(*a*) prose, (*b*) the art of language, (*c*) poetry.[2]

M. Schasler.   The two most recent systems of classification are furnished by Schasler and Hartmann, who have also submitted the schemes of their predecessors to searching criticism. Schasler [3] arranges the arts in two groups, adopting the criterion of simultaneity and succession : the arts of simultaneity are architecture, plastic and painting ; of succession, music, mimicry and poetry. He says that by following the series in the order indicated, it will be seen that simultaneity, originally predominant, yields place to succession, which predominates in the second group and subordinates without wholly displacing the other. Parallel with this, another division is evolved, deduced from the relation between the ideal and material elements in each separate art, between movement and repose ; which begins with architecture " materially the heaviest, spiritually the lightest of all the arts," and ends with poetry, in which the opposite relation is observed. Curious analogies are established by this method between the first and second group of arts : between architecture and music ; between plastic and mimicry ; between painting in its three forms of landscape, *genre* and historical, and poetry in its three forms of lyric (declamatory), epic (rhapsodic) and drama
E. v.   (representative). Hartmann [4] divides the arts into arts of
Hartmann.   perception and arts of imagination : the former tripartite

---

[1] *Ästh.* §§ 404, 535, 537, 838, etc.
[2] Gustav Gerber, *Die Sprache als Kunst*, Bromberg, 1871–1874.
[3] *Das System der Künste*, 2nd ed., Leipzig-Berlin, 1881.
[4] *Phil. d. Sch.* chs. 9, 10.

into spatial or visual (plastic and painting), temporal or
auditory (instrumental music, linguistic mimicry, expressive song) and temporal-spatial or mimic (pantomime,
mimic dances, art of the actor, art of the opera-singer) ;
the second contains but one single species, which is poetry.
Architecture, decoration, gardening, cosmetic and prose-
writing are excluded from this system of classification and
lumped together as non-free arts.

Parallel with this search for a classification of the arts, *The supreme*
the same philosophers were led into the quest of the *art. Richard*
supreme art. Some favoured poetry, others music or *Wagner.*
sculpture ; others again claimed the supremacy for
combined arts, especially for Opera, according to the
theory of it already advanced in the eighteenth century [1]
and maintained and developed in our day by Richard
Wagner.[2] One of the latest philosophers to raise the
question " whether single arts, or arts in combination, had
the greater value," concluded that single arts as such
possess their own perfection, yet the perfection of united
arts is still greater, notwithstanding the compromises and
mutual concessions enforced upon them by their union ;
that single arts, from another point of view, have the
greater value ; and lastly, that both single and combined
arts are necessary to the realisation of the concept of art.[3]

The capriciousness, emptiness and childishness of such *Lotze's*
problems and their solutions must have excited feelings of *attack on*
impatience and disgust, but we rarely find a doubt thrown *classifications.*
on their validity. One such dissentient is Lotze when he
writes : " It is difficult to see the use of such attempts.
Knowledge of the nature and laws of individual arts is
but little increased by indication of the systematic place
allotted to each." He further observed that in real life
the arts are variously conjoined, forming themselves into
no systematic series, while in the world of thought an
immense variety of orders can be created ; he therefore
selected one of these possible orders, not because it was

---

[1] *E.g.* by Sulzer, *Allg. Theorie*, on word *Oper.*

[2] Rich. Wagner, *Oper und Drama*, 1851.

[3] Gustav Engel, *Ästh. der Tonkunst*, 1884, abstracted in Hartmann,
Dtsche. Ästh. s. Kant, pp. 579-580.

the sole legitimate one, but because it was convenient (*bequem*). His series begins with music, " the art of free beauty, determined only by the laws of its matter, not by conditions imposed by a given task of purpose or of imitation " ; followed by architecture, " which no longer plays freely with forms, but subjects them to the service of an end " ; and then by sculpture, painting and poetry, excluding minor arts which cannot be co-ordinated with the others, since they are incapable of expressing with any approach to completeness the totality of the spiritual life.[1] A recent French critic, Basch, opens his treatise with the following excellent remarks : " Is it necessary to show there is no such thing as an absolute art, differentiating itself later by means of one knows not what immanent laws ? What exists is the particular forms of art, or rather artists who have striven to translate, as best they can, according to the material means at their command, the song of the ideal in their souls." But later on he thinks it possible to effect a division of the arts by starting " from the artist, instead of the art in itself," by proceeding " according to the three great types of fancy, visual, motor and auditory " ; and as for the debated point of the supreme art, he thinks it must be settled in favour of music.[2]

Schasler is not altogether wrong in his spirited counter-attack on Lotze's criticism ; he protests against the principle of indifference and convenience, and remarks that " the classification of the arts must be regarded as the real touchstone, the real differential test of the scientific value of an æsthetic system ; for on this point all theoretical questions are concentrated and crowd together to find a concrete solution." [3] The principle of convenience may be excellent as applied to the approximative grouping of botanical or zoological classifications, but it has no place in philosophy ; and as Lotze, in common with Schasler and other æstheticians, conformed

Contradictions in Lotze.

---

[1] Lotze, *Geschichte d. Ästh.* pp. 458-460 ; cf. p. 445.
[2] *Essai critique sur l'Esth. de Kant*, pp. 89-496.
[3] *Das System der Künste*, p. 47.

to Lessing's principle of the constancy, limits and peculiar nature of each art, and therefore held that the concepts of the individual arts were speculative and not empirical concepts, he could not evade the duty of fixing the mutual relations of these concepts, arranging them in series, subordinating and co-ordinating them, and arriving at each of them either deductively or dialectically. He ought, in order to get definitely rid of these barren attempts at classification and at discovering the supreme art, to have criticized and dissolved Lessing's principle itself : to keep the principle and deny the need for a classification, as Lotze did, was obviously inconsistent. But not a single æsthetician has ever re-examined or investigated the scientific foundation of the distinctions enunciated by Lessing in his fluent and elegant prose ; no one has probed to the bottom the truth which was illumined by Aristotle in a single lightning-flash, when he refused to allow an extrinsic difference, that of metre, as the real distinction between prose and poetry : [1] no one, that is to say, save *Doubts in* perhaps Schleiermacher, who at least called attention to *Schleier-* the difficulties of the current doctrine. He proposed to *macher.* start from the general concept of art and prove by deduction the necessity of all its forms ; and after finding two sides to artistic activity, the objective consciousness (*gegenständliche*) and the immediate consciousness (*un-mittelbare*), and observing that art stands wholly neither in the one nor in the other and that the immediate consciousness or representation (*Vorstellung*) gives rise to mimicry and music, while the objective consciousness or image (*Bild*) gives rise to the figurative arts, he then, proceeding to analyse a painting, found the two forms of consciousness to be in this case inseparable, and remarks : " Here we arrive at the precise opposite : searching for distinction, we find unity." Nor did the traditional division of the arts into simultaneous and successive seem to him very solid, for " when looked at attentively, it evaporates entirely " ; in architecture or gardening, contemplation is successive, while in the arts labelled as

---

[1] *Poet.* ch. I.

successive, such as poetry, the chief thing is coexistence and grouping : " from whichever side we look at it, the difference is but secondary and the antithesis between the two orders of art merely means that every contemplation, like every act of production, is always successive, but, in thinking out the relation of the two sides in a work of art, both seem indispensable : coexistence (*Zugleichsein*) and successive existence (*das Successivsein*)." In another passage he observes : " The reality of art as external appearance is conditioned by the mode, depending on our physical and corporeal organism, in which the internal is externalised : movements, forms, words. . . . That which is common to all arts is not the external, which is rather the element of diversification." When these observations are compared with the sharp distinction he himself drew between art and technique, it would be easy to deduce that he held the partitions of the arts and the concepts of the particular arts to be devoid of æsthetic value. But Schleiermacher does not draw this logical inference, he wavers and hesitates : he recognizes the inseparability of the subjective and objective, musical and figurative, elements in poetry, yet he struggles to discover the definitions and limits of the individual arts ; sometimes he dreams of a union of the various arts from which a complete art would spring ; and when composing the syllabus of his lectures on Æsthetic, he arranged the arts into arts of accompaniment (mimicry and music), figurative arts (architecture, gardening, painting, sculpture) and poetry.[1] Nebulous, vague, contradictory as this may be, Schleiermacher had the acumen to distrust the soundness of Lessing's theory and to inquire by what right particular arts are singled out from art in general.

[1] *Vorles. üb. Ästh.* pp. 11, 122-129, 137, 143, 151, 167, 172, 284-286, 487-488, 508, 635.

IV

OTHER PARTICULAR DOCTRINES

I. Schleiermacher also rejected the concept of Natural *The æsthetic*
Beauty, giving Hegel greater praise than he deserved in *theory of*
Natural
the matter, because Hegel's denial of this concept was, *Beauty.*
as we have seen, more verbal than real. At all events,
Schleiermacher's radical denial of the existence of a
natural beauty external to and independent of the human
mind marked a victory over a serious error, and appears
to us imperfect and one-sided only so far as it seems to
exclude those æsthetic facts of imagination which are
attached to objects given in nature.[1] Important contributions towards the correction of this imperfect and one-
sided element were supplied by the historical and psychological study of the " feeling for nature," promoted
successfully by Alexander Humboldt in his dissertation to
be found in the second volume of *Cosmos*,[2] and continued
by Laprade, Biese, and others in our own time.[3] In his
criticism of his own *Ästhetik*, Vischer completes the
passage from the metaphysical construction of beauty in
nature to the psychological interpretation of it, and
recognizes the necessity of suppressing the section devoted
to Natural Beauty in his first æsthetic system, and in-
corporating it with the doctrine of imagination : he says
that such treatments do not belong to æsthetic science,
being a medley of zoology, sentiment, fantasy and
humour, worthy of development in monographs in the
style of the poet G. G. Fischer's on the life of birds, or
Bratranek's on the æsthetic of the vegetable world.[4]
Hartmann, as heir of the old metaphysics, reproaches

[1] See above, pp. 98-99.

[2] *Das Naturgefühl nach Verschiedenheit der Zeiten und Volksstämme,*
in *Cosmos*, ii.

[3] V. Laprade, *Le Sentiment de la nature avant le christianisme,* 1866 ;
also *chez les modernes,* 1867 ; Alfred Biese, *Die Entwicklung des Natur-*
gefühls bei den Griechen und Römern, Kiel, 1882–1884 ; *Die Entwicklung*
des Naturgefühls im Mittelalter und in der Neuzeit, 2nd ed., Leipzig, 1892.

[4] *Kritische Gänge,* v. pp. 5-23.

Vischer for this exclusion, and maintains that, in addition
to the beauty of imagination introduced by man into
natural things (*hineingelegte Schönheit*), there exist a
formal and a substantial beauty in nature, coinciding
with realisation of the immanent ends or ideas of nature.[1]
But the way chosen ultimately by Vischer is the only one
by which Schleiermacher's thesis can be successfully
developed so as to show the precise meaning which may
be given to the assertion of (æsthetic) beauty in nature.

The theory of æsthetic senses.

II. That æsthetic senses or superior senses exist and
that beauty attaches to certain senses only, not to all, is
a very old opinion.   We have seen already [2] that Socrates,
in the *Hippias maior*, mentions the doctrine of beauty as
" that which pleases hearing and sight " (τὸ καλὸν ἐστὶ
τὸ δι' ἀκοῆς τε καὶ ὄψεως ἡδύ) : and he adds, it seems
impossible to deny that we take pleasure in looking at
handsome men and fine ornaments, pictures and statues
with our eyes, and hearing beautiful songs or beautiful
voices, music, speeches and conversations with our ears.
Nevertheless Socrates himself in the same dialogue con-
futes this theory by perfectly valid arguments, amongst
which is that, besides the difficulty arising from the fact
that beautiful things may be found outside the range of
the sensible impressions of eye and ear, there is no reason
for creating a special class for the pleasure arising from
impressions on these two senses, to the exclusion of others.
He also states the more subtle and philosophical objection
that that which is pleasing to the sight is not so to the
hearing, and *vice versa* ; whence it follows that the ground
of beauty must not be sought in visibility or audibility,
but in something differing from either and common to
both.[3]

The problem was never again, perhaps, attacked with
such acumen and seriousness as in this ancient dialogue.
In the eighteenth century Home remarked that beauty
depended on sight, and that impressions received by the
other senses might be agreeable but were not beautiful,

---

[1] *Dtsche. Ästh. s. Kant*, pp. 217-218 ; cf. *Philos. d. Schönen*, bk. ii.
ch. 7.   [2] See above, pp. 164-165.   [3] *Hippias maior, passim.*

and distinguished sight and hearing as superior to those of touch, taste and smell, the latter being merely bodily in nature and without the spiritual refinement of the other two. He held these to produce pleasures superior to organic pleasures though inferior to intellectual ; decorous pleasures, that is to say ; elevated, sweet, moderately exhilarating ; as far removed from the turbulence of the passions as from the languor of indolence, and intended to refresh and soothe the spirit.[1] Following suggestions of Diderot, Rousseau and Berkeley, Herder drew attention to the importance of the sense of touch (*Gefühl*) in plastic art : of this " third sense, which perhaps deserves to be investigated first of all, and is unjustly relegated to a place amongst the grosser senses." Certainly " touch knows nothing of surface or colour," but " sight, for its part, knows nothing of forms and configurations." Thus " touch cannot be so gross a sense as it is reputed, if it is the very organ by which we sensate all other bodies, and rules over a vast kingdom of subtle and complex concepts. As the surface stands to the body, so does sight stand in respect of touch, and it is merely a colloquial abbreviation to speak of seeing bodies as surfaces and to suppose that we see with our eyes that which we have gradually learnt in infancy simply by the sense of touch." Every beauty of form or corporeity is a concept not visible, but palpable.[2] From the triad of æsthetic senses thus established by Herder (sight for painting ; hearing for music ; touch for sculpture), Hegel returned to the customary dyad, saying that " the sensory part of art has reference only to the two theoretic senses of sight and hearing " ; that smell, taste and touch must be excluded from artistic pleasures, since they are connected with matter as such and the immediate sensible quality it may possess (smell with material volatilization ; taste with material solution of objects ; and touch with hot, cold, smooth and so forth) ; and that hence they can

---

[1] *Elements of Criticism*, introd., and cf. ch. 3.
[2] Herder, *Kritische Wälder* (in *Werke, ed. cit.* iv.), pp. 47-53 ; cf. *Kaligone* (*ibid.* vol. xxii.), *passim* ; and fragment on *Plastic*.

claim no concern with the objects of art, which are obliged to keep themselves in real independence, rejecting all relation with the merely sensory. That which pleases these senses is not the beautiful of art.[1]

It was Schleiermacher once more who recognized the impossibility of disposing of the matter in this summary fashion. He refused to admit the distinction between confused senses and clear senses, and asserted that the superiority of sight and hearing over the other senses lay in the fact that the others " are not capable of any free activity, and indeed represent the maximum of passivity, whereas sight and hearing are capable of an activity proceeding from within, and are able to produce forms and notes without having received impressions from outside " ; were eye and ear merely means of perception, there would be no visual or auditory arts, but they also operate as a function of voluntary movements which supply a content to the dominion of the senses. From another standpoint, however, Schleiermacher thinks that " the difference seems to be one rather of degree or quantity, and a minimum of independence must be recognized as existing in the other senses as well." [2] Vischer remains faithful to the traditional " two æsthetic senses," " free organs and no less spiritual than sensuous," which " have no reference to the material composition of the object," but allow this " to subsist as a whole and work upon them." [3] Köstlin was of opinion that the inferior senses offer " nothing intuitible separate from themselves, and are only modifications of ourselves, but taste, smell and touch are not devoid of all æsthetic importance, since they assist the superior senses ; without touch an image could not be recognized by the eye as being hard, resistant or rough ; without smell certain images could not be represented as sweet or scented." [4]

We cannot go into a detailed account of all doctrines connected with sensationalistic principles,[5] for all the

[1] Vorles. üb. Ästh. i. pp. 50-51.   [2] Op. cit. p. 92 seqq.
[3] Ästh. i. p. 181.   [4] Ästh. pp. 80-83.
[5] E.g. Grant Allen, Physiological Æsthetics, chs. 4 and 5.

senses are naturally accepted as æsthetic by the sensationalists, who use "æsthetic" interchangeably with
"hedonistic" : it will suffice if we recall the "learned"
Kralik, who was ridiculed by Tolstoy for his theory of
the five arts of taste, smell, touch, hearing and sight.[1]
The few quotations already given show the embarrassing
difficulty caused by the use of the word "æsthetic" as
a qualification of "sense," compelling writers to invent
absurd distinctions between various groups of senses, or
to recognize all senses as being æsthetic, thus giving
æsthetic value to every sensory impression, as such. No
way out of this labyrinth can be found save by asserting
the impossibility of effecting a union between such wholly
disparate orders of ideas as the concept of the representative form of the spirit and that of particular physiological organs or a particular matter of sense-impressions.[2]

III. A variety of the error of literary kinds is to be
found in the theory of modes, forms or kinds of style
(χαρακτῆρες τῆς φράσεως), considered by the ancients as
consisting of three forms, the sublime, the medium and
the tenuous, a tripartition due, it would seem, to Anti-
sthenes,[3] modified later into *subtile, robustum* and *floridum*,
or amplified into a fourfold division, or designated by
adjectives of historic origin as in the Attic, Asiatic or
Rhodian styles. The Middle Ages preserved the tradition
of a tripartite division, sometimes giving it a curious
interpretation, to the effect that the sublime style treats
of kings, princes and barons (*e.g.* the *Aeneid*) ; the mediocre,
of middle-class people (*e.g. Georgics*) ; the humble, of the
lowest class (*e.g. Bucolics*) ; and the three styles were for
this reason also called tragic, elegiac and comic.[4] It is
a well-known fact that kinds in style have never ceased
to afford matter for discussion in rhetorical text-books
down to modern times ; for instance, we find Blair distinguishing styles by such epithets as the diffuse, the

The theory of kinds of style

[1] Tolstoy, *What is Art?* pp. 19-22. Kralik is the author of *Welt-schönheit, Versuch einer allgemeinen Ästhetik*, Vienna, 1894.
[2] See above, pp. 18-20.
[3] Cf. Volkmann, *Rhet. d. G. u. Röm.* pp. 532-544.
[4] Comparetti, *Virgilio nel M. E.* i. p. 172.

concise, the nervous, the daring, the soft, the elegant, the flowery, etc. In 1818 the Italian Melchiorre Delfico, in his book on *The Beautiful*, energetically criticized the " endless division of styles," or the superstition " that there could be so many kinds of style " ; saying that " style is either good or bad," and adding that it is not possible " it should exist as a preconceived idea in the artist's mind," but that " it should be the consequence of the principal idea, *i.e.* that conception which determines the invention and the composition." [1]

The theory of grammatical forms or parts of speech.
IV. The same error reappears in the philosophy of language, as the theory of grammatical forms or parts of speech,[2] first created by the sophists (Protagoras is credited with having first distinguished the gender of nouns), adopted by the philosophers, notably by Aristotle and the Stoics (the former was acquainted with two or three parts of speech, the latter with four or five), developed and elaborated by the Alexandrian grammarians in the famous and endless controversy between the analogists and the anomalists. The analogists (Aristarchus) aimed at introducing logical order and regularity into linguistic facts, and described as deviations all such as seemed to them irreducible to logical form. These they called pleonasm, ellipsis, enallage, parallage, and metalepsis. The violence thus wrought by the analogists upon spoken and written language was such that (as Quintilian tells us) some one wittily (*non invenuste*) remarked that it appeared to be one thing to talk Latin and quite another to talk grammar (*aliud esse latine, aliud grammatice loqui*).[3] The anomalists must be credited with restoring to language its free imaginative movement : the Stoic Chrysippus composed a treatise to prove that one thing (one same concept) may be expressed by different sounds, and one and the same sound may express different concepts (*similes res dissimilibus verbis et similibus dissimiles esse vocabulis notatas*). Another anomalist was the celebrated grammarian Apollonius Dyscolus, who rejected the metalepsis,

[1] *Nuove ricerche sul bello*, ch. 10.
[2] See above, pp. 145-146.   [3] *Inst. Orat.* i. ch. 6.

the schemes, and the other artifices by which the analogists tried to explain facts which did not fit their categories, and pointed out that the use of one word for another, or one part of speech for another, is not a grammatical figure, but a blunder, a thing hardly to be attributed to a poet such as Homer. The upshot of the dispute between anomalists and analogists was the science of Grammar (τέχνη γραμματική), as handed down by the ancients to the modern world, which is justly considered as a sort of compromise between the two opposed parties because, if the schemes of inflection (κανόνες) satisfy the demands of the analogists, their variety satisfies those of the anomalists ; hence the original definition of Grammar as theory of analogy was changed subsequently to " theory of analogy and anomaly " (ὁμοίου τε καὶ ἀνομοίου θεωρία). The concept of correct usage, with which Varro hoped to settle the controversy, fell into the trap (common to compromises), merely stating the contradiction in set terms, like the " convenient ornament " of Rhetoric or the kinds accorded a " certain licence " in the literature of precept. If language follows usage (that is to say, the imagination), it does not follow reason (or logic) ; if it follows reason, it does not follow usage. When the analogists upheld logic as supreme at least inside the individual kinds and sub-kinds, the anomalists hastened to show that even this was not the case. Varro himself was forced to confess that " this part of the subject really is very difficult " (hic locus maxime lubricus est).[1]

In the Middle Ages grammar was cultivated to the point of superstition. Divine inspiration was found lurking in the eight parts of speech because " octavus numerus frequenter in divinis scripturis sacratis invenitur," and in the three persons of verbal conjugation, created simply " ut quod in Trinitatis fide credimus, in eloquiis inesse videatur." [2] Grammarians of the Renaissance and later recommenced the study of linguistic problems and

---

[1] For all this cf. the works of Lersch and of Steinthal, which contain the more important texts.

[2] Comparetti, Virgilio nel M. E., i. pp. 169-170.

worked to death ellipsis, pleonasm, licence, anomaly and
exception ;   only in comparatively recent times has
Linguistic begun to question the very validity of the
concept of parts of speech (Pott, Paul and others).[1]   If
they still survive, the reason may lie in the facts that
empirical, practical grammar cannot do without them ;
that their venerable antiquity disguises their illegitimate
and shady origin ; and that energetic opposition has been
worn down by the fatigue of an endless war.

Theory of
æsthetic
criticism.

V. The relativity of taste is a sensationalistic theory
which denies a spiritual value to art. But it is rarely
maintained by writers in the ingenuous categorical garb
of the old adage : *De gustibus non est disputandum* (concerning which it would be useful to enquire when the
saying was born, and what it first meant : whether, too,
the word *gustibus* referred solely to impressions of the
palate, and was only later extended to include æsthetic
impressions) ; as though sensationalists, as if dimly conscious of the higher nature of art, have never been able
to resign themselves to the complete relativity of taste.
Their torments in the matter really move one to pity.
" Is there," Batteux asks, " such a thing as good taste,
and is it the only good taste ?   In what does it consist ?
Upon what depend ?   Does it depend upon the object
itself or the genius at work upon it ?   Are there, or are
there not, rules ?   Is wit alone, or heart alone, the organ
of taste, or both together ?   How many questions have
been raised on this familiar often-treated subject, how
many obscure and involved answers have been given ! "[2]
This perplexity is shared by Home. Tastes, he says,
must not be disputed ; neither those of the palate nor
those of other senses. A remark which seems highly
reasonable from one point of view ; but, from another,
somewhat exaggerated. But yet how can one dispute it ?
how can one maintain that what actually pleases a man
ought not to please him ?   The proposition then must
be true. But now no man of taste will assent to it.

[1] Pott, introd. to Humboldt, *cit.*   Paul, *Principien d. Sprach-*
geschichte, ch. 20.   [2] Batteux, *Les Beaux Arts*, part ii. p. 54.

We speak of good taste and bad taste ; are all criticisms which turn upon this distinction to be considered absurd ? have these everyday expressions no meaning ? Home ends by asserting a common standard of taste, deduced from the necessity of a common life for mankind or, as he says, from a " final cause " ; for without uniformity of taste, who would trouble to produce works of art, build elegant and costly edifices, or lay out beautiful gardens and so forth ? He does not fail to draw attention to a second final cause ; that of the advisability of attracting citizens to public shows and uniting those whom class-differences and diversity of occupation tend to keep apart. But how shall a standard of taste be established ? This is a new perplexity, which one cannot think to be escaped by observing that, as in framing moral rules we seek the counsel of the most honourable of educated men, not of savages ; so to determine the standard of taste we should have recourse to the few who are not worn out by degrading bodily labour, not corrupted in taste, and not rendered effeminate by pleasure, who have received the gift of good taste from nature, and have brought it to perfection by the education and practice of a lifetime : if, notwithstanding, controversies arise, then reference must be made to the principles of Criticism as set forth by Home himself in his own book.[1] Similar contradictions and vicious circles reappear in David Hume's *Essay on Taste*, where Hume tries in vain to define the distinctive characteristics of the man of taste whose judgement must be law, and, while asserting the uniformity of the general principles of taste as founded in human nature, and warning the reader against giving undue weight to individual perversions and ignorances, at the same time asserts that divergences in taste may be irreconcilable, insuperable, and yet blameless.[2]

But a criticism of æsthetic relativism cannot be based upon the opposite doctrine which, by its affirmation of

[1] *Elem. of Criticism*, iii. ch. 25.
[2] *Essays, Moral, Political and Literary* (London ed., 1862), ch. 23 : *On the Standard of Taste*.

absoluteness, resolves taste into concepts and logical inferences. The eighteenth century offers examples of this mistake in Muratori, one of the first to maintain the existence of a rule of taste and a universal beauty whose rules are furnished by Poetics ;[1] in André, who said that " the beauty in a work of art is not that which pleases at the first glance of fancy through certain individual dispositions of the mental faculties or bodily organs, but that which has a right to please the reason and reflexion by its own inherent excellence or rightness and, if the expression be allowed, by its intrinsic agreeableness " ;[2] in Voltaire, who recognized a " universal taste " which was " intellectual " ;[3] and in very many others. This intellectualistic error, no less than the sensationalistic, was attacked by Kant ; but even Kant, by making beauty consist in a symbolism of morality, failed to grasp the concept of an imaginative absoluteness of taste.[4] Succeeding generations of philosophers met the difficulty by passing it over in silence.

Nevertheless, this criterion of an imaginative absoluteness, the idea that in order to judge works of art one must place oneself at the artist's point of view at the moment of production, and that to judge is to reproduce, gathered weight little by little from the beginning of the eighteenth century, when its first appearance is seen in the work of the Italian Francesco Montani already quoted (1705), and by the English poet Alexander Pope in his *Essay on Criticism*. (" A perfect judge will read each work of wit With the same spirit that its author writ." [5]) A few years later Antonio Conti recognized part of the truth in the *règle du premier aspect* advised by Terrasson as a test for judging poetry, while noting it to be more applicable to modern than to ancient works : " *quand on n'a pas l'esprit prévenu, et que d'ailleurs on l'a assez pénétrant, on peut voir tout d'un coup si un poète a bien imité son objet ; car, comme on connaît l'original, c'est-à-dire les hommes et les*

---

[1] *Perfetta poesia*, bk. v. ch. 5.   [2] *Essai sur le beau*, disc. 3.
[3] *Essai sur le goût, cit.*   [4] See above, pp. 280-282.
[5] *Essay on Criticism*, 1711, part ii. ll. 233-234.

mœurs de son siècle, on peut aisément lui confronter la copie, c'est-à-dire la poésie qui les imite." In judging ancient writers something more is necessary : " *cette règle du premier aspect n'est presque d'aucun usage dans l'examen de l'ancienne poésie, dont on ne peut pas juger qu'après avoir longtemps réfléchi sur la religion des anciens, sur leurs lois, leur mœurs, sur leurs manières de combattre et d'haranguer, etc. Les beautés d'un poème, indépendantes de toutes ces circonstances individuelles, sont très rares, et les grands peintres les ont toujours évitées avec soin, car ils voulaient peindre la nature et non pas leurs idées ; "* [1] the necessary criterion, therefore, is to be found in history. The end of the same century saw the concept of congenial reproduction sufficiently defined by Heydenreich : " A philosophical critic of art must himself be possessed of genius for art ; reason exacts this qualification and grants no dispensation, just as she will refuse to appoint a blind man as judge of colours. The critic must not pretend to be able to feel the attraction of beauty by means of syllogisms (*Vernunftschlüsse*) ; beauty must manifest itself to feeling with irresistible self-evidence and, attracted by its fascination, reason must find no time to linger over the why and wherefore ; the effect, with its delightful and unexpected possession and domination of the whole being, should suffocate at birth any inquiry into origins or causes. But this state of fanatical admiration cannot last long ; reason must inevitably recover consciousness of itself and direct its attention upon the state in which it was during the enjoyment of beauty and upon its present memories of that state. . . ." [2] This was the wholesomely impressionistic theory which prevailed among the Romanticists and was accepted even by De Sanctis.[3] Still there was even then no definite theory of criticism, which demanded as its condition of existence a precise concept of art and of the relations of the work of art with its historical antecedents.[4] The very possibility of

[1] Letter to Maffei, in *Prose e poesie*, ii. pp. cxx-cxxi.
[2] *System d. Ästhetik*, pref. pp. xxi-xxv.
[3] Amongst other places *Saggi critici*, pp. 355-358.
[4] See above, pp. 123-127.

æsthetic criticism was questioned in the second half of the nineteenth century, when taste was relegated to a place amongst the facts of individual caprice, and a so-called historical criticism was proclaimed the sole scientific criticism and expounded in works of irrelevant learning or buried beneath the preconceptions of positivists and materialists. Those who reacted against such externalism and materialism generally made the mistake of supporting themselves by a kind of intellectualistic dogmatism [1] or an empty æstheticism.[2]

Distinction between taste and genius.

VI. We have seen that in the seventeenth century, when the words " taste " and " genius " or " wit " were in fashion, the facts they designated were sometimes interchanged amongst themselves and came to be considered as one single fact, while sometimes each was conceived as distinct in itself, genius being the faculty of production, and taste the faculty of judgement, taste being further subdivided into the sterile and the fertile : a terminology adopted by Muratori [3] in Italy and Ulrich König [4] in Germany. Batteux said, " *le goût juge des productions du génie* " ; [5] and Kant speaks of defective works having genius without taste or taste without genius, and of others in which taste alone suffices ; [6] now we find him distinguishing the two concepts as the judging and producing faculties, now he speaks of them as a single faculty existing in various degrees. An inherent difference between taste and genius was accepted by later writers on Æsthetic and assumed its most rigid form in the hands of Herbart and his followers.

Concept of artistic and literary history.

VII. The evolutionary theory of art made its appearance towards the end of the eighteenth century. This was the time when the distinction between classical and romantic art was first made ; a classification later augmented by an introductory section on Oriental art, owing to the increase of knowledge concerning the pre-Hellenic

---

[1] *E.g.* A. Ricardou, *La Critique littéraire*, Paris, 1896.

[2] *E.g.* A. Conti, *Sul fiume del tempo*, Naples, 1907.

[3] *Perf. poesia*, bk. v. ch. 5.

[4] *Untersuchung v. d. guten Geschmack*, 1727.

[5] *Les Beaux Arts*, part ii. ch. 1.   [6] *Krit. d. Urtheilskr.* § 48.

world. Towards the end of his life Goethe told his friend Eckermann that the concepts of classical and romantic had been formed by himself and Schiller, for he himself had upheld the objective method in poetry, whilst Schiller, in order to champion the subjective form to which he inclined, had written the essay *On Naïve and Sentimental Poetry*, in which the word naïve (*naiv*) expresses the style later called classical and the word sentimental (*sentimentalisch*) that later called romantic. " The Schlegels," continues Goethe, " seized upon these ideas and disseminated them, so that to-day everyone uses them and speaks of classical and romantic, things perfectly unknown fifty years ago "[1] (Goethe was speaking in 1831). Schiller's essay bears the imprint of Rousseau's influence and is dated 1795–6.[2]   It contains such statements as this : " Poets are above all things the preservers of nature ; and when they cannot be so entirely, and have tried upon themselves the destructive force of arbitrary and artificial forms or have fought against such forms, they stand up to bear witness on her behalf. Poets, therefore, either are nature or, having lost her, seek her. Hence arise two wholly distinct kinds of poetic composition, exhausting between them the whole field of poetry ; all poets who are worthy of the name must belong, according to the times and conditions in which they flourish, either to the category of naïve or to that of sentimental poets." Schiller recognized three kinds of sentimental poetry : satirical, elegiac and idyllic ; he defined a satirical poet as one " who takes as his object the desertion of nature and the contrast of the real with the ideal." The weak point of this division is the concept of two distinct kinds of poetry, the reduction of the infinite forms in which poetry appears to individuals, to two kinds. If one of these two kinds be taken the perfect and the other as the imperfect kind, the mistake is made of converting imperfection into a kind or species, the negative into a positive.

---

[1] Eckermann, *Gespräche mit Goethe*, under date March 21, 1831.
[2] *Über naive und sentimentalische Dichtung*, 1795-1796 (in *Werke*, ed. Goedeke, vol. xii.).

Wilhelm von Humboldt pointed out to his friend that if form is the essence of art, there cannot be a kind of poetry, such as the sentimental or romantic is supposed to be, in which matter preponderates over form, for that would constitute a pseudo-art, not a separate kind of art.[1] Schiller attached no historical meaning to his classification, in fact he declared explicitly that in using the words " ancient " and " modern " as equivalent to " ingenuous " and " sentimental " he did not mean to deny that some " ancient " poets, in his sense of the word, could be found among contemporary writers ; the two characters might even be united in the same poet or the same poetical work, as (to give Schiller's own example) in *Werther*.[2] The first to assign a historical meaning to the division were Friedrich and Wilhelm von Schlegel ; the former in an early work of 1795, the latter in his celebrated lectures on literary history given at Berlin in 1801–4. But the two senses, systematic and historical, were variously alternated and mixed by literary men and critics, and other distinctions were added ; " classical " was sometimes used to describe poetry of a frigid and imitative style, while " romantic " poetry was the inspired ; in some countries the word " romantic " came to mean a political reactionary, in Italy it stood for " liberal " ; and so forth. In 1815, when Friedrich Schlegel spoke of ancient Persian romantic poems, or when in our times attention is called to the romanticism of the Greek, Latin or French classics, the historical signification is lost in the theoretical, the sense originally intended by Schiller.

But the historical sense was prevalent in German idealism, which inclined towards the construction of a universal history, including that of literature and art, upon a scheme of ideal evolution. Schelling made a sharp division between pagan and Christian art ; the second being held an advance upon the former which was the lowest step.[3] Hegel accepted this division and

---

[1] Quoted in Danzel, *Ges. Aufs.* pp. 21-22.
[2] *Ub. naive u. sentim. Dicht.*, ed. cit., p. 155, note.   [3] See above, p. 291.

introduced a final regress by dividing the history of art into three periods : symbolic (Oriental) art, classical (Hellenic) and romantic (modern). Just as he conceived Roman art (with its introduction of satire and other kinds indicative of a failure to maintain harmony between form and content) as the dissolution of classical art, a thought suggested by Schiller, so he found in the subjective humour of Cervantes and Ariosto [1] the dissolution of romantic art ; and he regarded this series as completing the possibilities of art, though some interpreters think that by a self-contradiction he admitted the possibility of a fourth period, an art of the modern or future world. Indeed amongst his disciples we find Weiss rejecting the Oriental period in order to save the triadic division, and placing as third the modern period, synthesis of the ancient and the mediæval : [2] Vischer too inclines to recognize a modern or progressive period.[3]

These arbitrary constructions reappear in the works of positivist metaphysicians in the shape of an evolutionary or progressive history of art. Spencer dreamed of writing some sort of treatise on the subject, and in the published programme of his system (1860) we read that the third volume of his *Principles of Sociology* was to contain amongst other things a chapter on æsthetic progress " with the gradual differentiation of fine arts from primitive institutions and from each other, with their increasing variety in development, their progress in reality of expression and superiority of end." No grief need be felt that the chapter was left unwritten when we remember the samples of it preserved in the *Principles of Psychology* and already reviewed in these pages.[4]

The strong historical sense of our own day is leading us further and further away from the evolutionary or abstractly progressive theories which falsify the free and original movement of art. Fiedler remarked not without justice that unity and progress cannot be introduced into

[1] *Vorles. üb. Ästh.*, vols. ii. and iii.
[2] Cf. von Hartmann, *Dtsche. Ästh. s. Kant*, pp. 99-101.
[3] *Ästh.* part iii.   [4] See above, pp. 388-390.

a history of art, and that the works of artists must be judged discretely as so many fragments of the life of the universe.[1] In recent times a remarkable student of the history of figurative art, Venturi, has tried to bring evolutionism into fashion, and has illustrated it in a *History of the Madonna,* in which the presentment of the Virgin is conceived as an organism which is born, grows, attains perfection, grows old and dies! Others have claimed for artistic history its true character, intolerant of outward curb and rule, drawing her ever-varied productions from the well-head of the infinite Spirit.[2]

Conclusion.   These hurried notes may suffice to show in how narrow a circle has hitherto moved the scientific criticism of the errors we have called " particular." Æsthetic needs to be surrounded and nourished by a watchful and vigorous critical literature drawing its life from her and forming in turn her safeguard and strength.

[1] C. Fiedler, *Ursprung d. künstl. Thätigkeit,* p. 136 *seqq.*

[2] Ad. Venturi, *La Madonna,* Milan, 1899. Cf. B. Labanca, in *Rivista polit. e lett.* (Rome), Oct. 1899, and in *Rivista di filos. e pedag.* (Bologna), 1900 ; and B. Croce, in *Nap. nobiliss., Rivista di topografia e storia dell' arte,* viii. pp. 161-163, ix. pp. 13-14 (reprinted in *Probl. di estetica,* pp. 265-272). On the theory of method in artistic and literary history cf. above, pp. 128-139.

BIBLIOGRAPHICAL APPENDIX

THE first attempt at a history of Æsthetic is the work of J. Koller (see above, p. 248) mentioned by Zimmermann (*Gesch. d. Ästh.* pref., p. v) as being so exceedingly rare that he had never been able to see a copy of the book. We ourselves have had the good fortune to find the book in the Royal Library of Munich in Bavaria, by the help of our friend Dr. Arturo Farinelli of Innsbruck University, and to obtain the loan of it. It bears the title *Entwurf | zur | Geschichte und Literatur | der Aesthetik, | von Baumgarten auf die | neueste Zeit.* | Herausgegeben | von | J. Koller. | Regensburg | in der Montag und Weissischen Buchhandlung | 1799 (pp. viii-107, small 8vo) ; in the preface the author declares his intention of supplying young men attending Lectures on the Criticism of Taste and the Theory of the Fine Arts in the German Universities with a " lucid summary of the origin and later progress of these studies," premising that he will treat of general theories only and that his judgements are frequently derived from reviews in literary periodicals. The introduction (§§ 1-7) treats of æsthetic theories from antiquity down to the beginning of the eighteenth century ; Koller observes that " the names and form of a general Theory of Fine Art and Criticism of Taste were unknown to the ancients, whose imperfect ethical theory prevented their producing anything in this field." He dedicates § 5 to the Italians, " who have produced little in theory " ; indeed the only Italian books mentioned are the *Entusiasmo* of Bettinelli and the small work of Jagemann, *Saggio di buon gusto nelle belle arti ove si spiegano gli elementi dell' estetica*, di Fr. Gaud. Jagemann, Regente agostiniano, In Firenze, MDCCLXXI, Presso Luigi Bastianelli e compagni ; 60 pp. (concerning this, see B. Croce, *Problemi di estetica*, pp. 387-390). The section on the History and Literature of Æsthetic begins with the oft-quoted passage from Bülffinger (" *Vellem existerent*, etc.") and passes at once to Baumgarten : " the theoretical epoch owes its existence undeniably to Baumgarten ; to him belongs the inalienable merit of having first conceived an Æsthetic founded on principles of reason and wholly developed, and of having tried to put it into practice by the means offered him by his own philosophy." Immediately after this, Meier is mentioned, followed by the titles, accompanied by brief extracts and remarks—a sort of *catalogue raisonné*—of many German books on Æsthetic from those of K. W. Müller (1759) to one by Ramler (1799), mixed with various French and English writings under the dates of their German translations. Special emphasis is laid on Kant (pp. 64-74), with the remark that, prior to the appearance of the *Critique of Judgment*, æstheticians were divided into sceptics, dogmatics and empiricists : the most powerful intellects of the nation inclined towards empiricism, so much so that had Kant himself " been asked by what literature he had been most strongly influenced in the development of his own thought, he would certainly have named the acute empirical writers of England, France and Germany " ; but " by no pre-Kantian method had it been possible to establish an agreement (*eine Einhelligkeit*) between men upon matters of taste." The last pages call attention to the revival of interest in æsthetic studies, which nobody would now dare call a waste of time as in former days. " May Jacobi, Schiller and Mehmel soon enrich literature by publication of their theories ! " (p. 104).

The rarity of Koller's book has led us to notice it at some length. Apart from this the first general history of Æsthetic worthy the name is that written by Robert Zimmermann, *Geschichte der Ästhetik als philosophischer Wissenschaft*, Vienna, 1858. It is divided into four books : " the first of these contains the history of philosophical concepts concerning the beautiful and art from the Greeks down to the constitution of Æsthetic as a philosophical science through the labours of Baumgarten " ; the second runs from Baumgarten down to the reform of Æsthetic brought about by the *Critique of Judgment* ; the third, from Kant to the Æsthetic of idealism ; the fourth, from the beginnings of idealistic Æsthetic down to the author's own day (1798-1858). The work is on Herbartian lines, and is remarkable for solid research and lucid exposition, although the erroneous point of view and neglect of all æsthetic movement other than Græco-Roman or German are grave defects ; besides, it is now sixty years out of date.

Less solid and more compilatory in nature, whilst retaining all the defects of the foregoing, is the history by Max Schasler, *Kritische Geschichte der Ästhetik*, Berlin, 1872, divided into three books treating of ancient Æsthetic and that of the eighteenth and nineteenth centuries. The author belongs to the Hegelian school and conceives his history as a propædeutic to theory, " in order, that is, to attain a supreme principle for the construction of a new system " ; he schematizes the material of facts for each period into three grades of Æsthetic of sensation (*Empfindungsurtheil*), of intellect (*Verstandsurtheil*) and of reason (*Vernunfturtheil*).

English literature has Bernard Bosanquet's *History of Æsthetics*, London, 1892 ; a sober and well-arranged work, written from an eclectic point of view between the Æsthetic of content and the Æsthetic of form. The author, however, is wrong in believing he has passed over " no writer of the first rank " ; he has passed over not only writers but some important movements of ideas, and in general he shows insufficient knowledge of the literature of the Latin races. Another general history of Æsthetic in English is the first volume of *The Philosophy of the Beautiful, being Outlines of the History of Æsthetics*, by William Knight, London, Murray, 1895 : it consists mainly of a rich collection of extracts and abridgements of ancient and modern books treating of Æsthetic. In this respect the most noteworthy chapters are those on Holland, Great Britain and America (10-13) ; the second volume, published in 1898, has in an appendix, pp. 251-281, notices upon Æsthetic in Russia and Denmark. Another recent publication is George Saintsbury's *A History of Criticism and Literary Taste in Europe from the Earliest Times to the Present Day* ; vol. i., Edinburgh and London, 1900, concerning classical and mediæval criticism ; vol. ii., 1902, criticism from the Renaissance to end of the eighteenth century : vol. iii., 1904, modern criticism. The writer of this History, equally skilled in literature and innocent of philosophy, has thought it possible to exclude æsthetic science in the strict sense, " the more transcendental Æsthetic, those ambitious theories of Beauty and artistic pleasure in general which seem so noble and fascinating until we discover them to be but cloud-appearances of Juno," and to limit his treatise to " lofty Rhetoric and Poetic, to the theory and practice of Criticism and literary taste " (book i. ch. 1). Thus is produced a book instructive in many ways but wholly deficient in method and definite object. What is lofty Rhetoric and Poetic, the theory of Criticism and literary taste, if not Æsthetic pure and simple ? how can the history of these be composed without due notice of metaphysical Æsthetic and other manifestations whose interaction and development are the fabric of history itself ? Perhaps Saintsbury hoped to be able to write a History of Criticism as distinct from that of Æsthetic ; if that be the case, he has been unsuccessful in writing either one or the other. Cf. *La Critica*, ii. (1904), pp. 59-63.

The generosity of the Hungarian Academy of Science has enabled us to handle the History of Æsthetic (*Az Æsthetika története*) of Bela Janosi, Budapesth, 1899–1901, in three volumes ; the first volume treats the Æsthetic of Greece ; the second, of Æsthetic from the Middle Ages to Baumgarten ; the third, from Baumgarten to the present day. For us it is a book sealed with seven seals, save for reviews which have appeared in the *Deutsche Litteraturzeitung* of Berlin, August 25, 1900, July 12, 1902, and May 2, 1903.

Amongst Latin countries, France has no special history of Æsthetic, for this title cannot be given to the portion of the second volume (pp. 311-570) of the work by Ch. Levêque, *La Science du beau* (Paris, 1862), under the heading *Examen des principaux systèmes d'esthétique anciens et modernes*, where eight chapters are devoted to an exposition of the theories of Plato, Aristotle, Plotinus and St. Augustine, Hutcheson, André and Baumgarten, Reid, Kant, Schelling and Hegel. Spain, on the other hand, possesses the work of Marcelino Menendez y Pelayo, *Historia de las idéas estéticas en España*, 2nd ed., Madrid, 1890–1901 (5 vols., variously distributed amongst the 1st ed., 1883–1891, and the 2nd), which is not restricted, as the title suggests, to Spain alone or to Æsthetic alone but, as the author observes in his preface (i. pp. xx-xxi), includes the metaphysical disquisitions on the beautiful, the speculations of mystics on the beauty of God and on love ; the theories of art scattered through the pages of philosophers ; the æsthetic considerations found in treatises upon individual arts (Poetics and Rhetoric, works on painting, architecture, etc.) ; and, finally, ideas enunciated by artists concerning their own particular arts. This work is of capital importance on everything to do with Spanish authors, and also in its general part contains good treatments of matters generally passed over by historians. Menendez y Pelayo inclines to metaphysical idealism, yet seems not disinclined to welcome elements from other systems, even empirical theories : in our opinion this vagueness has an unfortunate effect on the work as a whole. Some years ago Professor V. Spinazzola announced the forthcoming publication of a course of lectures given by Francesco de Sanctis in Naples in 1845 on *Storia della critica da Aristotele ad Hegel*. For the history of Æsthetic in Italy cf. Alfredo Rolla, *Storia delle idee estetiche in Italia*, Turin, 1904 ; on which see Croce, *Problemi di estetica*, pp. 401-415.

We need take no notice of the historical remarks or chapters that generally stand at the beginning of treatises on Æsthetic ; the most important occur in the volumes of Solger, Hegel and Schleiermacher. A general history of Æsthetic, from the rigorous point of view of the principle of Expression, has not been attempted before the present work.

For the bibliography down to the end of the eighteenth century, Sulzer's *Allgemeine Theorie der schönen Künste*, 2nd ed., with additions by von Blankenburg, Leipzig, 1792, in four volumes, is practically complete and is an inexhaustible mine of information. For the nineteenth century much material is collected by C. Mills Gayley and Fred Newton Scott in *An Introduction to the Methods and Materials of Literary Criticism. The Bases in Æsthetics and Poetics*, Boston, 1899. Besides Sulzer, we may mention æsthetic dictionaries by Gruber, *Wörterbuch z. Behuf d. Ästh. d. schönen Künste*, Weimar, 1810 : Jeithles, *Ästhetisches Lexikon*, vol. i. A-K, Vienna, 1835 : Hebenstreit, *Encyklopädie d. Ästhetik*, 2nd ed., Vienna, 1848.

The following notes contain for the convenience of the student several books which the author has not been able to see.

I. Concerning ancient Æsthetic no better or more comprehensive work can be found than the *Geschichte der Theorie der Kunst bei den Alten*, by Ed. Müller, Breslau, 1831–1837, 2 vols. For inquiries concerning the Beautiful special reference should be made to Julius Walter, *Die Geschichte der Ästhetik im Alterthum ihren begrifflichen Entwicklung nach*, Leipzig, 1893. See also Em. Egger, *Essai sur l'histoire de la critique chez les Grecs*, 2nd ed., Paris, 1886 : Zimmermann, Bk. I. : Bosanquet, ch. ii.-v. and Saintsbury, vol. i.

Of the innumerable special monographs : for Plato's Æsthetic see Arn. Ruge, *Die platonische Ästhetik*, Halle, 1832 : for Aristotle's, Döring, *Die Kunstlehre des Aristoteles*, Jena, 1876 : C. Bénard, *L'Esthétique d'Aristote et de ses successeurs*, Paris, 1890 : S. H. Butcher, *Aristotle's Theory of Poetry and Fine Art*, 3rd ed., London, 1902. For Plotinus, E. Vacherot, *Histoire critique de l'école d'Alexandrie*, Paris, 1846 : E. Brenning, *Die Lehre vom Schönen bei Plotin im Zusammenhang seines Systems dargestellt*, Göttingen, 1864. On the *Ars Poetica* of Horace, A. Viola, *L' arte poetica di Orazio nella critica italiana e straniera*, 2 vols. Naples, 1901–1907.

For the history of ancient Psychology see H. Siebeck, *Geschichte der Psychologie*, 1880 : A. E. Chaignet, *Histoire de la psychologie des Grecs*, Paris, 1887 : L. Ambrosi, *La psicologia dell' immaginazione nella storia della filosofia*, Rome, 1898. For the history of the philosophy of language see H. Steinthal, *Geschichte der Sprachwissenschaft bei den Griechen und Römern mit besonderer Rücksicht auf die Logik*, 2nd ed. Berlin, 1890–1891, 2 vols.

II. For the æsthetic ideas of St. Augustine and early Christian authors see Menendez y Pelayo, *op. cit.* pp. 193-266. For Thomas Aquinas, L. Taparelli, *Delle ragioni del bello secondo la dottrina di san Tommaso d' Aquino* (in *Civiltà cattolica* for 1859–1860) : P. Vallet, *L'Idée du beau dans la philosophie de St. Thomas d'Aquin*, 1883 : M. de Wulf, *Études historiques sur l'esthétique de St. Thomas*, Louvain, 1896.

For the literary doctrines of the Middle Ages see D. Comparetti, *Virgilio nel medio evo*, 2nd ed. Florence, 1893, vol. i., and G. Saintsbury, *op. cit.*, vol. i. pp. 369-486. For the early Renaissance see K. Vossler, *Poetische Theorien in d. italien. Frührenaissance*, Berlin, 1900. For the Poetics of the high Renaissance see J. E. Spingarn, *History of Literary Criticism in the Renaissance, with special reference to the influence of Italy*, New York, 1899 (Italian trans. with corrections and additions, Bari, 1905). See also F. de Sanctis, *Storia della letteratura italiana*, Naples, 1870, *passim*.

For the traditions of Platonic and neo-Platonic ideas in the

Middle Ages and Renaissance, for best and fullest information see
Menendez y Pelayo, *op. cit.*, vol. i. part ii. and vol. ii. For Italian
treatises on beauty and love see Michele Rosi, *Saggi sui trattati
d' amore del cinquecento*, Recanati, 1899, and F. Flamini, *Il
cinquecento*, Milan, Vallardi, N.D., ch. iv. pp. 378-381. For Tasso
see Alfredo Giannini, *Il " Minturno " di T. Tasso*, Ariano, 1899 :
see also E. Proto in *Rass. crit. lett. ital.* vi. (Naples, 1901) pp.
127-145. For Leone Ebreo see Edm. Solmi, *Benedetto Spinoza
e L. E., studio su una fonte italiana dimenticata dello spinozismo*,
Modena, 1903 : cf. G. Gentile in *Critica*, ii. pp. 313-319.

On J. C. Scaliger see Eug. Lintilhac, *Un Coup d'État dans la
république des lettres : Jules César Scaliger, fondateur du classi-
cisme cent ans avant Boileau* (in the *Nouv. Revue*, 1890, vol. lxiv.
pp. 333-346, 528-547). On Fracastoro, Giuseppe Rossi, *Girolamo
Fracastoro in relazione all' aristotelismo e alla scienza nel Rinasci-
mento*, Pisa, 1893. On Castelvetro, Ant. Fusco, *La poetica di
Ludovico Castelvetro*, Naples, 1904. On Patrizzi, Oddone Zenatti,
Fr. Patrizzi, Orazio Ariosto, e Torquato Tasso, etc. (Verona, per
le nozze Morpurgo-Franchetti, N.D.).

III. For this period of ferment see H. von Stein, *Die Entstehung
der neueren Ästhetik*, Stuttgart, 1886 : K. Borinski, *Die Poetik der
Renaissance und die Anfänge der litterarischen Kritik in Deutschland*, Berlin, 1886 (esp. the last chapter) : also same author's
Baltasar Gracian und die Hofliteratur in Deutschland, Halle a. S.,
1894 : B. Croce, *I trattatisti italiani del Concettismo e B. Gracian*,
Naples, 1899 (in *Atti dell' Acc. Pont.* vol. xxix., reprinted in
Problemi di estetica, pp. 309-345) : *Elizabethan Critical Essays*,
edited with an introduction by G. Gregory Smith, Oxford, 1904,
2 vols. : *Critical Essays of the Seventeenth Century*, edited by J. E.
Spingarn, Oxford, 1908, 2 vols. : Leone Donati, *J. J. Bodmer und
die italienische Litteratur* (in the vol. *J. J. Bodmer, Denkschrift z.
C. C. Geburtstag*, Zürich, 1900, pp. 241-312) : see also *Probl. di
estetica*, pp. 371-380.

On Bacon see K. Fischer, *Franz Baco von Verulam*, Leipzig,
1856 (2nd ed. 1875), cf. P. Jacquinet, *Fr. Baconis in re litteraria
iudicia*, Paris, 1863. On Gravina, Em. Reich, *G. V. Gravina als
Ästhetiker* (in the Trans. of the Viennese Academy, vol. cxx.
1890) : B. Croce, *Di alcuni giudizî sul Gravina considerato come
estetico*, Florence, 1901 (in *Miscellanea d' Ancona*, pp. 456-464),
reprinted in *Probl. di est.* pp. 360-370. On Du Bos, Morel, *Étude
sur l'abbé du Bos*, Paris, 1849 : P. Petent, *J. B. Dubos*, Tramelan,
1902. On Bouhours, Doncieux, *Un jésuite homme de lettres au
XVIIᵉ siècle*, Paris, 1886. On the Bouhours-Orsi controversy,
F. Fottano, *Una polemica nel settecento*, in *Ricerche letterarie*,
Leghorn, 1897, pp. 313-332 : A. Boeri, *Una contesa letteraria
franco-italiana nel secolo XVIII*, Palermo, 1900 (cf. *Giorn.
stor. lett. ital.* xxxvi. pp. 255-256) : B. Croce, *Varietà di storia*

dell' estetica, §§ 1-2, in *Rass. crit. lett. ital.* cit., vi. 1901, pp. 115-126, reprinted in *Probl. di est.* pp. 346-359.

IV. On Cartesianism in literature see É. Krantz, *L'Esthétique de Descartes étudiée dans les rapports de la doctrine cartésienne avec la littérature classique française au XVIIIe siècle*, Paris, 1882; see also the chapter on André, pp. 311-341, and the introduction by V. Cousin to the *Œuvres philosophiques du p. André*, Paris, 1843: on Boileau, Borinski, *Poetik d. Renaissance*, c. 6, pp. 314-329: J. Brunetière, *L'Esthétique de B.* in *Revue des Deux Mondes*, June 1, 1899.

On the English intellectualist æstheticians see Zimmermann, *op. cit.* pp. 273-301; also von Stein, *op. cit.* pp. 185-216. On Shaftesbury and Hutcheson see esp. Gid. Spicker, *Die Philosophie d. Grafen v. Shaftesbury*, Freiburg i. B., 1872, part iv. on art and literature, pp. 196-233: T. Fowler, *S. and Hutcheson*, London, 1882: William Robert Scott, *Francis Hutcheson, his life, teaching and position in the history of philosophy*, Cambridge, 1900.

On Leibniz, Baumgarten and contemporary German writers see Th. W. Danzel, *Gottsched und seine Zeit*, 2nd ed., Leipzig, 1855: H. G. Meyer, *Leibnitz und Baumgarten als Begründer der deutschen Ästhetik*, Inaugural Dissertation, Halle, 1874: Joh. Schmidt, *L. und B.*, Halle, 1875: Ém. Grucker, *Histoire des doctrines littéraires et esthétiques en Allemagne* (from Opitz to the Swiss writers), Paris, 1883: Fr. Braitmaier, *Geschichte der poetischen Theorie und Kritik von den Diskursen der Maler bis auf Lessing*, Frauenfeld, 1888-1889. In the last-named book the first part treats of the beginning of Poetics and criticism in Germany, considered in their relation to the doctrines of classical, French and English writers: the second part treats of an attempt to found an æsthetic philosophy and theory of poetry upon a basis of Leibnitian-Wolffian psychology: which includes a long discussion of Baumgarten and quotations from two dissertations, Raabe's *A. G. Baumgarten, Aestheticae in disciplinae formam parens et auctor*, and Prieger's *Anregung u. metaphysische Grundlage d. Ästh. von A. G. Baumgarten*, 1875 (cf. vol. ii. p. 2).

V. On Vico as æsthetician see B. Zumbini, *Sopra alcuni principî di critica letteraria di G. B. V.* (reprinted in *Studî di letter. italiana*, Florence, 1894, pp. 257-268): B. Croce, *G. B. V. primo scopritore della scienza estetica*, Naples, 1901 (reprinted from *Flegrea*, April 1901), incorporated in the present volume as has been mentioned already: see also G. Gentile in *Rass. crit. della lett. ital.*, cit., vi. pp. 254-265: E. Bertana, in *Giorn. stor. lett. ital.* xxxviii. pp. 449-451: A. Martinazzoli, *Intorno alle dottrine vichiane di ragion poetica*, in *Riv. di filos. e sc. aff.* of Bologna, July 1902: also the reply of B. Croce, *ibid.*, August 1902: Giovanni Rossi, *Il pensiero di G. B. V. intorno alla natura della lingua e all' ufficio delle lettere*, Salerno, 1901. The important

position occupied by Vico in respect to Æsthetic had been remarked earlier by C. Marini, *G. B. V. al cospetto del secolo XIX*,
Naples, 1852, c. 7, § 10. For the influence exercised by Vico, B.
Croce, *Per la storia della critica e storiografia letteraria*, Naples,
1903 (in *Atti d. Acc. Pont.*, vol. xxxiii.), pp. 7-8, 26-28 (reprinted
in *Probl. di est.* pp. 423-425), and G. A. Borgese, *Storia della
critica romantica in Italia*, Naples, 1905, *passim*.

On Vico's thought in general, as well as on his Æsthetic, see
B. Croce, *La filosofia di Giambattista Vico*, Bari, 1911 : English
translation by R. G. Collingwood, 1913. The copious literature
concerning Vico is given by B. Croce in *Bibliografia vichiana*,
Naples, 1904 (reprinted from *Atti dell' Acad. Pont.* vol. xxxiv.),
and *Supplemento, ibid.* 1907, and *Secondo Supplemento*, 1910
(*Atti* cit., vols. xxxvii. and xli.).

VI. On the literary doctrines of Conti see G. Brognoligo,
L' opera letteraria di A. Conti, in *Arch. veneto*, 1894, vol. i. pp.
152-209 : on Cesarotti, Vitt. Alemanni, *Un filosofo delle lettere*,
vol. i. Turin, 1894 : on Pagano, B. Croce, *Varietà di storia del-
l' estetica*, § 3 ; *Di alcuni estetici italiani della seconda metà del
secolo XVIII*, in *Rass. crit.* cit. vii. 1902, pp. 1-17 (reprinted in
Probl. di est. pp. 381-450).

On the German æstheticians, in addition to the various general
histories already quoted, see R. Sommer, *Grundzüge einer Geschichte der deutschen Psychologie u. Asthetik von Wolff-Baumgarten
bis Kant-Schiller*, Würzburg, 1892. Greatly inferior is M. Dessoir,
Geschichte d. neueren deutschen Psychologie, 2nd ed., Berlin, 1897
(the first half only is published, down to Kant exclusive).

On Sulzer, Braitmaier, *op. cit.* ii. pp. 55-71 : on Mendelssohn,
ibid. pp. 72-279 : for Elias Schlegel, *op. cit.* i. p. 249 *seqq.* : on
Mendelssohn see also Th. Wilh. Danzel, *Gesammelte Aufsätze*,
Leipzig, Jahn, 1855, pp. 85-98 : Kannegiesser, *Stellung Men-
delssohns in d. Gesch. d. Asth.*, 1868. On Riedel, K. F. Wize,
F. J. Riedel u. seine Ästhetik, Diss., Berlin, 1907. On Herder,
Ch. Joret, *H. et la renaissance littéraire en Allemagne au XVIIIe
siècle*, Paris, 1875 : R. Haym, *H. nach seinem Leben u. seinen
Werken*, 2 vols., Berlin, 1880 : G. Jacobi, *H.'s und Kant's Asth.*,
Leipzig, 1907. For the ideas of Hamann and Herder concerning
the origins of poetry see Croce in *Critica*, ix. (1911), pp. 469-472.
On the history of Linguistic, see Th. Benfey, *Geschichte d. Sprach-
wissenschaft in Deutschland*, Munich, 1869, introd. : H. Steinthal,
*Der Ursprung der Sprache im Zusammenhange mit d. letzen Fragen
alles Wissens, eine Darstellung, Kritik und Fortentwicklung der
vorzüglichsten Ansichten*, 4th ed., Berlin, 1888.

VII. On Batteux see E. v. Danckelmann, *Charles Batteux,
sein Leben u. sein ästhetisches Lehrgebäude*, Rostock, 1902. On
Hogarth, Burke and Home, Zimmermann, *op. cit.* pp. 223-273 ;
Bosanquet, *op. cit.* pp. 202-210. On Home esp. J. Wohlgemuth,

H. Home's Ästhetik, Rostock, 1894 : W. Neumann, *Die Bedeutung Homes für d. Ästhetik, u. sein Einfluss auf d. deutschen Ästhetik*, Halle, 1894. On Hemsterhuis, Ém. Grucker, *François H., sa vie et ses œuvres*, Paris, 1866.

On Winckelmann, Goethe, *W. u. sein Jahrhundert*, 1805 (in *Werke*, ed. Goedeke, vol. xxxi.) : C. Justi, *W. u. seine Zeitgenossen*, 2nd ed., Leipzig, 1898. A criticism of Winckelmann's theory, by H. Hettner, appeared in the *Revue Moderne*, 1866. On Mengs, Zimmermann, *op. cit.* pp. 338-355. On Lessing, Th. Wilh. Danzel, *G. E. Lessing, sein Leben und seine Werke*, Leipzig, 1849–1853 : Kuno Fischer, *L. als Reformator d. deutschen Litteratur*, Stuttgart, 1881 : Ém. Grucker, *Lessing*, Paris, 1891 : Erich Schmidt, *Lessing*, 2nd ed., Berlin, 1899 : K. Borinski, *Lessing*, Berlin, 1900.

On Spalletti see B. Croce, *Var.*, cit., § 3 (*Probl. d. est.* pp. 392-398). On Meier, Hirth and Goethe, Danzel, *Goethe und die Weimarsche Kunstfreunde in ihrem Verhältniss z. Winckelmann*, in *Gesamm. Aufs.* pp. 118-145. On Goethe's Æsthetic esp. see Wilh. Bode, *Goethes Ästhetik*, Berlin, 1901.

VIII. Critical expositions of Kant's Æsthetic are very numerous even in Italy : for example, O. Colecchi, *Questioni filosofiche*, Naples, 1843, vol. iii.: C. Cantoni, *E. Kant*, Milan, 1884, vol. iii. In German, esp. H. Cohen, *Kants Begründung der Ästhetik*, Berlin, 1889 : also an important chapter in Sommer, *op. cit.* pp. 337-352 ; a sufficient representative of a host of others is the elaborate work of Victor Basch, *Essai critique sur l'esthétique de Kant*, Paris, 1896. See also, on an Italian trans. of the *Kr. d. Urth.*, B. Croce in *Critica*, v. (1907), pp. 160-164.

For Kant's lectures and the historical antecedents of his *Critique of Judgment* (besides the dissertations of H. Falkenheim, *Die Entstehung der kantischen Ästhetik*, Heidelberg, 1890, and Rich. Grundmann, *Die Entwickel d. Ästh. Kants*, Leipzig, 1893) see the exhaustive work of Otto Schlapp, *Kant's Lehre vom Genie und die Entstehung d. Kritik d. Urtheilskraft*, Göttingen, 1901.

IX. For the whole of this period, beside the general histories already quoted which treat of it in great detail, see Th. Wilh. Danzel, *Über den gegenwärtigen Zustand d. Philosophie d. Kunst u. ihre nächste Aufgabe* (in the *Zeitschr. f. Phil.* of Fichte, 1844–1845, and reprinted in *Gesammelte Aufsätze*, pp. 1-84) : this treats of Kant, Schiller, Fichte, Schelling, Hegel and, more particularly, of Solger, pp. 51-84 : Herm. Lotze, *Geschichte der Ästhetik in Deutschland*, Munich, 1868 (in the coll. " History of the Sciences in Germany," published by the Royal Academy of Sciences of Munich in Bavaria) : first book, history of general points of view from Baumgarten to the Herbartian school : second book, history of individual fundamental æsthetic concepts : third book, contributions to the history of the theory of the arts : Ed. v.

484 ÆSTHETIC

Hartmann, *Die deutsche Ästhetik s. Kant* (first part, historico-critical), Berlin, 1886, divided into two books. The first book discusses the doctrine of the chief æstheticians and, after an introduction on the foundation of philosophical æsthetic by Kant, treats of the Æsthetic of the content, divided into that of abstract idealism (Schelling, Schopenhauer, Solger, Krause, Weisse, Lotze) ; of concrete idealism (Hegel, Trahndorff, Schleiermacher, Deutinger, Oersted, Vischer, Zeising, Carrière, Schasler) ; of the Æsthetic of feeling (Kirchmann, Wiener, Horwicz) ; the Æsthetic of form, subdivided into abstract formalism (Herbart, Zimmermann), and concrete formalism (Köstlin, Siebeck). The second book is concerned with the more important special problems.

On the Æsthetic of Schiller specially see, amongst numerous monographs, Danzel, *Schillers Briefwechsel mit Körner*, in *Ges. Aufs.* pp. 227-244 : G. Zimmermann, *Versuch einer schillerschen Ästhetik*, Leipzig, 1889 : F. Montargis, *L'Esthétique de Schiller*, Paris, 1890 : the chapter in Sommer, *op. cit.* pp. 365-432 : V. Basch, *La Poétique de Schiller*, Paris, 1901.

On the Æsthetic of Romanticism, R. Haym, *Die romantische Schule : ein Beitrag z. Geschichte d. deutschen Geistes*, Berlin, 1870 (cf. on Tieck, book i. ; on Novalis, book iii. : for criticism of the two Schlegels, bk. ii. and bk. iii. ch. 5) : N. M. Pichtos, *Die Ästhetik Aug. W. v. Schlegel in ihrer geschichtlichen Entwickelung*, Berlin, 1893. On the Æsthetic of Fichte, G. Tempel, *Fichtes Stellung z. Kunst*, Metz, 1901.

On the Æsthetic of Hegel, Danzel, *Über d. Ästhetik der hegelschen Philosophie*, Hamburg, 1844 : R. Haym, *Hegel u. seine Zeit*, Berlin, 1857, pp. 433-443 : J. S. Kedney, *Hegel's Æsthetics : a critical exposition*, Chicago, 1885 : Kuno Fischer, *Hegels Leben u. Werke*, Heidelberg, 1898-1901, chs. 38-42, pp. 811-947 : J. Kohn, *Hegels Ästhetik* in *Zeitschrift für Philosophie*, 1902, vol. 120, fasc. ii. : see also B. Croce, *Ciò che è vivo e ciò che è morto della filosofia di Hegel*, Bari, 1907, ch. 6; Engl. tr. by D. Ainslie, 1915.

X. For the Æsthetic of Schopenhauer, Fr. Sommerlad, *Darstellung u. Kritik d. ästh. Grundanschauungen Schopenhauers*, Diss., Giessen, 1895 : Ed. v. Mayer, *Schopenhauers Ästhetik u. ihr Verhältniss z. d. ästh. Lehren Kants u. Schellings*, Halle, 1897: Ett. Zoccoli, *L' estetica di A. Sch. : propedeutica all' estetica Wagneriana*, Milan, 1901 : G. Chialvo, *L' estetica di A. Sch., saggio esplicativo-critico*, Rome, 1905.

For the Æsthetic of Herbart, beside Zimmermann, *op. cit.* pp. 754-804, see O. Hostinsky, *Herbarts Ästhetik in ihrer grundlegenden Theilen quellenmässig dargestellt u. erläutert*, Hamburg-Leipzig, 1891.

XI. Of the Æsthetic of Schleiermacher, the fullest treatment is given by Zimmermann, pp. 609-634, and von Hartmann, pp. 156-169.

XII. For the history of the theory of Language, beside Benfey, *op. cit.* introd., see Max. Leop. Loewe, *Historiae criticae grammatices universalis seu philosophicae lineamenta*, Dresden, 1839 : A. F. Pott, *W. v. Humboldt und die Sprachwissenschaft*, introd. to the reprint of Humboldt's *Verschiedenheit d. menschl. Sprachbaues* (2nd ed., Berlin, 1880, vol. i.).

On Humboldt see esp. Steinthal, *Der Ursprung der Sprache*, pp. 59-81, and Pott's introd. cit., *Wilh. v. Humboldt u. die Sprachwissenschaft*.

XIII. For this period, treated with unnecessary fulness, see von Hartmann, *op. cit.* bk. i. : more concisely by Menendez y Pelayo, vol. iv. (1st ed.), part i. chs. 6-8.

For the doctrine of the modifications of beauty see Zimmermann, *op. cit.* pp. 715-744 : Schasler, *op. cit.* §§ 517-546 : Bosanquet, *op. cit.* ch. 14, pp. 393-440 : in greater detail, v. Hartmann, bk. ii. part i. pp. 363-461.

For the history of the Sublime see also F. Unruh, *Der Begriff des Erhabenen seit Kant*, Königsberg, 1898. For Humour see B. Croce, *Dei varî significanti della parola umorismo e del suo uso nella critica letteraria*, in the *Journal of Comparative Literature* of New York, 1903, fasc. iii. (reprinted in *Probl. di est.* pp. 275-286) : F. Baldensperger, *Les Définitions de l'humour*, in *Études d'hist. litt.* Paris, 1907. For the history of the concept of the Graceful, F. Torraca, *La grazia secondo il Castiglione e secondo lo Spencer* (in Morandi, *Antol. della critica lett. ital.* 2nd ed., Città di Castello, 1885, pp. 440-444) : F. Braitmaier, *op. cit.* ii. pp. 166-167.

XIV. For the history of Æsthetic in France during the nineteenth century there is nothing so good as Menendez y Pelayo, vol. iii. part ii. chs. 3-9 ; *ibid.* chs. 1-2 give full information concerning Æsthetic in England.

For Æsthetic in Italy in the first half of the nineteenth century, Karl Werner, *Idealistische Theorien des Schönen in d. italienischen Philosophie des neunzehnten Jahrhunderts*, Vienna, 1884 (from Trans. of the Imperial and Royal Viennese Academy). On Rosmini see esp. P. Bellezza, *Antonio Rosmini e la grande questione letteraria del secolo XIX* (in the collection *Per Antonio Rosmini nel primo centenario*, Milan, 1897, vol. i. pp. 364-385). On Gioberti, Ad. Faggi, *Vinc. Gioberti esteta e letterato*, Palermo, 1901 (from the *Atti della R. Accad. di Palermo*, s. iii. vol. vi.). On Delfico, G. Gentile, *Dal Genovesi al Galluppi*, Naples, 1903, ch. ii. On Leopardi, E. Bertana in *Giorn. stor. lett. ital.* xli. pp. 193-283 : R. Giani, *L' estetica nei pensieri di G. Leopardi*, Turin, 1904 (cf. G. Gentile in *Critica*, ii. pp. 144-147). See also a book quoted by A. Rolla and B. Croce, *loc. cit.*, containing a catalogue of Italian books on Æsthetic of the nineteenth century (*Probl. di est.* pp. 401-415).

On the theories of the Italian Romanticists, F. De Sanctis, *La poetica del Manzoni*, in *Scritti varî*, ed. Croce, i. pp. 23-45 ; and the same author's *La letteratura italiana nel secolo XIX*, ed. Croce, Naples, 1897, on Tommaseo, pp. 233-243 : on Cantù, pp. 244-273 : on Berchet, pp. 479-493 : on Mazzini, pp. 424-441. On Mazzini esp. F. Ricitari, *Concetto dell' arte e della critica letteraria nella mente di G. Mazzini*, Catania, 1896. For all these see G. A. Borgese, *Storia della critica romantica in Italia*, cit.

XV. For the life of De Sanctis and the bibliography of his works see *Scritti varî*, ed. Croce, ii. pp. 267-308, also the volume *In memoria di Fr. de S.* edited by M. Mandalari, Naples, 1884.

On De Sanctis as literary critic, P. Villari, *Commemorazione* : A. C. de Meis, *Commem.*, in the above-mentioned vol. *In memoria* : Marc Monnier in *Revue des Deux Mondes*, April 1, 1884 : Pio Ferrieri, *Fr. de S. e la critica letteraria*, Milan, 1888 : B. Croce, *La critica letteraria*, Rome, 1896, ch. 5 ; *Fr. de S. e i suoi critici recenti* (in *Atti dell' Accad. Pontan.* vol. xxviii. reprinted in *Scritti varî*, append. ii. 309-352), and prefs. to vols. already quoted, *La lett. ital. nel sec. XIX*, and *Scritti varî* ; *De Sanctis e Schopenhauer*, in *Atti della Pontaniana*, xxxii. 1902 : Enr. Cocchia, *Il pensiero critico di Fr. de S. nell' arte e nella politica*, Naples, 1899 : G. A. Borgese, *op. cit.* last chapter and *passim*.

XVI. On the last phase of metaphysical Æsthetic, G. Neudecker, *Studien z. Geschichte d. deutschen Ästhetik s. Kant*, Würzburg, 1878, which discusses and criticises more particularly Vischer (self-criticism), Zimmermann, Lotze, Köstlin, Siebeck, Fechner and Deutinger. On Zimmermann, von Hartmann, *op. cit.* pp. 267-304: Bonatelli, in *Nuova Antologia*, October 1867. On Lotze, Fritz Kogel, *Lotzes Ästhetik*, Göttingen, 1886 : A. Matragrin, *Essai sur l'esthétique de Lotze*, Paris, 1901. On Köstlin, von Hartmann, pp. 304-317. On Schasler, see the same, pp. 248-252, also Bosanquet, pp. 414-424. On Hartmann, Ad. Faggi, *Ed. H. e l' estetica tedesca*, Florence, 1895. On Vischer see M. Diez, *Fried. Vischer u. d. ästh. Formalismus*, Stuttgart, 1889.

For French and English æstheticians, besides Menendez y Pelayo, *op. cit.*, on Ruskin, see J. Milsand, *L'Esthétique anglaise, étude sur J. Ruskin*, Paris, 1864 : R. de la Sizeranne, *Ruskin et la religion de la beauté*, 3rd ed., Paris, 1898 ; cf. part iii. On Fornari, V. Imbriani, *Vito Fornari estetico* (reprinted in *Studî letterarî e bizzarri e satiriche*, ed. Croce, Bari, 1907). On Tari see Nic. Gallo, *Antonio Tari, studio critico*, Palermo, 1884 : Croce, in *Critica*, v. (1907), pp. 357-361 ; also in pref. to vol.: *A. Tari, saggi di estetica e metafisica*, Bari, 1910.

XVII. For positivist Æsthetic see Menendez y Pelayo, *op. cit.* iv. (1st ed.) vol. ii. pp. 120-136, 326-369 : N. Gallo, *La scienza dell' arte*, Turin, 1887, chs. 6-8, pp. 162-216.

XVIII. On Kirchmann, von Hartmann, pp. 253-265. For various recent German æstheticians, Hugo Spitzer, *Kritische Studien z. Ästhet. der Gegenwart*, Leipzig, 1897. On Nietzsche, Ettore G. Zoccoli, *Fred. Nietzsche*, Modena, 1898, pp. 268-344 : Jul. Zeitler, *Nietzsches Ästhetik*, Leipzig, 1900. On Flaubert, A. Fusco, *La teoria dell' arte in G. F.*, Naples, 1907 : cf. *Critica*, vi. (1908), pp. 125-134. For books on Æsthetic published during the last decade of the nineteenth century see Luc. Arréat, *Dix années de philosophie*, 1891–1900, Paris, 1901, pp. 74-116. A few remarks on contemporary Æsthetic are made by K. Groos in *Die Philosophie im Beginn. des XX^{en} Jahrh.*, ed. by W. Windelband, Heidelberg, 1904–1905. For latest books on Æsthetic see *Critica*, ed. B. Croce (Naples), from 1903 onward, which publishes reviews of them. There is also a review, started in 1906, published at Stuttgart (ed. F. Enke), *Zeitschrift für Ästhetik und allgemeine Kunstwissenschaft*, edited by Max Dessoir.

XIX. The history of particular problems is usually omitted, or, at best, erroneously treated in histories of Æsthetic : for example, see the difficulty experienced by Ed. Müller, *Gesch.*, cit., ii. pref. pp. vi-vii, in connecting his treatment of the history of Rhetoric with that of Poetics. Some writers attach Rhetoric to the individual arts or to artistic technique ; others treat the doctrines of the modification of beauty and of natural beauty (in the metaphysical sense) as special problems ; others, again, discuss the kinds or classifications in art in an incidental manner, without seeking to incorporate them in the principal æsthetic problem.

§ 1. On the history of Rhetoric in the ancient sense see Rich. Volkmann, *Die Rhetorik der Griechen und Römer in systematischer Übersicht dargestellt*, 2nd ed., Leipzig, 1885, of capital importance : A. Ed. Chaignet, *La Rhétorique et son histoire*, Paris, 1888 ; rich in material, but ill-arranged and with the preconception that Rhetoric is still a defensible body of science. For special treatment see Ch. Benoist, *Essai historique sur les premiers manuels d'invention oratoire, jusqu'à Aristote*, Paris, 1846 : Georg Thiele, *Hermagoras, ein Beitrag z. Geschichte d. Rhetorik*, Strasburg, 1893. There is no history of rhetoric in modern times. For criticism of Vives and other Spaniards see Menendez y Pelayo, *op. cit.* iii. pp. 211-300 (2nd ed.). For Patrizzi see B. Croce, *F. Patrizzi e la critica della rettorica antica*, in the vol. of *Studî* in honour of A. Graf, Bergamo, 1903 (*Probl. d. est.* pp. 297-308).

For Rhetoric as theory of literary form in antiquity see Volkmann, *op. cit.* pp. 393-566 : Chaignet, *op. cit.* pp. 413-539 : also Egger, *passim*, and Saintsbury, bks. i. ii. For purposes of comparison see Paul Reynaud, *La Rhétorique sanskrite exposée dans son développement historique et ses rapports avec la rhétorique classique*, Paris, 1884. For the Middle Ages, Comparetti, *Virgilio*

nel medio evo, vol. i., and Saintsbury, bk. iii. There is need for
a work on modern Rhetoric in this sense also. For the form it
assumed ultimately according to the theory of Gröber see
B. Croce, *Di alcuni principî di sintassi e stilistica psicologiche del
Gröber*, in *Atti dell' Accad. Pontan.* vol. xxix. 1899 : K. Vossler,
Literaturblatt für germ. u. roman. Philologie, 1900, N.I. : B. Croce,
Le categorie rettoriche e il prof. Gröber, in *Flegrea*, April 1900 :
K. Vossler, *Positivismo e idealismo nella scienza del linguaggio*,
Ital. trans. Bari, 1908, pp. 48-61 (cf. *Probl. d. est.* pp. 143-171).
Very incomplete observations on the history of the concept of
metaphor are made by A. Biese, *Philosophie d. Metaphorischen*,
Hamburg-Leipzig, 1893, pp. 1-16 ; but this book has the merit of
calling attention to the importance of the views and influence
of Vico.

§ 2. For the history of the literary kinds in antiquity see the
works above quoted by Müller, Egger, Saintsbury, and the vast
literature on Aristotle's *Poetics*. For comparison with Sanskrit
poetics, Sylvain Levi, *Le Théâtre indien*, Paris, 1890, esp. pp. 11
152. For mediæval poetry see esp. Gio. Mari, *I trattati medievali
di ritmica latina*, Milan, 1899 ; and his recent edition of *Poetica
magistri Iohannis ąnglici*, 1901.

For the history of the kinds under the Renaissance see princi-
pally Spingarn, *op. cit.* i. chs. 3-4 ; ii. ch. 2 ; iii. ch. 3. Also
Menendez y Pelayo, Borinski, Saintsbury, *passim*.

Special works : on Pietro Aretino, De Sanctis, *Storia della
letteratura italiana*, ii. pp. 122-144 : A. Graf, *Attraverso il cinque-
cento*, Turin, 1888, pp. 87-167 : K. Vossler, *P. A.'s künstlerisches
Bekenntniss*, Heidelberg, 1901. On Guarini, V. Rossi, *G. B.
Guarini e il Pastor Fido*, Turin, 1886, pp. 238-250. On Scaliger,
Lintilhac, *Un Coup d'État*, cit. For the three unities, L. Morandi,
Baretti contro Voltaire, 2nd ed., Città di Castello, 1884 : Breitinger, *Les Unités d'Aristote avant le Cid de Corneille*, 2nd ed.,
Geneva-Basle, 1895 : J. Ebner, *Beitrag z. einer Geschichte d.
dramatischen Einheiten in Italien*, Munich, 1898. On the Spanish
polemic concerning comedy see A. Morel Fatio on the defenders
of comedy and of the *Arte nuevo*, in the *Bulletin Hispanique* of
Bordeaux, vols. iii. and iv. : on the dramatic theories see Arnaud,
*Les Théories dramatiques au XVIIe siècle, étude sur la vie et les
œuvres de l'abbé D'Aubignac*, Paris, 1888 : Paul Dupont, *Un
Poète philosophe au commencement du XVIIIe siècle, Houdar de la
Motte*, Paris, 1898 : Alfredo Galletti, *Le teorie drammatiche e la
tragedia in Italia nel secolo XVIII*, part i. 1700–1750, Cremona,
1901. On the history of French Poetics, F. Brunetière, *L'Évolution
des genres dans l'histoire de la littérature*, Paris, 1890, vol. i. introd. :
" *L'évolution de la critique depuis la Renaissance jusqu'à nos
jours.*" On that of English Poetics, Paul Hamelius, *Die Kritik in
d. engl. Literatur des XVII^{en} u. XVIII^{en} Jahrh.*, Leipzig, 1897 :
also the well-filled chapter in Gayley-Scott, *op. cit.* pp. 382-422, the

sketch of a book on the subject. For the romantic period see Alfred Michiels, *Histoire des idées littéraires en France au XIXᵉ siècle, et de leurs origines dans les siècles antérieures*, 4th ed., Paris, 1863. For Italy see G. A. Borgese, *op. cit.*

§ 3. For the early history of the distinction and classification of the arts see the literature quoted above in relation to Lessing, and his *Laokoon*, with notes by Blümner. For subsequent history, H. Lotze, *Geschichte*, cit., bk. iii. : Max Schasler, *Das System der Künste auf einem neuen, im Wesen der Kunst begründeten Gliederungsprincip*, 2nd ed., Leipzig-Berlin, 1881, introd. : Ed. v. Hartmann, *Deutsche Ästh. s. Kant*, bk. ii. part ii. especially pp. 524-580 : V. Basch, *Essai sur l'esth. de Kant*, pp. 483-496.

§ 4. For the doctrine of styles in antiquity see Volkmann, *op. cit.* pp. 532-566. The history of grammar and parts of speech is treated fully so far as Græco-Roman antiquity is concerned in Laur. Lersch, *Die Sprachphilosophie der Alten*, Bonn, 1838-1841 : better still by Steinthal, *Geschichte*, cit. vol. ii. For Apollonius Dyscolus see Egger, *Apollon Dyscole*, Paris, 1854. For the history of grammar in the Middle Ages see Ch. Thurot, *Extraits de divers manuscrits latins pour servir à l'histoire des doctrines grammaticales au moyen âge*, Paris, 1869. For modern times, C. Trabalza, *Storia della grammatica italiana*, Milan, 1908. For the history of Criticism several books mentioned under § 2 may be consulted : in addition to these, B. Croce, *Per la storia della critica e storiografia letteraria*, containing Italian examples (*Probl. d. est.* pp. 419-448) : for the theories of recent French criticism see Ém. Hennequin, *La Critique scientifique*, Paris, 1888, and Ernest Tissot, *Les Évolutions de la critique française*, Paris, 1890. On the concept of " romanticism " see G. Muoni, *Note per una poetica storica del romanticismo*, Milan, 1906 : cf. B. Croce, *Le definizioni del romanticismo*, in *Critica*, iv. pp. 241-245 (reprinted in *Probl. di estetica*, pp. 285-294).

INDEX

NOONDAY PAPERBACKS